COMMERCIAL
FCC LICENSE
HANDBOOK

No. 582
$9.95

COMMERCIAL FCC LICENSE HANDBOOK

By Harvey F. Swearer

TAB BOOKS
Blue Ridge Summit, Pa. 17214

SECOND EDITION

FIRST PRINTING—JANUARY 1974

Copyright © 1971, 1974 by TAB BOOKS

Printed in the United States
of America

Hardbound Edition: International Standard Book No. 0-8306-4582-9

Paperbound Edition: International Standard Book No. 0-8306-3582-3

Library of Congress Card Number: 73-93692

Preface

Many years ago, someone said, "Radio is the field of the future," and a little later the word "electronics" was substituted to better cover the expanded growth of the radio art. There can no longer be doubt in anyone's mind regarding the veracity of the statement. I don't need to tell you, the reader, that there are dozens of jobs from serviceman to broadcast station engineer at locations not only all over the U.S but all over the world! In what other field of endeavor could you become an engineer without higher education? In fact, you do not even need a high school diploma, but you do need the recommendation of the U.S. Government in the form of an FCC license.

An FCC license is a valuable asset. Lots of times you may get by uninitiated sales or administrative personnel with a few prepared statements, but when you are face to face with the experienced electronic technician, how are you going to convince him that you know the job if you don't? This is where the FCC license helps you get the job, even though the "ticket" may not be required or even needed. He knows you had to have a darn good understanding of electronics to get a passing grade from that "tough" FCC examining officer. I know, some applicants memorize 500 or 600 answers and as a result a few probably "sneak by," but they are not ready to fill the job and will be carrying the "toolbox" for the regular man until they learn what they should have mastered before taking the exam. In the meantime, the pay will be that of a helper instead of a technician. If you want to be a commercial radio operator, with your sights on the bigger job of transmitter engineer, roll up your sleeves, learn the theory and how to use the formulas to figure out those answers.

A knowledge of electronic theory is not required for Elements 1, 2. Only basic law is covered in Element 1 and basic operating practice in Element 2. Each element requires an examination consisting of 20 multiple choice questions, with 5 percent credit allowed for each question. A passing grade of 75 percent entitles the applicant to a radiotelephone third class operator's permit. By also receiving a passing grade on Element 9 (Basic Broadcast, 20 questions), the permit is endorsed for broadcast operation. Although no examination is required for the restricted radiotelephone permit, all other permits or licenses do require the applicant to pass Elements 1 and 2. Actual requirements for each class are as follows:

Radiotelephone first class operator's license:
    Elements 1, 2, 3, 4.
Radiotelephone second class operator's license:
    Elements 1, 2, 3.
Ship radio endorsement on first or second class:
    Element 8.
Radiotelephone third class operator's permit endorsed for broadcast operation:
    Elements 1, 2, 9.

Examination on the elements are given in order; i.e., if applying for a first class operator's license, you are examined on Elements 1 and 2 which must be passed before taking Element 3. Element 3 has to be passed before taking the exam on Element 4. If you failed to pass Element 4, you would receive a second class operator's license until you were re-examined on Element 4. Then, if successful, the second class license would be cancelled and the first class issued. In other words, the highest grade for which the applicant passes the required test is issued at that time and when applying for examination again, only the additional elements for the higher grade are given.

Applications for a new operator's license must be accompanied by the following fees:

First class radiotelephone operator's license: $5.
Second class radiotelephone operator's license: $4.
Third class radiotelephone operator's permit: $3.
Restricted radiotelephone operator's permit: $2.

Application for renewal of an operator's license: $2.
Application for endorsement of operator's license: $2.
Application for duplicate or replacement license: $2.

No fee is required when applying for a verification card (FCC Form 758-F) or verified statement (FCC Form 759). When an application requests both an operator's license and an endorsement, the required fee is the fee prescribed for the license document involved.

Harvey F. Swearer

Contents

CHAPTER 1

Basic Law: Elements 1 & 2

The rules and regulations promulgated and enforced by the Federal Communications Commission serve a specific purpose. They do not exist just to make it tough on applicable parties. These regulations are for the common good and protection of all our people. This fact should remain in your mind as you pursue your studies.

The first hurdle is low, but must be cleared on your way to that goal just a little farther on. Element 1 consists of 20 questions of the multiple choice type like: Who may apply for an FCC license?

(a) Any male having reached the age of 21.
(b) Any female at least 18 years of age.
(c) Any citizen or intended citizen of the U.S.
(d) Any person with normal sight and hearing.
(e) Any citizen of the United States.

You probably selected answer (e) without hesitation because it is certainly for the common good and the only requirement the applicant must fulfill when applying. Sex, age, race, religion or country of origin have no bearing whatsoever, but you definitely must be a citizen of the United States. As in all FCC examinations, the passing grade is 75 percent and, since five points are allowed for each correct answer, you only need 15 correct answers to pass Basic Law Element 1.

After successfully completing Element 1, you are ready for Element 2, which covers Basic Operating Practice and also consists of 20 multiple choice questions with the same passing requirement of 75 percent. There are two types of exams for Element 2: Series "0" for general radiotelephone operating practice or series "M" for maritime operation. If you intend to operate aboard ship or a coastal station, choose the "M" series, if not, request the "O" type. The questions do overlap, so it may be wise to study both, as the similarities may be helpful later on.

The radiotelephone third-class permit is issued in two classes or categories—the restricted which requires no oral or written exam of any kind and which authorizes very limited responsibilities, and the regular third-class radiotelephone permit which requires a passing grade on Element 1 (Basic Law) and Element 2 (Basic Operating Practice). This latter class is the foundation from which you start building your way to the coveted first-class radiotelephone "ticket." After passing the first two elements, you may prepare for the broadcast endorsement exam on Element 9, covering the responsibilities of a third-class permit which allows you to operate an AM station with a power of 10 KW or less and a nondirectional antenna. You may also work in an FM station of 25 KW or less, but in either event, you will work under the wing of a first-class radiotelephone license holder. In some educational stations, the top operator may be a second-class radiotelephone licensee. The Element 9 broadcast endorsement requires a passing grade on a 20-question multiple choice exam, and is covered completely in Chapter 2.

The radiotelephone second-class license allows the holder to operate any AM, FM or TV broadcast station, but usually under the supervision of a first-class operator. The second-class licensee is permitted to make certain adjustments to compensate for power supply variations. These adjustments require the simple turning of a control knob to bring the transmitter within authorized limits in modulation or operating power. He may not **repair** or **maintain** transmitters in AM, FM or TV broadcast stations. However, the second ticket holder may maintain and repair or service certain low-power transmitters such as those used in two-way radio service. The radiotelephone first-class license allows its holder to operate, maintain, and repair any transmitting equipment not using Morse code, and in some cases this is even permissible under "special privileges" cited in the FCC regulations. This "major league status" opens just about every conceivable door in communications and the associated crafts. It's well worth the effort required, so aim your sights for the goal and don't settle for less!

The radiotelegraph first- or second-class license exam includes Elements 1, 2, 5 (Radiotelegraph Operating Practice), and 6 (Advanced Radiotelegraph). The first-class radiotelegraph operator must have one year of service as a second-class radiotelegraph operator, be at least 21 years of age, and copy 25 words text or 20 code groups per minute in Morse code. The second-class operator must copy 20 words text or 16 code groups per minute. Neither may operate, maintain or repair AM, FM or TV broadcast transmitters. The holder of a radiotelegraph first-class or second-class license may receive the Aircraft Radiotelegraph endorsement by passing Element 7, covering that subject. This allows the operation of the radiotelegraph transmitter aboard an aircraft and, since such jobs are seldom available today, interest is nonexistent.

BASIC LAW

During the course of our study, some words or phrases may seem foreign or even somewhat removed from the intended meaning, such as "ticket" which refers to the FCC license. Defining a ticket we find that the term means label, tag, certificate, license or permit. Actually, nothing could be truer than the reference to the first-class radiotelephone license as a first-class "ticket." The doors to opportunity in the field of radio communications are many, but those permitting passage without a ticket are few.

There is a total of nine elements dealing with commercial operator licenses and each is a complete examination. The required elements in each case must be taken in order for the specific license or permit desired. If you fail to pass an element, you are finished for that day, but you may take it again after 60 days. No doubt, early morning is the best time to take an exam, since you are fresher at that time; waiting until late morning will run you through lunch time if you are going for second-class or better. You may not leave the room during an element—only between elements. Since Element 3 consists of one-hundred questions, you are probably going to be working on it for a couple of hours or so. There is no time limit on any of the examinations, except FCC office hours, so allow yourself plenty of time, and don't have your stomach growling at you through lunch-hour—like I did!

The elements are: 1. Basic Law; 2. Basic Operating Practice (O & M series); 3. Basic Radiotelephone; 4. Advanced Radiotelephone; 5. Radiotelegraph Operating Practice; 6. Advanced Radiotelegraph; 7. Aircraft Radiotelegraph (Endorsement); 8. Ship Radar (Endorsement); 9. Basic Broadcast (Endorsement). All elements are covered in this volume, except those pertaining to Radiotelegraph (5, 6 & 7) which are of no practical interest to most applicants as a result of the dwindling number of jobs in this area.

WHAT'S THE EXAM LIKE

None of the questions require an essay type answer; rather, each offers a choice of answers following each question (multiple-choice). Only one is correct, of course, even though one or more of the others may seem to **almost** fit. You may also be asked to draw a few simple diagrams, and correct incomplete or incorrect diagrams. Always sign every sheet of paper, even that given for figuring. No books, notes, or paper of any kind may be taken into the examination room.

The basic law in Element 1 covers simple FCC Rules and Regulations and should be understood for proper retention, rather than memorized. If you rely solely on memorization, you'll probably forget the answers by tomorrow and you don't want that to happen, so reason them out instead. The language may seem stiff, but it is professional and quite important. Remember that the rules are for the common good and protection of all our people.

After reviewing the answers to each question as suggested in the study guide, you will want to reason them out for yourself and determine the logic involved. The common sense behind each is apparent, and this analysis will enable you to keep the information handy in your mind for future use, not only in your exams but later on in your work as well. When you feel confident that you know the material in Elements 1 and 2, try the sample test questions and see how you are doing. If you are a little weak in an area, go over it again until you are confident.

Question 1. Where and how are FCC licenses and permits obtained?

The application on the prescribed form along with any specified documents may be offered in person or by mail to the FCC regional office where you wish action to be taken and where the required examination will be taken by the applicant. A license or permit will be issued to the successful applicant upon satisfactory completion of the exam. He may be advised of the outcome before leaving the office in order to make any desired preparations, but the actual license or permit will be mailed to the applicant's home address by the regional office. Fees are accepted before taking the examination. **Note:** An applicant for the restricted radiotelephone permit need only fill out the application; no examination is required at any time.

Question 2: When a licensee qualifies for a higher grade FCC license or permit, what happens to the lesser grade license?

The lesser grade license must be cancelled upon issuance of the higher grade and, therefore, must be submitted to the examining officer upon passing the higher grade test. It will be returned by mail (cancelled) along with the new (higher grade) license.

Question 3: Who may apply for an FCC license?

Although commercial licenses are issued only to citizens of the United States, an alien holding an Aircraft Pilot Certificate issued by the Civil Aeronautics Administration or the Federal Aviation Agency, and lawfully in the United States, may have the requirement waived by the FCC if it finds that the public interest will be served thereby.

Question 4: If a license or permit is lost, what action must be taken by the operator?

He must notify the FCC immediately, and properly file an application to the office of original issue for a duplicate, informing them of the circumstances involved in the loss of the original license or how it was destroyed. A statement that a reasonable search has been made for the original license, and that if found later will be returned to the FCC office for cancellation shall be included. Documentary evidence or a sworn statement of service performed under the original license must also be submitted. While awaiting receipt of the duplicate license, an operator may continue his duties; however, a signed copy of the application for the duplicate license must be exhibited.

Question 5: What is the usual license term of radio operators?

Commercial radio operator license terms are five years from the date of issuance.

Question 6: What government agency inspects radio stations in the U.S.?

The Federal Communications Commission (FCC).

Question 7: When may a license be renewed?

Renewal application can be made at any time during the final year of the license term or during a one-year grace period following expiration. However, the expired license may not be used during the grace period.

Question 8: Who keeps the station logs?

Each log shall be kept by a competent person or persons having actual knowledge of the facts required. Program logs and maintenance logs must be signed before going on duty and again when going off duty.

Question 9: Who corrects errors in the station logs?

Any necessary correction must be made by the person who made the error.

Question 10: How may errors in the station logs be corrected?

Correction must be made by the person originating the entry by striking out the error, initialing the correction and date thereof. Erasing is prohibited.

Question 11: Under what conditions may messages be rebroadcast?

Rebroadcast is permissible only with the express authority of the originating station.

Question 12: What messages and signals may not be transmitted?

A licensed radio operator shall not transmit unnecessary, unidentified or superfluous radio communications or signals. Communications containing obscene, indecent, or profane works, language or meaning are likewise prohibited, along with deceptive or false signals or communications and call letters not assigned by proper authority to the station he is operating.

Question 13: May an operator deliberately interfere with any radio communication or signal?

No.

Question 14: What type of communication has top priority in the mobile service?

Distress calls, distress messages and distress traffic with an order of priority in the mobile service as follows:

(a) Distress calls, distress messages and distress traffic.

(b) Communications preceded by an urgency signal.

(c) Communications preceded by a safety signal.

(d) Communications pertaining to direction-finding.

(e) Communications relative to navigation and safe movement of aircraft.

(f) Communications relating to the navigation, movements and needs of ships, and weather observation messages destined for an official meteorological service.

(g) Government radiotelegrams: Priority nations.

(h) Government communications for which priority has been requested.

(i) Service communications relating to the working of radio communications previously exchanged.

(j) All other communications.

Question 15: What are the grounds for suspension of operator licenses?

Violation of any provision of an Act, Treaty or Convention, or any regulation made by the Commission under such Treaty, Act or Convention.

Failure to carry out a lawful order of one in charge of a ship or aircraft on which he is employed.

Willfully damaging radio equipment or permitting it to be damaged.

Transmitting prohibited signals or communications as outlined in Question 12.

Willfully or maliciously interfering with any other radio transmissions.

Aiding or abetting another to attempt to obtain a license by fraudulent means.

Question 16: When may an operator divulge the contents of an intercepted message?

Messages pertaining to ships in distress or those transmitted for the use of the general public may be divulged.

Question 17: If a licensee is notified that he has violated an FCC rule or provision of the Communications Act of 1934, what must he do?

Within 10 days from receipt of notice or such period as may be specified therein, the licensee must send a written reply in duplicate to the FCC office that originated the violation notice. If an answer or acknowledgment cannot be made within the 10-day period due to illness or other unavoidable circumstances, an answer must be made with satisfactory explanation for the delay at the earliest practicable date.

The answer to each notice shall be complete within itself, and abbreviation by reference to other communications or answers to other notices are not acceptable. In every instance, the answer shall contain a statement of action to correct the condition or omission complained of and to preclude its recurrence.

Note: If the notice relates to violations that may have resulted from the physical or electrical characteristics of transmitting apparatus and new apparatus is to be installed, the reply must give date of order, manufacturer and estimated date of delivery.

Question 18: If a licensee receives a notice of suspension of his license, what must he do?

The operator must send his license to the FCC on or before the effective date of the order. Actually, the notice of suspension is not effective until received by him, and from which date he has 15 days to mail an application for a hearing on the suspension order. Upon such compliance his license suspension will be held in abeyance pending conclusion of the hearing.

Question 19: What are the penalties provided for violating a provision of the Communications Act of 1934 or a Rule of the FCC?

Violation of the Act, upon conviction, carries a fine of not more than $10,000 or one year in prison, or both. The prison term may be increased to two years for second offenders. Violation of an FCC Rule, if convicted, provides a fine of not more than $500 for each and every day during such offense, in addition to any other penalties.

Question 20: What is meant by "harmful interference"?

Any emission, radiation or induction that endangers the proper functioning of the radionavigation service or of other safety services or seriously degrades, obstructs, or repeatedly interrupts a radiocommunication service operating in accordance with these regulations.

ELEMENT 1

Sample Test Questions

1. When may a license be renewed?
   (a) Any time within six months before or after expiration.
   (b) Within a year of expiration of current license.
   (c) At all times, if no violations have been made.
   (d) Only within one month of expiration date.
   (e) None of the above.
2. Urgency signals have second priority, what has first?
   (a) Overseas commercial messages.
   (b) Safety communications.
   (c) Distress calls and messages.
   (d) International bulletins.
   (e) D-F communications.
3. Who may make corrections in the station log?
   (a) Any second class licensed operator.
   (b) Only an officer of the station.
   (c) Any licensed operator on duty.
   (d) Any person competent and familiar with facts.
   (e) The person who made the initial entry.
4. What is the usual license term for radio operators?
   (a) Two years.
   (b) Eight years.
   (c) One year.
   (d) Five years.
   (e) Until 65 years of age.

5. Who may inspect radio stations in the U.S.?
   (a) The Federal Communications Commission.
   (b) The U.S. Dept. of Commerce.
   (c) The General Services Administration.
   (d) Internal Revenue Service.
   (e) Secretary of Interior.

6. When do the secrecy provisions of the law not apply?
   (a) Commercial bulletins.
   (b) Distress messages.
   (c) Position reports.
   (d) Private wire service messages.
   (e) Weather bulletins.

7. An operator who loses his license must take what action?
   (a) Notify the FCC within 30 days.
   (b) Exhibit a copy of the application for the duplicate while continuing work.
   (c) Stop operating until his duplicate is received.
   (d) Notify the field office the next business day.
   (e) Continue operating until FCC inspector arrives.

8. False signals of distress are:
   (a) Permissible with low power only.
   (b) Proper tests for rescue efficiency.
   (c) Prohibited by law.
   (d) Allowed when checking emergency equipment.
   (e) Permitted only from midnight to local sunrise.

9. If you receive a notice of violation from the FCC, what must you do regarding same?
   (a) Reply within 24 hours to the nearest field office of the FCC.
   (b) Reply within 10 days to the FCC office that originated the notice.
   (c) Reply within three days to the main office of the FCC.
   (d) Respond immediately to the nearest Federal District Court.
   (e) None of the above.

10. When a licensee qualifies for a higher grade FCC license:
   (a) The lower grade license should be destroyed.
   (b) The lower class license is valid until its expiration date.
   (c) The lower grade license remains in force.
   (d) The lower grade license must be returned to the FCC for cancellation.
   (e) Licensee may retain the lower class license.

11. A message may be rebroadcast:
   (a) If authorized by the operator in charge.

(b) Provided the FCC engineer in charge of the district is notified.

(c) With proper credit given to source.

(d) With the express authorization of the originating station.

(e) If the originating station is promptly notified.

12. How may errors in station logs be corrected?

(a) Erase the error and enter the correction in ink.

(b) Cross out the mistake, initial, and enter the time of correction.

(c) Remove the error with correction fluid and type in the correction.

(d) Line-out the error, initial the correction, and indicate the date made.

(e) Have corrections notarized and notify the FCC district office.

13. An operator's license may not be suspended for which of the following offenses?

(a) Allowing another to willfully destroy or damage radio equipment.

(b) Transmitting false or deceptive signals.

(c) Transmitting unnecessary communications.

(d) Transmitting obscene, indecent, or profane language.

(e) Refusal to carry out orders from the station manager.

14. If a notice of suspension is received, what must you do?

(a) Request a hearing within 15 days.

(b) Cease operating at once.

(c) Return your operator's license to the FCC immediately.

(d) Request a hearing within 30 days.

(e) None of the above.

15. To obtain a commercial FCC license or permit, you must be:

(a) Of average intelligence.

(b) A citizen of the United States.

(c) At least 21 years of age.

(d) A citizen of a friendly country.

(e) A licensed operator of a friendly country.

16. A transmitter in a public place:

(a) May never be left unattended unless turned off.

(b) Must be posted with a warning sign.

(c) Must be locked when unattended.

(d) Must be fenced in to keep children away.

(e) Must have the final tube removed when unattended.

17. A person willfully violating a provision of the Communications Act of 1934 is subject to:

(a) A fine of not more than $500.

(b) A fine not to exceed $10,000.

(c) A fine of $5,000 and two years imprisonment.

—(d) A fine not exceeding $10,000 and one year imprisonment.

(e) A fine not exceeding $5,000 and one year imprisonment.

—18. An operator violating a Rule of the FCC may be subject to:

(a) Two years imprisonment.

(b) Five years imprisonment.

—(c) $500 fine for each day during which the violation occurs.

(d) $1000 fine for each day the violation occurs.

(e) None of the above.

19. Under what conditions may an operator divulge the contents of an intercepted message?

(a) If the sender's permission is obtained.

(b) By notification of the FCC within 24 hours.

—(c) When receiving a distress message or a message intended for general public use.

(d) If the regular commercial rate is paid.

(e) Not permitted at any time.

20. Deliberate interference with radio communications is permissible:

(a) At SHF frequencies only.

(b) In the 500-kHz channel only at reduced power.

(c) When required to establish frequency checks.

(d) Under no conditions.

(e) When operating above 54 MHz (daytime only).

ELEMENT 2

Series O: General Broadcasting Station Operating

Question 1: What should an operator do when he leaves a transmitter unattended?

Transmitter must be locked or made inaccessible to unauthorized personnel.

Question 2: What are the meanings of: clear, out, over, roger, words twice, repeat and break?

Clear or out: The transmission is ended and no response is expected.

Over: My transmission is ended and a response is expected.

Roger: Your last transmission has been received and completely understood.

Words twice: Each word will be given twice, due to poor reception.

Repeat: Say again.

Break: This is the end of this part, another will follow shortly.

Question 3: How should a microphone be treated when used in noisy locations?

Shield the microphone with cupped hands to avoid background noise pickup.

Question 4: What may happen to the received signal when an operator shouts into a microphone?

This causes overmodulation and distorts the signal at the receiving station, making it difficult to understand. Interference with stations on adjacent frequencies may also result.

Question 5: Why should radio transmitters be off when signals are not being transmitted?

The transmitter may cause interference with other stations even when not modulated.

Question 6: Why should an operator use well known words and phrases?

Simple phrases and plain words are easy to understand; this reduces errors and avoids undue repetition, thus saving time.

Question 7: Why is the station's call sign transmitted?

This provides positive identification of the sending station, thereby avoiding possible confusion.

Question 8: Where does an operator find specifications for obstruction marking and lighting (where required) for the antenna towers of a particular radio station?

Simply examine the station authorization as issued by the FCC. (See Part 17 FCC Rules & Regulations for general specifications.)

Question 9: What should an operator do if he hears profanity being used at his station?

He should cut the speaker off, note the incident in the station log and forward a report of the infraction to the FCC.

Question 10: When may an operator use his station without regard to certain provisions of his station license?

During a period of emergency in which normal communications facilities are disrupted as a result of hurricane, flood, earthquake or similar disaster. Notice must be sent to the FCC in Washington, D.C. and to the engineer in charge of the district of the station location as soon as possible following beginning of such emergency use. Emergency use of the station shall be discontinued as soon as substantially normal communication facilities are again available, along with immediate notification to the Commission and the engineer in charge when such special use of the station is terminated.

(a) Soon as possible after beginning emergency use of the station, send notice to the FCC in Washington, D.C. and the engineer in charge of the district in which the station is located.

(b) Emergency use of the station must be discontinued as soon as substantially normal communication facilities are restored.

(c) The Commission at Washington, D.C., and the engineer in charge shall be notified immediately when special use of a station is terminated.

(d) Under no circumstances may any station engage in emergency transmission on frequencies other than, or with power in excess of, that specified in the instrument of authorization or as otherwise expressly provided by the Commission, or by law.

(e) Any emergency communication undertaken under this section shall terminate upon order of the Commission.

Question 11: Who bears the responsibility if an operator permits an unlicensed person to speak over his station?

The licensed operator in charge of the station, as he is responsible for the proper operation.

Question 12: What is meant by a "phonetic alphabet" in radiotelephone communications?

A list of 26 words, each starting with a different letter of the alphabet and used to avoid possible misunderstanding of similar sounding words. For example, the word "bad" would be easily recognized by the phonetic spelling, "Bravo, Alpha, Delta."

Question 13: How does the licensed operator of a station normally exhibit his authority to operate the station?

Simply by posting a valid operator license or permit at the transmitter control point.

Question 14: What precautions should be observed in testing a station on the air?

The operator should clearly indicate that he is testing, giving the station call sign or name of the station clearly. Tests must be brief, and before starting, check the frequency to make sure that the test will not interfere with other communications already in progress.

Series M: Maritime Services Operating Procedure

Question 1: What is the importance of the frequency 2182 kc (kHz)?

The frequency 2182 kHz is the international distress frequency for radiotelephony. It shall be used for this purpose by ship, aircraft and survival craft stations using frequencies in the authorized bands between 1605 and 4000 kHz when requesting assistance from the maritime services. It is also the international general radiotelephone calling frequency for the maritime mobile service, and it may be used as a carrier frequency for this purpose by ship stations and aircraft stations operating in the maritime mobile service.

Question 2: Describe completely what actions should be taken by a radio operator who hears (A) a distress message; (B) a safety message.

Distress message

1. Acknowledge receipt of the distress message.

a. Stations of the maritime mobile service which receive a distress message from a mobile station that is, beyond any possible doubt, in their vicinity, shall immediately acknowledge receipt. However, in areas where reliable communication with one or more coast stations is practicable, ship stations may defer this acknowledment for a short interval so that a coast station may acknowledge receipt.

b. Stations of the maritime mobile service which receive a distress message from a mobile station that is not, beyond any possible doubt, in their vicinity shall allow a short interval of time to elapse before acknowledging receipt of the message, in order to permit stations nearer to the mobile station in distress to acknowledge receipt without interference.

Form of acknowledgment

a. The acknowledgement of the receipt of a distress message is transmitted, when radiotelephony is used, in the following form: (1) The call sign of the station sending the distress message, sent three times; (2) The letters DE; (3) The call sign of the station acknowledging receipt, sent three times; (4) The group RRR; (5) The distress signal SOS.

b. The acknowledgement of receipt of a distress message is transmitted, when radiotelephony is used, in the following form: (1) The call sign or other identification of the station sending the distress message, spoken three times; (2) The words, "This is"; (3) The call sign or other identification of the station acknowledging receipt, spoken three times; (4) The word, "received"; (5) The distress signal MAYDAY.

Information furnished by the acknowledging station

a. Every mobile station that acknowledges receipt of a distress message shall, on the order of the master or person

24

responsible for the ship, aircraft, or other vehicle carrying such mobile station, transmit as soon as possible the following information in the order shown: (1) Its name; (2) Its position; (3) The speed at which it is proceeding towards, and the approximate time it will take to reach, the mobile station in distress.

b. Before sending this message, the station shall ensure that it will not interfere with the emissions of other stations better situated to render immediate assistance to the station in distress.

Transmission of distress message by station not in distress

a. A mobile or a land station that learns that a mobile station is in distress shall transmit a distress message in any of the following cases: (1) When the station in distress is not itself in a position to transmit the distress message; (2) When the master or person responsible for the ship, aircraft, or other vehicle not in distress, or the person responsible for the land station, considers that further help is necessary; (3) When, although not in a position to render assistance, it has heard a distress message that has not been acknowledged. When a mobile station transmits a message under these conditions, it shall take all necessary steps to notify the authorities who may be able to render assistance.

b. The transmission of a distress message under conditions prescribed shall be made on either or both of the international distress frequencies (500 kHz radiotelegraph; 2182 kHz radiotelephone) or on any other available frequency on which attention might be attracted.

c. The transmission of the distress message shall always be preceded by the call indicated below, which shall itself be preceded whenever possible by the radiotelegraph or radiotelephone alarm signal.

When radiotelegraphy is used, this call consists of:

DD SOS SOS SOS DDD
The letters DE
The call sign of the transmitting station, sent three times.

When radiotelephony is used, this call consists of:

The signal, MAYDAY RELAY, spoken three times;
The words, "This is";
The call sign or other identification of the transmitting station, spoken three times.

d. When the radiotelegraph alarm signal is used, an interval of two minutes shall be allowed, whenever this is considered necessary, before the transmission of the call.

Safety Message

The safety message contains information concerning the safety of navigation or important meteorological warnings. All such messages should be reported to the ship's master, and the radio operator should not make any transmission likely to interfere with a safety message.

Question 3: What information must be contained in a distress message? What procedure should be followed by a radio operator in sending a distress message? What is a good choice of words to be used in sending a distress message?

Distress Signals

1. The international radiotelegraph distress signal consists of the group, three dots, three dashes, three dots" (...------...), symbolized herein by SOS, transmitted as a single signal in which the dashes are slightly prolonged so as to be distinguished clearly from the dots.

2. The international radiotelephone distress signal consists of the word MAYDAY, from the French expression "m'aidez."

3. These distress signals indicate that a mobile station is threatened with grave and imminent danger and requests immediate assistance.

Distress Calls

1. The distress call sent by radiotelegraphy consists of:
   a. The distress signal SOS, sent three times;
   b. The letters DE;
   c. The call sign of the mobile station in distress, sent three times.

2. The distress call sent by radiotelephony consists of:
   a. The distress signal, MAYDAY, spoken three times;
   b. The words, "This is";
   c. The call sign, or name if no call has been assigned, of the mobile station in distress, spoken three times.

3. The distress call shall have absolute priority over all other transmissions. All stations that hear it shall immediately cease any transmission capable of interfering with the distress traffic and and shall continue to listen on the frequency used for the emission of the distress call. This call

shall not be addressed to a particular station, and acknowledgment of receipt shall not be given before the distress message which follows it is sent.

Distress Messages

1. The radiotelegraph distress message consists of:
   a. The distress signal, SOS;
   b. The name of the mobile station in distress;
   c. Particulars of its position;
   d. The nature of the distress;
   e. The kind of assistance desired;
   f. Any other information that might facilitate rescue.
2. The radiotelephone distress message consists of:
   a. The distress signal, MAYDAY;
   b. The name of the mobile station in distress;
   c. Particulars of its position;
   d. The nature of the distress;
   e. The kind of assistance desired;
   f. Any other information that might facilitate rescue (for example, the length, color and type of vessel, and number of persons aboard).
3. As a general rule a ship signals its position in latitude and longitude (Greenwich) using figures for degrees and minutes and either NORTH or SOUTH and EAST or WEST. In radiotelegraphy the signal, dot, dash, dot, dash, dot, dash (.-.-.-) is used for separation of the degrees and minutes. When practicable, the true bearing and distance in nautical miles from a known position is appropriate.

Radiotelephone Distress Call and Message Transmission Procedure

1. The radiotelephone distress procedure shall consist of:
   a. The radiotelephone alarm signal (if possible);
   b. The distress call;
   c. The distress message.
2. The radiotelephone distress transmissions shall be made slowly and distinctly, each word clearly pronounced to facilitate transcription.
3. After the transmission by radiotelephony of its distress message, the mobile station may be requested to transmit suitable signals, followed by its call sign or name, to permit a direction-finding station to determine its position. This request may be repeated at frequent intervals if necessary.
4. The distress message, preceded by the distress call, shall be repeated at intervals until an answer is received. This

repetition shall be preceded by the radiotelephone alarm signal whenever possible.

5. When the mobile station in distress receives no answer to a distress message transmitted on the distress frequency, the message may be repeated on any other available frequency on which attention might be attracted.

A good choice of words to be used when sending a distress message is: MAYDAY, MAYDAY, MAYDAY, THIS IS THE FREIGHTER BROWN, 32 degrees 28 minutes NORTH LATITUDE, 48 degrees 12 minutes WEST LONGITUDE, ABANDONING SHIP DUE TO FIRE. 23 CREWMEN ABOARD, LAUNCHING FOUR LIFEBOATS, SHIP WILL SINK IN 30 MINUTES. OVER.

Question 4: What are the requirements for keeping watch on 2182 kHz? If a radio operator is required to "stand watch" on an international distress frequency, when may he stop listening?

Each station on board a ship navigating the Great Lakes and licensed to transmit by telephony on one or more frequencies within the 1605- to 3500-kHz band shall, during its hours of service for telephony, maintain an efficient watch for reception of emissions on the authorized carrier frequency 2182 kHz, whenever the station is not being used for transmission on that frequency or for communication on other frequencies. Except for stations on board vessels required by law to be fitted with radiotelegraph equipment, each ship station (in addition to those ship stations specified in the above paragraph) licensed to transmit by telephony on one or more frequencies in the band 1605 to 3500 kHz shall, during its hours of telephony service, maintain an efficient watch for the reception of emissions on the authorized carrier frequency of 2182 kHz whenever such station is not being used for transmission on that frequency or for communication on other frequencies. When the ship station is in Region 1 or 3, such watch shall, insofar as is possible, be maintained at least twice each hour for three minutes commencing at x h.00 and x h.30, Greenwich mean time.

Question 5: Under what circumstances may a coast station contact a land station by radio?

For the purpose of facilitating the transmission or reception of safety communication to or from a ship or aircraft station.

Question 6: What do distress, safety, and urgency signals indicate? What are the international urgency, distress and safety signals? In the case of a mobile radio station in distress, what station is responsible for the control of distress message traffic?

The distress signal, MAYDAY or SOS, indicates that a mobile station is threatened by grave and imminent danger and requests immediate assistance.

The safety signal, SECURITY or TTT, indicates that the station is about to transmit a message concerning the safety of navigation or giving important meteorological warnings.

The urgency signal, PAN or XXX, indicates that the calling station has a very urgent message to transmit concerning the safety of a ship, aircraft, or other vehicle, or the safety of a person.

The international urgency signal in radiotelephony consists of the word PAN, spoken three times and transmitted before the call. In radiotelegraphy, the urgency signal consists of three repetitions of the group XXX, sent with the individual letters of each group and the successive groups, clearly separated from each other.

The international safety signal in radiotelephony consists of the word, SECURITY, spoken three times and transmitted before the call. In radiotelegraphy, the safety signal consists of three repetitions of the group TTT, sent with the individual letters of each group and the successive groups, clearly separated from each other.

The international distress signal in radiotelephony consists of the word, MAYDAY, spoken three times and transmitted before the call. In radiotelegraphy, the distress signal consists of the group SOS, sent three times.

The control of distress traffic is the responsibility of the mobile station in distress or of the station which, pursuant to FCC Rule 83.242a, has sent the distress message. These stations may, however, delegate the control of the distress traffic to another station.

Question 7: In regions of heavy traffic, why should an interval be left between radiotelephone calls? Why should a radio operator listen before transmitting on a shared channel? How long may a radio operator in the mobile service continue to attempt to contact a station that does not answer?

In regions of heavy traffic (many stations operating), the radio operator must leave an interval of time between radiotelephone calls to permit other stations to transmit on the same frequency without interference. This is required by FCC Rules, as many stations are sharing a few allotted channels.

A radio operator should listen before transmitting on a shared channel to make sure that no one else is transmitting on that channel.

Calling a particular station shall not continue for more than 30 seconds in each instance. If the called station does not respond, that station shall not be called again until after an interval of at least two minutes. When such station does not answer to a call sent three times at two-minute intervals, the calling shall stop and not be started again for an interval of 15 minutes unless it is obvious that harmful interference will not be caused to other communications in progress at the time. In the latter case, calls may be resumed after an interval of at least three minutes. However, the provisions of this paragraph shall not apply in case of an emergency involving safety.

Question 8: Why are test transmissions sent? How often should they be sent? What is the proper way to send a test message? How often should the station's call sign be sent?

Test transmissions are sent to make sure that the equipment is in proper operating condition. They should be sent on a regular basis, once a day, before the normal day's communications are scheduled. Regular tests often reveal defects which, if corrected promptly, may prevent needless delays when communications are necessary.

Ship stations must use every precaution to ensure that, when conducting operational transmitter tests, the emissions of the station will not cause harmful interference. Radiation must be reduced to the lowest practicable level and, if feasible, shall be entirely suppressed. The proper way to send a test message is as follows:

1. The licensed radio operator or other person responsible for operation of the transmitting apparatus shall ascertain by careful listening that the test emissions will not be likely to interfere with transmissions in progress; if they are likely to interfere with the working of a coast or aeronautical station in the vicinity of the ship station, the consent of that station or stations must be obtained before the test emissions occur.

2. The official call sign of the testing station, followed by the word "test," shall be announced on the channel being used for the test as a warning that test emissions are about to be made on that frequency.

3. If, as a result of the announcement prescribed in Subparagraph 2, any station transmits by voice the word "wait," testing shall be suspended. When, after an appropriate interval of time, such announcement is repeated and no response is observed with careful listening, indicating that harmful interference will not be caused, the operator shall proceed as set forth in Subparagraph 4.

4. The operator shall announce the word, "testing," followed, in the case of a voice transmission test, by the count "1, 2, 3, 4, etc." or by test phrases or sentences not in conflict with normal operating signals, or followed, in the case of other emissions, by appropriate test signals not in conflict with

normal operating signals. The test signals in either case shall have a duration not exceeding ten seconds. At the conclusion of the test, there shall be a voice announcement of the official call sign of the testing station, the name of the ship on which the station is located, and the general location of the ship at the time the test is being made. This test transmission shall not be repeated until a period of at least one minute has elapsed; on the frequency 2182 kHz or 156.8 MHz in a region of heavy traffic, a period of at least five minutes shall elapse before the test transmission is repeated.

5. When testing is conducted on any frequency within the bands 2170 to 2194 kHz, 156.75 to 156.85 MHz, 480 to 510 kHz (survival craft transmitters only), or 8362 to 8366 kHz (survival craft transmitters only), no test transmissions shall occur which are likely to actuate any automatic alarm receiver within range. Survival craft stations using telephony shall not be tested on the frequency 500 kHz during the 500-kHz silence periods. The test signal shall have a duration not exceeding ten seconds. The official call sign of the testing station shall be given at the conclusion of each test.

Question 9: In the mobile service, why should radiotelephone messages be as brief as possible?

This permits all stations to transmit their communications without undue delay, and the courtesy works both ways.

Question 10: What are the meanings of: Clear, Out, Over, Roger, Words twice, Repeat and Break?

Clear or out: Conversation is ended and no response expected.

Over: My transmission is ended and I expect a response from you.

Roger: I have received all of your last transmission and understood same clearly.

Repeat: Say again.

Break: Hold, I will continue the transmission.

Question 11: Does the Geneva, 1959, Treaty give other countries the authority to inspect U.S. vessels?

Yes. The governments of appropriate administrations of countries that a mobile station visits may require the production of the license for examination. The operator of the mobile station, or the person responsible for the station, shall facilitate this examination. The license shall be kept in such a way that it can be produced upon request. As far as possible, the license, or a copy certified by the authority that issued it, should be permanently exhibited in the station.

Question 12: Why are call signs sent? Why should they be sent clearly and distinctly?

Call signs are sent to enable other stations to identify all callers. They should be sent clearly and distinctly to avoid unnecessary repetitions.

Question 13: How does the licensed operator of a ship station exhibit his authority to operate a station?

When a licensed operator is required for the operation of a station, the original license of each such operator, while he is employed or designated as radio operator of the station, shall be posted in a conspicuous place at the principal location on board ship at which the station is operated; provided that in the case of stations of a portable nature, including marine-utility stations, or in the case where the operator holds a restricted radiotelephone operator permit, the operator may in lieu of posting have on his person either his required operator license or a duly issued verification card (FCC Form 758-F), attesting to the existence of that license.

Question 14: When may a coast station not charge for messages it is requested to handle?

No charge shall be made for the service of any public coast station unless effective tariffs applicable to such service are on file with the Commission.

No charge shall be made by any station in the maritime mobile service of the United States for the transmission of distress messages and replies thereto in connection with situations involving the safety of life and property at sea.

No charge shall be made by any station in the maritime mobile service of the United States for the transmissions, receipt, or relay of the information concerning dangers to navigation, originating on a ship of the United States or of a foreign country.

Question 15: What is the difference between calling and working frequencies?

A calling frequency is one on which all stations listen for incoming calls or on which they transmit a call for another station. Once a reply has been received to the initial call, both stations transfer to a working frequency to continue their communication.

ELEMENT 2
Basic Operating Practice (Series O)

Sample test questions

1. What should an operator do when leaving a transmitter unattended?

(a) Transmitter should be inaccessible to unauthorized persons.

(b) Notify the night watchman.

(c) Make a note of the time and date on the log.

(d) Turn the keys over to the security officer.

(e) Pull the main circuitbreaker.

2. What problem may result from shouting into a microphone?

(a) Overmodulation.

(b) Miller effect.

(c) Linear amplification.

(d) Demodulation.

(e) The amplifier fuse will blow.

3. How should a microphone be treated when used in noisy location?

(a) Reduce the audio gain.

(b) Speak in a normal tone at about six inches.

(c) Cover the microphone with a handkerchief.

(d) Cup hands over the microphone to help exclude noise.

(e) Speak softly into the microphone at close range.

4. The word "Clear" means

(a) I have received your last transmission fully.

(b) This message ended, another will follow.

(c) Message ended, no response expected.

(d) Speak each word more distinctly.

(e) My transmission ended, I expect response.

5. The word "Break" indicates

(a) End of this message, another will follow.

(b) My transmission is ended, response expected.

(c) My message ended, no response expected.

(d) Last transmission received completely.

(e) Standby for further instructions.

6. The word "Roger" indicates

(a) I have received all of your last transmission.

(b) My transmission is ended; no response expected.

(c) This completes my message; another will follow.

(d) Please repeat each group twice.

(e) None of the above.

7. Why should a transmitter be off when transmissions are not being made?

(a) For economy reasons.

(b) To avoid wear on equipment.

(c) In order to avoid interference with other stations.

(d) To prevent overheating the power supply.

(e) To check operation of the main switch and regulators.

8. Parts of a single message may be separated by the following:

(a) Stop

(b) Repeat

(c) Break

(d) Over

(e) Clear

9. **Responsibility for the proper operation of the radio station falls on:**
    (a) The station licensee.
    (b) The owner of the station.
    (c) The person using the microphone.
    (d) The licensed operator in charge of the station.
    (e) Any operator over 21 years of age.

10. **During an emergency, the operator should:**
    (a) Change frequency to avoid interference.
    (b) Reduce power to a predetermined level.
    (c) Discontinue operation at once.
    (d) Increase power above that authorized.
    (e) Standby for further instructions before cutting the carrier.

11. **How does the licensed operator show his authority to operate the station?**
    (a) Posting his license in the station manager's office.
    (b) Posting his license at the transmitter control room.
    (c) Posting his license inside the antenna house.
    (d) By carrying a card attesting to same (FCC Form 758-F).
    (e) Any of the above.

12. **What should the operator do if he hears profanity being used at his station?**
    (a) Send a copy of the incident to the FCC.
    (b) Enter the information in the station log.
    (c) Report the incident to the local authorities.
    (d) Turn off the speaker, enter a report in the station log, submit the report to the FCC.
    (e) Notify the station owner and cut off the audio.

13. **Where may specifications for obstruction marking and lighting of antenna towers be found?**
    (a) In the radio station authorization.
    (b) Extracts from the Geneva 1959 Treaty.
    (c) Part 74 of the FCC Rules and Regulations.
    (d) Part 17 of the FCC Rules and Regulations.
    (e) None of the above.

14. **Why is the station's call sign transmitted?**
    (a) To provide positive identification of the sending station.
    (b) To reveal the location of the transmitter.
    (c) To permit determination of the output power.
    (d) Checking the frequency by the monitoring services.
    (e) To identify station ownership.

15. **An operator testing the transmitter should:**
    (a) Omit a statement of test.
    (b) Make the test as brief as possible.

(c) Provide personal identification.

(d) Not listen for a clear channel before the test.

(e) Increase the power for the test only.

16. In radiotelephone communications, common words, representing letters of the alphabet used to spell out words positively, are called:

(a) The communications method.

(b) The Morse code.

(c) The Miller effect.

(d) Alternate alphabet.

(e) The phonetic alphabet.

17. If an unlicensed person speaks over the air, who bears the responsibility for his actions?

(a) Only the individual speaking.

(b) The general manager of the station.

(c) The licensed operator in charge at the time.

(d) The owner or owners of the station.

(e) None of the above.

18. Why should an operator use well-known words and phrases?

(a) To demonstrate familiarity with the use.

(b) To eliminate distortion.

(c) Avoids damaging the microphone internally.

(d) Reduces biasing requirements.

(e) None of the above.

19. If testing the radio transmitter, the operator should not:

(a) Test for a brief period.

(b) Interfere with normal communications.

(c) Clearly indicate that a test is in progress.

(d) Identify the station by the call sign.

(e) None of the above.

20. The word, out, used in radiotelephone communications indicates:

(a) Transmission complete, no response expected.

(b) Transmission complete, response expected.

(c) Ignore previous message and resume transmission.

(d) All of your last transmission understood.

(e) End of this message, another will follow.

ELEMENT 2
Basic Operating Practice (Series M)
Sample test questions

1. What is the radiotelephone distress signal word?

(a) S O S

(b) Hear this.

(c) Mayday.

(d) Attention

(e) Hertz

2. What is the importance of the frequency 2182 kHz?

(a) It is the international distress frequency for radiotelephone.

(b) It is the frequency for radio beacon purposes.

(c) It is the international distress frequency for radiotelegraph.

(d) This is the appropriate ship-shore working frequency.

(e) It is the frequency for commercial messages between ships.

3. The control of distress traffic must be handled by:

(a) A representative of the FCC.

(b) Anyone willing to volunteer the service.

(c) The station originating the distress signal.

(d) The nearest Coast Guard station.

(e) Any government aircraft in the area.

4. What does the word "Pan" indicate?

(a) Urgency message.

(b) Distress message.

(c) Safety message.

(d) Pan-American aircraft.

(e) Weather message.

5. What does the word "Security" indicate?

(a) Navigational message.

(b) Safety message.

(c) Distress priority message.

(d) Radio beacon signal.

(e) Urgency message.

6. When is it not necessary to acknowledge receipt of a distress message at once?

(a) If the ship is traveling in the opposite direction.

(b) If the ship is too far away to be assisted.

(c) To allow a closer station to acknowledge without interference.

(d) If the ship is nearer a Coast Guard vessel.

(e) When the ship in distress belongs to an unfriendly country.

7. What is the international general calling and distress frequency for radiotelephone in the maritime mobile service?

(a) 500 kHz

(b) 1650 kHz

(c) 2,182 MHz

(d) 88.5 MHz

(e) 2,182 kHz

8. What are the "top three" priority messages in order of their priority?

(a) Distress, safety, urgency
(b) Distress, urgency, safety
(c) Safety, distress, urgency
(d) Distress, navigational, urgency.
(e) Priority, distress, safety.

9. **When may a mobile station send a distress message for another mobile station in distress?**

(a) When the person not in distress considers further help needed.

(b) When a station in distress is not in a position to transmit.

(c) When it has heard a distress message not acknowledged.

(d) All of the above apply.

(e) None of the above apply.

10. **The safety signal would have priority over:**

(a) D-F bearing communications.

(b) Urgency messages.

(c) Distress messages.

(d) Communications preceded by an urgent signal.

(e) None of the above.

11. **When operating on a shared frequency, the radio operator must:**

(a) Never operate after local sunset.

(b) Leave an interval between calls.

(c) Limit transmissions to five minutes.

(d) Transmit on a fixed schedule only.

(e) Increase power to override others.

12. **What is the purpose of a test transmission?**

(a) To ensure proper operation of the equipment.

(b) To avoid antenna icing conditions.

(c) To locate Coast Guard stations in the area.

(d) Provide a check on power supply regulation.

(e) Acquire additional time on the air.

13. **A station may not make a charge for:**

(a) Distress messages.

(b) International commercial messages.

(c) News bulletins.

(d) Personal messages if under 50 words.

(e) Baseball scores.

14. **What is a calling frequency?**

(a) One used only for special messages.

(b) Frequency used after an initial call for communications.

(c) Frequency for personal use only.

(d) Frequency used for priority messages.

(e) Frequency on which stations listen for incoming calls.

15. Calling a particular station should be limited to about:
    - (a) 45 seconds
    - (b) 15 seconds
    - (c) 10 seconds
    - (d) five seconds
    - (e) one minute

16. When hearing the word "Security" repeated three times:
    - (a) Call all stations.
    - (b) Increase power to attract other stations.
    - (c) Continue listening until the message is completed.
    - (d) Contact the Coast Guard for urgent information.
    - (e) None of the above.

17. Why should all radiotelephone messages in the mobile service be as direct and to the point as possible?
    - (a) So all stations may transmit their messages without delay.
    - (b) To avoid a cross-talk problem.
    - (c) To avoid overmodulation of the carrier.
    - (d) To eliminate parasitic oscillations.
    - (e) Harmonic suppression is improved.

18. What information must be contained in distress messages?
    - (a) Position, nature of distress, kind of help needed.
    - (b) Output power, call sign, number of operators.
    - (c) Type of antenna, length of ship, and location.
    - (d) Approximate distance from port, number of persons.
    - (e) Speed and direction, assistance needed.

19. Under what circumstances may a coast station contact a land station by radio?
    - (a) To aid transmission of safety communications to the ship.
    - (b) When commercial messages are not getting through.
    - (c) When the channel is not clear from ship to shore.
    - (d) When power is not sufficient to contact the ship.
    - (e) To report a violation of priorities.

20. How does the operator of a ship station exhibit his authority to operate a station?
    - (a) Showing proficiency in Morse code.
    - (b) Posting his license in plain view at the control point.
    - (c) Exhibiting his school diploma.
    - (d) Showing his Navy discharge papers.
    - (e) Posting his latest proficiency certificate.

CHAPTER 2

Basic Broadcast Practices: Element 9

The basic broadcast endorsement covered in this chapter enables the third-class permit holder to perform certain duties in the broadcast station under the supervision of a first-class license holder. He may operate an AM station with a non-directional antenna and having a power output of 10 KW or less, or an FM station with 25 KW output or less.

OPERATING & PROGRAM LOGS

The FCC regulations pertaining to operating and program logs are quite important to the third-class applicant. Here again, good common sense will prevail as witnessed by the query, "May abbreviations be used in a log?" Yes, but the meaning of the abbreviations must be explained elsewhere; otherwise, of what use would they be to the FCC officer or inspector.

SIMPLE TRANSFORMATIONS

In your studies it is important to remember and understand terms such as "kilo" which means 1,000, 2 kilovolts equals 2,000 volts and 2 kilohertz (kHz) means 2,000 hertz (Hz). As we mention hertz and kilohertz let's remember exactly what hertz means. One hertz equals one cycle per second and the terms mean the same thing; cycle was used universally until a few years ago. However, hertz will eventually be used everywhere, but until it becomes the universal replacement, cycle may pop up every now and then. For example, the FM broadcast band is frequently described as 88 to 108 megacycles (Mcs) instead of megahertz (MHz).

METER READING

Reading meters is a matter of careful observation and practice, which you will find very easy to master. Let's take a look at the frequency meter shown in Fig. 2-2. The center of the scale is the zero point. When the meter pointer rests on zero, the station carrier is exactly on frequency. In the drawing the

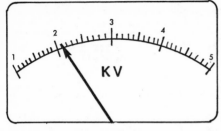

Fig.2-1. Plate voltage meters on some transmitters resemble this drawing.

pointer indicates the carrier is 2 Hz or cycles below the assigned frequency. If the deviation exceeds 20 Hz either way, a correction must be made, since an AM station which must be within 20 hertz (cycles) of its assigned frequency.

TOWER LIGHTING

The importance of tower lighting is emphasized by the several questions regarding tower construction and the many safeguards incorporated in the FCC regulations. The safety of aircraft in the area, as well as the lives and property of employees, crew and passengers, depends on the vigilance and prompt action of station operators. Many stations have an automatic indicator for the lights, but either way they must be checked at least once every 24 hours and full information pertaining to this inspection is entered in the log.

QUESTIONS AND ANSWERS

Many of the questions you may expect in the examination follow, along with answers which are drawn out to some extent where exceptions and specific provisions require. It is usually possible to find the more important text in the first several lines, and this will normally suffice, except for later reference purposes. Sample test questions follow the question and answer section of the chapter, and when you feel that you are

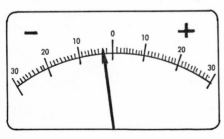

Fig. 2-2. On frequency monitor meters, the zero point is in the center of the scale.

ready to test yourself on the material covered, take a piece of scrap paper and run through the 20 questions, checking your score with the answers listed in Chapter 13.

ELEMENT 9

Basic Broadcast

Question 1: What is meant by the following words or phrases: standard broadcast station, standard broadcast band, FM station, FM band, daytime, nighttime, broadcast day, EBS?

Standard broadcast station means a broadcasting station licensed for the transmission of radiotelephone emissions primarily intended to be received by the general public and operated on a channel in the band 535 to 1605 kHz.

Standard broadcast band means the band of frequencies between 535 and 1605 kHz.

FM station is a station employing frequency modulation in the FM broadcast band and licensed primarily for the transmission of radiotelephone emissions intended to be received by the general public.

FM band indicates the band of frequencies extending from 88 to 108 MHz, which includes those assigned to non-commercial educational broadcasting.

Daytime covers that period of time between local sunrise and local sunset.

Nighttime is the period of time between local sunset and 12 midnight local standard time.

Broadcast day refers to that period of time between local sunrise and 12 midnight local standard time.

EBS signifies the Emergency Broadcast System and consists of broadcast stations and other authorized facilities or systems to operate in a controlled manner under the direction of the FCC during a war or grave national crisis.

Question 2: Make the following transformations: kilocycles to cycles (kHz to Hz), kilovolts to volts, milliamperes to amperes.

Since "kilo" means one thousand, we multiply by 1,000 to change kilocycles (kilohertz to hertz) to cycles, 1 kilocycle equals 1,000 cycles and 2 kilovolts equals 2,000 volts. The term "milli" means one thousandth or multiply by .001 to convert milliamperes to amperes (1,000 milliamperes X .001 equals 1 ampere). Remember that a mill is one tenth of a cent or one thousandth of a dollar, and a "mil" is 0.001 inch.

Question 3: Draw the "face" of the following meters and indicate you know how to read each: ammeter, voltmeter, frequency monitor meter, VU (volume unit) meter for percent modulation.

See Fig. 2-3A, B, C, D. Part A reads 6 amperes, B is 2.8 volts, C shows -25 cycles (hertz) frequency deviation from the

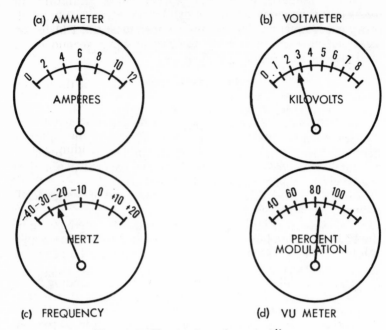

(a) AMMETER

AMPERES

(b) VOLTMETER

KILOVOLTS

(c) FREQUENCY

HERTZ

(d) VU METER

PERCENT MODULATION

Fig. 2-3. Typical meter readings.

assigned frequency, D indicates 85 percent modulation.

Question 4: What should an operator do if the remote antenna ammeter becomes defective?

Authority to operate without the remote antenna ammeter is not required, but the antenna base currents should be read and logged once a day for each mode of operation until the regular remote meter is returned to service.

Question 5: What should an operator do if the remote control devices at a station so equipped malfunction?

The malfunction of remote control circuits or any part thereof resulting in improper control or inaccurate metering should be reason for immediate suspension of remote control operation.

Question 6: What is the permissible percent of modulation for AM and FM stations?

Modulation percentage should be held as high as possible, consistent with good quality transmission and good broadcast practice, but no less than 85 percent on peaks of frequent recurrence, except when necessary to avoid objectionable loudness, and in no case exceeding 100 percent on negative peaks of frequent recurrence.

Question 7: What is the permissible frequency tolerance of standard broadcast stations? Of FM stations?

The standard broadcast station must maintain its operating frequency within 20 cycles per second (Hz) of its assigned frequency. The center frequency of the FM broadcast station must be within 2,000 cycles per second of its assigned center frequency.

Question 8: What stations may be operated by a third-class broadcast operator?

The holder of a third-class radiotelephone operator's permit with broadcast endorsement may operate the following stations, provided that a supervisory operator holding a first-class radiotelephone operator's license is employed or under contract for at least part-time work at the station: AM stations with a power of 10 KW or less and using a nondirectional antenna, or FM stations with a transmitter power output of 25 KW or less. The supervisory operator may hold a second class radiotelephone operator's license in the case of certain non-commercial educational stations.

Question 9: What are the power limitations on broadcast stations?

The operating power shall be held as near as practicable to the licensed power and not exceed +5 percent or -10 percent of the licensed power, except in an emergency when, due to causes beyond the control of the licensee, it becomes impossible to operate with full licensed power, the station may operate with reduced power for a period not exceeding ten days, and provided the Commission and the Engineer in Charge of the radio district in which the station is located shall be notified immediately after the emergency develops and also upon resumption of licensed power.

Question 10: What logs must be kept by broadcast stations according to the Rules and Regulations of the FCC?

The licensee or permitee of each standard broadcast station shall maintain program, operating and maintenance logs in an orderly and legible form and in proper detail.

Question 11: Who keeps the logs?

Each log shall be kept by competent station employees having an actual knowledge of the necessary information involved and, in the case of program and operating logs, he must sign the log when coming on duty and again when going off duty.

Question 12: What entries are made in the program log? In the operating log?

The following entries shall be made in the program log:

(a) Identification of each program by name or title.

(b) Time the program begins and ends.

(c) Classification of program type (music, drama, speech, etc.)

(d) Source of program and network.

(e) Program presenting a political candidate must show his name and political affiliation.

Commercial Material

(a) Identify the sponsor of the program, the person who paid for the announcement, or who furnished material or service.

(b) Total amount of commercial continuity within each commercially sponsored program.

(c) Duration of each commercial announcement and beginning time of each such announcement, or the 15-minute time segment (beginning on the hour) in which the announcement was transmitted.

(d) Show appropriate announcement of sponsorship, as those furnishing material or services, etc., as required by Section 317 of the Communications Act and Paragraph 73.119. A checkmark is sufficient, but it must clearly indicate the matter to which it relates.

Public Service Announcements

PSA indicates that a public service announcement has been made and the name of the organization or interest on whose behalf it is made must be indicated.

Other Announcements

(a) Time each required station identification is made with call letters and location.

(b) Each announcement for a political candidate must show the name and political affiliation of each candidate.

(c) Announcements made pursuant to the local notice requirements must show the time of broadcast.

(d) Entry showing that a mechanical reproduction announcement has been made.

Program entries may be made at the time of broadcast or prior thereto, but programs from a national network supplying all information as to programs, commercial matter, and other announcements for the composite week need not be logged, except as to the time of joining the network, the name of each network program broadcast, the sponsor, if commercially sponsored, time of leaving the network, and any matter not pertaining to the network. All information supplied by the network shall be kept with the station logs.

No part of this section shall be construed as prohibiting the recording or automatic maintenance of data required for program logs. The licensee must comply with the following requirements where automatic logging is used:

1. The licensee, whether employing automatic or manual logging or a combination, must be able to accurately furnish the FCC with all information required to be logged.

2. Each recording tape or other means employed shall be accompanied by a certificate of the operator or other responsible person on duty at the time or other duly authorized agent of the licensee to the effect that such reproduction accurately reflects what was actually broadcast.

The following entries shall be made in the operating log by the properly licensed operator actually in charge of the transmitting apparatus:

1. Time the station begins to supply power to the antenna and the time it stops.

2. Each interruption of the carrier wave, where restoration is not automatic, its cause and duration, followed by signature of the person restoring operation (if a licensed operator other than the licensed operator on duty).

3. At the beginning of operation and at intervals not exceeding one-half hour, the following actual readings observed prior to making any adjustments on equipment, and when appropriate, corrections made to restore parameters to normal operating values:

(a) Total plate voltage and current of the final radio amplifier stage.

(b) Antenna current or common point current on a directional antenna system without modulation, unless the meter is not affected.

(c) Reading of the frequency monitor.

4. Enter each day the following which apply:

(a) Antenna base current (without modulation if the meter readings are affected) for each mode where the remote meters are normally used but are defective, and as required by station license for directional antenna operation.

(b) In remote operation of a directional antenna station, common point readings must be taken for each pattern at the transmitter within two hours of the beginning of operation with each pattern (without modulation if the meter is affected); also base current without modulation unless the meter reading is not so affected, phase monitor loop current without modulation if modulation affects the reading and phase indication.

5. Other entries stipulated by the instrument of authorization or provisions of this section.

6. Accurately calibrated automatic instruments showing proper time and date, as well as circuit functions, may be used to record entries on the operating log, assuming certain conditions are fulfilled. In the final preparation of the operating log, original data could be recorded in rough form and later transcribed, but in all events the original memos are to be retained as a part of the complete record.

Question 13: When may abbreviations be used in the station's logs?

Abbreviations are permissible only if satisfactory explanations are available elsewhere in the log.

Question 14: How and by whom may a station's logs be corrected?

Corrections may be made only by the person making the entry originally, without erasure or obliteration. The erroneous portion shall be struck out, with correction made, initialed and dated.

Note: Any necessary corrections to be made after the log is signed must be accompanied by an explanation, dated, signed and attached either by the person keeping the log, station program director, station technical supervisor, inspecting operator or officer of the licensee.

Question 15: According to the Rules and Regulations of the FCC, how long must station logs be retained?

Standard broadcast station logs must be retained by the licensee or permitee for a period of two years, except those involving communications pertaining to a disaster or investigation by the Commission where the licensee or permitee has been notified. In such cases the logs must be retained until official notification from the Commission (in writing) is received to destroy them or until any claim or complaint has been fully satisfied or barred by a statute limiting the time.

Question 16: What information must be given an FCC inspector at any reasonable hour?

The following shall be made available upon request by an authorized representative of the FCC:

(a) Logs (operating, program and maintenance).

(b) Equipment performance measurements as ordered in Paragraph 73.47.

(c) Copy of the most recent antenna resistance or common-point impedance measurements submitted to the Commission.

(d) Copy of the most recent field intensity measurements to establish the performance of directional antennas as required by Paragraph 73.151.

Question 17: What is included in a station identification, and how often is it given?

The standard broadcast station licensee shall make station identification announcements, consisting of call letters and location, at the beginning and ending of each time of operation (broadcast day), and during such operation as follows:

(a) On the hour, and

(b) Either on the half-hour, or the quarter-hour following the hour and on the quarter-hour preceding the next hour. An identification announcement need not be made on the hour when it would interrupt a single consecutive speech, play, religious service, symphony concert, or operatic production of longer duration than 30 minutes. In such cases, identification announcement shall be made at the beginning of the program, at the first interruption in the entertainment continuity and at the program conclusion. The identification announcement need not be made on the half-hour or quarter-hour when such an announcement would interrupt a single consecutive speech, play, religious service, symphony concert, or operatic production. Here, the identification announcement shall be made at the first interruption of the entertainment continuity and at the program's conclusion. The announcement within five minutes of the times specified herein will satisfy the requirements of identification announcements. During variety shows, baseball broadcasts, or similar programs of longer duration than 30 minutes, the identification announcement shall be made within five minutes of the hour and of the times as specified above. In the case of all other programs, the identification announcement shall be made within two minutes of the hour and of the times specified above. In making identification announcements, the call letters shall be given only on the channel of the station identified thereby, except as otherwise provided in Paragraph 73.287 of the Commission's rules governing FM broadcast stations.

Question 18: What should an operator do if the modulation monitor becomes defective?

In the event the FCC type approved modulation monitor becomes defective, the station may be operated without the monitor, pending its repair or replacement, for a period not exceeding 60 days without further authority of the Commission. Proper entries shall be made in the maintenance log of the station showing date and time the monitor was removed from and restored to service. The Engineer in Charge of the radio district in which the station is located shall be notified immediately after the monitor is found to be defective and promptly after the repaired or replacement monitor has been installed and is properly operating. During the interim, modulation shall be monitored with a cathode-ray oscilloscope or other aceptable means.

Question 19: What should an operator do if the frequency monitor meter becomes defective?

In the event that the FCC type approved frequency monitor becomes defective, the station may be operated without the monitor, pending repair or replacement, for a period not to exceed 60 days without further authority of the Commission. Appropriate entries shall be made in the maintenance log of the station showing the date and time the monitor was removed from and restored to service. The Engineer in Charge of the radio district in which the station is located shall be notified both immediately after the monitor is found to be defective and again after the repair or replacement monitor has been installed and is properly operating. The station frequency shall be compared with an external frequency source of known accuracy at sufficiently frequent intervals to insure that the frequency is maintained within the tolerance prescribed in Paragraph 73.269. An entry is to be made in the station log as to the method used and the results thereof. Should conditions beyond the control of the licensee prevent the monitor from being restored to service within the allotted period, informal request should be made to the Engineer in Charge of the radio district in which the station is located for such additional time as may be needed to complete repairs.

Question 20: When should minor corrections in the transmitter be made, before or after logging the meter readings?

Minor corrections to the transmitter should be made after logging the meter readings.

Question 21: Should the sponsor's name ever be omitted when reading commercials on the air?

No.

Question 22: When should an operator announce a program as "recorded"?

All mechanically reproduced programs in which the element of time has special significance and which could cause the listening audience to believe the broadcast to be simultaneous must be preceded or immediately followed by an appropriate announcement that it was mechanically reproduced, whether such an impression was intentional or otherwise, unless the program is one minute or less.

Question 23: How often should the tower lights be checked for proper operation?

Any radio station antenna structure requiring illumination must be checked at least once each 24 hours either visually or by observing a properly maintained automatic indicator capable of registering the failure of such lights and to insure that all are functioning properly as required. As an alternative, an automatic alarm system shall be provided and properly maintained for the detection of any failure of such lights, with a means of indicating such failure to the licensee. All automatic or mechanical control devices, indicators and alarm systems associated with tower lignting to guarantee that such equipment is functioning properly must be inspected at periods not exceeding three months.

Question 24: What record is kept of tower light operation?

The licensee of any radio station which has an antenna structure requiring illumination shall make the following entries in the station record regarding the inspections required by Paragraph 17.47:

(a) The time the tower lights are turned on and off each day if manually controlled.

(b) Time the daily check of proper operation of the tower lights was made, if an automatic alarm system is not provided.

(c) In the event of any observed or otherwise known failure or improper functioning of a tower light:

(1) Nature of such failure or improper functioning.

(2) Date and time a failure or improper functioning was observed, or otherwise noted.

(3) Date, time and nature of the adjustments, repairs or replacements made.

(4) Identification of the Flight Service Station (Federal Aviation Administration) notified of the failure or improper functioning of any code or rotating beacon light or top light not corrected within 30 minutes, and the date and time such notice was given.

(5) Date and time notice was given to the Flight Service Station (Federal Aviation Administration) that the required illumination was resumed.

(d) Upon completion of the periodic inspection required at least once each 3 months, record:

(1) The date of the inspection and the condition of all tower lights and associated tower lighting control devices, indicator and alarm systems.

(2) Any adjustments, replacements or repairs made to insure compliance with the lighting requirements and the date such adjustments, replacements or repairs were made.

Question 25: What should an operator do if the tower lights fail?

If the tower lights fail, the operator must report immediately by telephone or telegraph to the nearest Flight

Service Station or office of the Federal Aviation Administration any observed or otherwise known failure or improper functioning of a code or rotating beacon light or top light not corrected within 30 minutes. Further notification by telephone or telegraph shall be given immediately upon resumption of the required illumination. A failure or improper functioning of a steady burning side or intermediate light or lights shall be corrected as soon as possible, but it is not necessary to notify the FAA of such failure or improper functioning.

Question 26: What is EBS?
Emergency Broadcast System, a system of facilities and personnel of nongovernment stations authorized by the FCC to operate in a controlled manner during war, disaster or other national crisis.

Question 27: What is an Emergency Action Condition?
The period of time between the transmission of an Emergency Action Notification and the transmission of the Emergency Action Condition Termination.

Question 28: What equipment must be installed in broadcast stations in regard to reception of an Emergency Action Notification?
All broadcast station licensees must install and operate, during their hours of broadcast operation, necessary equipment for receiving Emergency Action Notifications or Terminations transmitted by other radio broadcast stations. This equipment must be maintained in readiness, including arrangements for a human listening watch or automatic alarm devices terminated at the transmitter control point.

Question 29: How often should EBS test transmissions be sent? During what time period are they sent?
Test transmissions must be sent once each week on an unscheduled basis between 8:30 AM and local sunset. Noncommercial educational FM broadcast stations of 10 watts or less are not required to make these tests.

Question 30: During an Emergency Action Condition, what should all nonparticipating stations do?
These stations are required to discontinue operations for the duration of the Emergency Action Condition.

Question 31: If the tower lights of a station are required to be controlled by a light-sensitive device, and this device malfunctions, when should the tower lights be on?
The lights should be on continuously if the device malfunctions. The device should be adjusted to be on at a north sky light intensity level of 35-foot candles and off at a north sky light intensity level of 58-foot candles.

ELEMENT 9
Specific Operating Practices (Broadcast Endorsement)

Sample Test Questions

1. The standard broadcast station is:
   (a) Pulse modulated.
   (b) Phase modulated.
   (c) Frequency modulated.
   (d) Amplitude modulated.
   (e) None of the above.
2. How long must the station log be held?
   (a) 30 days
   (b) Two years
   (c) Five years
   (d) One year
   (e) Three years
3. May abbreviations be used in the station log?
   (a) Only if made in red ink.
   (b) Not unless the FCC gives permission.
   (c) Only when information requires extra log sheets.
   (d) If an explanation is given in the log.
   (e) Only when the short form is used.
4. Which of the following may be operated by a third-class broadcast operator?
   (a) 50-KW AM stations.
   (b) 10-KW AM stations with nondirectional antennas.
   (c) 10-KW AM stations with directional antennas.
   (d) 50-KW FM stations.
   (e) 5-KW AM stations with directional antennas.
5. The standard broadcast band refers to the following frequencies:
   (a) 88 MHz to 108 MHz
   (b) 455 kHz to 1600 kHz
   (c) 535 kHz to 1605 kHz
   (d) 535 MHz to 1600 MHz
   (e) 2182 kHz to 3480 kHz
6. What is EBS?
   (a) Evening Broadcast System
   (b) English Broadcast System
   (c) Eveready Battery Service
   (d) Engineering Broadcast Service
   (e) Emergency Broadcast System
7. Daytime operation means:
   (a) Sunrise to sunset
   (b) Noon to 6 PM
   (c) 7 AM to 6 PM

        (d) Sunrise to 4:30 PM
        (e) Sunrise to 6 PM
8. **Maximum modulation permitted is:**
        (a) 110 percent
        (b) 105 percent
        (c) 90 percent
        (d) 85 percent
        (e) 100 percent
9. **Proper station identification requires:**
        (a) Call sign, frequency, county
        (b) Call sign, street, city
        (c) Frequency, call sign, state
        (d) Call sign, city, state
        (e) None of the above
10. **If a broadcast station has an authorized power of 40 KW, what is the maximum power allowed?**
        (a) 42,000 watts
        (b) 44,000 watts
        (c) 48,000 watts
        (d) 50,000 watts
        (e) Any of the above
11. **How often should Emergency Broadcast System tests be made?**
        (a) Every month, on an unscheduled basis.
        (b) Every other week, when scheduled.
        (c) Once a week, between 8:30 AM and local sunset.
        (d) Each Monday between sunrise and sunset.
        (e) Tuesday or Friday after 4 PM.
12. **How often must tower lights be checked for proper operation?**
        (a) At least once every 24 hours.
        (b) At least once each week.
        (c) Daily at midnight or later.
        (d) Only when a low ceiling exists.
        (e) None of the above.
13. **The operating power of the station must not exceed the following:**
        (a) 5 percent above or 5 percent below the licensed power.
        (b) 5 percent above or 10 percent below the licensed power.
        (c) 10 percent above or 10 percent below the licensed power.
        (d) 10 percent above or 5 percent below the licensed power.
        (e) 15 percent above or 20 percent below the licensed power.

14. Minor corrections in the transmitter must be made:
    (a) While taking meter readings.
    (b) After taking meter readings.
    (c) Before logging the meter readings.
    (d) Only after tests are completed.
    (e) Only after reducing power.

15. What is the center frequency tolerance of a FM broadcast station?
    (a) 20 Hz
    (b) 200 Hz
    (c) 2 Hz
    (d) 2,000 Hz
    (e) 20 kHz

16. 50 milliamperes is:
    (a) 0.050 ampere
    (b) 0.500 ampere
    (c) 0.005 ampere
    (d) 0.0050 ampere
    (e) 50 million amperes

17. 1.75 kilovolts equals:
    (a) 175 volts
    (b) 1,750 volts
    (c) 17.5 volts
    (d) 17,500
    (e) 175,000 volts

18. When tower lights are controlled by a light-sensitive device which malfunctions, the lights must be on:
    (a) During operation of the station.
    (b) From sunset to sunrise.
    (c) 24 hours a day.
    (d) After sign-off until daylight.
    (e) As long as is considered necessary.

19. What is the voltmeter reading in Fig. 2-1?
    (a) 2.1 kilovolts
    (b) 1.9 kilovolts
    (c) 21 volts
    (d) 21 kilovolts
    (e) 0.21 kilovolts

20. What does the frequency meter in Fig. 2-2 indicate?
    (a) 2 Hz above the authorized frequency.
    (b) Practically on the authorized frequency.
    (c) Off frequency but within limits.
    (d) 2 Hz below the authorized frequency.
    (e) 2 kHz below the authorized frequency.

CHAPTER 3

Basic Radiotelephone, Part I:
Element 3

As we begin our study of Element 3, which is basic radiotelephone, an understanding of direct current is a good first step. Direct current or DC flows in one direction and it consists of a force or pressure known as a voltage. The amount of flow is the current or amperage, which is measured in amperes or milliamperes (thousandths of an ampere). Power is a multiple of the two; volts times amperes equals watts. In radio broadcasting, a term commonly used is kilowatts (KW) which is one thousand watts; ten kilowatts (10 KW) equals 10,000 watts, which incidentally is the maximum AM broadcast power output that a third class license holder is allowed to operate where nondirectional antennas are used.

CONDUCTORS AND NONCONDUCTORS

The physical structure of the atoms in a material determines whether or not it will conduct electric currents. In a ring around the nucleus of each atom there is a number of electrons. The fewer the number in this outer shell, the more easily other electrons can break away from each atom to become free electrons which are able to carry a current flow when a voltage is applied to the material. Thus, electric energy may be transferred from one point to another by the movement of free electrons as in a metallic conductor.

CURRENT DIRECTION

This term refers to a point of reference only and does not indicate the direction of movement for the electrical charges. Electron flow is from negative to positive, since electrons are negative and unlike charges attract; therefore, it is much simpler to consider the actual movement of electricity to be in the same direction.

POLARITY

Whether an electric charge is positive (+) or negative (-) may be determined very easily by connecting a voltmeter to the source. When connected correctly, across the battery or source of voltage, the meter pointer will indicate the actual DC voltage on the meter scale, but if the meter leads are reversed the meter pointer swings left against the pin, below zero. Aside from the positive, plus, (+) designations, the positive terminal may be red or have a red wire or lead, while the negative normally uses black as an indicator, in addition to minus or (-).

RESISTANCE

Just as the beaver's dam opposes the flow of water in the small stream, so does the resistance of a device or material oppose the flow of an electric current. Resistance converts electrical energy into heat and is the only form of opposition to DC. (Opposition to AC or alternating current is called impedance and is described in more detail shortly.) The resistance of a conductor depends on the cross-sectional area, length, and material and is measured in ohms. If a pressure of 1 volt causes a current of 1 ampere to flow through a device, its resistance must be 1 ohm. As we look at that most useful formula known as Ohm's Law, let's set up the usual letter abbreviation for the factors—resistance in ohms (R), voltage in volts (E), and current in amperes (I):

$$R = E/I, \quad E = IR, \quad \text{and} \quad I = E/R$$

These formulas will be used many times, along with others to be introduced, in your FCC exams.

If resistances are connected in series, simply add the resistance of each to find the total. If R1 is 2 ohms, R2 is 3 ohms, and R3 is 4 ohms, the total resistance of the group of 2 + 3 + 4 is 9 ohms. To calculate the parallel connection of the same three resistors, the formula below would apply to any number of resistors connected in parallel:

$$Rt = \cfrac{1}{\cfrac{1}{R1} + \cfrac{1}{R2} + \cfrac{1}{R3}} = \cfrac{1}{\cfrac{1}{2} + \cfrac{1}{3} + \cfrac{1}{4}} =$$

$$\cfrac{1}{\cfrac{6}{12} + \cfrac{4}{12} + \cfrac{3}{12}} = \cfrac{1}{\cfrac{13}{12}} = 0.923 \text{ ohms.}$$

If all resistors connected in parallel are the same value, simply divide that common value by the number of resistors so connected, or if three resistors are connected in parallel and each has a value of 3 ohms, 3 into 3 ohms equals 1 ohm. As a safeguard, when making quick decisions, the value of any parallel connection of resistors will always be less than the smallest of the group. This may be helpful in multiple choice questions if only one choice is less than the smallest; otherwise, figure it out and be sure. When only two resistors are connected in parallel, a simpler formula may be used:

$$Rt = \frac{R1 \times R2}{R1 + R2}$$

Larger resistors are usually wirewound with the ohmic values printed on the body, along with the tolerance, and having a rating of 4 watts or more. However, the common carbon-composition resistor in ¼-, ½-, 1-, or 2-watt sizes use the standard color code for proper identification. To read the color code, begin with the ring closest to one end of the resistor. The color of this first ring represents the first significant figure. The second or next ring provides the second significant figure, while the third ring indicates the multiplier (either the number of zeros or decimal). The fourth band or ring tells you how close to that value the resistor should be, or the tolerance in percentage. If the fourth band is silver, as most are, the ohmic value of the resistor should be within 10 percent of the indicated value. A gold band stipulates that the value must be a little closer or within 5 percent. If there is no fourth band at all, the tolerance is 20 percent. There are several catch-phrases for remembering the color code of small resistors, but the "automatic" way seems simpler than transposing slogans. If you see a red band on a resistor, it will always mean 2 or two zeros if the third band is red. In using the color code there are a couple of points that may be overlooked and even become confusing at times. The gold band often appears in the third position in these days of solid-state devices, and although it indicates a better than average resistor in the fourth position (5 percent tolerance), it means something entirely different in position 3—a multiplier of 0.1, and if band one is yellow and two is violet, that's 47 times 0.1 or 4.7 ohms. The silver band is also used at times as a multiplier in position 3, but not as often, and it would change the 47 to 0.47 ohms by indicating a 0.01 multiplier. The complete color code appears in Table 3-1.

Color	1st & 2nd band	3rd band multiplier or add zeros	
Black		1	(No. zeros)
Brown	1	10	1
Red	2	100	2
Orange	3	1,000	3
Yellow	4	10,000	4
Green	5	100,000	5
Blue	6	1,000,000	6
Violet	7	10,000,000	7
Gray	8	100,000,000	8
White	9	1,000,000,000	9
Gold	-	0.1	
Silver	-	0.01	

Tolerance value (4th band)

Gold $\pm$ 5 percent

Silver $\pm$ 10 percent

None $\pm$ 20 percent

Table 3-1. Resistor color code chart.

Resistors are often called by prefixes meaning one-thousand ohms, kilo or K, and one million ohms, megohm or M. In other words, a 4.7K resistor is 4.7 kilohms or 4,700 ohms and 2.2M means 2.2 megohms or 2.2 million ohms (2,200,000 ohms). The letter abbreviation is quite handy for crowded schematic drawings, but be careful of the decimal point; sometimes they don't come up as strong in print as the other lettering.

POWER

Power is the rate at which electrical energy is delivered and used up or consumed and it is measured in watts. The ordinary resistor opposes current flow and the resulting "friction" produces heat. If the resistor gets too hot, it will be damaged by the heat and crack, causing a change in value or even an open circuit. In order to figure the correct size resistor in watts, so it won't burn up or overheat, the power formula may be used, P equals I squared times R. If a 4.7-ohm resistor must carry a current of 0.5 amps or 500 ma, what size could we use without danger of overheating? Squaring the current 0.5 equals 0.25 times 4.7 or 1.175 watts, so a 2-watt resistor would do very nicely. If only the voltage and resistance values are known, the power may be found by: P equals E squared divided by R, but when voltage and current figures alone are handy, P equals EI.

RELAYS

A relay is a very useful electromechanical switching device which opens or closes one or more sets of contacts when its armature is actuated by a current flow through the relay coil. Problems are often given regarding relays. For example, if a relay coil resistance is 300 ohms and the current through it is 0.25 amperes from a 115-volt source, what value resistor must be connected in series with the coil? By Ohm's Law the voltage required across the relay coil is E equals IR equals 0.25 x 300 or 75 volts, so a series resistor capable of dropping the 115-volt source to 75 volts is required. This resistor value is determined by:

$$R = E/I = 40/.25 = 160 \text{ ohms.}$$

Naturally, the 0.25 ampere current flowing through the coil would also flow through the dropping resistor.

Relays may have one or more sets of contacts which are normally closed or open. The normally closed (NC) contact means that the contact points are closed when no current is flowing through the coil and the normally open (NO) contacts are open when the coil has no current flowing through it. As soon as current is applied to the coil the NC contacts open and the NO contacts close, and relay contacts are always shown in the inoperative position. The normal position is always without current applied to the coil unless otherwise noted.

IMPEDANCE

Impedance is the total opposition to an **alternating** (AC) current flow at a specific frequency and is a combination of the resistance and reactance. Usually, impedance is represented by the letter Z and is measured in ohms. The formula for impedance is:

$$Z = \sqrt{R^2 + X^2}$$

X is the reactance which varies according to the frequency of the current and the inductive or capacitive value. When dealing with AC circuits, the Ohm's Law formulas are changed by substituting the impedance (Z) figure (in ohms) in place of the usual R figure normally used in DC circuits. So E equals IZ, Z equals E divided by I, and I equals E divided by Z when we are dealing with AC circuits.

INDUCTANCE AND CAPACITANCE

Inductance, usually indicated by the letter L, is the property of a coil that causes an EMF or voltage to appear in opposition to any change in current flow through that coil. This property also causes an EMF to be induced in adjacent coils and is effective only in circuits where a varying current is available. The measure of inductance is the henry, which represents a change in current of 1 ampere per second which induces an EMF of 1 volt. Since henry is such a large unit of measure, the millihenry (mh), one thousandth of a henry, or the microhenry (uh), at one millionth of a henry, are often used. Inductance increases in direct proportion to the square of the number of turns, which means that a coil with twice the number of turns will have four times the inductance of the lesser coil. Inductance also varies with the cross-sectional area of the core and the permeability of the material used in the core. As the value of inductance increases, so does the coil's opposition to any change in current flowing through it. If two coils are wound in opposite directions and connected in series, they will oppose each other, and if the number of turns is the same, the total inductance of the pair is zero.

It should be remembered that a shorted turn in a coil or winding has a loading effect which, in fact, acts in opposition to remaining windings of the coil, causing the total inductance to decrease. The result is a power loss through overheating. This partially explains the problem that usually exists when a turn or two of a transformer winding becomes shorted due to an insulation breakdown. Minor heating results, which eventually causes more turns to short, and the heating increases until the transformer burns out completely or forces a protective device to open the circuit.

The formula for inductive reactance in ohms is:

$$X_L = 2\pi FL$$

where F is the frequency in Hz and L the inductance in henrys.

Capacitance is associated with a changing electric field instead of magnetic field and a capacitor is simply two conducting surfaces separated by an insulator known as the dielectric. The region between the two charged surfaces of the capacitor is an electrostatic field which blocks direct current but permits alternating current flow to a degree determined by the capacity and frequency of the current involved. The actual strength of the field is also dependent on the distance between the conducting surfaces and the dielectric constant (K) of the insulating material. Air has a K of 1, wax paper 2, and mica or glass about 5 or 6. If the dielectric constant is increased, the force between opposite charges is decreased, but the value of capacity of the unit is greater. The capacitor actually stores electrical energy as an excess of electrons on one plate, which causes an electric field in the dielectric because the plates are oppositely charged. Energy is stored in the dielectric, but the actual charge is on the inner surfaces of the plates or the outer surfaces of the dielectric. Being of opposite polarity, the charges are attracted to each other, but they can reach only the outer surfaces of the dielectric because they are unable to pass through it. When the capacitor is discharged, the charge on the plates is removed and the electric field in the dielectric collapses.

Capacitance or capacity is the measure of the ability of a capacitor to store a charge and depends on the voltage applied and the area of the plates. The capacitance is measured by the farad, but due to the very large size of this measure, the microfarad (mfd), which is one millionth of a farad, and the picofarad (pf), one millionth of a microfarad, are commonly used instead.

The amount of charge in a capacitor is the product of the capacitance C and the applied voltage E: Q equals CE. Q represents the charge in coulombs, C the capacitance in farads, and E the applied voltage in volts.

Capacitors are available in many sizes, shapes, and values according to the specific need and may be fixed or variable. The standard color code for EIA-MIL capacitors follows: Looking at a capacitor, with the arrows on the three top color dots pointing right, we read, the first top dot (reading left to right) is black for MIL mica or white for EIA mica. The second dot is the first significant figure, the third dot the second significant figure and the dot below the third dot denotes the decimal multiplier. The next bottom dot (middle) indicates tolerance percentage and the extreme left bottom dot the characteristic. The capacitor color code is listed in Table 3-2.

The energy stored in a capacitor is figured in watt-seconds (joules) and means one watt of power for a time of one second.

$$W = \frac{E^2 C}{2}$$

W is the energy in watt-seconds
E is the applied voltage across the capacitor in volts
C is capacitance in farads

An electrolytic capacitor provides a large amount of capacity in a small space as a result of a thin film manufacturing process. The space between two aluminum foil rolls is filled with a thick paste of aluminum borate and the DC applied across the electrodes forms a thin film on the positive plate. The thin oxide film is actually the dielectric material between the positive plate and the electrolyte, which is part of the negative plate, since it is in electrical contact with the foil. By acting as the dielectric, the thin oxide film, being only a few millionths of an inch thick, provides very high capacity in a very small space. The polarity of an electrolytic capacitor is extremely important and must never be reversed or damage will result. Such capacitors are used only in DC circuits.

The value of capacitors connected in parallel are simply added for the total capacitance and the combined voltage rating is the same as the lowest of the group. When capacitors are connected in series, the only advantage is an increase in working voltage, but this gain is at a considerable sacrifice in capacitance. There are other considerations which will be taken up as we progress. The formula for determining the total capacity of a series of capacitors is:

$$Ct = \frac{1}{\frac{1}{C1} + \frac{1}{C2} + \frac{1}{C3} \ldots}$$

Color	Fig. 1 & 2	Multiplier	Tolerance (percent)	Voltage	Characteristic
Black	0	1	±20		A
Brown	1	10	±1	100	B
Red	2	100	±2	200	C
Orange	3	1,000	±3	300	D
Yellow	4	10,000	GMV*	400	E
Green	5	100,000	±5	500	F
Blue	6	1,000,000	±6	600	G
Violet	7	10,000,000	±12.5	700	-
Gray	8	0.01	±30	800	-
White	9	0.1	±10	900	J
Gold	.	0.1	±5	1,000	.
Silver	.	0.01	±10	2,000	.

When no voltage is indicated, the EIA value is 500 volts. Voltage is shown by the left dot on the reverse side unless the capacitor is stamped with a value. The characteristic letter indicates the effect of temperature on the capacitance; A indicates a considerable change and J extremely small change.

* GMV is Guaranteed Minimum Value

Table 3-2. Capacitor color code chart.

The working voltages are added. Three 500-volt capacitors in series have an overall W.V. of 1500V.

Capacitive reactance is expressed by the formula:

$$X_C = \frac{1}{2\pi FC}$$

where 2pi equals 6.28, F is the frequency in hertz (Hz), and C is the capacitance in farads. X_C is the capacitive reactance in ohms. This expresses the opposition of the capacitor to an applied current. The opposition decreases as the frequency or capacitance is increased.

REACTANCE ($X_L + X_C$)

When the frequency of an applied voltage is increased, the reactance of the coil increases and the reactance of the capacitor decreases. If we lower the frequency, the reactance of the coil or inductor goes down accordingly but the reactance of the capacitor rises. Thus, the change in one component is opposed by the other, and in circuits where both are used, we determine the total reactance figure by subtracting the smaller value from the larger. Thus, our formula for impedance says that:

$$Z = \sqrt{R^2 + (X_L - X_C)^2}$$

so we are considering the resistance plus the difference between the capacitive reactance (X_C) and the inductive reactance (X_L) which is squared, added, and the square root of the answer is the actual impedance of the RLC combination in ohms.

So what is resonance? Nothing more than the X_L and X_C values being the same, in which case the total reactance of the pair is zero. Current flow in such a circuit is high because it is limited only by the pure resistance of the circuit. If no resistors are used in the circuit, there is nothing to oppose the current flow at resonance. This condition of equal reactances occurs at resonance regardless of whether the coil and capacitor are connected in series or parallel connected. The resonant frequency may be determined by:

$$Fr = \frac{1}{2\pi \ \sqrt{LC}}$$

where Fr is the resonant frequency in hertz, 2 pi equals 6.28, L is the inductance in henrys, and C is the capacity in farads.

VECTORS

In order to evaluate some quantities in electronics, it is necessary to use vectors. In a vector diagram, straight lines are drawn in the appropriate direction from a zero point for each value. The length of each line is proportional to the magnitude or quantity involved. If two voltages are applied in the same direction, that is negative of one to positive of the other (series connected), the total is obtained by adding the two voltages. But if 30 volts is applied in one direction and 50 volts in the opposite direction, the 50-volt potential would determine the combined direction with a net force of 50 less 30 or 20 volts, which is exactly what happens when two AC voltages are 180 degrees out of phase with each other. Between these extremes, the AC voltages may be out of phase to an extent less than 180 but more than 0 degrees and could be measured by drawing vectors accordingly.

POWER FACTOR

Power factor is a percentage rating determined by dividing the resistance of a circuit by its impedance figured at the operating frequency, and if we multiply the result by 100 the answer would be a percentage. This figure is the ratio between true power and apparent power. Therefore, the power factor is equal to the true power divided by the apparent power and the true power in watts is IE multiplied by power factor.

HIGH-PASS AND LOW-PASS FILTERS

When it is desirable to attenuate one frequency or group of frequencies, the use of a filter is indicated. If all frequencies above a specific cutoff point are to be passed without attenuation and those below that cutoff frequency must be attenuated, we would use a high-pass filter to do the job. By the same token, the frequencies below a selected cutoff may be passed while those above are attenuated; this is done with a low-pass filter. Filters are also designed to pass or reject a selected band or group of frequencies as desired, and these are known as bandpass or bandstop filters.

VACUUM TUBES

According to the number of elements or parts, vacuum tubes are known as diodes (2 elements), triodes (3 elements), tetrodes (4 elements), and pentodes (5 elements). All have a cathode to emit electrons when heated and a plate to attract those electrons. In order to attract the negative electrons, the plate must be positive, since unlike charges attract. The diode has only these two elements; therefore, they may be used only as a detector or rectifier. A diode does not amplify. You will see why in a minute. A diode is merely capable of passing current when the plate is provided with a positive voltage to attract the electrons from the cathode. The plate repels those electrons if negatively polarized. This causes the electrons to return to the cathode and no current is permitted to flow.

The triode has a third element known as the grid, or more specifically the control grid. The control grid is a wire mesh or spiral between the cathode and the plate which regulates electron flow from cathode to plate. When the control grid is supplied with a negative potential, called negative bias, some of the electrons are repelled and forced back to the cathode. Therefore, grid action regulates the actual amount of current that flows from cathode to plate. The more negative the grid, the more electrons are forced back to the cathode and the lower the current flow. The less negative bias applied to the control grid, the greater the cathode-plate current will be. As the grid is biased negative with no signal or input to the circuit, you can see that a tiny AC signal coming into the grid will cause the normally negative grid bias to become less negative when the incoming AC signal is positive and more negative as it swings through the negative half cycle. So the small input signal to the control grid is regulating the much heavier current flow between cathode and plate and this is basically what is meant by amplifying. The ordinary triode enables us to increase the magnitude of the input signal and, unlike the diode, provide an output that is many times the input.

Before looking at the tetrode, we must discuss the one major problem with the triode that actually led to the development of the tetrode. Whenever two conducting surfaces (grid and plate) are separated by an insulator, a capacitance exists between the two and, goodness knows, we do not need any built-in capacitors between the plate and grid. It is true, this capacity is very small, but it becomes very troublesome at radio frequencies and the higher the frequency the lower its reactance will be. The tetrode contains a fourth element, a screen grid between the plate and control grid which reduces that control grid-plate capacitance to an insignificant value by acting as a shield. The screen grid is positive, though to a lesser degree than the plate; therefore, electrons from the cathode pass through the control grid, and most go on through the holes in the wire mesh screen grid to the plate. The few that are attracted to the screen grid cause a small DC current flow in the circuit.

With introduction of the screen grid another problem arose: secondary emission. This results from the acceleration of the electrons by the positive screen grid. The fast-moving electrons strike the plate with sufficient force for many to bounce back to the screen grid. The undesirable effect of this action is more screen current and less plate current. Since most of the useful output signal is in the plate current, this presents a big disadvantage. The answer is the 5-element tube, the pentode, which has a fifth element called the suppressor grid between the plate and the screen grid. The suppression normally operates at the same potential as the cathode. As electrons pass the screen grid, they are slowed considerably by the suppressor grid and strike the plate at too low a speed to bounce off. Even the few that manage to bounce from the plate will return as the suppressor isolates them from the screen grid attraction, and the secondary emission problem is remedied.

SEMICONDUCTORS

The solid-state or semiconductor diode is available in many types and has replaced the vacuum tube type in most electronic equipment designed in recent years. Displaying more resistance than the usual conductor, but far less resistance than an insulator, semiconductor materials such as germanium and silicon find wide spread use today in diodes as well as transistors. The pure material is not useful for diodes or transistors until a small quantity of a suitable impurity is blended in to lower the resistance. The two basic materials treated in this way form N-types when antimony is blended with the pure semiconductor material to create additional free electrons, or by blending gallium with the semiconductor material P-types are formed because some electrons are taken away, leaving holes in the material which may conduct current. Since the holes always move in the opposite direction from electrons, they have a positive charge.

The solid-state diode consists of P-type material on one side and N-type material on the other; in other words, a PN junction forms the anode and cathode, respectively. The resistance of the junction is very low from cathode to anode but very high from anode to cathode, and, like its tube counterpart, it may be used to rectify, detect, or steer but not to amplify.

As we look at the 3-section semiconductor or transistor we will find out just how a solid-state device can amplify just as well and even more efficiently than the common vacuum tube triode. The transistor has many advantages, including its small size, no cathode to heat, no time lag, less expensive and many others of lesser import, over the vacuum tube. The transistor may be an NPN type or a PNP type and in either case the connections are the base, emitter, and collector. The emitter symbol for the PNP type always points in toward the base in a schematic diagram, while the emitter points out away from the base in the NPN symbol. The center letter designates the polarity of the base with regard to the emitter in either type.

During operation the emitter-base is forward biased while the collector-base is reverse biased. The resistance is always low when the transistor is forward biased as the carriers move through the junction between emitter and base. When the junction is reverse biased, the resistance at the junction is extremely high as would normally be the case between collector and base.

When comparing the terminals of the transistor to the elements of the vacuum tube, the emitter compares roughly to the cathode, the base to the control grid, and the collector to the plate. Applying a signal to the base of the transistor, the swing of the AC wave causes the base-emitter current to vary and the carriers in the base increase to result in a greater change in collector current.

As the signal is applied across the forward-biased base-emitter terminals, in a common-emitter amplifier, electrons flow from the emitter across the junction with the base and into the base according to the signal variation applied. When additional electrons flow into the base in excess of the base-emitter needs, some proceed to the base-collector junction and are promptly attracted by the positive charge at that junction and thus continue into the collector. This free movement of carriers into the reverse-biased junction results in a current flow through the collector load resistor into the common-emitter and provides an amplified potential across the high resistance of the collector load circuit.

Needless to say, additional study regarding the subject of electronics may be desirable in many cases and many texts are available from the publisher of this book to fit the direction of greatest interest. We are only able to scratch the surface lightly while proceeding toward our major goal and may not get too deeply involved in this most interesting subject, but if the inclination is there, the material is unlimited and you may enhance your technical know-how to any level you wish!

POWER SUPPLIES

The demand for DC power varies greatly in the quantity required, but the demand will always exist regardless of the size or type of electronic equipment being used. Only the smaller transistorized devices use batteries of the dry cell type. Mobile equipment operates from the car battery directly or indirectly through dynamotors, generators, or inverters and power supplies. Base stations draw from the old reliable 117v AC line and convert that power into direct current as needed. As a rule, this is done by using a rectifying device to convert the AC line current to pulsating DC which changes in value but not in direction. However, this pulsating current may be smoothed out very easily by a filter section. The rectifier may be either a vacuum tube diode or a solid-state (semiconductor) diode which allows the current to flow in one direction only. A rectifier converts AC to DC by allowing it to flow freely in one direction and stopping it completely in the other direction. The filter section may consist of one or more capacitors and a resistor or filter choke coil to smooth out the rectified voltage by removing the remaining AC ripple and increasing the average voltage. The larger the capacitor, the greater the filtering because its reactance to the AC component is less and the bypassing is more complete.

There are many types of rectifiers; the simple half-wave, the full-wave, and the bridge type (full-wave) which offers many advantages. We will look at these types along with the various filtering sections and regulation facilities later.

The "bleeder" resistor, by maintaining a minimum load on a power supply, improves the stability or regulation of the output and removes charges stored in the capacitors when the equipment is turned off. This charge could be hazardous in transmitters if allowed to remain, and the bleeder resistor which is across the output of the supply, will dissipate this dangerous potential harmlessly.

ELEMENT 3

Question 1: By what other expressions may a "difference of potential" be described?

Voltage, EMF, IR drop, fall of potential, electromotive force, voltage drop, voltage difference, difference of charge.

Question 2: By what other expression may an electric current flow be described?

Electron flow. If electrons pass a point at the rate of one coulomb per second, the current flow is one ampere.

Question 3: Explain the relationship between the physical structure of the atom and electric current flow.

The atom has an inner nucleus around which electrons revolve in rings, with the outer ring determining the electrical characteristics of the material. The loosely held electrons are free-moving and this movement is current flow. Such material is a conductor, and the movement of free electrons in a general direction under the influence of voltage force constitutes an electric current flow.

Question 4: With respect to electrons, what is the difference between conductors and nonconductors?

A conductor has a large number of free electrons which can move from atom to atom, since they are not bound tightly to their atom; therefore, we have a current flow. Nearly all of the electrons in a nonconductor are tightly bound to their atoms and are not free to travel when an EMF is applied.

Question 5: What is the difference between electric power and electric energy? In what units are each expressed?

Electric power is the rate of doing electrical work or work per unit of time. Electric energy is the amount or capacity for doing work. Electric power is expressed in watts, electric energy in joules. One watt is equal to one joule per second.

Question 6: If the diameter of a wire is doubled, how will the resistance be affected?

The resistance varies inversely with the cross-sectional area. By doubling the diameter, the area is increased four times and resistance reduced to one fourth.

Question 7: If a relay having a coil resistance of 400 ohms is designed to operate when 250 milliamperes flows through the coil, what value of resistance must be connected in series with the coil for operation from 115 volts DC?

Since the total resistance of the circuit is E divided by I, R equals 115 divided by .25 or 460 ohms. We know that the coil is 400 ohms, so the series resistor would be 460 minus 400 or 60 ohms.

Question 8: Draw a circuit with three resistors (50, 100 and 150 ohms) connected in a "pi" network to a 12 V battery as shown in Fig. 3-1.

(a) What is total current through each resistor?

(b) What is the voltage across each?

(c) What power is dissipated in each resistor, and the total power used in the circuit?

(a) Solving for R1, I equals E divided by R1 or 12 divided by 50, which is 240 mA. Since R2 and R3 are in series across the battery, I equals E divided by R2 + R3 or 12 divided by 100 + 150, or 12 divided by 250, which is 48 mA.

(b) The voltage across R1 is the battery voltage, 12 volts; the voltage across R2 is I2 x R2 or .048 x 100 which equals 4.8 volts, and the voltage across R3 is I3 x R3 or .048 x 150 which equals 7.2 volts. Since R2 and R3 are in series with each other

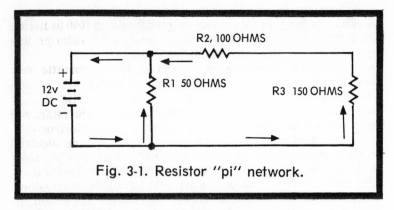

Fig. 3-1. Resistor "pi" network.

across the 12V battery, the voltage drop across the two must equal 12 volts.

(c) Power dissipated in R1 equals E x I or 12 x .240 which equals 2.88 watts; R2 equals 4.8 X .048 or .2304 watts; the power across R3 is 7.2 X .048 or .3456 watts. The total power dissipated in the circuit would be the sum of the three resistors R1 + R2 + R3 equals 2.88 + .2304 + .3456 or 3.456 watts.

Question 9: What is the relationship between wire size and resistance?

The resistance of the wire varies in an inverse proportion to the cross-sectional area.

Question 10: What is the meaning of "skin effect" in conductors carrying RF energy?

The term "skin effect" describes the tendency of RF currents to flow in that area of the conductor nearest the surface, rather than throughout the entire cross-sectional area. This causes the effective resistance of the conductor to increase with the frequency of the current.

Question 11: Why is impedance matching between electrical devices important? Is it always desired? Can it always be attained in practice?

Impedance matching is important between electrical devices where a maximum efficiency of energy transfer is required. This is especially desirable in circuits handling appreciable power, but in the case of others, such as an amplifier in a PA system, a mismatch can contribute to amplifier stability. Perfect impedance matching is seldom attained, although in a given frequency range satisfactory matching is normal.

Question 12: A loudspeaker with an impedance of 3.2 ohms is operating in a plate circuit with an impedance of 3200 ohms. What is the impedance ratio of an output transformer used to match the plate circuit to the speaker? What is the turns ratio?

The impedance ratio is 3200 divided by 3.2 or 1000 to 1. The turns ratio is the square root of the impedance ratio or the square root of 1000, which is 31.6 to 1.

Question 13: Compare some properties of electrostatic and electromagnetic fields.

An unchanging electric field, such as the static charge between the plates of a charged capacitor after the charging voltage has been removed, is an example of an electrostatic field. The current in a wire is composed of moving electric charges or electrons. Each electron produces an electric field in the space around the wire. Since this electric field moves with the electrons, a magnetic field is produced which surrounds the wire and we have an electromagnetic field. If the current is turned off, the electromagnetic field collapses and soon disappears, while the electrostatic field remains in the capacitor even after the charging voltage is removed. The electrostatic field may cause induction while stationary, but the electromagnetic field must be in motion to do this.

Question 14: In what way are the electrical properties of common circuit elements affected by electromagnetic fields? Are interstage connecting leads susceptible to these fields?

The electrical properties of most components are not usually affected by electromagnetic fields, although problems may be caused when electromagnetic fields exist near interstage leads. Unwanted voltages may be induced, resulting in hum, oscillation or distortion. To eliminate such problems, interstage leads must be separated or shielded to prevent electromagnetic lines of force from leaving the wire or outside ones from entering.

Question 15: Which factors determine the amplitude of the EMF induced in a conductor which is cutting magnetic lines of force?

Strength, rate, length and angle. In other words, the density or strength of the magnetic field, plus the speed at which the conductor cuts the lines of force, the length of the conductor and finally the angle at which it cuts the lines of force.

Question 16: Define the term "reluctance."

Reluctance is to magnetic circuits as resistance is to electrical circuits. It is the opposition to the formation of magnetic lines of force in a magnetic circuit and is equal to the magnetomotive force divided by the magnetic flux.

Question 17: Define the term "residual magnetism."

The magnetism remaining after the magnetizing force has been removed, as would be the case in DC generator field coils when the generator is turned off.

Question 18: In what way does an inductance affect the voltage-current phase relationship of a circuit? Why is the phase of a circuit important?

An inductance opposes a change in current but does not oppose a change in voltage. When an AC signal is applied to an inductive circuit, the output current will lag the output voltage by 90 degrees. Inductance, then, exhibits the same effect on current in an electric circuit as inertia does on the velocity of a mechanical object. The effects are advantageous in many respects and disadvantageous in others. By selectively using the phase-lag characteristics of inductance, we can effect a great deal of control over electrical circuits. One example is the series inductance of a power supply where the current-lag characteristic of a coil is used to maintain the supply's B+ at a constant level (through "inertia") even though the load on the supply may change considerably and often.

Question 19: Explain how values of resistance and capacitance in RC networks affect the time constant. How would the output waveform be affected by the frequency of the input in an RC network?

Since the time constant in seconds (T) equals the resistance in ohms times the capacity in farads (T equals RC), increasing either R or C would increase the time constant. The flow of current into or out of the capacitor is limited or slowed down by the series resistance; the greater the value of resistance, the more the flow of current is delayed. The greater the capacity, the longer the time it requires to charge. The time constant is the time in seconds needed for the voltage across the capacitor to reach 63 percent of the applied voltage when charging or a drop to 37 percent when discharging. T in seconds equals R in megohms times C in microfarads for simplification.

A simple sine wave would pass through an RC network with no change, but with a loss in amplitude and a phase shift increasing with frequency. A complex wave would pass with a far greater attenuation of its high-frequency component, tending to smooth the output waveform. By reversing the takeoff point of the RC network, by taking the output across the resistance instead of the capacitor, we have a differentiator or high-pass filter network producing the oppsoite characteristics. The low-frequency component of the complex wave is attenuated much more than the high; thus, the output consists almost entirely of frequencies above the designed cutoff point of the network.

Question 20: Explain how the values of resistance and inductance in an RL network affect its time constant.

Resistance shortens the period necessary for the current to reach its final level after a voltage is applied and the time constant is equal to the inductance divided by the resistance T equals L divided by R, with T in seconds, L in henries and R in ohms. The time constant is the time required in seconds for the current to assume 63 percent of its final value on charging or to drop to 37 percent of its original level upon discharge. Therefore, the greater the resistance, the lower the time constant, and the greater the value of inductance, the greater the time constant.

Question 21: Explain the theory of molecular alignment as it affects the magnetic properties of materials.

The theory assumes that magnetic materials contain tiny magnets known as magnetic dipoles. When properly aligned with all like poles pointing in the same direction, the material is completely magnetized with north and south poles appearing at opposite ends. In most materials the tiny magnets do not line up in the same direction because of collisions and temperature vibrations going on within the atomic structure, which keeps the electrons in constant motion. Thus metals like copper, aluminum, silver and numerous others have little or no magnetic property. Other materials like iron retain their molecular alignment only as long as an electric current is applied. When this EMF is removed, only slight magnetism (known as residual) remains. Although iron is "soft" magnetically, certain hard magnetic materials like Alnico retain their magnetic power indefinitely with reasonable care. Excessive heat or mechanical shock in addition to opposing electromagnetic fields may weaken or demagnetize even such "permanent" magnets.

Question 22: What factors influence the direction of the magnetic lines of force produced by an electromagnet?

The direction of the current flow and the way the coil is wound. By applying the "left-hand rule," which states the thumb points in the direction of the lines of force within the coil with the fingers wrapped around it in the same direction as the current is flowing. This indicates the north pole of the electromagnet. The lines of force from the north pole return to the south pole outside the coil to form a closed loop.

Question 23: Explain how self- and mutual inductance produce transformer action.

When AC flows in the primary winding of a transformer, the magnetic field around it collapses and builds up at the frequency of the applied sine wave, resulting in a counter EMF across the winding and adjacent turns. This action is self induction. The turns of the second coil (or secondary), if close to the primary, are cut by the continuously expanding and collapsing magnetic field, inducing a current in it. The secondary will also induce a current in the primary and the reaction between the coils or windings is mutual inductance as transformer action is produced. If there is no load on the secondary, primary current will be small due to the opposing voltage (resulting from self induction) cancelling out much of the source voltage. However, with the secondary loaded, the current flow tries to set up a magnetic field just as the current through the primary does, but opposing it and thus reducing the self induction bucking voltage of the primary winding and allowing its current to increase as a result.

Question 24: How does the capacitance of a capacitor vary with the area of the plates, the spacing between the plates, dielectric material between plates?

Capacitance varies in direct proportion to the area of the plates. The greater the area of each plate or the number of plates, the greater capacitance.

The capacitance is inversely proportional to the spacing between the plates. Doubling the spacing between the plates will halve the capacitance.

The dielectric material between the plates varies the capacitance in direct proportion to the dielectric constant. Dielectric constant is a measure of the ability of any given material to conduct electric lines of force as compared to air. If the dielectric constant is 7, as in the case of mica, a capacitor having a value of .0005 uF with air would increase to .0035 uF by using mica as the dielectric between its plates.

Question 25: What does coefficient of coupling mean?

Coefficient of coupling is a measure of how much of the flux from one coil cuts the turns of the other, when two inductances are positioned to interact with each other. When two coils are placed very close together (side by side), the coefficient of coupling is maximum—all the flux from one coil cuts all the turns of the other. In this case, the coefficient of coupling is said to be unity. When the coils are separated, or when one of the coils is turned on its axis, the coefficient of coupling decreases. Coefficient of coupling (K) is expressed as a decimal, and is equal to the mutual inductance of the coils divided by the square root of the product of the two inductances.

Question 26: Assuming the voltage on a capacitor is at or below the maximum allowable value, does the value of the capacitor have any relationship to the amount of charge it can store? What relationship does this storage of charges have to the total capacitance of two or more capacitors in series; in parallel?

74

The amount of charge a capacitor can store is equal to the capacitance C times the voltage across it E:

$$Q = C \times E$$

Q: charge in coulombs
C: capacitance in farads
E: voltage across capacitor in volts
The coulomb is a measure of quantity and is equivalent to one ampere per second.

The storage capacity of capacitors in series is reduced, and for two identical capacitors connected in series it is halved as the total capacitance but the working voltage is doubled. When connected in parallel, two identical capacitors have double the storage capacity as well as total capacitance.

Question 27: How should electrolytic capacitors be connected in a circuit in relation to polarity? Which type of low leakage capacitor is used most often in transmitters?

Electrolytic capacitors may be used only in DC circuits and must be connected with the positive terminal to the voltage point which is more positive than the voltage applied to the negative terminal. Simply stated, always observe polarity with electrolytic capacitors, otherwise they will be destroyed. Mica capacitors are used most often in transmitters where low leakage is a must, providing low values of capacity are required. If large values are needed, the oil-filled paper type is often used.

Question 28: How much would it cost to operate a 120-volt bulb having an internal resistance of 100 ohms for a period of 24 hours on power supplied at 9c per kilowatt hour?

In order to find the power used by the bulb:

$$P = \frac{E^2}{R} = \frac{14,400}{100} = 144 \text{ watts} \times 24 \text{ hours} = 3,456$$

watt-hours or 3.456 kilowatt-hours (kwh)

times 9¢ = 31¢

Question 29: Name four materials that make good insulators at low frequencies but not at UHF or above.

Glass, fiber, rubber and paper.

Question 30: In an iron-core transformer, what is the relationship between the transformer turns ratio and primary-to-secondary current ratio; between turns ratio and primary-to-secondary voltage ratio? (Assume no losses.)

The primary-to-secondary current ratio is about an inverse ratio to the actual turns ratio. The primary-to-secondary voltage ratio is proportional to the turns ratio. Taking ideal examples and ignoring normal losses, if the secondary has twice as many turns as the primary, the secondary voltage will be twice that applied to the primary, but the current will be only half as much as that in the primary. As we step voltage up, we step current down and vice versa.

Question 31: What prevents high currents from flowing in the primary of an unloaded transformer?

The inductance of the winding which presents a high inductive reactance to the flow of current.

Question 32: How is power lost in an iron-core transformer? In an air-core transformer?

Power is dissipated through iron losses and copper losses in the iron-core transformer. The copper loss is caused by the actual resistance of the winding, the iron loss results from hysteresis and eddy currents. The molecular friction in the iron core produces heat which is lost power and is known as a hysteresis loss. The eddy currents are induced in the iron core by the alternating current flowing in the windings of the transformer and tend to heat the core which again represents a loss known as eddy current loss. Transformer cores are constructed with thin sheets of metal insulated from each other to help reduce these eddy current losses. All the transformer losses appear as heat in the iron-core type.

In the air-core transformer, power is lost as a result of radiation, absorption and shield losses, skin effect and band-width loading resistance. Since air-core transformers are normally used at radio frequencies, the copper loss increases due to skin effect and radiation loss goes up sharply as the lines of force are no longer confined by an iron core. This results in absorption loss as the lines of force spread out and induce currents in surrounding metal parts.

Question 33: What is the value and tolerance of a resistor that is color coded (reading from left) yellow, violet, orange, silver? What if the silver band is replaced with gold? What if there is no fourth band?

The first resistor is 47,000 ohms, plus or minus 10 percent (47K), the second resistor (with gold band) is 47,000 ohms, plus or minus 5 percent, the third resistor with no fourth band has the value indicated by the first three bands and a tolerance of 20 percent.

Question 34: What is the impedance of a parallel circuit which is composed of pure inductance and pure capacitance at resonance? Of a series circuit at resonance?

The impedance of the parallel circuit would be infinite and the series zero. This is easy to remember because the impedance of the two are opposite at resonance, parallel is high (very high) and series is low (very low) and to avoid getting them twisted, they are in alphabetical order: parallel high, series low.

Question 35: Explain the operation of a break-contact relay; of a make-contact relay.

A break-contact relay is one in which the contacts are closed when the relay coil is not energized; in other words, NC or "normally closed." The make-contact relay is one in which the contacts are open when the relay coil is not energized and closed when energized; this is referred to as NO or "normally open." A spring holds the movable contact arm in the not-energized position and the energizing of the coil pulls this arm in the opposite position against the spring action. A relay in the energized position always reverses the contact position. NO contacts are closed and NC contacts are open. Contact positions are always stated in the "normal" not-energized position unless specifically noted otherwise.

Question 36: Draw a circuit diagram of a low-pass filter composed of a constant-K and an M-derived section.

See Fig. 3-2 for a 2-section low-pass filter.

Question 37: List three precautions that should be taken in soldering electrical connections to assure a permanent junction.

Clean well and join mechanically; apply sufficient heat to the connection to make the solder flow freely onto the connection. Rosin-core solder should be used, **NEVER** acid core.

Question 38: Explain how to determine the sum of two equal vector quantitites having the same reference point but whose directions are 90 degrees apart; 0 degrees apart; 180 degrees apart. How does this pertain to electrical currents or voltages?

A vector may be used to represent direction and magnitude of a quantity. In Fig. 3-3, two sine waves with differing phase relationships are represented by two vectors, E1 and E2. Thus, the solution of problems, such as adding out-

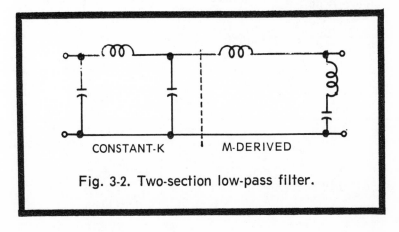

CONSTANT-K   M-DERIVED

Fig. 3-2. Two-section low-pass filter.

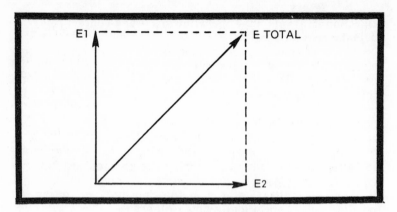

Fig. 3-3. Vector diagram representing two sine waves 90 degrees apart.

of-phase currents or voltages, is simplified by the use of vectors. Vectors may be subtracted only when their directions are exactly opposite and added only when their directions are the same.

Question 39: What would be the value, tolerance and voltage rating of an EIA-coded capacitor whose first row colors are (from left) white, red, green and second row green, silver, red?

Reading from the white dot, which merely indicates that the EIA system is used, the red dot indicates the number 2, the green dot the number 5 and the red dot on the bottom row the number of zeros, giving us the figure 2500 (picofarads). Continuing, the silver dots marks the tolerance 10 percent and the green dot indicates the temperature characteristic or variation due to change in temperature; green represents 0 to 70 parts per million per degree C.

Question 40: Draw a circuit composed of a voltage source of 100 volts at 1000 Hz, having a capacitor of 1 uF in series with the source and a T network composed of an inductor (2 mh), resistor (100 ohms) and inductor (4 mh). The load resistor following the network is 200 ohms.

What is the total current and the current through each circuit component?

What is the voltage across each component?

What is the apparent power consumed and what is the real or actual power consumed by the circuit? By the load resistor?

The total current is 621 mA and the current through the resistor C is 621 mA, inductor L1, 621 mA, inductor L2, 207 mA, resistor R1, 414 mA, and load resistor R2, 207 mA.

Voltage across each component: C, 98.86 volts; L1, 7.82 volts; L2, 5.2 volts; R1, 41.4 volts; R2 (load resistor), 41.4 volts.

The apparent power consumed is 62.1 watts and the actual power consumed by the circuit is 25.7 watts. The actual power used by load resistor R2 is merely 8.57 watts. See Fig. 3-4.

Question 41: Why are filters used? Explain the purpose of "band-stop," "high-pass" and "low-pass" filters.

Filters are used to pass all frequencies above or below a certain frequency, or to pass or reject certain bands of frequencies. A band-rejection (band-stop) filter is a combination of tuned circuits selected so as to provide a low-impedance short-circuit path for frequencies within a specific narrow range. All other frequencies (those not within the resonant band) see the shunt circuit as a high impedance. Such filters normally employ a parallel-resonant circuit in series with the line as well. The parallel-resonant circuit appears as a high impedance to the band that is to be rejected and as a low impedance to all other frequencies. Thus, all frequencies other than those within the resonant band are passed without opposition from input to output, while those within the resonant band are shunted to ground. A common application of the band-rejection filter is the familiar TV wavetrap, a pair of series-resonant circuits used on the lead-in of a transmission line to shunt out the signal from some interfering radio station.

A high-pass filter consists of a series capacitor and a shunt inductor. The capacitor is selected so as to pass all frequencies above a specific value, and the inductor is chosen so as to provide a low-impedance path for all frequencies below the desired value. Thus, high frequencies are passed and low

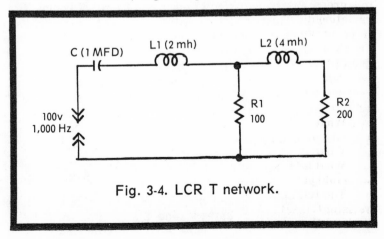

Fig. 3-4. LCR T network.

frequencies are short-circuited. High-pass filters are commonly used in the lead-in wires of television antennas—the objective is to prevent the signals from amateur or commercial transmitters operating below 54 MHz from interfering with the TV signals (which occur above 54 MHz).

A low-pass filter is used to pass low frequencies and attenuate high frequencies. The low-pass filter is the opposite of the high-pass filter constructionally; that is, the low-pass filter consists of a series inductance and a shunt capacitance. A common use for the low-pass filter is in the transmission line of an amateur or commercial radio station. Use of such a filter minimizes the chances of radiating spurious energy at frequencies above the design value of the antenna and transmitters.

Question 42: Discuss the physical characteristics and a common usage of each of the following electron tube types: diode, triode, tetrode, pentode, beam power, remote cutoff, duo-triode, cold-cathode, thyratron.

Diode. The simple diode tube contains a heated cathode and a cold plate. The plate of the tube collects electrons emitted by the heated cathode when the plate is supplied with a high positive dc voltage with respect to the cathode.

In an electronic circuit, the two electrodes of a diode act in the manner of a flow valve in a water pipe. The behavior of a diode is observed after connecting the plate and cathode elements in series with a battery and a milliammeter. The cathode is brought up to normal temperature by applying rated voltage across the heater terminals. If the battery is connected so that the plate is positive with respect to the cathode, the meter will indicate a current flow. This phenomenon, the emission of electrons from hot bodies, first observed by Thomas Edison in 1883, is known as the "Edison Effect." When the battery is connected in reverse polarity so that the plate is negative with respect to the cathode, the meter will indicate no plate-current flow.

The principal characteristics of the diode are these:

(1) When properly connected into a circuit, and with proper voltages, electrons "boil off" the cathode and are attracted to the plate. Since electrons flow from cathode to plate, and not from plate to cathode, the diode is a valve that allows current flow in one direction only.

(2) The diode has only two elements (hence the name), a cathode (or filament) and a plate (or anode).

(3) The diode cannot amplify because it has no tube element between the cathode and plate with which to introduce signal voltages to control the electron flow.

(4) Diodes have a point of sharp transition between the conducting (current gating) and nonconducting states, a factor that gives them a nonlinear characteristic that allows demodulation (detection) by rectifying the RF from modulated RF signals, leaving the audio for further processing.

Triode. The triode, or three-element tube, is similar in construction to the diode, except that a grid of fine-mesh wire is added between the cathode and plate. The addition of the grid gives the tube its most useful function—the ability to amplify. It is common practice to make the grid in the form of a spiral helix of circular or elliptical cross section with the cathode at the center. Other arrangements, however, may be used provided the essential requirement of being able to control the flow of plate current with the potential applied to the grid is met.

The space between the meshes is sufficiently large not to block the flow of electrons from cathode to plate, yet it is still small enough and close enough to the cathode to control effectively the amount of electrons that are allowed to pass from the cathode to the plate.

While plate current in a diode depends only on plate voltage and cathode temperature, plate current in a triode depends on these factors as well as on voltage on the grid with respect to the cathode. A very small change in grid voltage causes a relatively large change in plate current.

The principal uses of triodes are as amplifiers. Triodes can be used to amplify audio signals as well as radio-frequency signals. When a triode is used to amplify signals of very high frequency, certain precautions must be observed to minimize the coupling that takes place between the elements inside the tube.

Tetrode. The relatively large values of interelectrode capacitances of the triode, particularly the plate-to-grid capacitance, impose a serious limitation of the tube as an amplifier at high frequencies. To reduce the plate-to-grid capacitance, a second grid, referred to as a "screen" grid, is inserted between the grid and plate of the tube.

Because the screen grid is shunted by a screen bypass capacitor having a low reactance at the signal frequency, it acts as a shield between the plate and control grid. It effectively reduces the interelectrode capacitance coupling between the plate and the control grid circuits. The screen is supplied with a potential somewhat less positive than the plate. The positive voltage on the screen grid accelerates the electrons moving from the cathode to the plate. Some of these electrons strike the screen and produce a screen current. The larger portion of them, however, pass through the open-mesh screen grid to the plate.

Because of the presence of the screen grid, a variation in the plate voltage has little effect on the flow of plate current. The control grid, on the other hand, retains its control as in the triode. The tetrode has high plate resistance and a high amplification factor in comparison to the triode. The high amplification factor is brought about by the close proximity of the control grid to the cathode and the electrical isolation of the plate from the control grid. The transconductance of tetrodes is also relatively high when compared with that of triodes.

When the electrons flowing in a vacuum tube strike the plate with sufficient force, other loosely held electrons are knocked out of the plate material into the space near the plate. When the screen is at a higher positive potential than the plate the secondary electrons are attracted to the screen. The flow of these electrons to the screen is in the opposite direction to the normal flow from cathode to plate, so the plate current is decreased. This reduction in plate current continues until the potential of the plate approaches the screen grid potential. Further increase in plate voltage causes the secondary electrons to be pulled back to the plate and the plate current again increases. The tetrode's characteristic curve is thus considerably different from that of the triode.

The action in the region where plate current decreases as plate voltage increases is called "negative resistance." This action is opposite to that encountered in a normal resistor. When the tetrode is used as an amplifier, plate voltage should not fall below the screen voltage. If plate voltage does fall below that of the screen, plate current will fail to follow the grid-signal waveform and the output-signal plate voltage variation will be clipped. This distortion may be eliminated by reducing the amplitude of the grid signal or increasing the B-supply voltage. However, the relatively large screen current and the effects of secondary emission from the plate limit the usefulness of the tetrode as an RF voltage amplifier. Still, the tube has been successfully used in RF amplification applications, both for transmitting and receiving, for a number of years.

The most important single characteristic of the tetrode is the screen grid, which serves to overcome the disadvantageous interelectrode-capacitance problems of the triode.

Pentode. A pentode has, as the name implies, five elements. The secondary-emission problem of the tetrode is overcome with the addition of another grid element between the screen grid and the plate. This element, referred to as the suppressor grid, is typically at the same potential as the tube's cathode, so the effects of the screen's high potential are negated.

In the pentode, the suppressor grid serves to repel or suppress secondary electrons from the plate. It also serves to slow down the primary electrons from the cathode as they approach the suppressor. This action does not interfere with the flow of electrons from cathode to plate but serves to prevent any interchange of secondary electrons between screen and plate. The suppressor thus eliminates the negative-resistance effect that appears in a tetrode in the region where plate voltage falls below that of the screen. Thus, plate current rises smoothly from zero up to its saturation point as plate voltage is increased uniformly with grid voltage held constant. The amplification factor of pentodes is very high in comparison with triodes and tetrodes.

In the RF pentode, the chief purpose of the screen grid is to eliminate the effects of interelectrode-capacitance coupling between control grid and plate circuits. In the power pentode, at audio frequencies, the screen permits the output signal plate voltage variation to be relatively large without the degenerative action occurring as it does in the triode. Plate current is substantially independent of plate voltage in the power pentode since the screen voltage is the principal factor influencing plate current. With the addition of the suppressor, the allowable output voltage variation is larger than that of the tetrode, and the distortion effects of the tetrode are eliminated. Thus, an audio-frequency power pentode has an allowable output voltage variation in which the plate voltage can fall a large amount below that of the screen on the positive half-cycle of input signal without clipping the plate signal current. And the ratio of output power to grid driving voltage is relatively large.

Pentodes have traditionally been extensively used in applications where high amplification factors or high frequencies are involved.

Beam Power. The beam power tube has the advantages of both the tetrode and the pentode. This tube is capable of handling relatively high levels of electrical power for application in the output stages of receivers and amplifiers, and in different portions of transmitters. The power-handling capability stems from concentration of the plate-current electrons into beams, or sheets of moving charges. In the usual type of electron tube, the plate-current electrons advance in a predetermined direction but without being confined into beams.

The external appearance of these tubes is like that of other standard receiving-type tetrodes or pentodes; they are slightly larger in dimension because they are called upon to handle somewhat more power, but they have no distinctive external identifying features.

The beam-forming plates influence the movement of the plate-current electrons from the time they pass the screen electrode until they strike the plate. The beam electrodes are connected internally to the cathode, and consequently they are at the same potential as the latter.

Because of this potential of the beam-forming plates, an effect equivalent to a space charge is developed in the space between the screen and the plate. The effect is as if a surface existed in the screen-plate space. This is identified as the "virtual cathode." The presence of this electric plane repels secondary electrons liberated by the plate and prevents them from moving to the screen.

In some tubes, the effect of a virtual cathode is achieved by the use of a third grid in the place of the beam-forming plates. The results are identical in both versions. Because the plate current becomes substantially independent of plate voltage at much lower values of plate potential than in the conventional pentode, the beam power tube can handle greater amounts of electrical power at lower values of plate voltage. In addition, the beam power tube produces less distortion than the ordinary pentode while accommodating an increased grid swing and plate-current change.

Remote Cutoff. The amplification constant, or "mu," of an electron tube has been described as being a function of the geometry of the tube—that is, of the shape and organization of the electrodes. Slight variations in its value may occur under different operating voltages, but for practical purposes it is considered to remain substantially constant. This accounts for the fact that each vacuum tube bears a single "mu" rating which is assumed to be fixed.

The amplification constant of a tube expresses the relationship between plate current cutoff and negative grid voltage when a fixed value of plate voltage is applied. High-mu tubes such as tetrodes and pentodes, especially the latter, reach plate-current cutoff at relatively low values of negative grid voltage. Low-mu tubes allow the application of much higher negative grid voltages before cutoff is reached.

Such plate-current / grid-voltage relationships and the fixed-mu constant stem from the kind of control-grid structure used in most of the tubes discussed previously—that is, the turns of the control grid are uniformly spaced throughout the length of the tube structure. Application of a voltage to the control grid results in the same effect on the plate-current electrons all along the control-grid wires. The fixed-mu state poses a problem when high-mu tubes are used in communications systems. Frequently large amplitude signals are encountered and they must be controlled in the equipment in order to produce the desired intelligence with a minimum of distortion.

To minimize these effects, special kinds of tetrodes and pentodes are used. These are known as variable-mu, or "remote cutoff" tubes, and they differ from ordinary tubes in the construction of the control grids. In these tubes, the grid wires are unequally spaced. Turns are closer together at the top and bottom of the winding and wider apart at the center. This form of control grid construction produces a tube which does not have a constant mu; instead, mu changes with the value of grid voltage applied to the control grid.

At low values of bias, the grid operates in a normal manner. As the control grid is made more negative, the effect of the closely spaced grid wires becomes greater and the electron flow from the space charge in this region is cut off completely. The center of the grid structure also displays a greater effect but still allows electrons to advance to the screen and plate. The overall reduction in plate current, therefore, is gradual. Eventually, with sufficient negative voltage on the grid, all parts of the grid electrode winding act to cut off the plate current, but the negative grid voltage required to attain this is perhaps three to four times as much as for the conventional tube operated at like screen and plate voltages.

Remote-cutoff tubes are used in locations in communications equipment where high bias voltages may be necessary to provide control of the signal level.

Duo-Triode. The term "duo" means that two tubes are incorporated within the same glass envelope. There are a large number of multiunit tubes.

A multiunit tube has the advantage of being more compact and considerably more economical than a pair of tubes, each having the capability of one of the tubes in a combined pair. Duo-diodes and duo-triodes are the most common combined-pair tubes. Frequently, a single common cathode is used which supplies electrons to both sets of elements in a multielement tube. Occasionally, an electrode of one set of elements is connected internally to an electrode of another set of elements.

There are many types of multiunit tubes, used for a wide variety of purposes. A duo-diode can be used as a full-wave rectifier, an FM discriminator, or a combination detector and AVC rectifier.

Cold Cathode. A gas-filled tube in which two electrodes are inserted is called a gas diode. The electrode to which the positive potential is applied is called the plate and the other is called the cathode, as in ordinary vacuum tubes. The cathode in a gas diode can be an electrode like the plate or it can be a thermionic emitter. The former is known as a **cold cathode** and the latter is known as a **hot cathode.**

Cold-cathode tubes are used for many purposes; among these are voltage regulation, rectification, oscillation, circuit protection, and light production—as for neon signs.

Cold-cathode tubes rarely are used as rectifiers because of their high voltage drop, although a variation of the cold-cathode tube is used where filament power for a heater-cathode rectifier is difficult to obtain. An example of a cold-cathode rectifier was once used in vehicular equipment (it has since been replaced by semiconductors). The principle of operation is based on the heating of the cathode under ionic bombardment.

Thyratron. If a grid is placed between the cathode and the plate of a gas tube, the voltage at which breakdown occurs can be controlled by the voltage on the grid. The entire plate surface in this tube usually is shielded by the grid before breakdown. The grid is placed close to the plate to prevent discharge between the two elements. In a grid-controlled gas-discharge tube, the plate supply voltage exceeds the plate-to-cathode breakdown voltage and the grid is held either zero or negative with respect to the cathode. Under these conditions, breakdown does not take place.

If the grid voltage is raised, breakdown occurs between the grid and the cathode. This ionizes all the gas in the tube, and the discharge continues with plate-cathode current flow. Resistance in series with the grid limits its current on breakdown to a safe value. After breakdown, the grid can no longer control the discharge. If it is made negative with respect to the cathode, positive ions surround the grid wires, and electrons are repelled from them. The discharge, then, is shielded completely from the grid. To reestablish grid control, the plate voltage must be reduced to the extinction potential of the cathode-plate discharge.

This principle of grid control can be applied to almost any gas-discharge tube. It is used with cold-cathode, hot-cathode, and arc tubes. All of these types are given the generic name of "thyratron."

Question 43: What is the principal advantage of a tetrode tube over a triode tube as a radio-frequency amplifier?

The tetrode tube has a screen grid to act as a shield between the control grid and plate. Thus, the interelectrode capacitance normally found in the triode is eliminated. This makes the tetrode useful in many amplifier circuits without the neutralization required for a triode.

Question 44: Compare tetrode tubes to triode tubes in reference to high plate current and interelectrode capacitance.

Since the screen grid in a tetrode normally operates at a lower positive potential than the plate, the plate current is not dependent on the plate voltage. Therefore, the tetrode is capable of handling higher plate current at lower voltages than the triode, other factors being equal, and higher gain is attained. The interelectrode capacitance is greatly reduced in the tetrode as a result of the screen grid shielding provided between the offending elements (control grid and plate).

Question 45: Are there any advantages or disadvantages of filament-type vacuum tubes when compared with the indirectly heated types?

There are several advantages and disadvantages, with the indirectly heated tube apparently more desirable as more electrons are emitted from the specially coated cathode, and the AC filament variation does not affect electron emission, which prevents hum. In battery-operated (DC) circuits, the filament type is desirable for its instant-heating characteristic. Of course there would be no AC hum problems.

Question 46: Draw a simple circuit diagram consisting of each of the following and describe its operation. Show a signal source and include coupling and bypass capacitors, power supply connections and plate load.

AF "grounded-cathode" triode amplifier with cathode resistor biasing, as for Class A operation.

AF "grounded-cathode" pentode amplifier with battery biasing, for Class A operation.

RF "grounded-grid" triode amplifier with LC tank plate-load for Class B operation.

AF "cathode-follower" triode amplifier.

AF "push-pull" pentode amplifier operated Class B with transformer coupling to a speaker.

Audio Amplifier, Triode, With Cathode Bias Resistor. The most common method of obtaining bias in Class A amplifier tubes is to incorporate a series resistor in the cathode circuit, as shown in the circuit diagram of Fig. 3-5. In this circuit, the bias voltage is developed across the cathode resistor. Under quiescent conditions (the no-signal state), plate current flows continuously from cathode to plate and back to the cathode through its series resistor. Since the plate current flows from chassis ground to the cathode through the resistor, the chassis is negative with respect to the cathode.

In the figure, the signal source is shown by the symbol e_S. The output signal is designated e_O (as it appears at the grid of the succeeding stage).

Assume that the voltage drop across the cathode resistor is 5V. This makes the cathode 5V positive with respect to the grid (or the grid 5V negative with respect to the cathode). The grid resistor is part of the coupling network for the input signal (e_S). If the input signal is sinusoidal, the plate current will vary sinusoidally about an average DC value. The varying plate current flows through the cathode resistor. Since the required bias is a fixed voltage (5V), the AC component of plate current through the cathode resistor must be removed. This is accomplished by means of the bypass capacitor across the cathode resistor. The capacitor acts as a short circuit to the alternating current. The value of the capacitor is large so that its capacitive reactance is small compared with the resistance of the cathode resistor at the frequency of operation (within the audible spectrum). The value for audio applications would be in the general range of 10 to 50 uF. The value of the cathode resistor is usually from 250 to 3000 ohms.

The plate-current flow is a direct result of grid bias. When the grid goes slightly more negative, plate current drops considerably, but in direct proportion to the negative-going grid signal. For a 1V variation in grid voltage, the plate current may vary as much as 10 mA.

The proportional variation in output current is passed through a resistor in the plate lead, called the load resistor (R_L). In accordance with Ohm's law, the voltage drop across a resistor changes according to the current applied to the resistor. The changing voltage here, brought about by the changing current, is the signal that is applied to the next stage. However, since this voltage is DC, it cannot be applied directly to the next stage without upsetting that stage's own biasing. The coupling capacitor (DC) is used to pass the amplified signal while blocking the high DC potential.

The variations produced in the plate current of a vacuum tube when a signal voltage is applied to the control grid are exactly the same as would be produced in a generator developing a voltage and having an internal resistance equal to the plate resistance of the tube.

Audio Amplifier, Grounded Cathode, With Battery Biasing. The circuit diagram shown in Fig. 3-6 is for a single-triode Class A amplifier that obtains all its operating voltages, including grid bias, from batteries. The bias battery in series with the signal source is 8V, which sets the operating point for the tube. The phase and character of the input signal is described by the sine wave labeled e_c. The varying plate current in the output is labeled i_b. The plate load resistor signal is labeled e_{RL}. The output signal, 180 degrees out of phase with the input, is labeled $e_{b(out)}$. The signal on the control grid of an electron tube is always in phase with the plate current, but is 180 degrees out of phase with the output plate voltage. This statement holds true for all types of electron tubes, whether they are triodes, tetrodes, or pentodes.

Grounded-Grid RF Triode Amplifier, LC Tank-Plate Load, Class B. In the grounded-grid amplifier (Fig. 3-7) the signal is applied between the cathode and ground, the grid is grounded, and the output is taken across a load between plate and ground—in this case, the LC tank plate load.

The grounded-grid circuit permits the use of a triode (with its lower noise figure) and does not require neutralization. However, the voltage gain of the amplifier is not as great as that of the grounded-cathode circuit because the input impedance is very low. The tuned circuit has little voltage step-up to overcome tube noise, and the overall noise performance tends to suffer somewhat. The low-impedance input circuit permits the attainment of wide bandwidth and a reasonable noise figure without sacrificing too much voltage gain in the input circuit.

The gain of the grounded-grid amplifier may not be great enough to override the noise produced by some converter tubes; thus, it is common practice to find two grounded-grid amplifiers in cascade. The added complications arising from this necessity and the need for special tubes limit its use. The tubes themselves must have very low effective plate-to-cathode capacitance if the shielding effect of the grounded grid is to be realized.

Audio-Frequency Cathode Follower. A cathode follower is a single-stage degenerative amplifier in which the output is taken from across the cathode resistor, as shown in Fig. 3-8. This circuit is essentially a device for matching a high-impedance circuit to a low-impedance circuit without discriminating against any frequency. Its voltage output is always less than the input voltage, but it is capable of power amplification. Two of the advantages of cathode followers are low input capacitance and distortion-free output.

The cathode follower introduces very little amplitude distortion into the output; it is a degenerative circuit in which negative feedback is always produced by an unbypassed cathode resistor, and its output is taken from across the cathode resistor and not from the plate.

The input impedance in a cathode follower is quite high. Since cathode followers are operated with the grid negative with respect to the cathode, a high-amplitude voltage can be applied between the grid and ground without causing grid current to flow. This is due to the degenerative action of the cathode resistor and the high input impedance during the positive input signal. Because of its high input impedance, the cathode follower has negligible loading effect on the circuit which drives it.

Class B Push-Pull Pentode With Transformer Coupling to Loudspeaker. The diagram in Fig. 3-9 shows a push-pull audio amplifier using beam-power pentodes. The circuit is essentially the same as if it were a triode type, except that provisions are made for screen-grid voltages. The screen voltage is usually the same as the plate voltage.

Referring to a manufacturer's tube manual, a comparison between the 6V6 Class A single-ended and the 6V6 Class B push-pull amplifiers can be made. With a plate voltage of 250V, the single-ended power output is about 4.5W. For the same plate voltage, the push-pull power output is 10W. This larger output power is a result of using a larger input signal, which is possible with push-pull operation. The upper tube in the push-pull pair may be operated at the lower end of the linear portion of the dynamic curve, and the lower tube is operated in the same manner, with curve reversed. A positive-going signal, then, can go much further without distortion, and a negative-going signal can go much further negative without distortion, since each tube has its own dynamic characteristic over which to amplify Class B signals.

The single-ended stage is biased for Class A, while the push-pull stage may be operated Class B.

In the circuit shown, the input signal is transformer-coupled to the push-pull pair. The centertap on the input coupling transformer serves to keep the polarities of the two tubes properly opposed. The two output waveforms are applied to an output transformer that is similarly centertapped. The upper tube supplies positive half-cycles to the transformer, and the lower tube supplies negative half-cycles. The output of the transformer, whose impedance matches the speaker, is a composite of the positive and negative half-cycles—this composite is a replica of the original input waveform.

Question 47: What kind of vacuum tube responds to filament reactivation, and how is reactivation accomplished?

Thoriated tungsten filaments usually respond to reactivation. The filament voltage is raised to about two to three times its normal value for one minute and then is reduced to approximately 25 percent above normal for at least 10 minutes. Actually, reactivation is recommended only in emergencies; it's more practical to replace with a new tube rather than risk failure at some critical time with a "repaired" tube. The figures and times for reactivation are quite flexible, so don't worry about splitting hairs if you use them.

Question 48: Draw a rough graph of plate-current versus grid-voltage (I_p vs E_g) for various plate voltages on a typical triode vacuum tube.

(a) How would output current vary with input voltage in Class A amplifier operation? Class AB operation? Class B operation? Class C operation?

(b) Does the amplitude of the input signal determine the class of operation?

(c) What is meant by "current-cutoff" bias voltage?

(d) What is meant by plate current "saturation"?

(e) What is the relationship between distortion in the output current waveform and:

1. The class of operation?

2. The portion of the transfer characteristic over which the signal is operating?

3. Amplitude of the input signal?

(f) What occurs in the grid circuit when the grid is "driven" positive? Would this have any effect on biasing?

(g) In what way is the output current related to the output voltage?

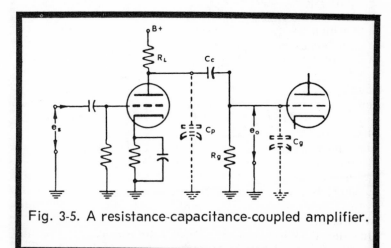

Fig. 3-5. A resistance-capacitance-coupled amplifier.

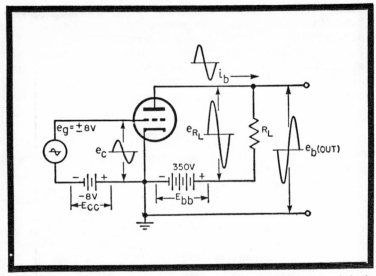

Fig. 3-6. Current and voltage phase relations in triode amplifier circuit.

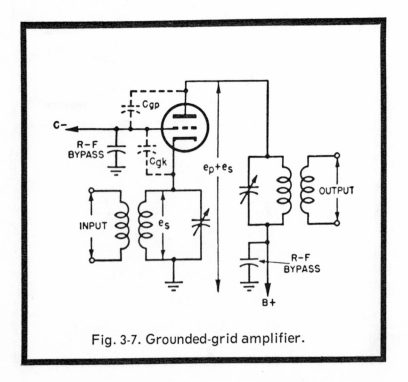

Fig. 3-7. Grounded-grid amplifier.

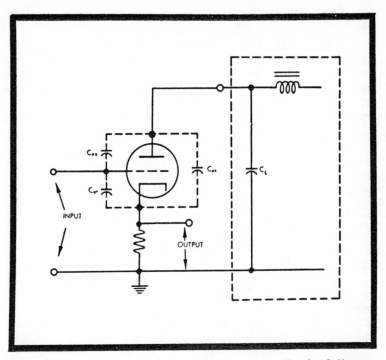

Fig. 3-8. Interelectrode capacitance in cathode follower circuit.

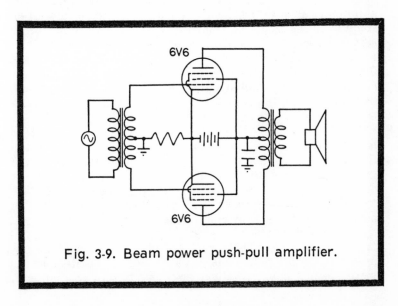

Fig. 3-9. Beam power push-pull amplifier.

Each curve in Fig. 3-10 is identified by a specific value of applied plate voltage, and is therefore the resultant of the stated plate voltage and changes in the grid voltage. The curve is formed by noting the plate current as the control-grid voltage is increased in the negative direction, beginning at zero volts. These points are joined and form a curve. The change in plate current corresponding to a fixed change in bias voltage (grid voltage) is a function of the operating region on the plate-current curve.

(a) In all classes of amplifier operation, the output current varies in direct proportion to input voltage as long as the input signal is swinging positive. In Class A operation, the plate current follows the input signal completely, increasing when the grid signal goes positive, decreasing when the grid signal goes negative. In Class B operation, the output current follows the grid voltage during positive half-cycles, but current is cut off completely during negative half-cycles. In Class C operation, since the tube is biased well below plate-current cutoff, plate current flows only during the latter two-thirds or so of its positive swing, so the tube is not drawing current at all during the greater portion of each input cycle. Class AB operation is quite similar to Class B, except that the tube is biased so that its operating point is slightly above cutoff; actually, the operating point is often midway between the center of the linear region and cutoff.

(b) The amplitude of the input signal does not in itself determine the class of operation; however, the input-signal amplitude can alter the class. For example, when an amplifier stage is biased to operate Class AB, and a very small input signal is applied to the grid, the tube will conduct during the complete input cycle and the tube can be said to be operating Class A.

So long as the input signal keeps the tube operating within its linear region, the amplifier is operating Class A regardless of the biasing point.

(c) The current-cutoff bias voltage is the amount of negative grid bias required to cause plate current to stop flowing at a particular value of applied plate voltage. As the grid voltage goes more and more negative, plate current decreases. At some point, called plate-current cutoff, the plate current will drop to zero. The value of the grid potential at this point is called "current cutoff bias voltage."

(d) Saturation occurs when plate current ceases to increase despite changes in grid voltage. As grid voltage approaches zero (from some negative value), plate current increases in a linear relationship. Close to zero grid voltage,

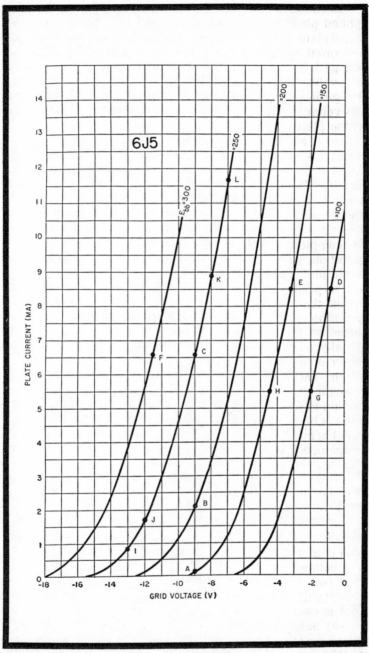

Fig. 3-10. Grid family of characteristic curves for 6J5 triode.

though, the plate current increase does not follow the same constant rising characteristic as it did at the negative value.

(e) There is a direct relationship between distortion and class of operation. Class A operation is the only class that results in distortion-free operation, because it is the only class where the output waveform religiously follows the input waveform. Distortion occurs when the output waveform ceases to change in accordance with the changes of the input waveform.

The portion of the transfer characteristic is also a determining factor with respect to total distortion. If the transfer characteristic is linear and the tube is biased so that its no-signal current drain is plotted at the center of this linear region, the output signal will be undistorted so long as the input voltage does not go beyond the limits established by plate-current cutoff and saturation. When a Class A amplifier is improperly biased—so that the no-signal operating point is above or below the center point on this transfer line—signal excesses will result in distortion.

The amplitude of the input signal is important in maintaining any given class of operation. A Class C amplifier, for example, requires a very high-amplitude signal in order to bring the grid voltage up to the level required to make the amplifier conduct. If the driving signal is of insufficient amplitude, the tube may never be made to conduct at all. At best, it will be made to conduct for an insufficient period of the total signal's cycle.

(f) If the grid of an amplifier is driven positive, the grid circuit will draw current. A current drain in the grid circuit is objectionable in most amplifier circuits because such drain represents a power loss and does not contribute to amplifier performance. The result of such power consumption is deterioration in amplifier operating efficiency. Similarly, a current drain in the grid circuit causes a change in biasing under most amplifier biasing arrangements.

(g) An increase in output current causes a proportionate drop in plate voltage; thus, the output voltage of a grounded-cathode amplifier is precisely out of phase with the input voltage; and the plate-current waveform is equal and opposite to the plate-voltage waveform.

Question 49: What is meant by "space charge"? By secondary emission?

The "space charge" is a cloud of electrons that form around the cathode, and, being negative, it repels electrons nearest the cathode. Secondary emission is the effect caused by electrons striking the plate, knocking other electrons loose from the plate material.

Question 50: What is meant by the "amplification factor" (mu) of a triode vacuum tube (amplifier)? Under what conditions would the amplifier gain approach the value of the mu?

Amplification factor is the change in plate voltage caused by a change in grid voltage with plate current constant. It is the maximum voltage gain of an amplifier.

When the highest possible plate load resistance is used, and when that load impedance is many times the plate resistance of the tube, amplifier gain will approach the mu of the tube.

Question 51: What is meant by "plate resistance" of a vacuum tube? Upon what does its value depend?

Plate resistance is the opposition to current flow through a vacuum tube and actually is a measure of change in plate current caused by change in plate voltage with grid bias constant.

$$r_p = \frac{\text{change in } E_p}{\text{change in } I_p} \; (E_g \text{ constant})$$

The value indicates the effectiveness of the plate voltage in producing a change in plate current and depends on the physical and electrical properties of the tube in question. The plate resistance of a triode is much less than that of a tetrode or pentode. Since the addition of screen and suppressor grids tends to isolate the control grid from the plate, changes in plate voltage have less effect on plate current and plate resistance increases.

Question 52: What is meant by the voltage "gain" of a vacuum tube amplifier? How is this gain achieved?

Voltage gain is the ratio of output (plate) voltage to input (grid) voltage. Gain equals E output divided by E input. Voltage gain is achieved as a result of the amplifying ability of the tube and is related directly to the amplification factor.

Question 53: Draw a rough graph of plate current vs plate supply voltage for three different bias voltages on a typical triode vacuum tube.

(a) Explain, in a general way, how the value of the plate load resistance affects the portion of the curve over which the tube is operating. How is this related to distortion?

(b) Operation over which portion of the curve produces the least distortion?

(a) The higher the plate voltage, the higher the value of negative grid bias required to cut off the tube; nonetheless, at some maximum plate-voltage value, there will be a determinable negative grid voltage that will cause the tube to cut off, or stop conducting. The lower right terminal of the load line of Fig. 3-11 is plotted at the point where applied plate voltage is maximum and current is zero. At the other extreme, there is a point at which plate current will be at its maximum—a point where further decreases in negative grid voltage will not result in additional plate-current flow, and where plate voltage will actually drop to zero. At this point, the factor that determines plate current is the plate load resistance. The maximum supply voltage divided by the plate load resistance will yield the total plate current at this extreme. The load line is plotted from this maximum-current point to the no-current, maximum-voltage point, as shown.

(b) The least distortion will be observed when the tube is operated over the lower part of the curve. The lower on the curve the load line is drawn, the more linear will be the operation of the amplifier and the more symmetrical the waveshape.

Question 54: A triode "grounded cathode" audio amplifier has a mu (amplification factor) of 30, a plate impedance of 5000 ohms, load impedance of 10,000 ohms, plate voltage of 300 volts, plate current of 10 mA and cathode resistor bias is used.

(a) What is the stage gain of this amplifier?

(b) What is the cutoff bias voltage E_{co}?

(c) Assuming the bias voltage is one-half the value of E_{co}, what value cathode resistor would be used to produce the required bias?

(d) What size capacitor should be used to sufficiently bypass the cathode resistor if the lowest approximate frequency desired is 500 Hz? (cps)

(a) The stage gain of this amplifier is 20. Stage gain is independent of plate current and voltage, and is a function of the plate and load resistances and the individual tube's amplification factor, or mu. The equation for calculating stage gain is $(uR_L)/(R_L + R_p)$

where u (Greek letter mu) is amplification factor and the other symbols represent the resistance of the plate and load. With a mu of 30, a load resistance of 10K, and a plate impedance of 5K, the equation becomes

$$\frac{30 \times 10,000}{10,000 + 5,000} = \frac{300}{15} = 20$$

(b) The stage's cutoff bias is equal to the plate voltage divided by the amplification factor, or E_{bb}/u. The plate voltage is 300V and the amplification factor is 30; so the cutoff bias value is 10. As a negative grid bias voltage: —10V.

(c) The grid of the triode amplifier is biased at —5V during the no-signal state. To maintain this 5V bias, the cathode resistor must keep the grid 5V negative with respect to the cathode. Given a plate current of 10 mA and a cathode-resistor drop of 5V, the value of the resistor may be determined from Ohm's law, R=E∕I. (The 10 mA of plate current flows through the cathode resistor, across the space charge, and out through the plate circuit.) Since E is 5V, and I is 0.01A (10 mA), the cathode resistor value is 500 ohms.

(d) The value of the cathode bypass capacitor must be such that its capacitive reactance is small compared with the resistance of the cathode resistor at 500 Hz. A practical value for audio applications would be in the range from 10 to 50 uF. Since there is no set rule for what constitutes "small" when compared with the cathode resistor value, some design specialists like to stay with an arbitrary percentage of the cathode resistance—such as 10 percent. If we say that the capacitive reactance at 500 Hz must not exceed 50 ohms (10 percent of 500 ohms), we can apply this formula: $X_C=1/(2\pi fC)$ using an arbitrary value of capacitance—say, 10 uF. By using the value of 10 uF and 500 Hz, the capacitive reactance works out to 31 ohms, well below the 10 percent established as our maximum.

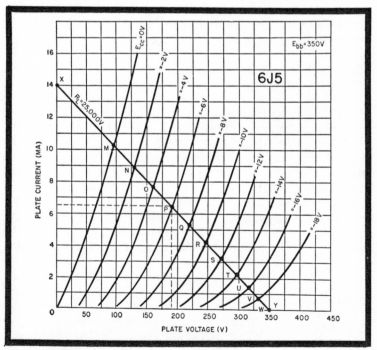

Fig. 3-11. Plate family of characteristic curves for 6J5 triode, including load line.

Question 55: Why is the efficiency of an amplifier operated Class C higher than one operated Class A or Class B?

Since the efficiency of an amplifier depends on the time that plate current flows, which in the case of Class C is the least per cycle, less power is dissipated within the tube and more output power is provided in Class C operation than any other.

Question 56: The following are excerpts from a tube manual rating of a beam pentode. Explain the significance of each item.

(a) Control grid-to-plate capacitance: 1.1 pF
(b) Input capacitance: 2.2 pF
(c) Output capacitance: 8.5 pF
(d) Heater voltage: 6.3 volts
(e) Maximum DC plate supply voltage: 700 volts
(f) Maximum peak positive pulse voltage: 7,000 volts
(g) Maximum negative pulse plate voltage: 1,500 volts
(h) Maximum screen grid voltage: 175 volts
(i) Maximum peak negative control grid voltage: 200 volts
(j) Maximum plate dissipation: 20 watts
(k) Maximum screen grid dissipation: 30 watts
(l) Maximum DC cathode current: 200 mA
(m) Maximum peak cathode current: 200 mA
(n) Maximum control grid circuit resistance: 0.47 megohm.

Control-Grid-To-Plate Capacitance. This important vacuum-tube specification gives valuable information with regard to the inherent coupling between the two key tube elements: the control grid and plate. The value of this interelectrode capacitance helps you to know the frequency limitations on the tube without neutralization. The lower the value here, the higher the signal frequency can be without neutralization. The specification is based on a measurement made with the screen and suppressor grids connected to the cathode element.

Input Capacitance. It would be hard to imagine a tube whose grid-to-plate capacitance was 1.1 pF having a total input capacitance of only 2.2 pF. This number is supposed to be the total sum of all the capacitances relative to the control grid; that is, it is the sum of these capacitances: control grid to plate, control grid to suppressor grid (and cathode, when no internal connection between the two is provided), and control grid to screen grid. The specified value is important because the values of capacitance on the control grid are additive to the capacitances in this part of the circuit, and will form part of any resonant circuit connected between these electrodes. A more realistic value for the total capacitance of a beam power pentode would be 10 - 20 pF.

Output Capacitance. The output capacitance is the sum of all capacitances associated with the plate, which include plate-to-grid, plate-to-suppressor, plate-to-screen, and plate-to-cathode. The importance of the specification lies in the fact that all these capacitance values are additive in nature and must be considered when a resonant network is part of the plate circuit.

Heater Voltage. The heater voltage specified is that voltage on which all tube performance ratings are based. Since most tubes will behave quite differently under different heater temperatures, it is important to adhere to this specified value when the tube is employed as an amplifier. Heater voltage ratings affect such important parameters of performance as tube life, maximum plate current, and total output power.

Max DC Plate Voltage. As implied by the specification, this value is the highest permissible DC operating voltage the tube can tolerate under maximum-load conditions.

Max Peak Positive Pulse Voltage. In many applications, an amplifier tube will be subjected to pulse voltages far above the maximum safe value that can be applied under normal operating conditions. This specification permits the user to assess a tube's qualifications for such applications as **horizontal output,** where extremely high pulse voltages are applied to the plate for brief (microseconds) periods. Exceeding the design values here could result in destruction of the tube, serious internal arcing, or erratic performance.

Max Negative Peak Pulse Plate Voltage. In inductive plate loads, high negative voltages often develop for brief "flash" periods as the opposing EMF builds across the load. This specification establishes the maximum flash-voltage value that can be tolerated without tube deterioration.

Maximum Screen-Grid Voltage. Since the screen voltage (rather than plate voltage) is a determining factor with respect to the plate current capabilities of tetrodes and pentodes, this specification becomes one of particular importance. The value given represents the maximum working voltage that can be applied to the screen grid.

Max Peak Negative Control-Grid Voltage. This specification describes the maximum safe value of negative voltage that can be tolerated by the tube without internal arcing. The value shown indicates that levels below 200V can be handled without deleterious effects.

Max Plate Dissipation. This specification describes the maximum power the plate can safely dissipate under a normal, sustained-load operation. The value may be exceeded where the tube is cooled by some external means (unless the specification is based on operation while tube is being cooled, as with many RF power amplifiers).

Max Screen-Grid Dissipation. The screen, being positioned opposite to the control grid and in line with the cathode, is capable of dissipating power in the same manner as a plate, and many circuits involve use of the screen grid as a plate element. Nonetheless, the value listed (30 watts) is very likely a misprint, since it is unrealistic to rate the screen grid at a greater dissipation value than the plate. A more likely figure would be some value between 10 and 15 percent of the plate-dissipation capability.

Max DC Cathode Current. The cathode supplies the current required in the plate circuit. The value specified here is the maximum current the cathode can deliver without premature burnout or weakening of the heater/cathode material. This current rating is not the maximum current the filament will draw from its low-voltage supply; this value would be considerably higher (perhaps more than an order of magnitude).

Max Peak Cathode Current. Beyond the normal steady-drain value specified above, the cathode of many types of amplifiers is called upon to deliver very large surge currents. Understandably, the surge capability of a cathode is considerably higher than the normal DC constant-drain capability. The value given under this specification describes the maximum safe value of any high-current pulse. Exceeding the value even briefly may cause serious tube deterioration.

Max Control-Grid Circuit Resistance. This specification describes the maximum grid-to-ground resistance of the tube's control grid, and must not be exceeded in design of the circuit in which the tube will be used. Higher values than that listed could result in cancellation of the grid bias, with the result that excessive voltage is applied to the grid, thereby destroying the tube or prohibiting normal operation.

Question 57. Name at least three abnormal conditions which would tend to shorten the life of a vacuum tube. Also name one or more probable causes of each condition.

Excessive heater voltage, excessive power dissipation (plate), excessive DC operating voltage, operating the filaments from a DC supply, operating out of resonance, and improper bias are typical abnormal operating conditions that tend to degrade a tube's performance and result in premature failure. Causes are as follows.

Excessive Heater Voltage. In mobile equipment, improper adjustment of the car's voltage regulator results in excessive heater voltage. High line voltage is another common cause of this condition. An overheated heater boils off more electrons than the plate can handle; the condition results in rapid deterioration of the filament or heater, which weakens as electrons from its surface are spent.

Excessive Power Dissipation. As mentioned in the answer to the preceding question, each tube designed for "power" applications has a rated dissipation, which can be exceeded to the detriment of the tube. Excessive plate voltage on the tube will result in a commensurate increase in plate current, the combination of which must be delivered to the load or dissipated by the tube. Excessive dissipation can also be caused by improper load impedance or an out-of-resonance condition in the output circuit.

Excessive DC Operating Voltage. This condition may be caused by improper design of the tube's power supply, excessive line voltage, too low a value of plate load resistor, and—in mobile equipment—operation of the equipment when the voltage regulator in the automobile is adjusted for too high a voltage output. In the latter case, the excesses can be quite severe. The supply voltage should be about 12.6 volts (to a maximum of around 14.3 or so). Considering the turns ratio of step-up transformers, it is not surprising that this condition has probably been responsible for the demise of more tubes than all the other faults combined. A transformer designed to produce 480V from a 12V source will produce 640V when supplied with a source of only 16V.

Filament Operation From a DC Supply. Prolonged operation of a tube's filaments from a DC voltage supply will cause deterioration of one side of the heater before the other. Since one end of the heater winding is negative with respect to the other, it will release more electrons than the other end. This is why many economy-minded experimenters reverse the DC heater leads of their expensive power amplifiers from time to time.

Operating Out of Resonance. This condition is common with RF power amplifiers operated Class C. When the output circuit is in resonance, the plate current is at its minimum value. If any out-of-resonance condition occurs—such as any change in the plate load, change in the antenna, or a change in the setting of the capacitor in the final plate tank circuit—will cause the plate current to rise steeply, exceeding the maximum ratio value of the tube.

Improper Bias. This is particularly true with Class C and Class B amplifiers, which are designed to operate only during portions of the input-signal's complete cycle. When a Class C amplifier's operating point is moved closer to the tube's plate - current cutoff point (as happens with component value changes or other such causes), the tube is made to conduct for longer periods of each cycle. The maximum ratings for a particular class of operation are not necessarily applicable when the tube is operated under other classes.

Question 58: Name at least three circuit factors (not including tube types and component values) in a one-stage amplifier circuit that should be considered at VHF but are not of particular concern at VLF.

Low-loss, high-quality components should be used. Length of wiring must be kept short to avoid capacitive and inductive feedback that result in circuit oscillation. Use of a common ground point for bypassing, and grounded-grid type amplifiers to reduce feedback problems. Neutralization may be necessary in many cases.

Question 59: What is a "lighthouse" triode? An "acorn tube"? These tubes were designed for operation in what frequency range?

UHF tubes are especially constructed for operation at higher frequencies, where it is necessary to reduce interelectrode capacitances and to cut down transit time (the time electrons require to travel from the cathode to the plate). This is done by making the electrodes quite small and spacing them very closely together. Because of these construction features, the power-handling ability of this type of tube is somewhat less than that of tubes used at lower frequencies.

In UHF tubes, there is frequently no tube base. Connections to the electrodes are made through pins which protrude through the envelope in a way that keeps the leads short and minimizes capacitance between them. Three special types of UHF tubes—the acorn tube, the doorknob tube, and the lighthouse tube—are so named because of their shapes and sizes. Acorn and doorknob tubes are available in diodes, triodes, and pentodes. The lighthouse tube is designed to fit directly into the end of a concentric tubing used to form the tuned or tank circuit in UHF systems. By directly connecting the tube in this manner, losses due to connecting wires are eliminated.

Question 60: Why are special tubes sometimes required at UHF and above?

As the operating frequency is increased, capacitive reactance between electrodes in a vacuum tube decreases. At frequencies higher than 100 MHz, the interelectrode capacitance of an ordinary vacuum tube bypasses radio frequencies very effectively. The electron transit time is about one-thousandth of a microsecond (0.001 usec). Although this may seem an insignificant amount of time, it approaches and sometimes equals the time of a cycle within the tube, thus causing an undesirable shift in phase.

A small number of ordinary vacuum tubes can be operated at frequencies higher than 100 MHz under certain critical operating conditions. The most suitable tubes of this type are triodes having low interelectrode capacitances, close spacing of the electrodes to reduce the transit time, a high amplification factor, and a fairly low plate resistance. Since some of these requirements are conflicting, tubes which strike a happy medium are generally selected. The operation of certain ordinary vacuum tubes at extremely high plate voltages is sometimes permitted in radar circuits to reduce the electron transit time.

The amount of interelectrode capacitance, the effect of the electron transit time, and other objectionable features of ordinary vacuum tubes are minimized considerably in the construction of special tubes for use at UHF. The UHF tubes have very small electrodes placed close together and often have no socket base. By reduction of all physical dimensions of a tube by the same scale, the interelectrode capacities are decreased without affecting the transconductance or the amplification factor. Transit time, likewise, is reduced, as is also the power-handling capacity of a tube of small dimensions.

Question 61: Describe the difference between positive (P-type) and negative (N-type) semiconductors with respect to:

(a) The direction of current flow when an external EMF is applied.

(b) The internal resistance when an external EMF is applied.

In an NPN transistor, the emitter injects free electrons into the P-type base region, where they are attracted across the collector junction by the positive potential. In a PNP transistor, the battery polarities would have to be reversed and the flow through the transistor would be by "holes" rather than electrons. NPN transistors are biased negatively at the emitter and positively at the collector (when the base is common).

With the application of voltage to a transistor's input circuit, a current flows through the base-emitter junction. The action of the transistor is such that the same current density is caused to flow in the output circuit, which has a high internal resistance (considerably higher than the input circuit). Since the same current appears in both the input and output circuits, and the output circuit has a higher resistance than the input circuit, the result is a high equivalent power in the output circuit than the input circuit for any given input signal current.

Question 62: What is the difference between forward and reverse biasing of transistors?

Forward bias provides a free flow of current through the transistor junction, due to the movement of the majority carriers along the P and N type material. Forward biasing is illustrated for a PNP transistor in Fig. 3-12. You will recall that holes are the majority carriers in P-type material, electrons in N-type material.

Reverse bias retards or restricts current flow in a transistor. The small current flow is the result of the activity of the minority carriers. The minority carriers are few in number and consist of excess electrons in P material or excess holes in N material. The application of an external EMF to reverse bias a junction actually widens the barrier region at that junction and stops the movement of majority carriers through it. See Fig. 3-12.

Question 63: Show the connections of external batteries, resistance load and a signal source as would appear in a properly (fixed) biased, common-emitter transistor amplifier.

A properly biased common-emitter amplifier stage is shown in Fig. 3-13. It is common practice to show a signal source as a sine wave in a circle in series with the grid resistor (Rg). The stage could just as easily have been an NPN transistor rather than a PNP. With an NPN, the battery and electrolytic capacitors would be reversed in polarity. The

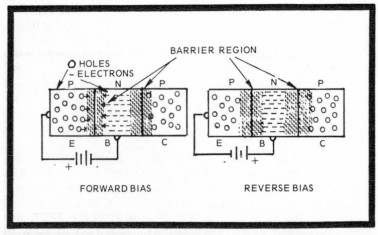

Fig. 3-12. Drawings showing the effect of forward and reverse biasing of a PNP transistor.

current movement through a PNP is said to be by virtue of "holes" rather than electrons. (A hole is the absence of, or an attraction for, a free electron.) In a common-emitter amplifier stage, the output signal is 180 degrees out of phase with the input signal; that is, as the input signal goes more positive the output signal goes more negative, and vice versa.

Question 64: The following are excerpts from a transistor handbook describing the characteristics of a PNP alloy-type transistor as used in a common-emitter circuit configuration. Explain the significance of each item.

Maximum and minimum ratings:

(a) Collector-to-base voltage (emitter open): -40 volts maximum

(b) Collector-to-emitter voltage, (base-to-emitter volts is 0.5): -40 volts maximum

(c) Emitter-to-base voltage: -5.0 volts maximum

(d) Collector current: 10 mA maximum

Transistor dissipation:

(e) At an ambient temperature of 25 degrees C, for operation in free air: 120 mW maximum

(f) At a case temperature of 25 degrees C, for operation with a heat sink: 140 mW maximum

(g) Ambient-temperature range, operating and storage: -65 to +100 degrees C.

(a) Collector-to-base voltage (emitter open) is the maximum voltage that may be applied between these elements without danger of breakdown of the junction. (No connection to emitter terminal.)

(b) Collector-to-emitter voltage (base-to-emitter reverse biased at -5 volts) refers to the maximum safe voltage that may be applied between the collector and emitter without danger of a breakdown.

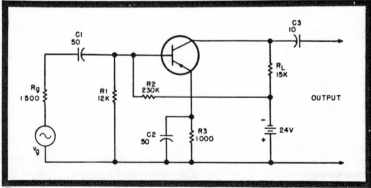

Fig. 3-13. Common-emitter amplifier circuit using PNP transistor.

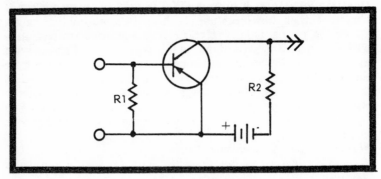

Fig. 3-14. Common-emitter amplifier circuit with self-bias.

(c) Emitter-to-base voltage is the maximum forward bias voltage that may safely be used to limit emitter-to-collector and base-to-emitter current.

(d) Collector current is the value that may not be exceeded without possible permanent damage to the collector-emitter junction.

(e) Transistor dissipation at an ambient temperature of 25 degrees C for operation in free air is the maximum power that can safely be dissipated by the transistor without a heat sink.

(f) Transistor dissipation at a case temperature of 25 degrees C with a heat sink refers to the greatest thermal rating at which the transistor may be safely operated with a heat sink.

(g) Ambient temperature range for operating and storage is the temperature limit within which no electrical characteristic damage to the transistor will occur. Either simple storage or operation outside of these limits could be expected to result in degradation of the unit.

Question 65: Draw a circuit diagram of a method of obtaining self-bias with one battery, without current feedback, in a common-emitter amplifier. Explain the voltage drops in the resistors.

See Fig. 3-14. Base-to-emitter negative bias is developed across R1, forming part of a voltage divider network. The network consists of R2 and R1, with electron flow from the negative battery through R1, then R2 and back to the positive battery terminal. Voltage drop is negative at the negative battery and positive at the transistor base end of R1. The R2 voltage drop is negative at the base end and positive at the battery terminal. The emitter is also connected to the positive battery which places the base negative with respect to the emitter.

Question 66: Draw a circuit diagram of a common-emitter amplifier with emitter bias. Explain its operation.

See Fig. 3-15, which places the emitter at ground potential with respect to the signal, due to the capacitor across V_{ee}, but at a positive DC level. Reverse biasing of the collector-emitter junction is accomplished by the negative terminal of V_{ee} feeding the collector through R_L and the positive battery connection to the emitter. Forward biasing of the base-emitter junction is carried out by current flowing from negative Vee through current-limiting resistor R_b and on through the base-emitter junction back to positive battery.

Question 67: Why is stabilization of a transistor amplifier usually necessary? How would a "thermistor" be used in this respect?

Stabilization of the transistor amplifier is normally required because the reverse-bias collector current or leakage current increases with temperature and changes the operating point of the transistor. Collector current may be stabilized by lowering the base current to compensate for the increase in leakage current. This can be done with a thermistor, which is a temperature-sensitive resistor with a negative temperature coefficient. Connecting the thermistor between the base and emitter provides the desired circuit stabilization, since the constant current through the base biasing resistor is divided between the transistor base and the thermistor. As temperature increases, the resistance of the thermistor decreases, causing more current to flow through it and leaving less for the base bias current. By the use of proper values, the decrease in base current may be sufficient to cause a decrease in collector current that is equal to the increase in

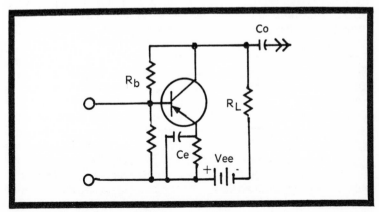

Fig. 3-15. Common-emitter amplifier circuit with emitter bias.

collector leakage current. Thus, the collector current is constant under varying temperature conditions.

Question 68: The value of the alpha cutoff frequency of a transistor is primarily dependent upon what one factor? Does the value of alpha cutoff frequency normally have any relationship to the collector-to-base voltage?

Alpha cutoff frequency is primarily dependent on the physical thickness of the transistor base. The thinner the base the higher the alpha cutoff frequency. Indirectly related to the collector-to-base voltage, the alpha cutoff frequency increases as the permissible collector-to-base voltage decreases. This makes sense if we consider the fact that the thinner the base, the lower the allowable base-to-collector voltage.

Question 69: Draw a diagram of each of the following power supply circuits. Explain the operation of each, including the relative input and output voltage amplitudes, waveshapes, and current waveforms.

(a) Vacuum-tube diode, full-wave rectifier with a capacitive-input pi-section filter.

(b) Vacuum-tube diode, full-wave rectifier with choke-input filter.

(c) Silicon-diode doubler circuit with a resistive load.

(d) Nonsynchronous-vibrator power supply, with silicon-diode bridge circuit and capacitive-input, pi-section filter.

(e) Synchronous-vibrator power supply with capacitive-input pi-section filter.

Tube-Type Full-Wave Supply, Capacitive-Input Pi Section. The two-page drawing of Fig. 3-16 shows a complete power supply, from the step-up transformer to the output line. Each section is labeled according to its function, and a functional description is included with each section. Immediately below the diagram sections are shown waveforms that represent the output voltage of that section. As shown, the transformer section of the supply is driven from the 115V primary power line. The transformer is shown with two windings—one for the rectifier's filaments and the other for the high voltage. The rectifier stage allows current to pass in one direction only. The pi-section filter is named because of its shape; notice the resemblance between the filter and the Greek letter "pi." The regulator and voltage-divider sections, though not required by the FCC, are presented to allow a better understanding of power supply circuits.

It should be noted that each section is applicable to virtually any power supply. For example, the transformer section can be used for any of the various power supply configurations, and the filter—a capacitive-input type—is applicable to all power supply circuits, be they half- or full-wave.

The explanations of the circuit functions shown in the drawing are applicable to all other illustrated power-supply types except as noted.

Figure 3-17 illustrates all the basic power-supply circuits. It should be noted that the silicon-diode symbol—the arrow with a perpendicular line crossing the point—may be used for diodes of either vacuum-tube, silicon, or selenium construction; thus, the supplies pictured are applicable to either silicon-diode or vacuum-tube circuits.

Tube-Type Full-Wave Supply, Choke-Input Filter. The diagram for this supply is precisely the same as that shown in Fig. 3-16, except that the left-side 10 uF capacitor is removed from the filter section. Use of a choke-input filter results in a slight reduction of total supply voltage output, but results in better regulation when a regulator section is not incorporated into the supply.

A capacitor-input filter with no load produces a terminal voltage which is nearly equal to the peak value of the applied AC. As the load is increased, however, the terminal voltage falls, because the current drawn by the load prevents the capacitor from retaining its full charge. As shown in Fig. 3-18, the output voltage of a capacitor-input filter depends substantially on the drain of the load. As long as the load is quite light or constant, the output voltage is relatively stable; variations in load, though, cause variations in the output voltage. The capacitor-input filter is thus said to have relatively poor regulation. The choke-input filter's output voltage is constant so long as the load is above a certain minimum value. Since the output voltage remains essentially the same over a wide range of current drains, the choke-input filter is said to have good regulation.

Silicon-Diode Doubler Circuit With Resistive Load. The basic doubler circuit is shown in Fig. 3-17B. A resistive load is provided by connecting a resistor across each of the capacitors in the output line.

The waveform of a power supply with a highly resistive load is shown in the lower portion of Fig. 3-19A. By contrast, note the waveform of the DC voltage output of the supply shown in Fig. 3-19B. As indicated, a highly resistive load offers better regulation when a capacitor-input filter system is used, regardless of whether the supply type is a doubler, conventional full-wave, or bridge.

Nonsynchronous-Vibrator Supply With Diode Bridge and Pi-Section Filter. The basic nonsynchronous vibrator supply is shown in Fig. 3-20. The two output lines (identified by the arrows) may be connected to any of the diode rectifier circuits illustrated in Fig. 3-17 in place of the transformer pictured.

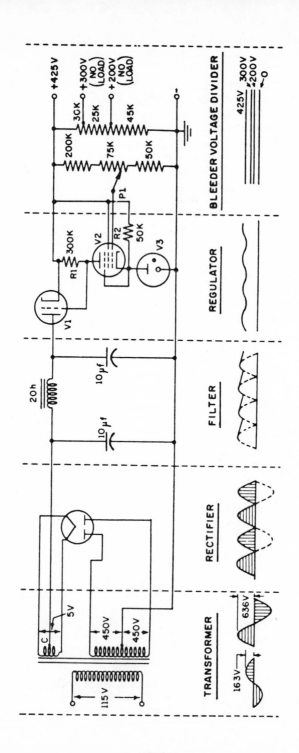

Low voltage is stepped up by the transformer from 115 volts to 900 volts. Center tap provides a dividing point so that 450 volts are applied to each section of the 5U4G rectifier. The ends of the transformer alternately become positive and negative.

Center tap C on heater winding is used to force plate current to divide equally in each filament lead. If there is no center tap, a voltage divider of two equal 50 ohm resistors may be put across the secondary to produce the same effect.

Alternately positive and negative voltage is applied to the plates of the rectifier.

The two plates conduct alternately as each plate is made positive in turn by the secondary of the transformer. Pulses of current flow from the filament line to each plate in turn. The ends of the transformer alternately become positive and negative with the applied a. c., but the filament line will show a one-directional flow.

Capacitors charge when the rectifier conducts, and they discharge through the bleeder resistor when the tube is not conducting.

Choke builds up a magnetic field when the tube draws current. The field collapses as current decreases, tending to keep a constant current flowing in the same direction through the bleeder resistor and the load.

Capacitor input (illustrated) gives higher voltage output with low current loads.

Choke input gives steadier output with less ripple under load conditions.

If the load draws more current or if the a-c input voltage falls, the terminal voltage of the power supply falls.

Resistor R1, tube V2, and gas-tube V3 are in series across the rectifier terminals. V3 holds the cathode of V2 at a constant positive potential with respect to ground, and setting of P1 determines bias on V2. A fall in terminal voltage causes more negative bias on V2, less current through V2, hence, less current through R1. Less IR drop across R1 causes less negative bias on V1. V1, then acts as a lower value resistor, and terminal voltage decrease is checked.

As a bleeder, the resistor is for safety to discharge the capacitors when power is removed.

As a load resistor, it acts as a stabilizer to protect the voltage regulator at no load, and to improve the regulation.

A voltage divider meets the requirements of a load resistor and a bleeder, but in addition has taps placed at intervals for voltage at less than the maximum.

It is usually grounded at the lower end but may be grounded at any higher point to get a negative output.

Fig. 3-16. Complete power supply.

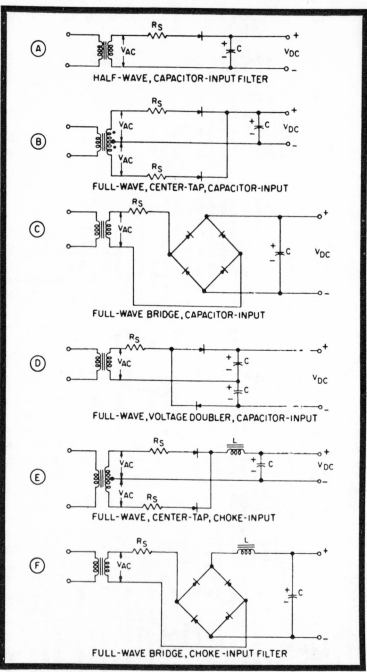

Fig. 3-17. Basic semiconductor rectifier circuits.

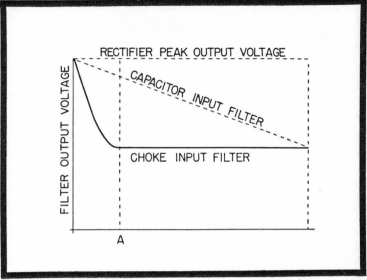

Fig. 3-18. Effect of load on terminal voltage of capacitor and choke input filters.

Thus, to show a nonsynchronous-vibrator bridge circuit, the vibrator supply's output lines would be connected in place of the transformer shown in Fig. 3-17C. The capacitor (C) in Fig. 3-17C represents the first leg of the pi-section filter (which is illustrated in complete form in Fig. 3-16).

It is important to emphasize that power supplies are, by their nature, modular. That is, the vibrator-transformer section can be replaced with a line-transformer section. Any of the rectifier circuits may be connected to the transformer, and any of the filters may be used with the rectifier circuits.

Synchronous-Vibrator Supply, Pi-Section Filter. No rectifier is necessary with the synchronous vibrator supply (Fig. 3-20B). As shown, a second set of contacts provides a ground that alternates about the output line at the same rate as the input; the rectification is purely mechanical, but effective. As shown, the output is passed through a pi-section filter.

Question 70: What advantage may a bridge rectifier have over a conventional full-wave rectifier?

The main advantage of the bridge rectifier over the conventional full-wave rectifier is that twice the voltage output from the same input is available. However, the current would be half as much in such cases, with the transformer limiting the VA or power output to the rectifier. The bridge rectifier does not require a center-tapped secondary, or in

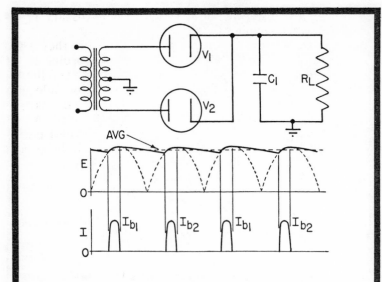

Fig. 3-19A. Full wave rectifier / high resistance load.

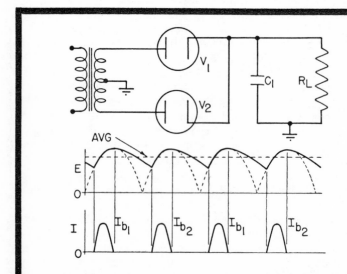

Fig. 3-19B. Full wave rectifier / low resistance load.

fact, even a transformer of any kind as is necessary in the other full-wave supplies.

Question 71: What are swinging chokes? How are they used?

A swinging choke varies in inductance according to the actual load or inversely with the load current. The smaller the load, the greater the inductance required for adequate filtering. Aside from being more economical, voltage regulation under varying loads is greatly improved. An air gap in the iron core with the proper width provides partial saturation from the DC load. The greater the load, the greater the core saturation and the lower the inductance value. An ideal use for the swinging choke is the Class B modulator supply where the load changes from nearly zero to extremely high levels for peak audio inputs.

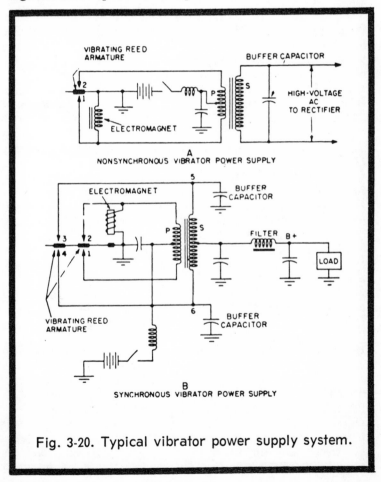

Fig. 3-20. Typical vibrator power supply system.

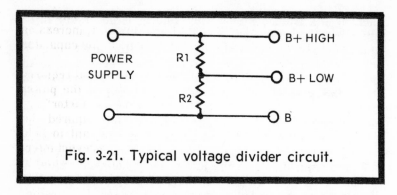

Fig. 3-21. Typical voltage divider circuit.

Question 72: Show a method of obtaining two voltages from one power supply.

See Fig. 3-21 for a voltage divider circuit which provides the best regulation. The resistance of the dropping resistor is found by Ohm's Law, R equals E divided by I, or the desired voltage drop divided by the sum of the current through the reduced voltage terminal plus the bleeder current.

Question 73: What are the characteristics of a capacitor input filter system as compared with a choke input filter system? What is the effect on a filter choke of a large value of direct current flow?

Comparative characteristics of the capacitor input are higher DC output voltage, higher peak surge current, poorer voltage regulation. Capacitor input filters are not satisfactory for mercury vapor rectifiers. Large values of DC current have no adverse effect on a filter choke if properly designed; otherwise, if the normal rating is exceeded, core saturation occurs, causing reduced inductance and overheating.

Mercury vapor tubes are unable to withstand the initial surge current in a capacitor input filter, which acts as almost a dead short with no charge.

Choke-input filters offer better voltage regulation, lower peak surge current, more efficient use of tubes and transformers, but lower voltage output (90 percent of the secondary RMS).

Question 74: What is the purpose of a "bleeder" resistor as used in conjunction with power supplies?

The bleeder resistor improves the regulation of the supply output by maintaining a constant load. It also offers a safety factor by discharging filter capacitors after shut down.

Question 75: Would varying the value of the bleeder resistor in a power supply have any effect on the ripple voltage?

Decreasing the value of the bleeder resistor would increase the output ripple in either capacitor input or choke input filters, while increasing the bleeder value would have little or no effect on the choke input type. However, increasing bleeder value would reduce the output ripple in the capacitor input arrangement.

Question 76: What effect does the amount of current required by the load have upon the voltage regulation of the power supply? Why is voltage regulation an important factor?

As a rule, the greater the amount of current required, the poorer the voltage regulation. It is very important to hold output voltages constant under varying loads to prevent inter-modulation of circuits, possible damage to components, and to maintain power output limits. The formula used to determine the percentage of regulation in power supplies is:

$$\text{Percentage of regulation} = \frac{E_{NL} - E_{FL}}{E_{FL} \times 100}$$

E_{NL} =voltage, no-load; the voltage when no current is drawn, E_{FL} = voltage, full load; when **maximum** current for which the circuit was designed is being delivered.

Question 77: What is meant by the peak inverse voltage rating of a diode? How can it be computed for a full-wave power supply?

The peak inverse voltage rating of a diode (PIV) is the maximum peak voltage to which it may safely be subjected in the reverse direction. The silicon diodes are very critical in this regard, since exceeding the ratings even momentarily will destroy the unit.

Full-wave peak inverse voltage is computed by multiplying the entire secondary (end-to-end) RMS voltage by 1.414, or take the actual peak-to-peak reading end-to-end. When no transformer is used, multiply the line voltage (RMS) by 1.414. The point most often overlooked in figuring PIV is that the voltage rating of a transformer, either side of center tap, must be multiplied by 2.83 to come up with the correct figure. Add a little extra for a safety factor, too; remember that a line surge is possible and your silicon diodes may not survive.

Question 78: Discuss the relative merits and limitations of the following types of rectifiers as used in power supplies.

(a) Mercury-vapor diode
(b) High-vacuum diode
(c) Copper-oxide diode
(d) Silicon diode
(e) Selenium diode

(a) Mercury-vapor diodes have a low internal voltage drop of 10 to 15 volts, which provides a higher voltage output and improves voltage regulation because the loss in the tube is small. Disadvantages are numerous and hard to overlook; the need to preheat the filament before applying plate voltage, low peak inverse rating, a source of RF interference, vertical operation required, and it cannot be used with capacitive-input filter to name the most important faults.

(b) High-vacuum diodes have a high peak inverse voltage rating. They will stand considerable abuse without damage, may be used in any position and do not generate RF hash. Disadvantages are few and with varying importance according to specific requirements. They are less efficient due to the relatively high internal voltage drop, poor regulation, high heater current requirement and considerable heat loss.

(c) Copper-oxide diodes, an early semiconductor type, are more rugged than tubes but limited to low voltages and small currents. Characteristics vary greatly with temperature and most have been replaced with silicon or germanium types.

(d) Silicon diodes represent top, overall efficiency with a very low internal voltage drop, compact size, inexpensive, good regulation and high current ratings. The only disadvantage of this diode is its sensitivity to PIV ratings. Even momentary transient voltages will cause a silicon diode to be destroyed if its ratings are exceeded.

(e) Selenium diodes are more efficient than copper-oxide types: They have a lower internal voltage drop and are not as sensitive to voltage transients as the silicon diode. Unlike the silicon, which has a lower internal voltage drop, the selenium forward resistance increases with age until replacement is mandatory. Selenium diodes are much larger than silicon units having the same rating.

Question 79: Explain the action of a voltage regulator (VR) tube.

Voltage drop across a VR tube is nearly constant over the designed range of the tube (frequently 5 to 30 ma) and when connected across the load they maintain a constant voltage under varying conditions by drawing more current as the load draws less and less as the load draws more. In other words, the VR tube takes up the "slack." The gaseous regulator tube has a wire cathode surrounded by the anode in a glass envelope containing argon or neon gas. The tube should never be used without a series resistor to protect it against a current overload which could destroy it. The VR tube requires a normal conducting voltage and a slightly higher voltage to start conduction. After the "firing voltage" reaches the tube, conduction causes a voltage drop across the series resistor in the amount required to reduce the power supply voltage to the normal operating voltage of the tube.

Question 80: If the plate, or plates, of a rectifier tube suddenly become red hot, what might be the cause and could remedies be effected?

As rectifier plates do not normally become red hot, this condition would indicate that excessive current was being drawn. The likely cause is a shorted filter capacitor or load. The remedy would be to disconnect the load and if this corrects the condition, look for the short circuit in the load; otherwise, turn off the supply, locate the shorted filter and replace it. The defective electrolytic will probably be warm and often may be quickly found by checking for this. If the supply uses a choke coil between the input capacitor and load, an overheated choke would place the trouble beyond it, either in the following filter capacitor, bleeder or load. Of course, the trouble could be in the wiring or even the rectifier tube socket, but these are almost too rare to mention.

Question 81: If a high-vacuum type of high-voltage rectifier tube should suddenly show severe internal sparking and then fail to operate, what elements of the rectifier filter system should be checked for possible failure before installing a new rectifier tube?

In this case, trouble may be in the tube itself, in the power supply or in its load. Check the supply and the load both carefully before trying another tube, and if possible check the tube in a tester if nothing else shows up. Here again, the filter capacitors should be the prime suspect.

Question 82: What does a blue haze in the space between the filament and plate of a high-vacuum tube rectifier indicate?

A blue haze between the elements of any tube is indicative of the presence of gas. The flow of current through a gassy tube may be erratic; the result is generally rapid deterioration, sporadic operation, severe internal arcing, and a markedly fluctuating voltage drop across the tube. Gassiness in tubes results from a leaky envelope (which allows external gases to enter the evacuated chamber) and from contamination of the evacuated chamber with vapor molecules that have been heated excessively.

CHAPTER 4

Basic Radiotelephone, Part II: Element 3

As we continue with our study, a close look at the basic indicating instrument movement known as the D'Arsonval is important. Most of the meters used for electronic measurements employ this movement with necessary modifications, and by understanding its construction and operation, the entire field of measuring instruments is greatly simplified.

INDICATING INSTRUMENTS

By merely adding resistance in series with the ordinary milliammeter, voltage readings may be made, or by using a shunt resistance across the meter, its current measuring capability may be increased as desired. Although the meter may only be used to measure direct current or voltage, the addition of a small diode rectifier will permit AC to be measured as well. The sensitivity of a meter is dependent on the current drawn by the meter movement for full-scale deflection; the less current required the greater the sensitivity. Voltmeters are rated according to ohms per volt and this is equal to the reciprocal of the current required for full-scale deflection. In other words, a voltmeter rated at 20,000 ohms per volt would have a current of 1 over 20,000 or 50 microamperes for full-scale deflection. This would be considered to be a good meter, but not good enough for measurements where circuit loading would result in inaccurate readings, such as most amplifier input circuits and many control circuits, too. In such cases, the volt-ohm-milliammeter (VOM) is no longer useful, but the VTVM (or vacuum tube voltmeter) is capable of accurately reading the most delicate circuits. This is actually a vacuum tube amplifier which boosts the sensitivity of the D'Arsonval meter movement and provides extremely high input impedance (usually about 11 megohms). Even the most critical circuits are not loaded with such an insignificant burden. Currently, there is considerable progress in meters, with the new FET multimeters having a capability of measuring resistors, transistors, and other components in the circuit. Using the field-effect transistor as an amplifier, the input impedance ranges to 15 megohms and the high-low voltage arrangement prevents transistors from conducting during in-circuit resistor measurement on low and allows them to conduct on high for accurate measurement of the semiconductors.

OSCILLATORS

Oscillators are generators of alternating current with the output frequency dependent on the characteristics of the circuitry. The fact that they are capable of generating signals at various frequencies dictates their use in radio and television receivers and transmitters. Needless to say, oscillators have many other uses in electronic equipment, but the receiver and transmitter applications are of primary interest at this time.

Although oscillators fall into many categories, most may be labeled feedback oscillators and have similar basic principles. If a charged capacitor is connected across an inductor, the capacitor will cause a current to flow through the coil from negative to positive and form an electromagnetic field around the inductor, energy will be stored in that field. As the capacitor becomes fully discharged, the electromagnetic field around the coil collapses and causes a back EMF to recharge the capacitor in the other direction. As the capacitor is recharged, the field around the coil is set up again with the energy stored therein, which collapses and recharges the capacitor in the original direction. This current reversal in the circuit generates an alternating wave and the ability of the LC circuit at resonance to cause oscillations is the flywheel effect. This action could continue except for the loss of power in the resistance of the coil and capacitor in the form of heat. The gradual decrease in amplitude of the oscillations in our parallel resonant circuit is called damping and the wave produced is a damped wave.

The oscillating frequency depends on the values of the inductance and capacitance. The frequency is lowered as either or both values are increased. Since it takes longer for the capacitor to charge and also longer to discharge as the value of capacitance is increased, it means fewer oscillations are possible per second. Naturally, decreasing the values of capacitance or inductance in the LC parallel resonant circuit results in less time to charge and discharge with more oscillations per second or a higher frequency. The formula for determining the resonant frequency is,

$$F_r = \frac{1}{2\pi \sqrt{LC}}$$

F_r is the resonant frequency in Hz, 2 pi equals 6.28, L is the inductance in henrys, C is the capacitance in farads.

Since the LC circuit needs much more energy to be useful, DC is furnished so that it will not stop oscillating when loaded, and by using an amplifier arrangement with a vacuum tube or transistor, we sustain oscillations by feeding back a portion of the output to the input. So now it becomes obvious that the oscillator is actually a self-excited amplifier and no signal or trigger is needed to start it. As soon as DC power is applied, circuit noise will be amplified and fed back, causing a weak signal at the input. The input signal is amplified to a strong signal and more is fed back until oscillations snowball to full strength.

AUDIO AMPLIFIERS

Audio or sound amplifiers increase the voltage or power of an audio frequency signal in the 20- to 20,000-Hz range. The level of the input is always very low and one or two stages of voltage amplification are usually required to build the weak input signal to a sufficient amplitude to drive a power amplifier. When vacuum tubes are used, the voltage of the signal is increased and with transistors the current is increased, but the end result is the greater signal amplitude necessary for the power stage. Impedance coupling, RC coupling, or transformer coupling may be used. Direct coupling, while superior to all other methods in low-frequency response, lacks the stability of the rest. Transistor amplifiers may be used in cascade for additional gain, and using RC coupling, high power gain is available with the common-emitter arrangement.

In an audio amplifier, the output waveform must be the same as the input. Any deviation is distortion. One common form, known as frequency distortion, results when signal gain varies with frequency. Amplitude distortion is a variation in gain with amplitude and may result from a defective tube or transistor, improper bias, too much drive, defective coupling capacitor, or low output impedance. The gain of an amplifier is less than the amplification factor of the selected vacuum tube, and the amplification factor, which is the theoretical maximum, should always be high when using a triode. A pentode should be chosen with a high value of trans-conductance for best amplifier stage gain.

Voltage or current amplifiers serve only limited output power needs and are usually operated Class A, which is low in efficiency but high in quality. Since these amplifiers operate with low power, the efficiency of operation is not important but the quality of the output is extremely important. The output waveform should be an exact replica of the input except for the level or amplitude. The power amplifier can only reproduce the applied signal; it cannot improve the quality. Power amplifiers are operated Class B, as a rule, to provide the large output required.

The impedance of a power amplifier output must be matched to the impedance of the load in order to realize maximum power, and a transformer may be used to provide such a match. An output transformer should have the correct turns ratio to provide a correct match. The correct turns ratio is equal to the square root of the ratio of the impedances we are using. If the power amplifier has an output impedance of 8,000 ohms and the loudspeaker an impedance of 16 ohms, the ratio of the impedances is 8,000 to 16 equals 400, so the proper transformer turns ratio is the square root of 400 or 20. The primary of the output transformer must have 20 turns for every single turn in the secondary, and could be something like 1,000 to 50. The winding with the greater number of turns would be connected to the higher impedance, with the lower number going to the lower impedance.

MICROPHONES

A microphone converts sound waves into electrical waves or impulses, and these tiny impulses are amplified thousands of times by audio amplifiers. There are several types of microphones but all make use of the pressure provided by the sound wave against a diaphragm or plate. This pressure causes a variation in resistance by shifting carbon granules in a button for the carbon microphone, and these changes in electrical resistance produce a variation in the current flowing in the primary of the microphone transformer. Another method is the piezoelectric effect which produces an electrical voltage when a mechanical strain or pressure is applied. The ordinary crystal microphone operates this way by using two thin crystals cemented in an arrangement called a bimorph cell. Sound waves striking the diaphragm cause a twisting or strain on the cell and produce a tiny electrical output voltage. A third method uses a moving coil that cuts magnetic lines of force in a permanent magnet which produces a small voltage across that coil. In a dynamic microphone sound waves strike a diaphragm attached to the coil, causing it to move in and out, thus generating a tiny voltage which corresponds to the sound-pressure changes. A more thorough coverage on microphones is given in the question and answer section, along with an evaluation of the different types.

RADIO FREQUENCY AMPLIFIERS

Radio frequency (RF) amplifiers are used to boost signal power. Normally, they operate Class C, since it is more practical due to the much greater efficiency and power output. However, if a modulated signal is being amplified, Class B must be used to avoid distorting the modulation. RF voltage amplifiers often operate Class A, since small amounts of power are needed and even with the low efficiency, the losses amount to very little.

It is important to remember that plate current flows all the time in a Class A amplifier, about one-half the time in Class B, and only for short pulses in Class C. The short pulses of the Class C RF amplifier output are rounded into a clean sine wave by the flywheel effect of the plate tank circuit. Bias requirements for Class C are never critical and quite easy to supply. Grid-leak bias is often used, but a resistor and bypass capacitor should be included in the cathode to limit plate current in cases where grid drive may be lost. Otherwise, a loss of grid drive would permit the plate current to rise to a degree where the vacuum tube would be damaged permanently.

TRANSMITTERS AND AM MODULATION

A transmitter may consist of a number of simple stages in which each performs a specific function. The oscillator generates the RF and applies it to the buffer stage, which isolates the load from the delicate oscillator and prevents that load from affecting frequency stability. The next stage is a multiplier to change the output frequency of the oscillator to the desired higher level, and sometimes more than one stage is necessary because single stages never multiply more than four times (quadrupler). If we need to multiply the oscillator frequency by six, a doubler followed by a tripler would do the job very well.

Since the oscillator determines the frequency of the transmitter, it is most important that it operates on the correct frequency at all times and does not drift even slightly from that frequency. This means crystal control of the oscillator for best frequency stability, and since even crystals change frequency slightly with temperature, most transmitters house crystals in temperature-controlled ovens. These sealed units start at 3 parts per million for an ambient range of 32 degrees F to 140 degrees F and range to about one thousand times that accuracy. Power supply regulation is also a necessity for good oscillator frequency stability; therefore, a separate oscillator supply is desirable.

The primary purpose of the buffer amplifier is isolating the oscillator from the stages following, which could very well change the frequency by load variations. Since the buffer operates Class A or B, the input draws only negligible power from the oscillator.

Frequency multipliers are normally doublers or triplers, although the quadrupler is used at times. The multiplier stage or stages must have a high Q plate tank, high grid bias, sufficient grid drive, and operate Class C. Triode tubes may be used for frequency multipliers without neutralization because input and output circuits are tuned to different frequencies.

The power amplifier provides the big boost in the signal and supplies the carrier to be coupled through the transmission line to the antenna. As a result of the large amount of power handled, spurious oscillations frequently show up in this stage. Aside from wasting power, these oscillations may get to the antenna and cause interference, so it is important that they be eliminated. The Faraday screen or shield forms a comb-like screen between primary and secondary of the output to reduce the transfer of harmonics.

Transmitter power output is determined by the indirect method with reasonable accuracy, but in some cases, such as AM broadcast transmitters, the direct measurement of output power must be used. Both methods are taken up in detail a little later.

While holding the carrier frequency constant, the amplitude is varied by the modulating signal. Amplitude modulation is accomplished by introducing the audio signal from the modulator to an element of the final power amplifier. The plate is the most popular, but the screen grid, control grid, suppressor grid or cathode may be used. As the carrier varies in amplitude with the modulating signal, two sidebands are generated with one above and one below the carrier, and their widths are limited by the FCC according to the service, as you will learn shortly.

SINGLE SIDEBAND, SUPPRESSED CARRIER

Single sideband makes use of the fact that two of the three frequencies normally radiated in AM transmission may be eliminated, with additional advantages resulting. Since at least 50 percent of the radiated power is in the carrier (which carries no intelligence), it is suppressed in single sideband (SSSC) transmission. We now have the two sidebands, the upper and lower, which are the same except for frequency, so one is eliminated, and the result is single sideband, suppressed carrier transmission. There is a very large plus when compared to the conventional AM in efficiency. In an ordinary AM transmitter with a power of 1,000 watts, there is only about 250 watts in each sideband, so by using SSSC transmission it is possible to raise the power to four times that value or 1,000 watts for the single sideband radiated—without exceeding plate dissipation ratings or even the capacity of the power supply. The required bandwidth is halved, and this reduction means a better signal-to-noise ratio at the receiver. The BFO (beat frequency oscillator) of the ordinary superheterodyne receiver serves a useful purpose in detecting single sideband, as well making reception of A-1 (code) transmissions easier and more pleasant to hear as the pitch of the note is adjustable.

ALIGNMENT PROCEDURES

The step-by-step alignment of an AM receiver is described in detail in the Q & A study section, along with explanations and the importance of certain indicating devices while making such adjustments.

Question 1: Make a sketch showing the construction of the D'Arsonval type meter and label the various parts. Draw a circuit diagram of a vacuum-tube voltmeter and a wattmeter.

D'Arsonval Movement. The principle of the D'Arsonval movement is clearly shown in Fig. 4-1A. In the diagram, only one turn of wire is shown, though in practice the coil consists of many turns of very fine wire, each turn adding more effective length to the coil. The coil is usually wound on an aluminum frame or bobbin, to which the pointer is attached. Oppositely wound hairsprings are also attached to the bobbin, one at

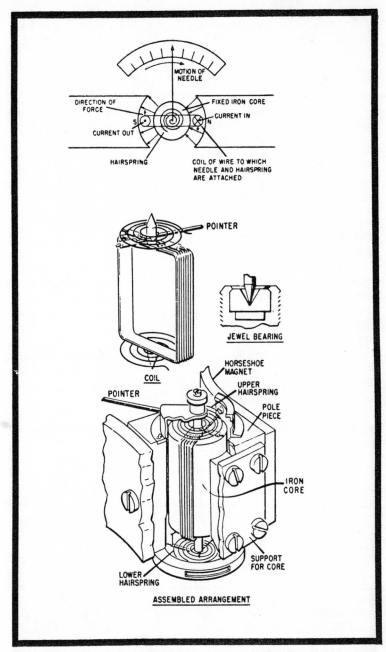

Fig. 4-1. (A) D'Arsonval movement. (B) Detailed view of basic D'Arsonval movement.

either end. The circuit to the coil is completed through the hairsprings. In addition to serving as conductors, the hairsprings serve as the restoring force that returns the pointer to the zero position when no current flows.

In the movement, the deflecting force is proportional to the current flowing in the coil. The deflecting force tends to rotate the coil against the restraining force of the hairsprings. The angle of deflection, then, is proportional to the deflecting force. When the deflecting force and the restraining force are equal, the coil and pointer cease to move further.

The deflecting force is proportional to the current in the coil; the angle of rotation is proportional to the deflecting force; thus, the angle of rotation is proportional to the current through the coil. When current ceases to flow in the coil, there is no longer a force to oppose the restraining force of the hairspring, and the pointer returns to its resting position. Figure 4-1B is a detailed view of the D'Arsonval movement in which the various parts have been labeled.

Vacuum-Tube Voltmeter. Needless to say, the vacuum-tube voltmeter has all but vanished from the inventory of modern test equipment; it has been replaced by high-impedance meters employing field-effect transistors rather than tubes. The question about vacuum-tube voltmeters may occur on the exam, however, regardless of the VTVM's antiquity—so it will pay to know the workings of this device. In the AC version of the VTVM, the AC voltage to be measured is applied to the AC probe (Fig. 4-2A). It is rectified by V1 and filtered by the RC network in the probe.

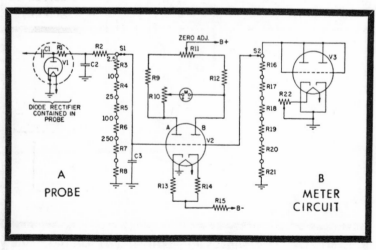

Fig. 4-2. VTVM circuit.

The meter circuit is a balanced bridge network. When the input voltage between the probe and ground is zero, the bridge is balanced and the voltages across the two arms containing the plate load resistors of V2 are equal. Thus, the DC meter indicates zero. If a voltage is applied between the probe and ground, the bridge becomes unbalanced and current flows through the meter. The meter is calibrated in RMS volts. The input impedance is very high. At the lower frequencies, the input capacitance is negligible, but as the frequency increases, the input capacitance introduces an additional load on the circuit under test and causes an error in the meter reading.

Diode V1 causes a contact potential to be established across the voltage-divider network connected to the grid of V2A. This voltage would unbalance the bridge. Therefore, a similar contact potential is introduced across the grid of V2B and V3 and its associated voltage divider to balance the bridge before the AC voltage to be measured is applied to the probe.

The DC electron-tube voltmeter circuit is shown in Fig. 4-2B. The DC voltage to be measured is applied between the DC input terminal and ground. The DC input voltage is therefore applied through R23 to the divider network feeding the grid of V2A. The grid of V2B is grounded. The meter is connected across a normally balanced bridge so that the application of the DC voltage unbalances the bridge and causes the meter to deflect. The calibration is in DC volts. Bias is obtained for V2A and B through the voltage drop across R13, R14, and R15. The cathodes are positive with respect to B— by an amount equal to the bias. Thus, the grids are correspondingly negative with respect to the cathodes. In Fig. 4-2B, no

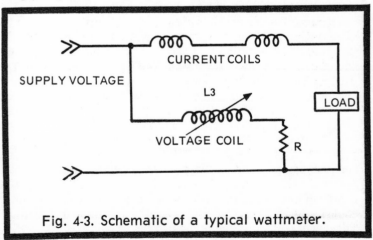

Fig. 4-3. Schematic of a typical wattmeter.

diode is used in the probe, so no contact potential is established, and V3 (with its associated voltage-divider network) is omitted from the circuit.

Wattmeter. Electric power is measured by means of a wattmeter. This instrument is of the electrodynamometer type. It consists of a pair of fixed current coils and a movable potential coil, as shown in Fig. 4-3. The fixed coils are made up of a few turns of comparatively large-conductor wire. The potential coil consists of many turns of fine wire; it is mounted on a shaft carried in jeweled bearings so that it may turn inside the stationary coils. The movable coil carries a pointer which moves over a suitably graduated scale. Flat coil springs hold the pointer to a zero position.

The current coil (stationary) of the wattmeter is connected in series with the circuit (load), and the potential coil (movable) is connected across the line.

When line current flows through the current coil of a wattmeter, a field is set up around the coil. The strength of this field is proportional to the line current and in phase with it. The potential coil of the wattmeter generally has a high-resistance value resistor connected in series with it. This is for the purpose of making the potential-coil circuit of the meter as purely resistive as possible. As a result, current in the potential circuit is practically in phase with line voltage. Therefore, when voltage is impressed on the potential circuit, current is proportional to and in phase with the line voltage.

The actuating force of a wattmeter is derived from the interaction of the field of its current coils and the field of its potential coil. The force acting on the movable coil at any instant (tending to turn it) is proportional to the product of the instantaneous values of line current and voltage.

The wattmeter consists of two circuits, either of which will be damaged if too much current is passed through them. This fact is to be especially emphasized in the case of wattmeters, because the reading of the instrument does not serve to tell the user that the coils are being overheated. If an ammeter or voltmeter is overloaded, the pointer will be indicating beyond the upper limit of its full-scale range. In the wattmeter, though, both the current and voltage circuits may be carrying such an overload that their insulation is burning and yet the pointer may be only part of the way up the scale. This is because the position of the pointer depends upon the power factor of the circuit as well as upon the voltage and current. Power of course, can easily be calculated in a DC circuit by connecting an ammeter and voltmeter as shown in Fig. 4-4. The power is the product of the two readings.

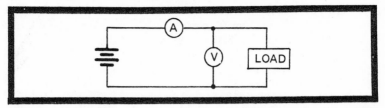

Fig. 4-4. Measurements used to determine power in a DC circuit.

Question 2: Show by a diagram how a voltmeter and ammeter should be connected to measure power in a DC circuit.

See Fig. 4-4. The power of the circuit is determined by multiplying the voltage by the current as indicated by the meters. In a DC circuit the power in watts is equal to the voltage in volts times the current in amperes, P equals E X I.

Question 3: If a 0-1 mA DC milliammeter is to be converted into a voltmeter with a full-scale calibration of 100V, what value of resistance should be connected in series with the milliammeter?

This is easily determined from Ohm's Law: We want 1 mA of current to flow (to deflect the meter full-scale) when 100V DC is applied. Resistance is equal to 100V divided by 0.001 ampere; thus, the value of the resistor would be 100,000 ohms.

Question 4: A one-milliampere meter having a resistance of 25 ohms was used to measure an unknown current by shunting the meter with a 4-ohm resistor. It then read 0.4 milliampere. What was the unknown current value?

The unknown current was 2.9 milliamperes as determined by the basic formula $R_m I_m = R_s I_s$, where R_m is the meter resistance, I_m the current through the meter, R_s the resistance of the shunt and I_s the current through the shunt. As we know, the current and resistance through the meter, $R_m I_m$ equals E_m, and the voltage drop E_m is equal to the voltage drop across the shunt, since they are in parallel. This enables us to quickly solve for I_s which is E_s divided by R_s.

Question 5: An RF VTVM is available to locate the resonance of a tunable primary tank circuit of an RF transformer. If the VTVM is measuring the voltage across the tuned secondary, how would resonance of the primary be indicated?

Resonance would be indicated by a peak reading (maximum voltage) on the VTVM. In a parallel LC circuit, impedance is greatest at resonance and with a voltage drop proportional to impedance, it would be maximum at resonance also. Since the signal voltage across the primary is maximum at resonance, maximum voltage would be induced into the secondary, and tuning the primary for a peak reading of the VTVM in the secondary would show resonance in the primary tank circuit.

Question 6: Define the following terms and describe a practical situation in which they might be used.

    (a) **RMS voltage**
    (b) **peak current**
    (c) **average current**
    (d) **power**
    (e) **energy**

RMS Voltage. The term "RMS" means "root mean square," and is applied to alternating voltages as a means of comparison with an equivalent DC voltage value. In AC, then, RMS is the equivalent DC voltage value required to deliver the same effective heating power to a load. The effective, or RMS, value of a sine wave is 70.7 percent (0.707) of the peak AC voltage value. A practical situation where RMS voltage is used is in an AC voltmeter, which uses a rectifier to measure an AC value in RMS volts.

Peak Current. One of the most frequently measured characteristics of a sine wave is its amplitude. Unlike DC measurements, the amount of alternating current or voltage present in a circuit can be measured in various ways. In one method of measurement, the maximum amplitude of either the positive or the negative alternation is measured. The value of current or voltage obtained is called the "peak" voltage or current. To measure the peak value of current or voltage, an oscilloscope or special meter (peak reading) must be used. The peak value of a sine wave is 100 when the average value is 63.7 and the RMS value is 70.7. Peak current measurements are often made on antennas, transmission lines, audio circuits, and RF amplifiers.

Average Current. The average value of a complete cycle of a sine wave is zero, since the positive alternation is identical to the negative alternation. In certain types of circuits, however, it is necessary to compute the average value of one alternation. This can be accomplished by adding together a series of instantaneous values of the wave between zero degrees and 180 degrees and then dividing the sum by the number of instantaneous values used. Such a computation would show one alternation of a sine wave to have an average value equal to 63.7 percent of the peak value. Average values of current and voltage are useful in calculating the unfiltered output voltages and currents of rectifiers. The DC output of an unfiltered rectifier is equal to the average value of the applied voltage alternations.

Power. A value of power is a means for measuring the rate at which work is accomplished, and it may be calculated in

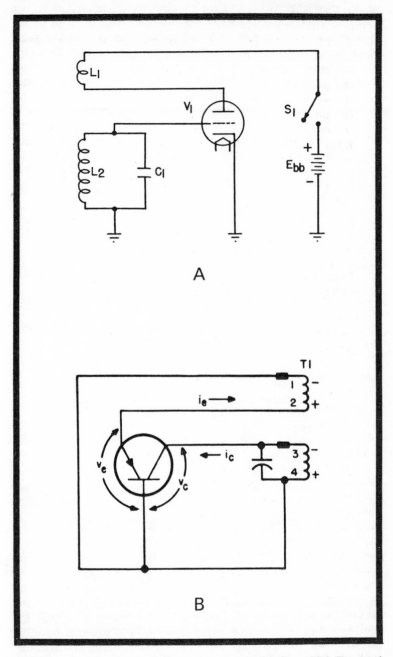

Fig. 4-5. (A) Tube-type Armstrong oscillator. (B) Typical transistor oscillator and current waveforms, bias circuits omitted.

purely resistive circuits by multiplying a load's current by its source voltage. If the source voltage is unknown, power may be calculated by multiplying the square of the current drain by the resistance of the load. Power is an extremely common measurement in electronics, for it offers the principal means for measuring circuit efficiencies, circuit performance capability, and requirements of a source to adequately drive a load. The watt is the unit of electrical power, and is equal to work done at the rate of 1 joule of work per second. Typical practical applications where power measurements are made include RF output strength, measurement of audio output volume, and an almost unlimited number of other functions, both AC and DC.

Energy. The term "energy" represents the ability to perform work electrically. In other words, a certain amount of energy must be available in order for a source to be able to deliver a certain amount of power to a load. Energy, then, is the capacity to perform work, the basic unit of which is the joule. Practical uses for the term occur in studies related to nuclear physics and in computing the value of laser discharges.

Question 7: Draw circuit diagrams of each of the following types of oscillators (include any commonly associated components). Explain the principles of operation of each.

(a) Armstrong.
(b) tuned-plate, tuned-grid (LC and crystal)
(c) Hartley (series- and shunt-fed)
(d) Colpitts
(e) electron-coupled
(f) multivibrator
(g) Pierce (crystal-controlled)

Armstrong. The simplest of all the oscillators is the Armstrong. The vacuum-tube Armstrong circuit is shown in Fig. 4-5A and the transistor equivalent is shown in Fig. 4-5B. In the tube circuit, L2-C1 forms the tank circuit, which determines the resonant frequency, and L1 is the feedback coil (often referred to as a tickler). In both the tube and the transistor circuit, the bias voltages have been omitted for simplicity.

Oscillations begin in the circuit when the bias conditions of the amplifier tube or transistor are normal and power is applied. The amplitude of current flow in the circuit will increase, causing an expanding magnetic field around the tank circuit. This induces a voltage in the tank coil and charges the tank capacitor. The charge of the tank capacitor causes output current to increase by increasing the potential on the tube's grid (or collector, in the common-base transistor Armstrong oscillator). This regeneration continues until the nonlinear characteristics of the amplifying device cause a difference in the rate of change of the output current.

When the induced voltage of the tank coil falls below the charge of the capacitor, the tank capacitor begins to discharge. The discharge of this capacitor causes the input potential to decrease, thereby decreasing output current. When the tank capacitor is completely discharged, the field of the tank coil collapses and charges the capacitor with the opposite polarity. Partway through this portion of the cycle of operation, the input potential will become sufficiently negative to cut the amplifier's conduction off. When the field of the tank coil is completely collapsed, the capacitor will begin to discharge. As the tank voltage comes nearer the bias point, the input potential will approach the point where the amplifier comes out of cutoff (this oscillator is biased for Class C operation). As the amplifier begins to conduct, regenerative feedback occurs and replaces the lost energy. Oscillations can now continue until DC power is removed from the circuit.

Tuned-Plate, Tuned-Grid. In the TPTG oscillator, the grid circuit (L1-C1, Fig. 4-6A) is tuned to the resonant frequency desired. When the first surge of current starts this circuit oscillating, the oscillations appear at the grid and are amplified in the plate circuit. The plate circuit consists of L2-C2. The feedback path in the TPTG oscillator occurs through the plate-to-grid capacitance of the triode. Energy is coupled from the plate circuit to the grid circuit. If L2-C2 is tuned to the same frequency as L1-C1, the phase of the feedback is not proper to sustain oscillations; for this reason, the plate circuit is made inductive at the frequency of oscillation of the grid circuit to make the feedback regenerative. This is done by tuning the plate circuit to a slightly higher frequency.

In the TPTG oscillator circuit shown in Fig. 4-6B, the grid tank has been replaced with a crystal (which itself serves the function of a complete, highly stable tank circuit consisting of a capacitance, an inductance, and a resistance).

Series-Fed Hartley. The principal identifying characteristic of the Hartley oscillator is the split tank coil, half of which feeds the input of the tube or transistor, and the other half of which feeds the output circuit. Figure 4-7A shows the basic series-fed vacuum-tube circuit, and 4-7B shows the transistor version.

In the tube oscillator, one tank circuit is actually made to serve as both grid and plate resonant circuits. The grid is coupled to one end of the tank and the plate is connected to the other end. The cathode is attached to a point on the inductor. This divides the coil between the grid and the plate circuits in

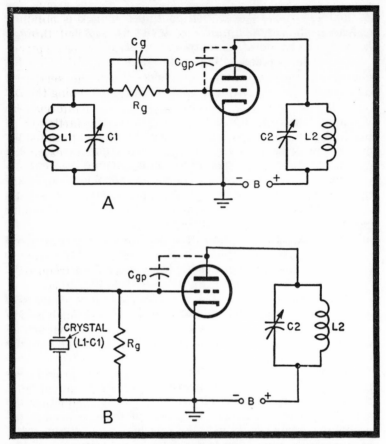

Fig. 4-6. (A) Tuned-plate tuned-grid oscillator. (B) Crystal oscillator.

the form of an inductive voltage divider, as shown. The voltage across L1 is between the grid and cathode, thereby applying a signal to the grid. The amplified voltage at the plate appears across L2. This provides the necessary feedback.

In the Hartley, the DC plate current must pass through inductor L2 before it can return to the cathode. The disadvantage in this arrangement is that the plate supply is placed at a high AC potential with respect to the cathode. Also, the supply has a large distributed capacitance to ground, and this capacitance is shunted across the tank coil (L2).

In the transistor version of the series-fed Hartley, resistors R_B and R_F provide the necessary bias for the base-emitter circuit. Collector bias is obtained through transformer winding 1-2. Capacitor C_E provides an AC bypass around the emitter swamping resistor (R_E). The feedback is obtained from the induced voltage in winding 2-3 coupled through capacitor C_C to the base of the transistor. Capacitor C2 places terminal 2 of the tank coil at AC ground potential.

Shunt-Fed Hartley. The disadvantage of the series-fed circuit (discussed above) can be overcome by keeping the DC plate supply (tube circuit) and the oscillating plate current separate. This is accomplished in the shunt-fed Hartley (Fig. 4-7C). The plate current oscillations are coupled to the split-inductance tank by means of capacitor C2. The capacitor prevents the plate current from returning to the cathode through the tank. The plate current, therefore, can return only through the choke in series with the B+ source. This choke prevents any oscillations from appearing in the supply because its reactance is very large.

The transistor version of the shunt-fed Hartley is pictured schematically in Fig. 4-7D. Resistors R_B, R_C and R_F provide the necessary bias conditions for the circuit. The frequency-determining network consists of the series combination of windings 1-2 and 2-3 in parallel with capacitor C1. Since this capacitor is variable, the circuit may be tuned through a wide range of frequencies. Capacitor C2 is a DC blocking capacitor. Capacitor C_E provides an AC bypass around the emitter swamping resistor (R_E).

The coil functions as an autotransformer to provide the regenerative feedback signal. The feedback is obtained from the induced voltage in winding 2-3 coupled through capacitor C_C to the base of the transistor. By shunt-feeding the collector through resistor R_C, direct current flow through the tank coil is avoided.

Colpitts. The Colpitts, like the Hartley, is a split-tank oscillator; the difference is that the Hartley incorporates a split inductance, whereas the Colpitts uses a split capacitance in the tank circuit. The capacitance of the tank circuit in the Colpitts (Fig. 4-8A) is provided by capacitors C1 and C2, which form a capacitive voltage divider between the grid and plate circuits. By adjusting C1 and C2, it is possible to control the frequency and amount of positive feedback.

Figure 4-8B illustrates the transistor Colpitts oscillator circuit. Regenerative feedback is obtained from the tank circuit and applied to the emitter of the transistor. Base bias is provided by resistors R_B and R_F. Resistor R_E develops the emitter input signal and also acts as the emitter swamping resistor. The tuned circuit consists of capacitors C1 and C2 in parallel with inductor winding 1-2. Capacitors C1 and C2 form the voltage divider. The voltage developed across C2 is the

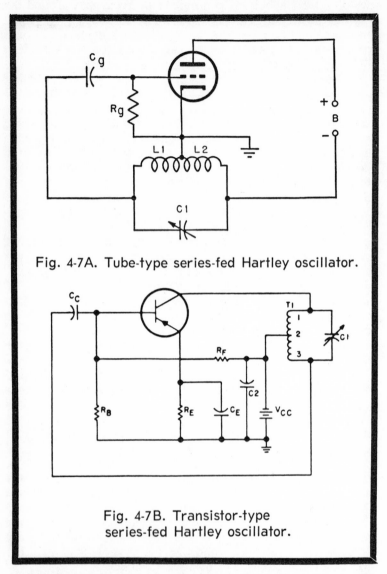

Fig. 4-7A. Tube-type series-fed Hartley oscillator.

Fig. 4-7B. Transistor-type
series-fed Hartley oscillator.

feedback voltage. The manner of operation is the same as with the tube circuit.

Electron-Coupled. By using a multielectrode tube, the oscillator and buffer stages of a transmitter can be replaced by a single circuit that performs both functions. Such a circuit is called an electron-coupled oscillator. Figure 4-9 is a typical circuit arrangement using a pentode. In this circuit, the cathode, the control grid, and the screen grid perform the

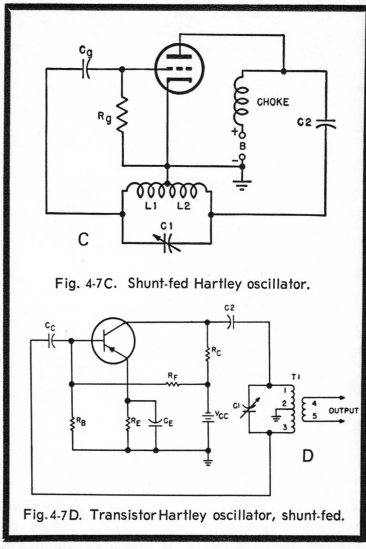

Fig. 4-7C. Shunt-fed Hartley oscillator.

Fig. 4-7D. Transistor Hartley oscillator, shunt-fed.

function of the triode in the Hartley oscillator. The cathode of the pentode taps the split-inductance tank consisting of L1, L2, and C1. The control grid is coupled to one end of the tank, and the screen grid takes the place of the triode plate. The screen voltage is taken from the voltage divider, consisting of R1 and R2 across the B+ supply. This part of the circuit can be compared to the Hartley oscillator previously described.

The signal appearing at the grid causes the current through the tube to oscillate. In the ordinary Hartley, this

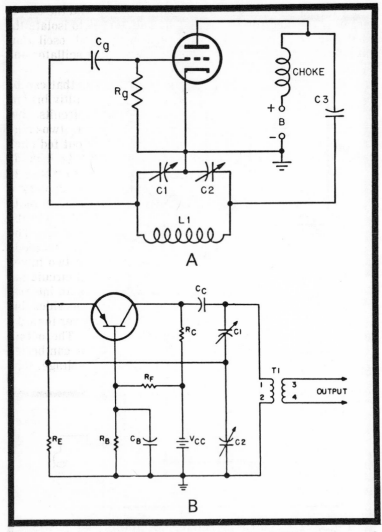

Fig. 4-8. Tube-type (A) and transistorized (B) versions of the common Colpitts oscillator,

current is collected at the plate, where one portion of it is used for feedback and the rest for output. In the electron-coupled oscillator, however, the screen grid collects only that portion of the current needed for feedback. The output portion of the current passes through the screen grid to the pentode plate, where it is collected and passed through the output tank circuit consisting of C3 and L3. Capacitors C2 and C4 serve to bypass oscillations around the power supply.

The only connection between the oscillator and the output circuit is the electron stream itself. This serves to isolate the oscillator from the load. The electron-coupled oscillator, therefore, has all the advantages of a separate oscillator and buffer.

Multivibrator. One of the simplest oscillators that can be used as a frequency divider is the synchronized multivibrator. There are many varieties of multivibrator circuits, but essentially they are all modifications of a two-stage resistance-coupled amplifier circuit with the output fed back to the input. When the grid voltage of a vacuum tube is made more positive the plate voltage decreases. This decrease in plate voltage is coupled into the grid of one tube, causing a decrease of grid voltage. This results in an increase in plate voltage which is applied to the grid of a second tube, and the cycle reverses. The circuit is shown in Fig. 4-10A. The variations possible consist in using direct coupling, cathode coupling, or mixed types of coupling between the two tubes.

A small amount of voltage applied to the grid circuit can be used to trigger oscillation. Any voltage that is an integral multiple of a natural frequency of the oscillator provides this triggering action. The frequency can be much higher than the actual frequency of operation of the oscillator. The output from one multivibrator controlled in this manner can be ten times less in frequency than the controlling voltage. The

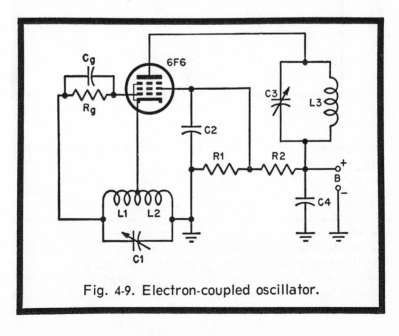

Fig. 4-9. Electron-coupled oscillator.

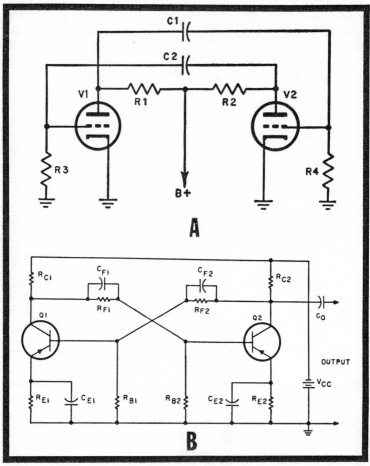

Fig. 4-10. (A) Simple multivibrator circuit. (B) Transistor multivibrator.

output of this multivibrator can be connected to another multivibrator that also divides by a like amount, providing division by 100. In this way, the high frequency of the crystal oscillator and the master oscillator in an FM system can be reduced to a frequency that falls in the audio range.

The basic transistor version of the multivibrator is shown in Fig. 4-10B. This is a two-stage RC-coupled common-emitter amplifier with the output of the first stage coupled to the input of the second stage, and the output of the second stage coupled to the input of the first stage. Since the signal in the collector circuit of a common-emitter amplifier is reversed in phase with respect to the input of that stage, a portion of the output of each stage is fed to the other stage in phase with the signal on the base electrode. This regenerative feedback with amplification is required for oscillation. Bias and stabilization are established identically for both transistors.

Pierce. The Pierce oscillator, also frequently known as the ultra-audion (or simply ultraudion), is shown in its vacuum-tube form in Fig. 4-11A. This is considered to be the simplest of the tube-type **crystal** oscillators, for all that is required are a few resistors and capacitors. As with the Colpitts oscillator, oscillation occurs because of the voltage feedback provided by the voltage divider formed by the grid-plate capacitance and the grid-cathode capacitance.

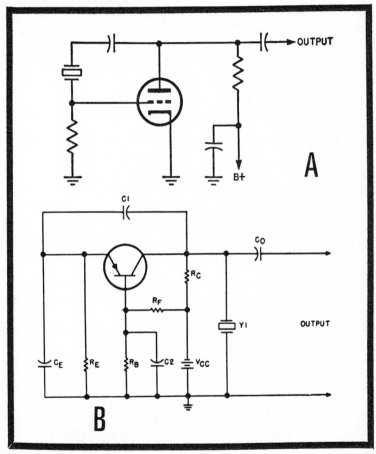

Fig. 4-11. Colpitts-type crystal oscillator, collector-emitter regeneration. The crystal in these circuits makes them "Pierce" oscillators.

The transistor version of the Pierce oscillator is shown in Fig. 4-11B. If the crystal were to be replaced by its equivalent LCR circuit, the functioning of the circuit would become analogous to that of the Colpitts oscillator. The circuit of Fig. 4-11B shows the common-base configuration with the feedback supplied from collector to emitter through capacitor C1. Resistors R_B, R_C, and R_F provide the proper bias and conditions for the circuit. The emitter resistor is the emitter swamping resistor(R_E). Capacitors C1 and C_E form a voltage divider connected across the output. Capacitor C2 is an AC bypass around base-biasing resistor R_E. Since no phase shift occurs in this configuration, the feedback signal must be connected so that the voltage across the emitter capacitor will be returned to the emitter with no phase shift occurring. The oscillating frequency of this circuit is determined not only by the crystal but by the parallel capacitance offered by capacitors C1 and C_E. These are normally made large to swamp both the input and output capacitances of the transistor and make the oscillations comparatively independent of changes in transistor parameters.

Since the parallel capacitance of C1 and C_E affects the oscillator frequency, the operation of the crystal is in the inductive region of the impedance-versus-frequency characteristic between the series- and parallel-resonant frequencies.

Question 8: What are the principal advantages of crystal-controlled oscillators over tuned circuit oscillators?

Stability is improved by the crystal-control which enables the transmitter to the "locked" closer to its assigned frequency. Quality of transmission is also improved, since the extremely high Q of the crystal circuit insures less distortion. Compact size of the crystal, as opposed to the somewhat bulky LC tank, is another attractive feature. The only disadvantage is the additional problem in changing operating frequencies and this would be a consideration only in some transmitters. As a rule, the disadvantage would not apply.

Question 9: Why should excessive feedback be avoided in a crystal oscillator?

Excessive feedback could cause overheating which would result in fracturing or cracking of the crystal. Frequency stability depends on the level of feedback; abnormal amplitudes could cause frequency deviation that could not immediately be corrected without changing crystals.

Question 10: Why is a separate source of plate power desirable for a crystal oscillator stage in a radio transmitter?

This ensures against frequency shift or dynamic instability during modulation which causes a change in load on the supply, and can, in turn, affect the oscillator frequency.

Increasing the oscillator plate voltage with the screen constant makes the oscillator frequency higher due to the decrease in tube input capacity. A similar increase in screen voltage would cause the oscillator frequency to decrease. The frequency stability of the transmitter is considerably improved by providing a separate supply for the crystal oscillator plate.

Question 11: What may result if a high degree of coupling exists between the plate and grid circuits of a crystal-controlled oscillator?

This could result in excessive feedback and the usual undesirable effects of dynamic instability.

Question 12: Explain some methods of determining if oscillation is occurring in an oscillator circuit.

There are a variety of ways to check oscillation with little indicator lamps. One of the simplest of these is to connect a small length of wire as a loop to a Christmas-tree lamp (low-voltage, series type). The wire, about 5-6 inches in length, is soldered so as to make a continuous loop from the base of the lamp to its shell. When held near the oscillator tank coil, the lamp will glow. The brilliance of the lamp indicates the energy lost at the tank.

Occasionally, when testing RF amplifiers and transmitters, it may become necessary to determine whether a radiated signal is being generated in the transmitter's oscillator circuit. In this case, you can rule out the oscillator by merely unplugging the crystal to see if the oscillation ceases. If it does not stop when the crystal is removed, parasitic oscillations and possibly inadequate neutralization of a stage or stages are indicated.

Other methods for checking oscillation of a stage include listening to the frequency on a receiver or other device capable of tuning to the signal frequency of the oscillator, monitoring the oscillator at close proximity with a diode connected across a sensitive meter, and holding a small fluorescent lamp near the tank coil (lamp will fluoresce if circuit is oscillating).

Question 13: What is meant by parasitic oscillations? How may they be detected and prevented?

Parasitic oscillations are signals generated within a transmitter other than by design.

The most noticeable features of parasitic oscillation in an amplifier are erratic tuning and the radiation of spurious signals at other than the design frequency. When an RF amplifier is operating properly, the plate current dips sharply as the tank circuit is tuned through resonance. This plate-current dip also corresponds to maximum power output and (usually) maximum grid current into the final amplifier. If a tetrode is operating normally, the plate current change may not be too great, but the screen current dip will still be significant. With parasitic oscillation, the plate current may not dip at all; the minimum may not correspond to maximum power output; several dips may appear in the tuning range; or grid current to the final amplifier will not coincide with the dip in the final amplifier plate current reading. Parasitics can be cured sometimes by inserting a parallel inductance and resistance in the grid or plate lead. This detunes one of the parasitic circuits sufficiently to prevent oscillation. (Usually, the process is no more complex than wrapping a few turns of solid, 16-gage wire around a carbon resistor so that both the resistance and the inductance are paralleled.) Another method is to insert a small resistance in series with circuit leads to introduce sufficient loss to stop oscillation. A third alternative is to incorporate a tuned parallel-resonant trap that actually inserts a very high impedance in the parasitic frequency path. In addition to the trap circuit, it is common to find small high-frequency capacitors connected from plate and control grid to cathode; these bypass the harmonic path.

Question 14: What determines the fundamental frequency of a quartz crystal?

The fundamental is the lowest frequency of vibration for a specific mode of operation and is determined by the thickness, type of cut, substance and type of mounting. The thicker crystal has a lower vibrating frequency than the thinner one. The modes of operation are flexure, longitudinal, face shear, thickness shear and third-overtone. Crystal substances are quartz, tourmaline and rochelle salts, all of which exhibit piezo-electric powers. Capacity of the holder and temperature both affect the crystal frequency, although the latter may be closely controlled by the use of a constant-temperature oven.

Question 15: What is meant by the temperature coefficient of a crystal?

Temperature coefficient expresses the holding power of the crystal with changes in temperature and may be either positive or negative, as well as low or high. A low temperature coefficient indicates that the crystal frequency will vary only slightly with larger changes in temperature and, of course, is a most desirable factor. A negative temperature coefficient signifies an increase in crystal frequency with a decrease in temperature and positive means the opposite. The pertinent information is normally printed on the crystal holder and refers to + or - parts per million per degree centigrade.

Question 16: What are the characteristics and possible uses of an "overtone" crystal? A "third-mode" crystal?

The "overtone" crystal is ground to oscillate at an odd harmonic of its fundamental frequency, each as the third, fifth, seventh, etc., harmonic. This procedure permits control at much higher frequencies than would be possible otherwise, and at the same time reduces the number of frequency multiplier stages required at high frequencies, such as VHF and UHF. Needless to say, specially designed "overtone" crystals are far superior to the usual fundamental type crystal, although the latter will operate in such a circuit. The "third mode" crystal is one that is ground for the third overtone of the fundamental and will perform well at three times the fundamental.

Question 17: Explain some of the factors involved in the stability of an oscillator (both crystal and LC-controlled).

Several important factors are involved:

(a) Stray capacitance changes the total capacitance of the tank circuit and causes the oscillator to "drift." Included are tube interelectrode capacitance and reflected reactance, all of which should be held as low as possible to ensure a high C-L ratio in the tank circuit.

(b) Loading of the oscillator lowers the Q of the tank and reduces stability. Isolation of the oscillator from its load as provided by a buffer amplifier between the oscillator and load is desirable.

(c) Voltage must be constant and preferably regulated to keep it that way.

(d) Temperature should be constant with high temperature coefficient crystals enclosed in a temperature-controlled oven. Temperature compensating components should also be utilized.

(e) Q should be high for good stability; keep the resistance of the tank coil low by using heavy wire or crystal control.

(f) Shielding with material having good electrical conductivity reduces stray fields, humidity and air.

(g) Bias resistors and capacitor values must be suitable for stable operation. The Q value is considerably higher with a crystal type oscillator than one of the LC type and stability of the former circuit is far superior to that of the latter as a result.

Question 18: Is it necessary or desirable that the surfaces of a quartz crystal be clean? If so, what cleaning agents may be used which will not adversely affect the operation of the crystal?

The crystal surfaces must be clean. Dirt, lint or grease will interefere with proper operation. Even grease or oil from the skin is harmful and a soft tissue is best for cleaning, along with soap and water, followed by a thorough rinsing. Carbon tetrachloride is also an excellent cleaner and will insure good contact with the holder. If the crystal is hermetically sealed in its holder, foreign material could not possibly reach the crystal and there is never any problem of clean surfaces.

Question 19: What is the purpose of a buffer amplifier stage in a transmitter?

A buffer amplifier improves the frequency stability of the oscillator by isolating it from the load. It acts as a buffer by lessening the effect of the load on the critical oscillator output and presents a high-impedance load on the oscillator with little or no effect on circuit Q. Tuning of the final amplifier, antenna circuit or swinging of the antenna could cause the oscillator frequency to shift without the buffer stage to separate it from such loading effects.

Question 20: Draw simple schematic diagrams illustrating the following types of coupling between audio amplifier stages and between a stage and a load.

(a) Triode vacuum tube inductively coupled to a loud-speaker.

(b) Resistance coupling between two pentode vacuum tubes.

(c) Impedance coupling between two tetrode vacuum tubes.

(d) A method of coupling a high-impedance loudspeaker to an audio frequency amplifier tube without a flow of plate current through the speaker windings, and without the use of a transformer.

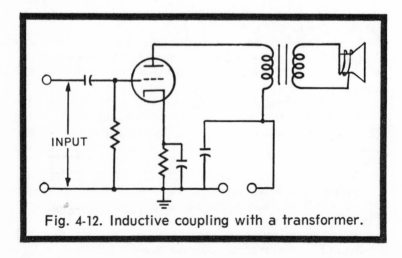

Fig. 4-12. Inductive coupling with a transformer.

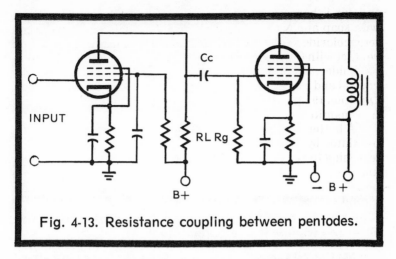

Fig. 4-13. Resistance coupling between pentodes.

(a) Inductive coupling by a transformer is shown in Fig. 4-12. This is a series-fed circuit, since the DC plate current flows through the transformer primary.

(b) Resistance coupling between pentode stages is shown in Fig. 4-13. RL, Rg and Cc form the coupling network. The reactance of Cc must be low at the lowest frequency amplified to avoid poor low-frequency response due to excessive loss across Cc.

(c) Impedance coupling between tetrodes is clarified by Fig. 4-14. The coupling network consists of L, Cc and Rg. Here again, proper frequency response depends on the ability of coupling capacitor Cc to pass the desired frequencies without loss.

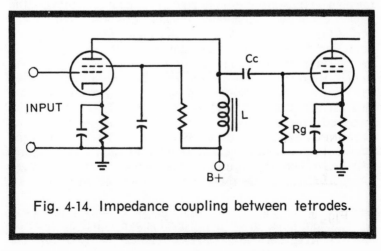

Fig. 4-14. Impedance coupling between tetrodes.

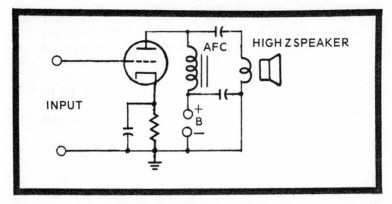

Fig. 4-15. A capacitor couples a high-impedance loud-speaker directly to the output stage.

(d) Fig. 4-15 shows a high-impedance loudspeaker coupled to an audio frequency amplifier without plate current flow through the speaker windings and without using a trans-former. A coupling capacitor in series with the speaker coil keeps the DC in the plate circuit from entering the speaker but passes the audio. The audio choke AFC passes the DC and rejects the audio signal.

Question 21: What would probably be the effect on the output amplitude and waveform if the cathode resistor bypass capacitor in an audio stage were removed?

The bypass capacitor places the cathode at ground potential with respect to audio passing through the stage. The audio component must be removed from the cathode stage if the bias on the amplifier is to remain constant. Removing the bypass capacitor would cause the audio AC voltage to appear across the cathode resistor, thus causing a varying bias on the amplifier. Without a fixed bias point, the amplifier would no longer be capable of operating in the center of its linear region. However, since current flow through an unbypassed cathode resistor develops a voltage that varies at the same rate as the plate voltage, negative signal feedback is in-troduced. Negative feedback has a canceling effect, which negates any distortion introduced by the stage and reduces the overall amplitude drastically. Thus, while the operating point will tend to drift, the amplitude of the signal will be low enough to keep it within the linear region, and distortion will be minimal.

Question 22: Why do vacuum tubes produce random noise?

Random noise in vacuum tubes is generated by electron emission irregularities as the electrons are emitted from the cathode at random rather than in a smooth, continuous stream. This is known as random or shot noise and it results in thermal noise in the control grid circuit and partition noise from the variations in the division of screen and plate currents. Microphonic noise is caused by mechanical vibration of the cathode, grids and plate inside the tube but normally triggered by external sound waves.

Question 23: Why are decoupling resistors and capacitors used in stages having a common power supply?

Decoupling networks prevent multistage amplifiers from oscillating due to unwanted signal voltages passing from one circuit to another through the common power source. Signal voltage variations from the output stage plate across the B+ bus are fed back into the input stage, causing it to oscillate.

Question 24: How would saturation of an output transformer create distortion?

Saturation causes the output transformer to operate in a nonlinear way, because an increase in the primary current no longer increases the flux and the secondary signal is not an accurate pattern. Actually, the secondary response is flattened and severe audio distortion results. Excessive primary signals may drive the core flux to saturation and the DC plate current in the primary often adds to this primary signal, causing the core to saturate at a lower signal amplitude than it would otherwise. Push-pull operation permits much stronger signals to be handled before saturation, since DC plate currents cancel in the split primary winding. Summarizing, saturation of the output transformer reduces its inductance causing a lower load impedance and amplitude, especially at lower frequencies.

Question 25: Why is noise often produced when an audio signal is distorted?

Noise is produced when an audio signal is distorted due to the presence of harmonics which, if sufficient in strength, will cause the original signal to be noisy. When nonlinear audio amplification appears, the resulting amplitude distortion produces harmonics of the original wave and intermodulation. The output signal consists of desired and undesired signals; the latter, of course, are "audio noise."

Question 26: What factors determine the correct bias voltage for the grid of a vacuum tube?

In an audio amplifier, the bias is chosen so that the tube operates as closely as possible to the center of its linear transfer characteristic during the no-signal state, and so that no amount of input signal will cause the grid to draw current. When properly biased, a Class A amplifier will allow maximum-level input signals to approach saturation of the

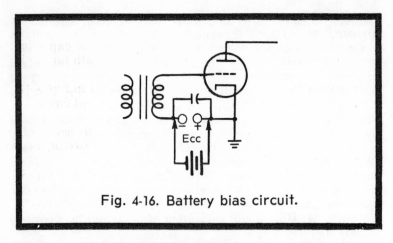

Fig. 4-16. Battery bias circuit.

tube on positive alternations and **approach** cutoff on negative alternations. At saturation, the grid begins to draw current; at cutoff, the tube does not conduct.

Question 27: **Draw a schematic diagram illustrating each of the following types of grid biasing and explain its operation.**
  (a) **Battery**
  (b) **Power supply**

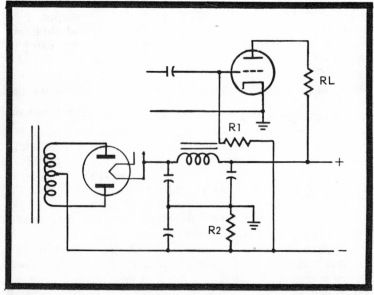

Fig. 4-17. Bias is drawn from the power supply in this circuit.

(c) Voltage divider

(d) Cathode resistor

(a) Fig. 4-16 shows battery grid bias with a capacitor across the battery to furnish a low-impedance path for audio signals.

(b) Grid bias from a power supply is shown in Fig. 4-17. The center tap of the transformer returns to ground through a resistor.

(c) The voltage divider in Fig. 4-18 provides the necessary grid bias and this arrangement is suitable when two or more different voltages are required.

(d) A basic method of cathode bias is illustrated in Fig. 4-19 with the cathode returned to ground through a resistor. As plate current flows, a voltage drop across the resistor places the cathode positive with respect to the control grid. A capacitor across the cathode resistors provides a low-impedance path for the signal voltage and prevents variations in the voltage drop.

Question 28: Is grid-leak biasing practical in audio amplifier stages?

Grid-leak biasing is not practical in audio amplifier stages because they normally operate without drawing grid current. A constant value of grid bias is required for audio amplifiers while grid-leak bias varies with the signal amplitude applied to the grid. This would cause more bias to be developed on strong signals than on weaker ones and distort the output.

Question 29: Draw a diagram showing a method of obtaining grid bias for a filament type vacuum tube by using a resistance in the plate circuit of the tube.

There are several ways to obtain grid bias by using resistances in the plate circuit, but none of them are too

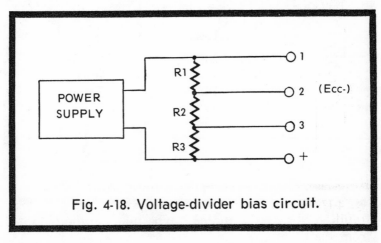

Fig. 4-18. Voltage-divider bias circuit.

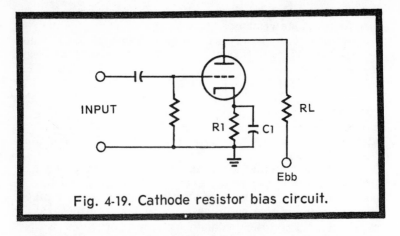

Fig. 4-19. Cathode resistor bias circuit.

practical because obtaining bias through other schemes is so much simpler. The circuit of Fig. 4-20 is one possible arrangement. The output of the full-wave supply is dropped across a divider consisting of a resistor (high value) and a zener (whose breakdown voltage is the bias required). As shown, the anode of the zener is kept below ground potential. A pair of voltage divider resistors split the filament voltage so that the filament sees a voltage that is slightly above ground on one side and slightly below ground on the other. The zener can be replaced by a resistor, but the operating point is considerably more stable with the zener than with a resistor.

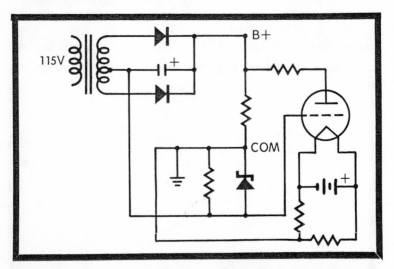

Fig. 4-20. Bias for a filament-type tube can be obtained from the plate circuit.

Question 30: Explain how you would determine the approximate value of cathode resistance necessary to provide correct grid bias for any particular amplifier.

The approximate cathode resistance may be figured by a simple application of Ohm's Law:

$$R_k = \frac{E_g}{I_k} = \frac{\text{Required grid voltage}}{\text{Total cathode current}}$$

The cathode current is the same as the plate current in triodes, but for tetrodes or pentodes, screen current must be added to the plate current for the total cathode current figure. Cathode bias is developed by the voltage drop across the series resistor as current flows in the cathode circuit.

Question 31: Why does a Class B audio-frequency stage require considerably more driving power than a Class A amplifier?

Bias is adjusted in Class A operation so that grid current does not flow at any time and the input is a high impedance. Class B amplifiers are biased so that grid current flows during the positive peak of each cycle of the input waveform which represents appreciable power loss in the grid circuit. Consequently, more driving power is required to overcome the current loss in the Class B input.

Question 32: Show by use of a circuit diagram two ways of using single-ended stages to drive a push-pull output stage.

Fig. 4-21 shows an interstage transformer coupling a push-pull output stage to the driver with a center-tapped

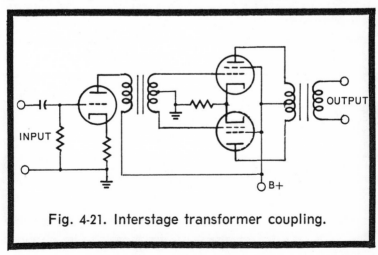

Fig. 4-21. Interstage transformer coupling.

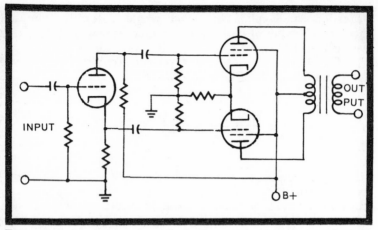

Fig. 4-22. Inverter circuit designed to feed a push-pull output stage.

secondary winding. This provides signals to the push-pull control grids that are 180 degrees out of phase as required. The inverter circuit in Fig. 4-22 provides signals from the single-ended stage that are 180 degrees out of phase to feed the push-pull stage.

Question 33: Draw circuit diagrams and explain operation (including input-output phase relationships, approximate practical voltage gains, approximate stage efficiency, uses, advantages, and limitations) of each of the following types of audio circuits.

(a) Class A amplifier with cathode resistor biasing.

(b) Cathode-follower amplifier.

(c) At least two types of phase inverters for feeding push-pull amplifiers.

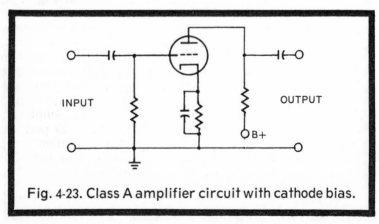

Fig. 4-23. Class A amplifier circuit with cathode bias.

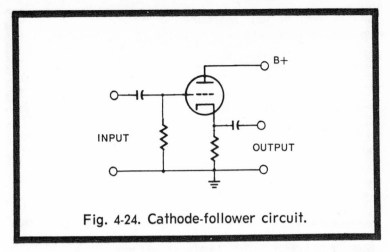

Fig. 4-24. Cathode-follower circuit.

(d) Cascaded Class A stages with a form of current feedback.

(e) Two Class A amplifiers operated in parallel.

(f) Class A push-pull amplifier.

(a) Fig. 4-23 is a Class A amplifier circuit with cathode resistor biasing. The output voltage is 180 degrees out of phase with the input. The practical voltage gain would vary, depending on the mu of the tube as well as whether a triode or pentode was used. Much higher voltage gains would be possible with the pentode. Approximate efficiency is 25 percent and it is normally used as a voltage amplifier driver. Its advantages are simplicity, no separate bias voltage is needed and bias is self-adjusting. Distortion is minimal and low drive is required. The limitations include low efficiency and low power output.

(b) The cathode-follower circuit is shown in Fig. 4-24, where the input is applied between grid and ground and the output taken between cathode and ground. Since the output is taken from across the cathode resistor, it is not bypassed. With the degenerative resulting, stage voltage gain is less than unity. The output voltage is in phase with input voltage. The input impedance is higher than average and the output impedance low, making it a useful impedance-matching circuit. The cathode-follower operates as a Class A amplifier; therefore, efficiency usually is about the same 25 percent. Applications include that of a matching or isolation stage between high- and low-impedance circuits and its only important limitation is the no power gain is offered.

(c) Figs. 4-25A and 4-25B show two basic types of phase inverters. The first is a single tube split-load type. One output is taken from the plate 180 degrees out of phase and the other from the cathode in phase with the input. Voltage gain is less than unity because of negative feedback and the efficiency is 25 percent as usual with Class A. Simplicity, excellent balance and frequency response are advantages worthy of note, and a lack of voltage gain is the only significant disadvantage. The second phase inverter (Fig. 4-25B) is a cathode-coupled type. The output of V1 is 180 degrees out of phase with the input. The voltage gain is about equal to half the normal for each stage because of the cathode action, and efficiency is 25 percent. The important advantage is the fair amount of voltage gain available and the disadvantage the poorer frequency response.

(d) Fig. 4-26 is a cascaded two-stage amplifier with current feedback. The cathode resistors are not bypassed,

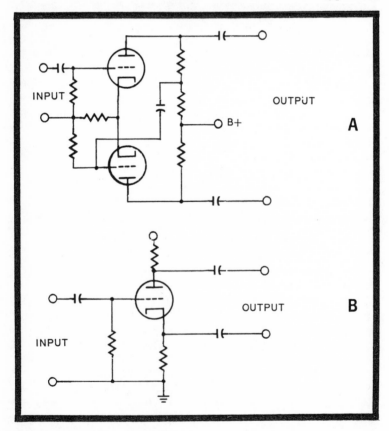

Fig. 4-25. Split-load phase inverter circuit (A). Cathode-coupled phase inverter (B).

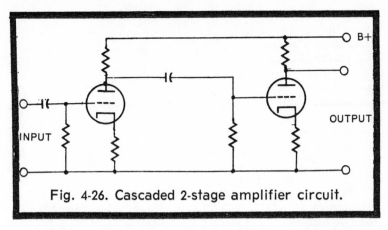

Fig. 4-26. Cascaded 2-stage amplifier circuit.

resulting in degenerative feedback. This negative feedback is a current in nature because the voltage at each cathode is dependent on the plate current of each tube as it flows through the individual cathode resistor. Since the signal has a phase reversal of 180 degrees in each stage, the output signal is in phase with the input signal after the double reversal. Voltage gain overall is equal to the product of the two stages and since it operates Class A, the efficiency is 25 percent. The popular application is a voltage amplifier with reduced distortion and good frequency response as a result of the elimination of the cathode bypass. The only limitation is that gain is somewhat reduced in comparison to a conventional type circuit.

(e) Fig. 4-27 illustrates the use of two Class A amplifiers in parallel. Operation is basically the same as with a single tube.

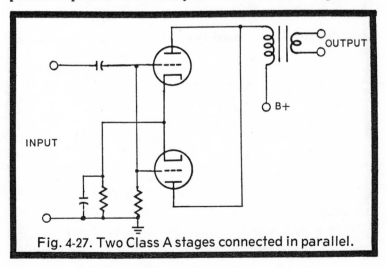

Fig. 4-27. Two Class A stages connected in parallel.

Varying input signals to the control grids result in corresponding plate current variations. There is 180-degree phase reversal from input to output and power gain is obtained with the usual 25 percent efficiency. Power amplification is the usual application and double the single tube output is obtained, but there is more distortion than would be found in the more popular push-pull circuit. The only possible advantage of the parallel hookup is the elimination of the phase splitter that is essential for push-pull. Disadvantages of consequence are the special output transformer required double the DC plate current, no reduction in distortion and the larger cathode bypass capacitor required because the cathode resistor is lower in value.

(f) A Class A push-pull amplifier circuit is shown in Fig. 4-28. Proper inputs supplied by a center-tapped input transformer instead of a phase inverter. Power gain is double that of a single tube and efficiency is 25 percent. Its most popular application is as a power amplifier in an audio output stage and it displays many advantages in such an arrangement. Even harmonic distortion is eliminated, hum and regenerative feedback are reduced, there's no DC core saturation in the output transformer and no cathode bypass capacitor is required, although in the case of the latter, improvement is possible in some cases by using the cathode bypass to compensate for a lack of balance in the tubes. Limitations are few and may be summed up in the possible need for bias controls to insure exact balance, matched tubes for improved operation and the need for out-of-phase input signals.

Question 34: Draw circuit diagrams and explain the operation of two commonly used tone control circuits.

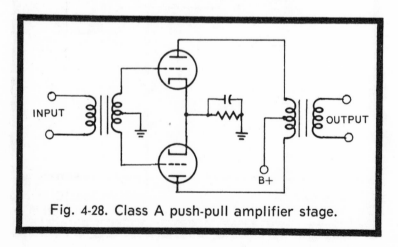

Fig. 4-28. Class A push-pull amplifier stage.

Two control circuits are presented in Fig. 4-29. The circuit shown in sketch A is a tone control for bass signals and that at B is the equivalent circuit for treble signals. Note that one circuit is the complement of the other in component placement. The first circuit (for bass signals) uses a high-pass filter network to pass high frequencies while shunting lower frequencies through an attenuator. Conversely, the circuit in B uses a low-pass filter so that low frequencies are passed to the amplifier stage directly while the high-frequency signal components are shunted to an attenuator.

Question 35: Name some causes of hum and self-oscillation in audio amplifiers and suggest methods of reducing it.

Hum originates in the AC power source and may enter the circuit through heater-to-cathode capacitance or emission. Center-tapped filament transformers or a potentiometer across the filament with its slider grounded may eliminate or greatly reduce the hum if this is actually the source. Frequently, hum problems arise as a result of insufficient filtering of the B+ supply. Filtering components should always be checked first to ascertain if any of the hum is originating there. Hum pickup from a power transformer located too close to a high-gain amplifier or with improper shielding may be reduced by carefully dressing grid leads and

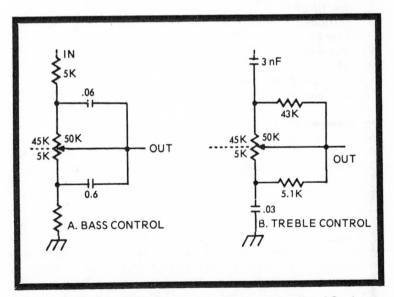

Fig. 4-29. Bass and treble controls used in the IC stereo preamp. Notice that one is the complement of the other in component placement.

shielding of the tubes involved. In an occasional stubborn case, transformer replacement may be necessary. Twisting the leads carrying AC will usually eliminate electrostatic and magnetic coupling with amplifier circuits. Also, placing transformers (power) with cores perpendicular instead of parallel to chassis will reduce hum.

Self-oscillation in audio amplifiers normally results from interaction between stages and often takes place in the power supply if decoupling filters are not used. Good regulation and RC decoupling filters in individual B+ leads will correct the problem. Mechanical vibrations, called microphonics, between stages may be corrected by shock or rubber mounting of high-gain sections. An open grid resistor or a coupling circuit with too long a time constant could also result in self-oscillation and may, of course, be eliminated by the indicated replacement.

Question 36: What factors should be taken into consideration when ordering a Class A audio output transformer; a Class B audio output transformer feeding a speaker of known ohmic value?

Considerations for Class A audio output transformers include: Normal operating power rating, direct current in the primary, frequency response, primary and secondary impedance, and shielding.

Factors for Class B include the above, plus the fact that Class B audio amplifiers require a center-tapped secondary for the input transformer and a center-tapped primary for the output transformer, since push-pull operation is always used. In push-pull amplifiers lead inductance in the output transformer primary must be held to a minimum to avoid distortion.

The importance of sufficient power handling capability cannot be emphasized too strongly because overheating will result in a breakdown of insulation and permanent damage. Even a slight overload in signal power can cause distortion on peaks. In single-ended Class A stages, the DC flowing in the primary must never exceed the transformer's rated specifications or core saturation will result. The frequency response of the transformer is marked by a drop-off in extremes at the low and high ends with a flat response between the two. Needless to say, the quality of the amplifier or system will only be as good as the ability of the transformer to response to the frequencies involved and the curve should be carefully noted when making a selection. The primary impedance should match or load the amplifying device coupled to it properly and the secondary impedance must match the speaker impedance exactly to afford maximum transfer of output power. The magnetic and electrostatic shielding of the transformer should be sufficient for the intended location.

Question 37: Draw a diagram of a single-button carbon microphone circuit, including the microphone transformer and source of power.

In Fig. 4-30 a step-up transformer is used to match the low impedance of a carbon microphone to the high impedance input of an amplifier grid. A battery in series with the transformer primary and the microphone provides the source of power. As the sound vibrations produce a variation in pressure on the carbon granules, the resistance of the button is varied accordingly, resulting in changes in current flow in the transformer primary.

Question 38: If low-impedance headphones in the order of 75 ohms are to be connected in the output of a vacuum tube amplifier, how may this connection be made to permit most satisfactory operation?

The plate circuit of a vacuum tube is one characterized by a very high impedance value; 75 ohms represents a low value. If the plate of the tube were coupled directly into the headphones, an impedance mismatch would occur which might serve to introduce distortion and compromise circuit efficiency. The best approach is to use a transformer whose primary impedance matches the characteristics required by the tube, and whose secondary impedance is 75 ohms.

Question 39: Describe the construction and explain the characteristics of a crystal-type microphone; of a carbon-button type microphone.

Crystal-Type. When a quartz crystal is subjected to a mechanical pressure, the crystal produces a minute alternating voltage that can be measured with ordinary test equipment. Similarly, a crystal will produce mechanical energy when an electrical signal is applied to it. (This is called the piezoelectric effect.) Since the electrical energy emitted by the crystal is proportional to the mechanical energy required to drive it, the crystal is indeed an energy converter—or transducer.

The crystal responds to sonic vibrations by producing a voltage that reverses polarity in exact correspondence with the physical movement; low-frequency sounds produce voltages that alternate slowly, and high-pitched sounds produce output voltages that shift polarity with high frequency. Sound vibrations are coupled to the crystal by means of a diaphragm. The electrical signals generated by the crystal can be used to drive a high-impedance amplifier directly.

The frequency response of the crystal mike is not too uniform. This is due to the inertia of the crystal itself; however, for applications such as amateur radio or any other noncritical application, they are widely used. Because of its high impedance, the crystal microphone may be directly connected to the input of the grid circuit of a speech amplifier. The output of the crystal microphone is on the order of about —55 dB, although this figure tends to vary from manufacturer to manufacturer, depending on quality of microphone and other factors. The diaphragm type has a frequency response of 80 to about 6000 Hz. The type of crystal most widely used is Rochelle salt, because its sensitivity is somewhat higher than that of natural quartz.

Carbon-Type. If a piece of pure carbon were split up and made granular, the resulting pile would possess a value of specific resistance and would pass a current if the pile were enclosed in an insulated container. If a variable pressure is applied to the pile its density changes. If the source of the pressure variations is the human voice, the compressions and rarefactions of air applied to the carbon pile will cause its resistance to vary at an audio rate. The variable-resistance characteristic of the carbon pile is the underlying principle on which the operation of the microphone is based.

In the single-button carbon microphone, the granules are placed in a cup-like button, and are permitted to make contact with the suspended perpendicular element called the "diaphragm." If a stress is placed on the diaphragm, the pressure exerted on the carbon granules is increased and the resistance of the carbon pile decreases. Relaxation of the pressure restores the button's resistance to its original value.

The microphone button is placed in series with a battery, as shown in Fig. 4-30. Any current flowing in the microphone circuit will also flow through the primary of the transformer.

Question 40: What precautions should be observed when using and storing crystal microphones?

Ordinary crystal microphones using Rochelle-salt crystals should be stored in a cool, dry place and not subjected to mechanical vibrations or physical abuse. Even though a measure of protection against moisture is provided by the wax seal, moisture-proof wrapping is standard procedure for storage. Protection from high temperatures is also mandatory during storage, since the salt crystal will not withstand temperatures in excess of 120 degrees F. The ceramic type may be subjected to much higher temperatures with no problem.

Question 41: What is an RFC? Why is it used?

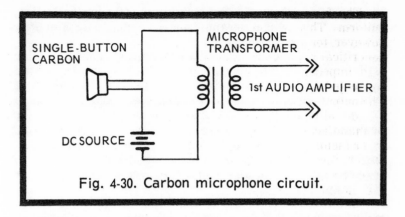

Fig. 4-30. Carbon microphone circuit.

RFC is the abbreviation for "radio-frequency choke." Such chokes are used to prevent the flow of (choke out) radio-frequency signals in a DC circuit. Depending on the value of the RFC, the device will impede the flow of RF at certain frequencies without interfering in any way with the passage of direct current through the series-connected winding.

Question 42: What are the advantages of using a resistor in series with the cathode of a Class C RF amplifier tube to provide bias?

The use of a cathode resistor in a Class C RF amplifier will protect the tube against damage in the event excitation is lost or interrupted. If grid-leak bias only is used in the stage, a loss of grid drive due to interruption of the input signal will reduce grid bias to zero, causing excessive DC plate current to flow and destroy the tube. By having a portion of the bias obtained from the cathode resistor, bias will never be reduced to the danger zone because the DC plate current flowing through the cathode will result in a voltage drop across the resistor and produce some negative bias. Since plate current only flows during a small portion of the cycle in Class C operation, the voltage drop across the cathode resistor is available only during that period and may supply only a portion of the grid bias as a safety measure.

Question 43: What is the difference between RF voltage amplifiers and RF power amplifiers in regard to applied bias? What type of tube is generally employed in RF voltage amplifiers?

The RF voltage amplifier is normally operated Class A, but the RF power amplifier in Class B or Class C. Power amplifier tubes are often larger to dissipate and properly handle the additional power. Triodes, tetrodes or pentodes are acceptable. The RF voltage amplifier uses a pentode in most

167

cases for its higher gain and stability without neutralization.

Question 44: Draw a diagram of a grounded-grid RF amplifier and explain its operation.

Fig. 3-7 is a schematic for a grounded-grid RF amplifier with the signal fed to the cathode and the output taken at the plate. The grid at RF ground acts as a shield between the input and output circuits, thus reducing cathode-plate capacitance to an insignificant value and eliminating the need for neutralization. Although more input power is required with this circuit, most of it appears in the plate circuit as output power. The triode is less noisy than the tetrode or pentode.

Question 45: Explain the principle involved in neutralizing an RF stage.

Neutralization in a radio-frequency amplifier involves the reduction to an absolute minimum, by cancellation, the signal transferred between input and output circuits through grid-to-plate capacitance, thus eliminating the tendency toward self-sustained oscillations. By feeding back a voltage from the output circuit to the input circuit about equal the opposite in phase to that fed through the grid-plate capacitance, the voltages cancel and the stage is neutralized.

Question 46: Explain, step-by-step, at least one procedure for neutralizing an RF amplifier stage.

There are three common neutralization methods—plate, grid and push-pull. The step-by-step procedure for plate neutralization, sometimes referred to as the Hazeltine method, follows:

1. Remove plate voltage from the tube so that any signal appearing in the plate circuit will be due to grid-plate capacitance.

2. Tune the preceding stages and the grid of the stage to be neutralized for maximum signal.

3. Connect or loop-couple an RF indicator to the plate tank circuit. (Oscilloscope, AC-VTVM, neon bulb or even a flashlight bulb attached to a loop of a few turns of wire).

4. Adjust the neutralizing capacitor, after tuning the plate tank to resonance or maximum indication, until minimum RF is indicated. Retune the grid circuit for any additional RF indication and recheck the plate tuning for any possible increases. Then, retouch the neutralizing capacitor setting for minimum or zero reading, after which the stage may be considered to be neutralized. In the event that the final indication is not satisfactory, the complete procedure should be repeated and preferably with a more sensitive indicator.

The undesirable effects of oscillation in the RF amplifier are many, such as possible tube failure from overheating, excessive plate current, component damage, generation of spurious frequencies and modulation distortion.

Question 47: What class of amplifier is appropriate for an RF doubler stage?

A Class C amplifier is best because it is rich in harmonics.

Question 48: Draw a circuit diagram of a push-pull frequency multiplier and explain its principle of operation.

Fig. 4-31 illustrates a push-pull multiplier with the grids connected in push-pull and the plates connected in parallel. The balanced grid circuit applies out-of-phase voltages to the grids of the tubes. The grid with the positive voltage conducts while the other with a negative grid is cut off. When the excitation impulse is reversed, the cut off tube receives the positive pulse at the grid and conducts while the other tube receiving the negative is promptly cut off. As the plates are connected in parallel, a single cycle of the input frequency produces two cycles in the plate circuit. Thus, the frequency is automatically doubled and the output circuit may be tuned to any even harmonic. In the push-pull circuit, the fundamental and all odd harmonics are eliminated.

Question 49: Push-pull frequency multipliers normally produce what order of harmonics—even or odd?

Push-pull frequency multipliers generally produce odd-order harmonics and operate Class C for best results. Since plate current output is badly distorted, even harmonics are cancelled because the output from each tube is opposite in phase.

Question 50: State some indications of and methods of testing for the presence of parasitic oscillations in a transmitter.

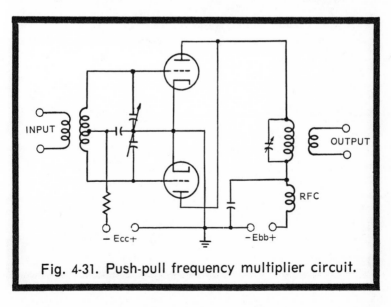

Fig. 4-31. Push-pull frequency multiplier circuit.

Not all combinations of input and output circuits can be used together successfully, since some of them permit the amplifier stage to oscillate at frequencies that are relatively unrelated to the frequency to which it is tuned. These parasitic oscillations are distinct from the sort of oscillation that occurs in an amplifier which is improperly neutralized or one in which the input circuit is not shielded sufficiently from the output. They are undesirable because they cause the transmission of spurious signals, thus impairing the efficiency of the amplifier.

The most noticeable features of parasitic oscillation in an amplifier are erratic tuning and the radiation of spurious (unwanted) frequencies. When an amplifier is operating properly, the DC plate current dips sharply as the tank circuit is tuned through resonance. This plate-current minimum also corresponds to maximum power output. If a tetrode is operating normally, the plate-current change may not be too great, but the screen current's dip will be significant. With parasitic oscillation, the plate current may not dip at all; the minimum may not correspond to maximum power output; or several dips may appear in the tuning range. Since the symptoms presented by a stage which is not properly neutralized are somewhat similar, it is difficult to tell the two effects apart unless neutralization is checked first. (Refer also to Question 13 in this section.)

Question 51: Draw a schematic diagram and explain the operation of a harmonic generator stage.

Fig. 4-32 is an RF doubler harmonic generator schematic. The output is rich in harmonics with the grid biased at about ten times cutoff. Grid excitation exceeds the bias for very

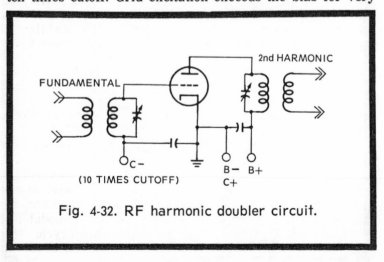

Fig. 4-32. RF harmonic doubler circuit.

short periods during the cycle, causing a short pulse of current in the output. Because the plate tank has a high Q, sufficient "flywheel effect" is available to sustain oscillations during cutoff of the tube between excitation peaks. During the cutoff interval, the tank oscillates at the selected harmonic as determined by the resonant tank frequency and the drive frequency.

Question 52: What is the meaning of the term "carrier frequency"?

The frequency of the unmodulated RF carrier wave as assigned for transmission.

Question 53: If a carrier is amplitude modulated, what causes the sideband frequencies?

Whenever modulation of the carrier takes place, as in AM, there are new frequencies present at the transmitter output, in addition to the carrier frequency. These are known as sidebands and are formed by the distorting of the sinusoidal carrier wave to produce a nonsinusoidal wave that is equal to the sum of three sinusoidal waves—carrier frequency, carrier plus audio frequencies and carrier minus audio frequencies. Since many audio frequencies are present in the complex speech waveform, a group of sideband frequencies are produced with an upper sideband above the carrier frequency and a lower sideband below the carrier.

Question 54: What determines the bandwidth of emission for an AM transmitter?

The actual width of the channel of frequencies of a radiated AM signal is equal to twice the highest audio modulating frequency. For an AM station with audio modulation at frequencies from 50 to 20,000 cycles (Hz), the upper sideband extends 20 kHz above the carrier and the lower 20 kHz below it. Assume the carrier frequency as 600 kHz; the upper sideband would extend to 620 kHz and the lower to 580 kHz. Thus, the bandwidth in this exaggerated example would be 40 kHz or 40 Kcs. Once again it should be noted that the term cycles per second (cps) comes up time after time and will probably "pop up" often in your FCC examination, so it is important to use it when asked to do so and at the same time remember that it is synonymous with Hertz (Hz).

Question 55: Why does exceeding 100 percent modulation in an AM transmitter cause excessive bandwidth?

It is first important to understand that some waveforms are more efficient harmonic generators than others. Square waves, in particular, are very effective in creating harmonic signals. An overmodulated AM signal produces a modulation envelope that is clipped off at the negative half-cycle. This clipped waveform resembles a square wave and is rich in harmonics of the modulating signal. Since the harmonic of a signal appears at a multiple of the fundamental signal—and since the bandwidth of a carrier is a function of the frequency content—it stands to reason that an overmodulated signal produces a larger proportion of sidebands over a broader range of frequencies than a 100-percent-modulated RF carrier.

Question 56: What is the relationship between the percentage of modulation and the shape of the waveform envelope relative to carrier amplitude?

The amplitude of the transmitter output varies according to the audio voltage; it increases above the unmodulated carrier level during the positive swing of the audio and decreases below it during the negative excursion. The peak modulation amplitude expressed as a percentage of the actual carrier level is the modulation percentage, the formula:

$$A_m = \frac{M \times A_c}{100} = \frac{A_m}{A_c} \times 100$$

Ac is the level of the carrier, Am is the maximum increase or decrease, and M is the modulation percentage.

During 100 percent modulation, the transmitter output drops to zero on negative peaks in the audio cycle and, since increasing modulation above 100 percent can't drive the transmitter output below that, the zero time is extended, and the envelope flattened during negative peaks.

Question 57: Draw a simple schematic diagram showing a method of coupling a modulator tube to an RF power amplifier tube to produce grid modulation of the amplified RF energy. Compare some advantages or disadvantages of this system of modulation with those of plate modulation.

Fig. 4-33 is a schematic showing a modulator tube connected to an RF amplifier to produce control grid modulation. The modulator output is coupled in series with the amplifier grid bias by the modulation transformer. Much less power in the modulator is needed for this form of modulation, thus there is a considerable saving realized with a smaller tube and modulation transformer. The disadvantage of note is lower efficiency because the RF output from the power amplifier is much lower with the same amount of power drawn from the supply as would be required for plate modulation. Unless grid modulation is very carefully handled, appreciable distortion will result.

Question 58: What is the relationship between the average power output of the modulator and the plate circuit input of the

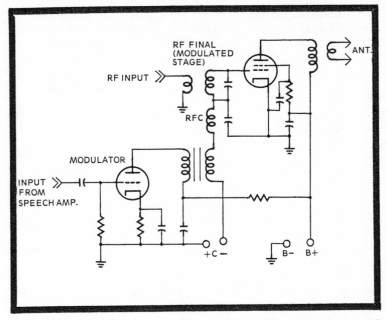

Fig. 4-33. Schematic of the connection used for grid modulation.

modulated amplifier under 100 percent sinusoidal plate modulation? How does this differ when normal voice modulation is employed?

In order to get 100 percent modulation with a sine wave, the modulator must be capable of suppling 50 percent as much power as is normally required by the modulated power amplifier plate. If the power amplifier draws 500 watts, the modulator would need 250 watts of audio power to modulate it 100 percent with a sine wave. A speech wave has a lower average power, and since peaks may not exceed 100 percent, less average power is required from the modulator. The modulator supplies power for the sidebands and the DC supply the power for the carrier.

Question 59: What is the relationship between the amount of power in the sidebands and the intelligibility of the signal at the receiver?

The greater the amount of power in the sidebands, the more intelligible will be the signal at the receiver. Unfortunately, it is impossible to get more power into the sidebands than an amount equal to 50 percent of the unmodulated carrier...that is, at 100 percent modulation. Sideband power decreases as modulation percentage decreases. Total RF power decreases and the signal distorts when modulation percentage is increased beyond the 100-percent point.

Question 60: What might cause FM in an AM radiotelephone transmitter?

Dynamic instability resulting from a common power supply, and if the modulator is not operating Class A, undesired frequency modulation can result since the oscillator frequency will shift with changes in loading.

Question 61: What is meant by "frequency shift" or "dynamic instability" with reference to a modulated RF emission?

Frequency shift in an AM transmission is a deviation from the desired carrier frequency as a result of changes in the DC plate current of an RF oscillator. In severe cases, particularly where the AM transmitter is mobile and the plate current is affected by variations that are attributable to insufficient isolation between stages or oscillator instability, frequency drift can be extreme and rapid enough to appear as FM.

Question 62: What would cause a dip in the antenna current when AM is applied? What are the causes of carrier shift?

This condition, commonly experienced by radio amateurs, is referred to as "downward modulation." It may be caused by a number of problems, including:

1. Inadequate regulation on a power supply used to provide voltages to all transmitter stages.

2. Insufficient RF drive to the final amplifier.

3. Soft tube in the final amplifier stage.

4. Inability of the final RF amplifier to handle peak currents of twice the normal unmodulated value (which may be attributable to a wide variety of problems, including poor design).

5. Modulation transformer problems, including arcing because of excessive voltage or RF leakage.

Question 63: Explain the principles involved in a single-sideband suppressed-carrier (SSSC) emission. How does its bandwidth and required power compare with that of full carrier and sidebands?

The principle of single-sideband suppressed-carrier emission is to transmit only one sideband while suppressing the carrier and one of the sidebands. Each sideband carries the same information, so only one is needed, and the carrier contains no intelligence, thus most of the power in AM transmission is wasted. Since one third of the power is conventional AM is in the sidebands with two thirds in the carrier, only one sixth of the power to the antenna is necessary for communication. In SSB transmission, all the power is fed into one sideband which affords a considerable power advantage. The single-sideband carrier requires only one half of the bandwidth of the AM signal and offers a gain of many db over AM. Noise pickup would naturally be reduced by one half at the same time.

Question 64: Draw a block diagram of a SSSC transmitter (filter type) with a 20-kHz oscillator and emission frequencies in the range of 6 MHz. Explain the function of each stage.

A filter type SSSC transmitter block diagram is illustrated in Fig. 4-34. The 20-kHz oscillator generates a reference signal which is fed to a balanced modulator. Combining the usual audio, 30 to 10,000 Hz, with the 20-kHz oscillator signal balances the carrier and only the two sidebands remain. These are applied to the sideband filter which passes only the upper sideband while eliminating the lower. The first mixer combines the 2-MHz oscillator with the upper sideband and passes frequencies 2.02 to 2.03 MHz to the second mixer where the 4-MHz oscillator signal is added. The band of frequencies now available are 6.02003 to 6.03 MHz, and, after amplification by the linear RF amplifier which prevents distortion, the output is fed to the antenna.

Question 65: Explain briefly how an SSSC emission is detected.

The SSSC signal is detected by mixing the low-frequency local oscillator output (20 kHz) with the single-sideband output of the last IF amplifier in the second detector. An AM signal is thus produced and detected as usual. Although single or double conversion may be used, the single-sideband receiver differs primarily in the way detection takes place. The reinserted carrier at the receiving point must have the identical frequency of the transmitter carrier, so that normal AM detection is possible.

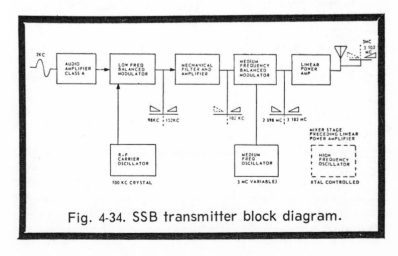

Fig. 4-34. SSB transmitter block diagram.

Question 66: Draw a block diagram of a single-conversion superheterodyne AM receiver. Assume an incident signal and explain briefly what occurs in each stage.

The block diagram of a typical superheterodyne receiver is shown in Fig. 4-35. Below corresponding sections of the receiver are shown the waveforms of the signal at that point. The RF signal from the antenna passes first through an RF amplifier, where the amplitude of the signal is increased. A locally generated unmodulated RF signal of constant amplitude is then mixed with the carrier frequency in the mixer stage. The mixing (heterodyning) of these two frequencies produces an intermediate-frequency signal which contains all of the modulation characteristics of the original signal. The intermediate frequency is equal to the difference between the station frequency and the oscillator frequency associated with the mixer. The intermediate frequency is then amplified in one or more stages called intermediate-frequency (IF) amplifiers and fed to a detector for recovery of the audio signal. The detected signal is amplified in the AF section and then fed to a headset or loudspeaker.

Question 67: Explain the relation between the signal frequency, oscillator frequency and the image frequency in a super heterodyne receiver.

If the oscillator is tuned above the incoming frequency, it will equal the sum of the incoming frequency and the intermediate frequency. The image frequency is the incoming frequency plus twice the intermediate frequency. When the local oscillator is below the incoming frequency, as in VHF, the oscillator frequency is equivalent to the incoming minus the intermediate frequency. The image frequency now appears at the incoming frequency minus two times the intermediate frequency.

Question 68: Draw a circuit diagram of an AM second detector and an AF amplifier (in one envelope), showing AVC circuitry. Also show coupling to and identification of all adjacent stages.

(a) Explain the principles of operation.

(b) State some conditions under which readings of AVC voltage would be helpful in troubleshooting a receiver.

(c) Show how this circuit would be modified to give DAVC.

The diagram shown in Fig. 4-36A is a typical AVC circuit.

(a) Diode section D1 (Fig. 4-36B) detects the audio in the usual way and diode D2 receives RF from D1 through the coupling capacitor. After rectification the RF produces a negative DC voltage across AVC load resistor RL. The filtering action of R1 and CF removes any remaining RF and

AF. This is the negative AVC voltage which is proportional to the level of the received signal.

(b) The AVC becomes more negative as the amplitude of the incoming signal increases and is applied to the grid of the RF and IF amplifiers, which reduces stage gain accordingly. On weaker signals, the bias provided by the AVC is less negative and stage gain increases.

(c) The negative AVC voltage often interferes with the reception of weak signals and this problem is corrected by employing the delayed AVC (DAVC) action. The circuit in Fig. 4-36B prevents AVC action until the received signal reaches a predetermined level. On strong s gnals the AVC voltage is applied immediately. Modification of the circuit is clarified in Fig. 4-36B with the addition of cathode resistor R_k. Since the AVC voltage across R_k is in series with D2, it will not conduct until sufficient RF is applied to exceed the DC across R_k. Thus, AVC action is prevented on weak signals. The cause of trouble may often be apparent by measuring the AVC voltage.

Question 69: Draw a beat frequency oscillator (BFO) circuit diagram and explain its use in detection.

The beat frequency oscillator (BFO) is necessary when CW signals are to be received because these signals are not modulated with an audio component. In superheterodyne receivers the incoming CW signal is converted to the intermediate frequency at the first detector as a single frequency signal with no sideband components. The in-

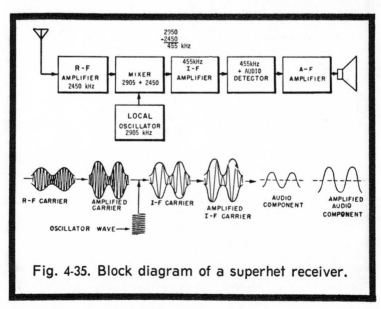

Fig. 4-35. Block diagram of a superhet receiver.

termediate-frequency signal is heterodyned (with a separate tunable oscillator known as the beat frequency oscillator) at the second detector to produce an AF output. In the circuit shown in Fig. 4-37, the Hartley oscillator (BFO) is coupled to the plate of the second detector by capacitor C3.

If the intermediate frequency is 455 kHz and the BFO is tuned to 456 kHz or 454 kHz, the difference frequency of 1 kHz is heard in the output. Generally the switch and capacitor tuning control are located on the front panel of the receiver.

The BFO should be shielded to prevent its own output from being radiated and combined with desired signals ahead of the second detector. If AVC voltage is to be used it should be obtained from a separate diode isolated from the second detector. One way is to couple the output of an IF amplifier stage ahead of the second detector to the AVC diode. Otherwise, the output of the BFO would be rectified by the second detector and would develop an AVC voltage even on no signal.

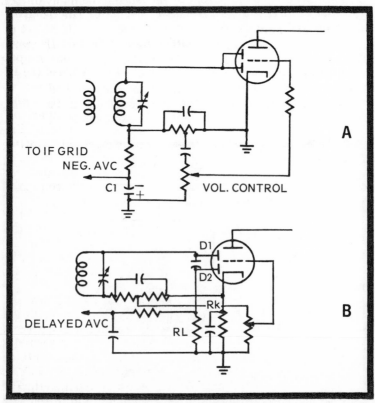

Fig. 4-36. Basic AVC circuit (A). Delayed AVC circuit (B).

Question 70: Explain, step-by-step, how to align an AM receiver using the following instruments. In addition, discuss what is occurring during each step.

(a) Signal generator and speaker.

(b) Signal generator and oscilloscope.

(c) Signal generator and VTVM.

The alignment procedure is the same regardless of the type of indicating instrument used. The signal generator must be AM modulated and should be reasonably well calibrated, especially if the receiver to be aligned is badly out of adjustment. Although the speaker may be used to indicate maximum response of the tuned circuits in a preliminary way, small signal changes are just about impossible to detect by ear. This is where the oscilloscope or VTVM prove quite useful.

The oscilloscope should be connected across the voice coil of the speaker. A VTVM connected between AVC and ground is satisfactory for the DC type or across the speaker voice coil if an AC type VTVM is used. Maximum indication on any device used signifies correct alignment at that point. The usual IF frequency is 455 kHz, so the signal generator should be set to this frequency and connected to the grid of the last IF stage through a .01-mfd capacitor. Using the minimum output necessary, peak the primary and secondary windings of the IF transformer for maximum indication on the meter or scope.

Now, move the generator to the grid of the next to last stage of the IF and peak that transformer for maximum, just as was done on the last stage. Continue by moving the generator to the grid of the IF stage being aligned until the first stage has been completed. It is necessary to keep reducing the generator output as alignment progresses, always maintaining the lowest level possible to insure proper performance of the amplifiers.

The IF transformer coupling the plate of the mixer to the grid of the first IF amplifier is the last to be aligned and the signal generator should be connected to the mixer grid in this case. It should be remembered that the generator output will have to be increased at this point because the mixer is not tuned to the IF frequency.

After completing the alignment of the IF section, proceed with RF alignment by connecting the signal generator to the antenna terminal through a small series capacitor and ground the other side to the chassis. Begin with a setting at 1400 kHz (both the generator and receiver), and adjust the oscillator trimmer for maximum indication on the scope or VTVM. Continue by adjusting first the mixer trimmer and then the RF trimmer for peak response. Reset the tuning dial to 600 kHz and the generator to the same frequency. Adjust the oscillator

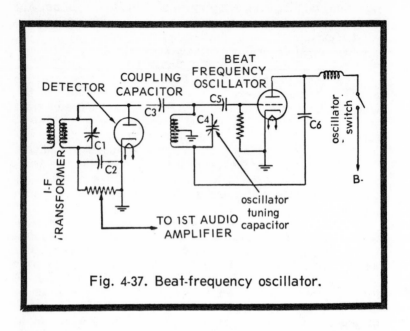

Fig. 4-37. Beat-frequency oscillator.

and low-frequency trimmer for maximum reading. Repeat the complete RF alignment procedure for possible improvement of your original settings. As each circuit is adjusted for resonance at the proper settings, stage gain will be maximum and the receiver is completely aligned.

Question 71: What are the advantages and disadvantages of a bandpass switch on a receiver?

The quality of a received signal is proportional to the bandwidth of that signal, since higher frequencies require wider passbands. Narrowing the bandpass of a receiver allows a receiver's selectivity to be increased substantially, but it often causes intelligibility of a received signal to deteriorate, particularly when the frequencies contained in the received signal are relatively high. It must be remembered that all the intelligence of an AM signal is contained in the sidebands, and the sidebands are displaced from the carrier frequency by an amount of spectrum that is equal to the audio frequency being transmitted.

Question 72: Explain sensitivity and selectivity of a receiver. Why are these important quantities? In what typical units are they usually expressed?

Sensitivity is the strength of a signal, usually measured in microvolts at the receiver input terminals, capable of producing a certain audio output. Its importance stems from the fact that it gives the receiver a merit rating according to its ability to perform adequately under weak signal conditions. Selectivity is the ability of the receiver to separate the selected frequency distinctly from adjacent undesirable frequencies and may be expressed in Hz or kHz, which is the bandwidth, and measurement may be quoted in points where response is down a definite number of db in relation to the IF center frequency (usually 6 db and 60 db).

CHAPTER 5

Basic Radiotelephone, Part III: Element 3

At this point, most of Element 3 is already behind us and the study ahead will come much easier as mental reference is made to the material previously discussed. Our first subject in this chapter is frequency modulation.

FREQUENCY MODULATION SYSTEMS

Since static, lightning, and other disturbances create amplitude modulated interference, frequency modulated waves may be received with comparative freedom from such annoyances. The carrier of the FM transmitter remains at its center or resting frequency without modulation. As modulation is introduced, the carrier varies in frequency by swinging higher and lower on either side of the normal center or resting point. Meanwhile, the amplitude of the wave does not vary and the antenna current of the FM transmitter is unchanged with modulation. The transmitter is constructed so that the frequency swing of the carrier is proportional to the amplitude of the modulating voltage and the frequency variation of the carrier is in step with the audio voltage, so the rate of carrier swing is actually equal to the modulating voltage. The reactance tube modulator varies the frequency of the oscillator in the FM transmitter in step with the audio modulating voltage. Frequency multipliers enable a small deviation in the oscillator frequency to cause a much larger deviation in the output frequency. If you shout in the FM microphone, the deviation or swing of the carrier will be greater, but as you raise the pitch of your voice, the **rate** of deviation becomes greater. FM receiver alignment is detailed in the Q & A section, along with the correction of interference problems that may occur with mobile installations.

ANTENNAS

An antenna is a conductor that radiates or picks up electromagnetic and electrostatic fields. It varies in size according to the need and may be mounted horizontally or vertically. The polarization of the radio wave is horizontal if the electrostatic field is traveling parallel to the surface of the earth, or vertical if they are traveling perpendicular to the earth's surface. The polarization of the wave depends on the position of the radiating antenna. The receiving antenna must be polarized or positioned similarly for satisfactory results. FM and television waves are horizontally polarized because the annoying reflections from tall buildings and man-made types of interference are not as likely to cause difficulties. The characteristics of several antennas are discussed later. The Marconi antenna is usually grounded at one end, while the Hertz antenna is not. Both can be horizontally or vertically polarized according to the specific need.

TRANSMISSION LINES

A transmission line is simply a means of transferring RF energy from the source to the load with maximum efficiency. Since transmission lines are made up of two parallel conductors, inductance results, so the current lags the applied voltage. The lines have capacitance, but neither the inductance nor capacitance results in a power loss. The real losses are due to RF resistance, leakage paths across the lines, and also radiation. A line terminated in its characteristic impedance acts like a line of infinite length regardless of its actual length. Thus, it may be termed an untuned line since its action does not depend on its length. Untuned lines have numerous advantages and are frequently used to transfer RF because of the absence of standing waves. Current handling capability is maximum and power losses are much smaller. The line performs equally well at all frequencies.

If a line is terminated in a value other than its characteristic impedance, the wave may be partially or completely reflected from the far end rather than being absorbed by the load. This forms a new wave on the line. Since the reflected wave attempts to travel back at the same speed as the original wave travels forward, the result is a wave that is not able to move along the line—a standing wave.

FREQUENCY MEASUREMENTS

There are several methods of frequency measurement, including the simple grid-dip meter which is merely an ordinary tube or transistor oscillator with a low-range current meter (mA or uA) to indicate grid collector current. The absorption frequency meter has a parallel resonant circuit that is inductively coupled to the circuit to be measured. It indicates a maximum reading on the milliammeter when tuned through resonance. The heterodyne frequency meter offers excellent accuracy in determining frequency and uses a calibrated variable frequency oscillator (VFO) and a nonlinear mixer amplifier. Its output contains the input frequencies as well as the sum and difference. Since the difference frequency is in the audio range, phones or a speaker may be used to monitor the output.

An FM deviation meter consists of an FM receiver with a good peak-reading voltmeter to sample the FM transmitter output and combine it with the local oscillator in the mixer to produce the difference frequency. A vernier scale assists in reading a dial with much greater accuracy; it is merely a short scale graduated so that 11 of its divisions are equal to 10 divisions of the scale being read. By sliding the zero of the vernier scale to the large scale point between the divisions being read, the decimal reading is indicated by the point where a small-scale division coincides with a large-scale division.

FORMULAS

Sinusoidal Voltages

Effective value equals 0.707 x peak
Average value is 0.637 x peak
Peak value is 1.414 x effective
Effective value is 1.11 x average
Peak value is 1.57 x average
Average value is 0.9 x effective

Resonant Frequency

$$Fr = \frac{1}{2\pi\sqrt{LC}}, \text{ or } \frac{.1592}{\sqrt{LC}}$$

$$L = \frac{1}{4\pi^2 F^2 C}, \text{ or } \frac{25,330}{F^2 C}$$

$$C = \frac{1}{4\pi^2 F^2 C}, \text{ or } \frac{25,330}{F^2 L}$$

$$X_C = \frac{1}{2\pi FC} \qquad C = \frac{1}{2\pi F X_C}$$

$$X_L = 2\pi FL \qquad L = \frac{X_L}{2\pi F}$$

X in ohms
C in farads
L in henrys
F in hertz

Question 1: Draw a schematic diagram of a frequency-modulated oscillator using a reactance-tube modulator. Explain its principle of operation.

Fig. 5-1 is a reactance-tube FM oscillator which is one basic way of producing frequency modulation. Frequency is variable by adjusting the tank circuit capacitor. With the modulator connected to the Hartley type oscillator, the reactance tube functions as capacitance in parallel to the regular tank capacitor. Therefore, the oscillator frequency is dependent on the sum of the two capacitance values. Since the reactance tube capacitance varies with the audio amplitude, the frequency of the oscillator will vary according to the audio modulating input. There are several types of reactance tube modulators, but basically all are similar in operation. The tube appears as a capacitance since its plate signal current leads its plate signal voltage by 90 degrees. A portion of the signal voltage on the modulator plate is fed back its grid through the voltage divider, and with the capacity value small, reactance is quite high compared to the resistance. This results in a 90-degree phase shift in the signal voltage fed back to the grid and places the plate current 90 degrees out of phase as it leads the plate voltage to that extent. By acting as a capacitor, the reactance tube grid voltage variations (audio input) modulate the oscillator RF plate current in direct accord with the modulating signal applied.

Question 2: Discuss the following with reference to frequency modulation:

(a) The production of sidebands.

(b) The relationship between the number of sidebands and the modulating frequency.

(c) The relationship between the number of sidebands and the amplitude of the modulating voltage.

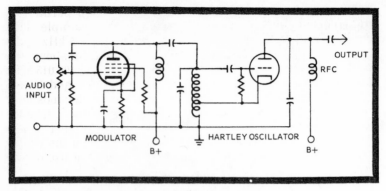

Fig. 5-1. FM oscillator circuit with reactance tube modulator.

(d) The relationship between percent modulation and the number of sidebands.

(e) The relationship between the modulation index or deviation ratio and the number of sidebands.

(f) The relationship between the spacing of the sidebands and the modulating frequency.

(g) The relationship between the number of sidebands and the bandwidth of emission.

(h) The criteria for determining bandwidth of emission.

(i) Reason for pre-emphasis.

(a) Sidebands are those groups of modulating components arranged above and below the carrier. In AM, the upper sideband is formed by the modulating frequencies plus the carrier frequency; the lower sideband is formed by the modulating frequencies subtracted from the carrier frequency. The carrier frequency is constant in amplitude modulation and only the amplitude of the transmitted wave is varied according to the modulating voltage. In FM, the modulating signal causes the carrier frequency to vary in frequency according to the frequency of the modulation. As modulation results in slightly higher or slightly lower excursions of the carrier frequency, sidebands are produced by this distortion of the carrier wave. The actual number of sidebands produced in the case of FM varies according to the degree of carrier deviation or swing; the greater swing produces the greater number of significant sidebands. However, sidebands at greater distances from the center frequency are too weak to be considered.

(b) The number of sidebands is directly proportional to the modulation index and inversely proportional to the modulating frequency. Adjacent sidebands are separated by the frequency of the modulating signal. For example, let's consider an FM transmission on 108 MHz with a 5-kHz audio tone modulation. Sidebands would be produced above the center frequency (108 MHz) at 108.005, 108.010 and 108.015 MHz and below the center frequency at 107.995, 107.990 and 107.985 MHz. The lower audio frequencies form more sidebands near the center carrier frequency and as a result, these sidebands are more significant in amplitude. Since higher audio frequencies produce sidebands farther away from the center frequency, they carry much less energy and can usually be ignored.

(c) The number of sidebands bears a direct relationship to the amplitude of the modulating voltage. As the modulating voltage is applied to the reactance tube modulator, it causes the oscillator frequency to vary. The higher that voltage, the greater the deviation and the greater the number of sidebands produced.

(d) The relationship between the percentage of modulation and the number of sidebands is governed by the fact that the higher the percentage of modulation the greater the frequency swing. This, in turn, results in a greater number of sidebands of significant amplitude. Therefore, the number of sidebands is directly proportional to the modulation percentage. Regular FM broadcast service at 100 percent modulation has a bandwidth of 150 kHz or 75 kHz above and below the carrier (center) frequency.

(e) The number of sidebands is directly proportional to the modulation index. The higher that index or deviation ratio, the greater the number of significant sidebands. The modulation index is equivalent to the carrier frequency deviation divided by the audio modulating frequency causing that deviation.

(f) The relationship between the spacing of the sidebands and the modulating frequency produces a spacing equal to the frequency of the audio modulation. If the sidebands were spaced 2 kHz apart, we could assume that the audio modulating frequency was 2000 Hz.

(g) The bandwidth of emission, which must contain 99 percent of the radiated power, depends on the number of significant sidebands multiplied by the modulating frequency. Although sidebands exist beyond this width, their power is small enough to be ignored.

(h) The criteria for determining the bandwidth of emission are the modulation index and frequency, which determines the frequency deviation. The bandwidth of emission is twice the sum of the frequency deviation and modulating frequency. Bandwidth of emission is always wider than the frequency swing as may be noted by FCC regulations for commercial transmitters operating below 450 MHz. Authorized bandwidth is 20 kHz, frequency deviation 5 kHz or a frequency swing 10 kHz. Remember that the authorized bandwidth contains 99 percent of the power and any sideband having at least .25 or ¼ of 1 percent of the total radiated power must be considered as part of that bandwidth.

(i) The reasons for pre-emphasis may be explained by the fact that very little energy is contained in higher frequencies of the audio range, and as a result they may be lost in the noise. Their importance should not be underestimated because they improve speech quality and add to the identity of various musical instruments. Amplifying the high frequencies more than the low before modulation enables them to override the noise and is known as pre-emphasis. Overmodulation is not caused by this amplification, since the additional amplification of highs does not raise their signal level above that of the lower. The opposite of pre-emphasis used in an FM transmitter is de-emphasis in a receiver to bring the amplitude of the higher frequencies down to its normal level with regard to the lower frequencies.

Question 3: How is good stability of a reactance tube modulator achieved?

An automatic frequency control (AFC) circuit is used to maintain the carrier frequency within tolerance. Although the reactance tube modulator cannot be crystal controlled, the AFC circuit can utilize the reference of a good stable crystal oscillator. In the AFC system, the phase detector receives signals from the modulated oscillator and the crystal oscillator for comparison. In the event the modulated oscillator differs, a DC error voltage is produced which is fed to the modulator. The error voltage corrects the error by bringing the modulated oscillator to its proper frequency at which time the error voltage is reduced to zero. As long as the modulated oscillator remains on frequency, the error voltage is zero, but by drifting in either direction, an error voltage is developed which biases the modulator grid and causes the master oscillator to return to its center frequency. When the modulated oscillator is locked on center frequency, the phase detector output will not be zero because it varies at the audio rate with an average value of zero. In order to prevent this output from upsetting the modulated oscillator frequency through the modulator, an RC low-pass filter is connected between the phase detector and reactance tube modulator, which prevents the audio output of the phase detector from reaching the modulator.

Question 4: Draw a diagram of a phase modulator, explain its operation, and label adjacent stages.

The phase modulator circuit shown in Fig. 5-2 is frequently used in mobile equipment. It uses a crystal-controlled oscillator with the output tank tuned to the crystal frequency. The output is coupled by phase networks to the dual modulators, with R3-C3 supplying the input to modulator V3. Since the reactance of C3 is equal to the resistance of R3 at the oscillating frequency, the phase shift resulting at the V3 grid lags by 45 degrees. Modulator V2 is supplied through phasing network L2-R2 and the reactance of L2 is equivalent to the resistance of R2 at the oscillator frequency, so the grid input to V2 leads the oscillator signal by 45 degrees. These signals are equal in voltage with no modulating signal and the RF plate currents of the modulators are in phase with the oscillator voltage as a unit. As a result, the output of the modulation transformer is in phase with the oscillator signal frequency when no modulation is applied to the transformer. The application of a signal to the modulator cathodes causes V2 to go positive while V3 is negative; V3's plate current increases as V2's decreases. As V3 conducts more than V2 and its output contains a lagging current, the output frequency of the oscillator is decreased. When the other modulator (V2) conducts more than V3, the leading current produced as a result causes the output frequency to be increased. Thus, we have a frequency modulation characteristic as with the reactance tube modulator. By following the phase-shift modulator with

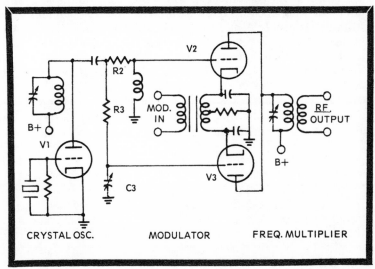

Fig. 5-2. Phase modulator circuit.

frequency multiplying stages, the deviation of the FM wave may be greatly increased.

Question 5: Explain, in a general way, why an FM deviation meter (modulation meter) will show an indication if coupled to the output of a transmitter which is phase-modulated by a constant-amplitude constant audio frequency. To what will this deviation be proportional?

The meter reading is proportional to the frequency swing, although the transmitter is phase-modulated, since there will be a frequency swing at the output which the meter will indicate. Phase modulation always produces a frequency swing and the meter reading is proportional to the amplitude and frequency of the modulation. Phase modulation of the same amplitude will read just twice as much for a 4-kHz signal as it will show for 2 kHz on the meter. The FM deviation meter, like the FM superhet receiver, uses a local oscillator, mixer, IF amplifier and discriminator. If the transmitter is not modulated, the discriminator reads zero, providing the transmitter is not off frequency. However, center frequency drift will result in an output voltage from the discriminator and this voltage is applied to the modulation meter through a rectifier and DC amplifier. This provides instant response to the slightest deviation voltage. Normally, the modulation meter is calibrated in percent and decibels; 100 percent or 0 db usually indicates maximum authorized swing.

Question 6: Explain briefly what occurs in a waveform when it is phase-modulated.

Shifting the waveform in phase by audio modulation in a phase-shifting network causes the phase to be varied smoothly from the original. If the network phase shift causes it to lag the original wave, the resulting wave takes a longer time to reach its peak. As its wavelength is increased, frequency is decreased. If the phase shift leads the original, it peaks sooner and wavelength is decreased with frequency.

Question 7: Discuss wideband and narrowband reception in FM voice communication systems with respect to frequency deviation and bandwidth.

Wideband FM communication systems are a luxury of the past. Because of increased demands for more and more spectrum, the two-way bands have been undergoing a "squeezing" process for several years. Today, most of the popular communications bands are restricted to use by narrowband equipment (± 5 kHz deviation). A few years ago, the standard transmitter frequency deviation was ± 15 kHz, which allowed a total bandwidth of 30 kHz (plus sidebands) for every user. To minimize interference, the FCC maintained a spacing of 50 kHz between user stations. This broad bandwidth and wide deviation capability allowed such user benefits as superior signal-to-noise ratio, high-fidelity transmission capability, and—theoretically—interference-free communications capability.

In recent years, the increasing numbers of user stations have dictated the need for additional spectrum. In response, the FCC lowered the maximum deviation standard to ±5 kHz and split the spacing between allocated channels. The bandwidth of user transmitters thus halved, a great many more stations have been accommodated. The early problems of high signal-to-noise ratio and generally lower signal level have been solved by the advent of receivers that are not only more sensitive but sharply selective within the allowable passband. As a result, the overall performance of a narrowband communications system is comparable to that of a wideband system.

Question 8: Could the harmonic of an FM transmission contain intelligible modulation?

Since there is harmonic radiation of the carrier, there is harmonic radiation of the sidebands. Adjacent sidebands are separated by the harmonic multiple of the audio modulating frequency which makes the intelligence less realistic and subject to much distortion if the receiver is not able to pass the wider bandwidth. This could be two or three times as wide as the fundamental, depending on the harmonic.

Question 9: Explain briefly the principles involved in frequency-shift keying (FSK). How is this signal detected?

Frequency-shift keying, known as F1 emission, provides keying of the radio-telegraph transmitter by changing the output frequency when the key is depressed, in place of turning it off and on. By connecting a reactance tube across the master oscillator and keying the former, the resonant frequency is changed (about 850 Hz) as the tube is keyed. The oscillator operates at a low frequency and, since the frequency shift is small, good stability is maintained. Two levels are used, the mark at 425 Hz above the carrier and at 425 Hz below is the space. The method of detection is similar to that required for regular FM, a ratio detector tuned to the center frequency. A communications receiver could also be used for reception of FSK by tuning as for CW and adjusting the BFO so the audio note varies accordingly.

Question 10: Under what conditions of maintenance and-or repair should a transmitter be retuned?

A transmitter should be retuned after any change has been made to the transmitter's circuitry, power supplies, or load. Replacing a tube usually requires retuning, since each tube has slightly different characteristics from all other tubes.

Question 11: What might be the effect on the transmitted frequency if a tripler stage in an otherwise perfectly aligned FM transmitter were slightly detuned?

The output signal may not be on the assigned transmitter frequency.

Question 12: If an indirect FM transmitter without modulation is within carrier frequency tolerance, but with modulation it is out of tolerance, what would be some possible causes?

The indirect (Armstrong) system of FM depends on a balanced modulator to generate sidebands and if the transmitter is out of tolerance only during modulation, the modulator must be out of balance. This would cause unequal sidebands to be produced which, in turn, would cause the average frequency to be raised or lowered. The actual trouble could be a defective modulator tube, capacitor or excessive drive.

Question 13: In an FM transmitter, what would be the effect on antenna current if the grid bias on the final power amplifier were varied?

High-quality FM transmitters are operated Class C, which means that the final amplifier is biased well below the stage's cutoff point. If the grid bias were increased (operating point established at a more negative position), antenna current would decrease so long as the drive signal were held constant. In this case, distortion would increase but circuit efficiency would be improved; a high-power signal would be required to drive the amplifier into its saturation region. If the grid bias were decreased (operating point brought closer to tube cutoff), antenna current will increase if no change is made to the excitation signal, but the amplifier's efficiency will diminish and the tube will run much hotter than it should.

Question 14: Draw a schematic diagram of each of the following stages of a superheterodyne FM receiver. Explain the principles of operation. Label adjacent stages.

(a) Mixer with injected oscillator frequency.
(b) IF amplifier.
(c) Limiter.
(d) Discriminator.
(e) Differential squelch circuit.

(a) Fig. 5-3 is a mixer circuit with grid shunt injection. The RF input is applied across the grid tank. As the tube operates nonlinearly, the two frequencies heterodyne to form the desired IF to the tuned converter plate circuit.

(b) The IF amplifier circuit shown in Fig. 5-4 operates Class A with the tuned circuits resonant at the selected IF frequency. The typical receiver has two or three stages of IF with a bandwidth of about 150 kHz.

(c) A limiter stage is illustrated in Fig. 5-5. Its function is to remove amplitude variations from the IF signal prior to detection in the discriminator. This stage removes most of the noise which is usually amplitude modulated and, being a sharp cutoff type, operates with low screen and plate voltages, which ensures limiting on even the weakest signals or noise.

(d) A discriminator schematic appears in Fig. 5-6. A discriminator produces a conventional audio output from the frequency variations of the FM input. The discriminator also supplies AVC and AFC voltages. As the FM carrier deviates in one direction, the DC output voltage increases; it decreases as

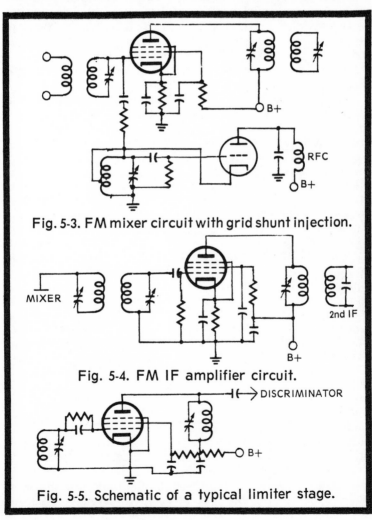

Fig. 5-3. FM mixer circuit with grid shunt injection.

Fig. 5-4. FM IF amplifier circuit.

Fig. 5-5. Schematic of a typical limiter stage.

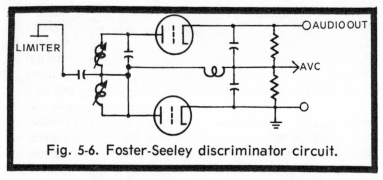

Fig. 5-6. Foster-Seeley discriminator circuit.

the carrier swings the other way. Since the broadcast FM wave deviates exactly with audio modulation, the DC variations from the discriminator reproduce the original modulation information. Since this stage lacks the ability to reject amplitude modulation (noise), one or two limiter stages must precede it to handle this problem.

(e) An FM differential squelch circuit is displayed in Fig. when no carrier is being received. The high noise level from the discriminator with no carrier present is amplified by the noise amplifier and rectified by the noise diode (detector). This positive DC voltage is applied to the squelch amplifier grid and forces it to conduct heavily. This large current flow biases the audio amplifier to cutoff, thus there is no noise output. When a carrier is received, a limiting signal appears which cuts off the noise amplifier. The small coupling capacitor in the noise amplifier grid passes only high-frequency impulses. Since the noise amplifier is now cut off, the squelch tube no longer conducts; it is cut off by the fixed cathode bias. The audio amplifier now operates normally. The squelch circuit control may be adjusted to avoid weak signal squelching by setting it at a point where the noise is just barely reduced to a tolerable level.

Question 15: Explain how spurious signals can be received or created in a receiver. How could this be reduced in sets having sealed untunable filters?

Spurious signals may be received from adjacent channels due to poor receiver selectivity, or such signals may be created by oscillating IF stages, local oscillators or multipliers which generate heterodyne frequencies. The sealed untunable filter improves receiver selectivity considerably by its flat response over the desired IF bandwidth and sharp drop off on either side. This enables the receiver to reject most of the undesired signals.

Question 16: Describe step-by-step, the proper procedure for aligning an FM double-conversion superheterodyne receiver.

IF Stages. The meter alignment of the IF stages in a receiver measures the voltage developed at the detector circuit as the IF amplifiers are tuned. In the ratio detector, the meter is connected across the load capacitor, and in the gated-beam and locked-oscillator circuits, and audio output meter is used when the detector is altered so that it responds to AM. When aligning a receiver that uses a discriminator-limiter detector, connect the meter across the limiter grid resistor. If two resistors are used in series, connect the meter between the junction of the two and ground. As the signal to the limiter increases, the grid current increases, and consequently the voltage across the grid resistor rises.

Always work from the detector or the limiter toward the mixer. In the limiter-discriminator circuit, align the discriminator first. If a dual limiter is used with tunable coupling between the two stages, align the first limiter by connecting the meter across the grid resistor of the second limiter. Connect the signal generator to the grid of the first limiter. Then tune the interstage coupling circuit for maximum reading of the meter. Connect the meter to the grid resistor of the first limiter and proceed with the IF alignment.

When all of the IF amplifiers are known to be single-peaked—that is, when none of them are overcoupled—tune each secondary and primary, working toward the mixer from the first-limiter grid or from the grid of the last IF stage, depending on the type of detector. Adjust each tuning control for maximum deflection of the meter. The signal generator must be unmodulated when the discriminator and ratio detector are aligned, and modulated for other detectors.

RF, Mixer, and Oscillator Stages. The alignment of RF and mixer stages requires an accurately calibrated RF signal source that can be tuned to frequencies in the low, high, and center portions of the receiver. The mixer and the oscillator must track over the desired range if the receiver is continuously tuned, and tracking adjustments may vary widely with the type of receiver.

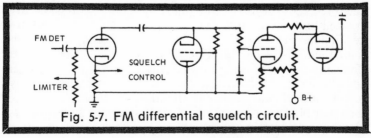

Fig. 5-7. FM differential squelch circuit.

The mixer trimmer and the oscillator trimmer are adjusted at the high frequency end of the tuning range for optimum gain and calibration. Set the receiver control at the designated alignment frequency. Connect a signal generator to the grid of the RF amplifier. Set its frequency to the highest calibration point called for in the equipment manual. Vary the oscillator trimmer until the signal is heard in the output circuit, or until the meter in the detector circuit indicates maximum deflection. Peak the mixer grid-circuit trimmer for maximum output. Tune the receiver to the designated low-frequency alignment point. Tune the signal generator to the low end of the frequency range and set it at the low-frequency calibration point. Adjust the oscillator padder until the signal is a maximum at the detector. Then return the signal generator and receiver to the high-frequency calibration point. Retune the oscillator trimmer, if necessary, to bring the dial calibration of the receiver into correspondence with the frequency of the generator. Repeat these steps until both the low and the high frequencies are in calibration without the need for touching either the oscillator trimmer or the padder. Set the signal generator to a point midway in the frequency range, and check the calibration. When these steps have been carried out carefully, the calibration should be correct.

Alignment of the RF stage is done best with a noise generator. For the first rough initial alignment, antenna noise or a weak external signal supplied by the leakage from the signal generator or any other source will do. Peak the trimmer for maximum signal at the high end of the frequency range, and apply the noise-generator technique at the highest frequency to obtain the maximum signal-to-noise ratio.

Question 17: Discuss the cause and prevention of interference to radio receivers installed in motor vehicles.

Most man-made noises fall into two general classifications: impulse noise and fluctuation noise. Impulse noise consists of sharp pulses of RF voltage which, when detected in a receiver, take the form of equally sharp pulses of audio voltage. They are often many hundreds of times greater in amplitude than the desired signal and make it impossible for the desired signal to be received. Perhaps the most common producers of impulse noise are the ignition systems of gasoline engines. Since many radio applications call for the installation of communication equipment in vehicles, impulse noise is a problem. Steps can be taken to eliminate much of this noise, but such elimination measures can never be perfect. There is always a residual component of the noise which may cause serious difficulties if the received signals are weak. The second kind of man-made noise, called fluctuation noise, is of a more continuous character. It appears as a broad band of many pulses which bear little or no relation to each other. Such noises are produced to a great extent by rotating electrical machinery, gas rectifiers, high-voltage transmission lines, and similar power devices. The noise from a small motor, although frequently weaker than the signal by a considerable amount, is capable of causing severe interference and possible interruption to reception.

After the source of the interference is determined, steps to eliminate it can be initiated. The methods include **active** steps—that is, attempts to decrease the amplitude of the signals at the source of the noise—and **passive** steps—or attempts to combat the problem at the receiver. Active measures include the bypassing of radiating components, use of resistive spark-plug elements, insertion of choke coils in supply circuits. Passive measures include installation of noise limiters, clippers, and silencers at the receiver; shielding and improved grounding of receiver and power-supply circuits.

Question 18: Explain the voltage and current relationship in a full-wavelength antenna; half-wavelength (dipole) antenna; quarter-wavelength "grounded" antenna.

An antenna may be considered an inductance. Since an inductance opposes current changes, antenna current always lags antenna voltage by 90 degrees. When antenna current is maximum, voltage is minimum, and vice versa. On a full-wave antenna, the current may be thought of as a sine wave whose value is essentially zero at the ends and center. A half-wave antenna is characterized by a current pattern that resembles the left half of a sine wave—that is, the antenna current in a half-wave line is maximum at the center and minimum at the ends. A quarter-wave antenna takes on the appearance of the left half of the pattern of a half-wave antenna—that is, current is minimum at the free-space end and maximum at the end being fed.

Question 19: What effect does the magnitude of the voltage and current, at a point on a half-wavelength antenna in "free space" (a dipole), have on the impedance at that point?

Antenna impedance at any point must equal the voltage-to-current ratio as Z equals E divided by I. Magnitude is of no importance except to establish the ratio; the greater the voltage or smaller the current, the greater the impedance will be.

Question 20: How is the operating power of an AM transmitter determined by antenna resistance and antenna current?

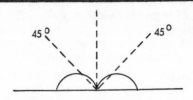

Fig. 5-8. Vertical radiation pattern,
quarter-wave vertical antenna.

There is nothing particularly esoteric about calculating RF power. By extension of Ohm's Law for power ($P = I^2R$); simply multiply antenna resistance by the square of antenna current.

Question 21: What kinds of fields emanate from a transmitting antenna and what relationships do they have with each other?

Radio waves in space have two kinds of fields, magnetic and electric. They are perpendicular to each other and both are at right angles to their direction of movement.

Question 22: Can either of the two fields that emanate from an antenna produce an EMF in a receiving antenna? If so, how?

The fields radiated from the transmitting antenna induce an EMF in the receiving antenna as they pass, somewhat like the transformer where the fields around the primary "cut" the secondary windings and induce a voltage in that winding. It is true that the receiving antenna gets maximum pickup when parallel to the passing electromagnetic wave.

Question 23: Draw a sketch and discuss the horizontal and vertical radiation patterns of a quarter-wave vertical antenna. Would they apply to a similar type of receiving antenna?

Fig. 5-8 illustrates the radiation pattern of a quarter-wave vertical antenna. The horizontal radiation is equal in all directions around the antenna, while the vertical radiation pattern forms an arc with a height of about 40 degrees at its maximum. As a result of the curvature of the earth and other influential obstacles between transmitting and receiving points, the antenna at the receiving point may not be parallel to the electric field as it passes. In such cases, current distribution would differ considerably from that of the transmitting antenna and the pattern would be altered accordingly.

Question 24: Describe the directional characteristics, if any, of horizontal and vertical loop antennas.

The horizontal loop antenna is nondirectional with a minimum of radiation or reception capability vertically.

Needless to say, it is seldom used in the horizontal plane as its primary purpose is not met. The vertical loop antenna has a bidirectional pattern horizontally, forming a figure 8 with the two maximum lobes in the plane of the loop and little or no radiation or pickup perpendicular to that plane. The vertical pattern is nondirectional.

Question 25: In speaking of radio transmissions, what bearing do the angle of radiation, density of the ionosphere, and frequency of emission have on the length of the skip zone?

The smaller the angle of radiation, the greater the length of the skip zone. If the angle between the direction of the wave and the earth's surface is too large, the wave will not return at all. The critical angle is the maximum angle at which the radiated wave will be reflected back to earth. As the density of the ionosphere increases, the greater the bending of the wave and the shorter the skip zone. This heavily ionized region extends from about 25 to several hundred miles above the earth's surface, and exists in several layers. The "D" layer ranging to about 55 miles high, exists only in sunlight. The "E" layer at 65 miles is the lowest permanent layer and makes long distance communication better, but the "F2" layer is most important in that regard. This layer ranges from 150 to 250 miles in height and is most consistent in density overall. Although high-frequency waves readily pass through the lower layers, the denser F2 layer may reflect or bend them back to earth.

The higher the frequency of emission below a critical value, the greater the skip zone as the degree of wave bending decreases. However, the frequency may be increased to a point where the wave is not bent enough to return and no skip zone is possible. The energy of low-frequency sky waves is completely absorbed by the ionosphere, and skip above 50 MHz is not reliable. There is an area at the transmitting antenna where the sky wave is not returned due to the angle of radiation, and a skip zone exists between the limit of the ground wave and point where the sky wave may again be returned to earth as the radiation angle decreases.

Question 26: Why is it possible for a sky wave to "meet" a ground wave 180 degrees out of phase?

When signals are radiated from an antenna, they radiate in many directions. Those signals radiated parallel to the earth are called ground waves, and those radiated into space are called sky waves. Sky waves strike atmospheric reflective layers of ionic material and reflect back to the earth. If a receiver is situated so as to receive both sky and ground waves from a single transmitter, signal cancellation could occur simply because the sky wave's path is longer than the ground wave. If the sky wave arrives later than the ground wave by a period equal to the duration of one-half cycle (or any multiple thereof), the two arriving signals will be 180 degrees out of phase and cancellation results.

The degree of cancellation depends on the relative strengths of the two signals. When both out-of-phase signals are of equal strength, there is complete cancellation; when one signal is stronger, only partial cancellation takes place.

Question 27: What is the relationship between the operating frequency and ground-wave coverage?

The longer the wave, the more effective the ground-wave communications. Low-frequency waves actually follow the curvature of the earth. Conversely, very high-frequency signals tend to be attenuated during propagation and are thus not reliable for communications except on a line-of-sight basis.

Question 28: Explain the following terms with respect to antennas (transmission or reception):

(a) **Field strength**
(b) **Power gain**
(c) **Physical length**
(d) **Electrical length**
(e) **Polarization**
(f) **Diversity reception**
(g) **Corona discharge**

(a) Field strength is signal strength induced in an antenna and measured in microvolts (uV) or millivolts (mV) per meter. If the field strength of a signal at a certain point from the transmitter measures 100 mV per meter, an induced voltage 100 mV would be neasured in a conductor one meter in length.

(b) Power gain is a figure of merit for a directional antenna and is the ratio of power that must be supplied to a standard (dipole) antenna to reach a specific field strength figure at a certain distance as compared to the directional antenna power required to show the same field strength at the same distance. The same polarization must be used on each, and in order to figure the power gain of an antenna, the fielu gain figure is needed. Since the field gain is equivalent to the voltage induced in the directional antenna divided by the voltage induced in the comparison antenna, the power gain would be the square of that figure. Power is proportional to the square of the voltage.

(c) The physical length of an antenna is its actual length in feet or meters, and the physical length is shorter than the same wavelength in free space.

(d) The electrical length of an antenna is the physical length expressed in wavelength, radians or degrees. It may be in degrees of a full hertz of the operating frequency, such as a resonant half-wave dipole which is 180 degrees. The electrical length may also be expressed in wavelengths in free space. A half-wave dipole operating on 20 meters would be one half of 20 meters in length at resonance or 10 meters long (39.37 inches per meter). The actual physical length of the dipole would be 5 percent shorter because it is not entirely free of surrounding forces that would decrease the velocity of a wave over that in free space. The length of a half-wave antenna in free space is 300,000,000 divided by 2 times the frequency in hertz which gives the frequency in meters. The resonant frequency is determined by the time required for a wave to travel the length of the antenna (180 degrees) and return (360 degrees). Since the usual approximation of the reduction in velocity is 5 percent, simply multiply the electrical length by .95 for the physical length.

(e) Polarization is determined by the physical position of the antenna with regard to the earth and this indicates how the electric field propagates. Vertically polarized waves are generated by a vertical antenna, and the horizontal antenna radiates horizontally polarized waves.

(f) Diversity reception is an efficient way of reducing· fading by the use of more than one antenna. They are normally. spaced several wavelengths (5 to 10) apart so that fading is not likely in all antennas at the same time. Each antenna is coupled to a separate amplifier with all feeding the same audio output stage. The use of a special type AVC blocks all amplifiers except the one carrying the strongest signal, so the automatic use of the antenna receiving the strongest signal at the time reduces the fading effect to an absolute minimum. Diversity antenna systems are quite common in transoceanic communications.

(g) Corona discharge is an electrical discharge resulting from ionization of air, quite like a lightning discharge on a very small scale. Corona results from a voltage build-up around an HV conductor that tends to ionize the air near it. By rounding or balling all sharp or rough points, corona effect may be reduced considerably. Uninsulated or braided wire should never be used in high-voltage areas where corona discharge is likely to occur.

Question 29: What would constitute the ground plane if a quarter-wave grounded (whip) antenna 1 meter in length were mounted on the metal roof of an automobile? Mounted near the rear bumper of an automobile?

An antenna mounted on the roof of an automobile has a good ground plane in the roof itself, which is a reasonable part of a wavelength in this case. Mounted near the rear bumper, a quarter-wave whip could use the bumper as a ground plane and possibly a portion of one fender or the trunk. However, at this wavelength, the bumper would probably suffice.

Question 30: Explain why a "loading coil" is sometimes associated with an antenna. Under this condition, would absence of the coil mean a capacitive antenna impedance?

A "loading coil" makes it possible to operate the antenna at a lower frequency than its actual length would permit. The inductance of the coil in series with the antenna makes it possible to resonate an antenna that is too short physically for the operating frequency and one that would look like a capacitive reactance without the "loading coil." This reactance could make it impossible to feed power into the antenna.

Question 31: What radio frequencies are useful for long-distance communications requiring continuous operation?

Sky waves must rely on the presence of densely packed atmospheric layers for reflection. Since these layers are inconsistent in their density and reflecting ability, ground waves are inherently more reliable than sky waves. Very short-wavelength signals are readily absorbed by foliage and air and are thus dissipated more readily than longer wavelengths.

The U.S. Navy states that shore-based transmitters are able to transmit long-range ground-wave transmissions by using frequencies between 18 and 300 kHz with extremely high power. Since the electrical properties of the earth along with the paths the ground wave travels are relatively constant, the signal strength from a given station at a given point is nearly constant.

Question 32: What type of modulation is largely contained in "static" and "lightning" radio waves?

Virtually all pulse-type interference takes the form of an amplitude-modulated signal—which gives FM one of its most striking advantages. Static, lightning discharges, ignition noises, and other impulse disturbances are effectively minimized or eliminated in FM receivers with adequate limiting circuitry.

Question 33: Will the velocity of propagation differ in different materials? What effect, if any, would this difference have on the wavelength or frequency?

The velocity of propagation of radio waves differs according to the dielectric constant of the medium. It is always less than the speed of light by the factor "K" which is 1 for air. It may be assumed that radio waves travel at maximum speed through air, atmosphere or space (vacuum). The use of insulating material with a dielectric constant (K) greater than 1 will decrease the speed of the wave and will cause the physical length to be shorter than the electrical length. Velocity of propagation is lowered whenever the constant K is greater than unity (1).

Question 34: Discuss series and shunt feeding of quarter-wave antennas with respect to impedance matching.

A series-fed quarter-wavelength antenna is normally called a "whip." When the whip length is such that it is a quarter-wavelength at the operating frequency, the antenna will appear as a pure resistance at the point where energy is fed to the base of the antenna. The base of a series-fed quarter-wave antenna is insulated from ground, but a large metallic surface or ground plane must be in the immediate vicinity of the antenna's base for resonance and radiation to occur.

When the input impedance of the quarter-wave series-fed antenna is comprised primarily of radiation resistance, the efficiency of the antenna is high. At frequencies above or below antenna resonance, inductive or capacitive reactances dominate the input impedance, and efficiency is low. When such reactances are unavoidable, they can be effectively canceled by introducing more inductance or capacitance in the series input circuit to cancel the effects. That is, series capacitance can be used to cancel an inductive reactance, and inductance can be added to tune out capacitive reactance.

A shunt-fed antenna is a grounded vertical quarter-wavelength radiator, often called a Marconi antenna. This system is also known by the generic term "image antenna." The ground is a fairly good conductor and acts as a large "mirror" for radiated energy. The ground surface reflects a large amount of energy that is radiated downward from an antenna mounted over it. It is just as though a mirror image of the antenna is produced; the image being located the same distance below the surface below the ground as the actual antenna is located above it. Even in the high-frequency range and higher, many ground reflections occur, especially if the antenna is erected over highly conducting earth, water, or a grounded screen.

Using this characteristic of the ground, a shunt-fed quarter-wave antenna can be made into the equivalent of a half-wave antenna. If such an antenna is erected vertically (its lower end is connected electrically to the ground), the quarter-wave behaves like a half-wave. Here, the ground takes the place of the missing quarter wavelength, and the reflections supply that part of the radiated energy that normally would be supplied by the lower half of an ungrounded half-wave antenna.

The input impedance of a series-fed quarter-wave radiator varies, depending on the plane of the metallic ground surface. When the ground surface is perpendicular to the plane of the upright antenna, the impedance is precisely half that of the half-wave antenna, or 36-37 ohms. The grounded (shunt-fed) quarter-wave radiator cannot be fed at the base because the base itself is grounded directly. Since the impedance increases with the distance towards the end of the whip from ground, a suitable feed point may be found by attaching the feed line to a point somewhat above the ground surface. The point at which the antenna should be fed depends on the characteristic impedance of the feed line; the higher up the antenna the feed point is, the higher the feed-point impedance will be. Higher efficiency will be observed when the feed point is less than halfway between the ground and the antenna's center.

Question 35: Discuss the directivity and physical characteristics of the following types of antennas:
- (a) Single-loop
- (b) V-beam
- (c) Corner reflector
- (d) Parasitic array
- (e) Stacked array

(a) A single loop refers to the small loop antenna which consists of one or more turns of wire enclosed in an electrostatic shield. Generally circular, the loop acts as an inductance coil with a large diameter-to-length ratio and has maximum response in the direction of the plane of the loop. There is little or no pickup in a direction perpendicular to the plane.

(b) The V-beam consists of two radiating conductors arranged to form a V. It is directional in the open face. If each leg of the V is one wavelength long, the angle should be about 75 degrees. If unidirectional operation is desired, the ends of each leg should be terminated by load resistors to ground.

(c) The corner reflector has a driven element, which is a simple half-wave dipole, and two metal sheets forming a corner to act as a reflector. Its direction of radiation is principally away from the corner and may be further concentrated by decreasing the angle between the reflector sheets.

(d) The simplest form of parasitic array is a half-wave horizontal dipole acting as the driven element and a single parasitic element acting as a reflector. Placed at a distance of ¼ wavelength from the driven element, the parasitic element, in this case a reflector, should be about 5 percent longer than the driven dipole. Intercepting some of the energy from the driven element, the reflector reradiates energy to combine with that radiated by the main element and concentrates it in that direction. The use of additional parasitic elements, with reflectors longer and behind the driven element and directors shorter and in front of the driven element, offers exceptional unidirectional characteristics and gain. This type antenna is commonly known as a yagi, and is extremely popular for a specific frequency or channel.

(e) The stacked array makes use of yagi elements mounted above each other (parasitic arrays) for exceptional gain. Aside from excellent directivity, stacking confines radiation to low angles, cutting ground losses and energy normally wasted in vertical radiation. These directional characteristics in the horizontal plane offer improvement in field strength and range.

Question 36: Draw a sketch of a coaxial (whip) antenna, identify the positions, and discuss the purposes of the following components:

(a) Whip   (e) Support mast
(b) Insulator   (f) Coaxial line
(c) Skirt   (g) Input connector
(d) Trap

(a) Fig. 5-9 shows a sketch of a coaxial (whip) antenna. The whip is the upper radiating section and its length is about 95 percent of the free space quarter-length. It is an extension of the coaxial transmission line inner conductor.

(b) The insulator separates the upper and lower radiating sections and insulates the center conductor so that it will not short against the skirt.

(c) The metal cylinder mounted below the insulator is the skirt and it forms the lower radiating part of the antenna. It is also a quarter-wavelength and along with the whip is a half-wave dipole. A very high impedance is offered at the end near the insulator which minimizes current flow and prevents high vertical radiation.

(d) The trap is a portion of the skirt forming the outer conductor with part of the support mast forming the inner conductor of a quarter-wave coaxial section shorted at the bottom. The purpose of the trap is to eliminate current flow on the mast and the coax transmission line.

(e) The support mast is a good, strong pipe that holds up the entire antenna and also provides the inner conductor for the trap.

(f) The coaxial line is the transmission line used to carry energy from the transmitter to the antenna. Coaxial line, because of its low impedance (75 ohms) matches the input impedance or radiation resistance of the antenna, which is about 75 ohms.

(g) The input connector is a fitting for the coaxial cable to provide a convenient connection from transmitter to whip antenna.

The coaxial antenna is constructed to offer a handy, unbalanced feed arrangement and is a vertical half-wave type. Vertically polarized, it radiates at right angles to its plane and equally in all directions.

Question 37: Why are insulators sometimes placed in antenna guy wires?

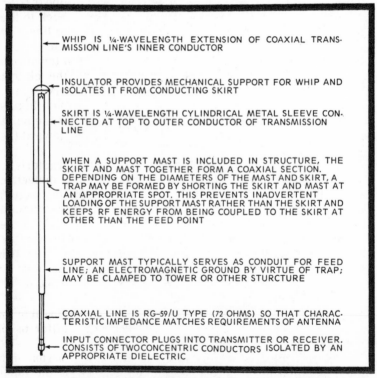

WHIP IS ¼-WAVELENGTH EXTENSION OF COAXIAL TRANSMISSION LINE'S INNER CONDUCTOR

INSULATOR PROVIDES MECHANICAL SUPPORT FOR WHIP AND ISOLATES IT FROM CONDUCTING SKIRT

SKIRT IS ¼-WAVELENGTH CYLINDRICAL METAL SLEEVE CONNECTED AT TOP TO OUTER CONDUCTOR OF TRANSMISSION LINE

WHEN A SUPPORT MAST IS INCLUDED IN STRUCTURE, THE SKIRT AND MAST TOGETHER FORM A COAXIAL SECTION. DEPENDING ON THE DIAMETERS OF THE MAST AND SKIRT, A TRAP MAY BE FORMED BY SHORTING THE SKIRT AND MAST AT AN APPROPRIATE SPOT. THIS PREVENTS INADVERTENT LOADING OF THE SUPPORT MAST RATHER THAN THE SKIRT AND KEEPS RF ENERGY FROM BEING COUPLED TO THE SKIRT AT OTHER THAN THE FEED POINT

SUPPORT MAST TYPICALLY SERVES AS CONDUIT FOR FEED LINE; AN ELECTROMAGNETIC GROUND BY VIRTUE OF TRAP; MAY BE CLAMPED TO TOWER OR OTHER STURCTURE

COAXIAL LINE IS RG-59/U TYPE (72 OHMS) SO THAT CHARACTERISTIC IMPEDANCE MATCHES REQUIREMENTS OF ANTENNA

INPUT CONNECTOR PLUGS INTO TRANSMITTER OR RECEIVER. CONSISTS OF TWO CONCENTRIC CONDUCTORS ISOLATED BY AN APPROPRIATE DIELECTRIC

Fig. 5-9. The coaxial vertical antenna.

This makes the wires too short to resonate at the operating frequency by keeping their length below a half-wavelength, at which point they would absorb energy from the transmitting antenna and reradiate, distorting the planned pattern. By using the familiar "egg type" insulators, the guy wire remains intact even if the insulator breaks.

Question 38: What is meant by the characteristic impedance of a transmission line? On what physical factors is its value dependent?

Any length of wire has a specific resistance. Wire lengths also represent inductances. And when two wires are spaced proximally to each other, a capacitance exists between them. When an AC signal is fed to a resistive, capacitive, inductive circuit, the circuit represents a finite impedance. The characteristic impedance of a transmission line is the impedance it would have if it were infinite in length. This impedance is considered to be purely resistive, and is constant for a given transmission line. The characteristic impedance is important in determining how well energy is transferred from the source of the signal to the load. For the infinitely long line, of course, all the energy sent out on the line would appear to be dissipated in the line and none would be reflected back to the source because of subsequent impedances down the line that might represent values other than the line's characteristic. Since lines are not infinitely long, it is important to terminate a transmission line in a load that represents the closest possible equivalent of the line's characteristic; otherwise, not all the energy on the line will be transferred to the load. In this case, some value of RF power would be reflected at the point of termination, and would travel back down the line toward the source.

The physical factors that determine a line's characteristic impedance are: resistivity of the conductors, dielectric material separating the conductors (including the actual spacing between them), and the diameter of the conductors. For a given impedance value, the larger the diameter of the conductors, the more they must be spaced. The closer the spacing between conductors, the lower the characteristic impedance. The characteristic impedance of a line may be expressed mathematically by taking the square root of inductance divided by capacitance.

Question 39: Why is the impedance of a transmission line an important consideration when matching a transmitter to an antenna?

The characteristic impedance of the transmission line must be equal to the antenna input impedance or the input impedance at the transmitter will appear to vary with the length of the line, making maximum transfer of energy impossible. When the line is a quarter-wave or a multiple of this length, the formula for the characteristic impedance of the line is:

$$Z(line) = \text{square root of } Z (in) \times Z (load)$$

where Z (in) is the input impedance at the transmitter end, Z (load) is the antenna impedance and Z (line) is the characteristic impedance of the transmission line. If the transmitter output impedance is 140 ohms to a 40-ohm antenna impedance, by the above formula, the characteristic impedance would be 80 ohms for the transmission line cut to an odd multiple of a quarter-wave.

Question 40: What is meant by "standing waves"; "standing-wave ratio (SWR)"; and "characteristic impedance" as referred to transmission lines? How can standing waves be minimized?

When a transmission line is not terminated in its characteristic impedance, energy is reflected from the antenna (load) and combined with the power flowing out to the antenna to form standing waves. The "standing wave ratio" or SWR is the ratio of the maximum voltage to the minimum voltage along the line.

Standing waves may be reduced or even eliminated by terminating the line in an impedance equivalent to the characteristic impedance of that line. In other words, the line must be matched to the antenna impedance.

The "characteristic impedance" of a transmission line is the input impedance of a line having infinite length, such as the input signal would "see" when flowing into a line of infinite length. Values of characteristic impedance actually vary from 25 to 600 ohms according to the type of line. Coaxial lines usually range from 25 to 90 ohms, parallel lines (twinlead, etc.) 100 to 600 ohms, with "open line" running to 600 ohms.

Question 41: If standing waves are desirable on a transmitting antenna, why are they undesirable on a transmission line?

Standing waves in a conductor cause that wire or line to radiate energy, which is desirable in the antenna but definitely undesirable in a transmission line. The fact that standing waves exist in the transmission line indicates that a mismatch between the transmitter and antenna is causing a lower efficiency of energy transfer than is necessary or desirable.

Question 42: What is meant by stub tuning?

Stub tuning is a method of tuning a transmission line. A short length of transmission line is attached to the main line to eliminate standing waves. The stub effectively serves as an impedance-matching device and actually assists in matching the transmission line to the antenna. This reduces line losses and permits maximum power transfer from the transmitter to the antenna.

Question 43: What would be the consideration in choosing a solid-dielectric cable over a hollow pressurized cable for use as a transmission line?

Solid cables use a resilient dielectric material such as polyethylene which is flexible and easy to install. It is lower in cost, has a higher loss tolerance and requires no special plumbing. The air-insulated cables are much more expensive but considerably more efficient. Some types are fully evacuated and filled with an inert gas under pressure and sealed to prevent moisture from accumulating within the cable, which results in losses. Seals are required at the ends and all joints as well, and the mechanical faults along with bulky accessories restrict this type of transmission line to non-movable transmitters.

Question 44: Draw a simplified circuit diagram of a grid-dip meter. Explain the operation and give some possible applications of the meter.

The circuit of a grid-dip meter is shown in Fig. 5-10. With this instrument it is possible to determine the resonant frequency of an antenna system, detect harmonics, and check relative field strengths. The meter can also be used as an absorption wavemeter to check frequency when the oscillator portion is not energized.

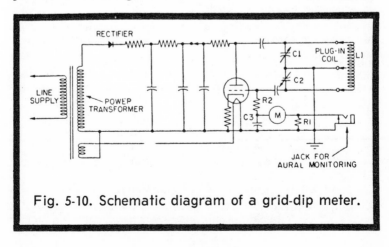

Fig. 5-10. Schematic diagram of a grid-dip meter.

The grid-dip meter is a calibrated oscillator with a meter in the oscillator's grid circuit. With the oscillator functioning, energy is coupled from the tuned circuit to the circuit under test, which is supplied a small amount of energy from the tank coil of the dip meter. Except for the field of the tank coil, the circuit under test is deenergized. Capacitors are adjusted to the point where the oscillator tank frequency is equal to the resonant frequency of the circuit under test. At resonance, the grid current decreases, as indicated by the dip in the grid meter. The energy absorbed from the tank coil by the circuit under test decreases the AC component of plate voltage, thus causing a decrease in feedback energy from the plate to the oscillator grid. The grid voltage is driven less positive, and the grid current decreases.

Question 45: Draw a simplified circuit diagram of an absorption wavemeter (with galvanometer indicator). Explain the operation and give some possible applications.

The schematic in Fig. 5-11 is simply a calibrated LC circuit with an indicating device. The galvanometer and diode may be replaced with a simple flashlight bulb as an indicator at a slight sacrifice in accuracy.

Probably the major disadvantage of the absorption wavemeter is a tendency to detune the circuit under test as energy is absorbed from it. Nevertheless, this condition may be minimized by keeping the coupling between the two circuits as loose as possible. As resonance is approached, coupling should be reduced by moving the wavemeter farther away from the circuit being measured until the meter is just barely off zero. Tuning becomes much sharper as coupling is loosened, and when ready for final adjustment, the meter may be switched to maximum sensitivity for a more accurate indication.

Question 46: Draw a block diagram showing only those stages that would illustrate the principle of operation of a secondary frequency standard. Explain the function of each stage.

The counter type of frequency meter is a high-speed electronic counter with an accurate crystal-controlled time base. These counters are typically used as secondary frequency standards. The combination time base and electronic counter provides a frequency meter which automatically counts and displays the number of events or cycles occurring in a precise time interval. A simplified block diagram of a representative counter-type frequency standard is shown in Fig. 5-12.

In addition to making direct frequency measurements, the counter can measure periods, frequency ratios, and total events. A self-check feature enables an operator to verify

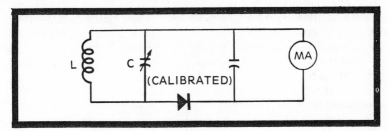

Fig. 5-11. Schematic of an absorption wavemeter with a galvanometer indicator.

instrument operation for most types of measurements. The internal oscillator is extremely stable. A secondary transfer standard is calibrated for accuracy against a primary standard (National Bureau of Standards' WWV broadcasts).

Question 47: Draw a block diagram of a heterodyne frequency meter, which includes the following stages:

    Crystal oscillator
    Crystal oscillator harmonic amplifier
    Variable frequency oscillator
    Mixer
    Detector and AF amplifier
    AF modulator

Show the RF input and RF, AF and calibration outputs. Assume a bandswitching arrangement and a dial having arbitrary units, employing a vernier scale.

(a) Describe the operation of the meter.

(b) Describe, step-by-step, how the crystal should be checked against WWV, using a suitable receiver.

(c) Under what conditions would the AF modulator be used?

(d) Describe, step-by-step, how the unknown frequency of a transmitter could be determined by the use of headphones; by the use of a suitable receiver.

(e) What is meant by calibration check points; when should they be used?

(f) If in measuring a frequency, the tuning dial should show an indication between two dial-frequency relationships in the calibration book, how could the frequency value be determined?

(g) How could this meter be used as an RF generator?

(h) Under what conditions would it be necessary to recalibrate the crystal oscillator?

(a) The heterodyne frequency meter consists of a stable variable-frequency oscillator, a crystal oscillator (and harmonic amplifier), a mixer / detector, an audio amplifier, and

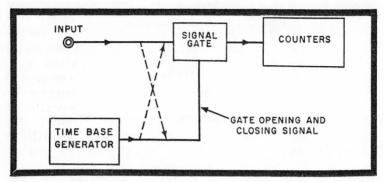

Fig. 5-12. Frequency counter, simplified block diagram.

sometimes an audio modulator, as shown in Fig. 5-13. The detector measures the difference frequency between the variable oscillator and the accurate standard crystal (or one of its harmonics). The resulting frequency difference is in the audio range, so that the beat frequency is audible in headphones (or other suitable reproducer) after amplification. The variable-frequency oscillator is tuned by means of a corrector knob to get a zero-beat; then the variable oscillator is known to be at the same frequency as the crystal. The RF input from the transmitter is then connected in place of the crystal oscillator. The variable oscillator is tuned to obtain a zero-beat; this oscillator is now at the same frequency as the transmitter. The setting of the calibrated dial is read directly or converted to frequency by means of a chart.

(b) To check the crystal frequency when one of the crystal's harmonics falls on the frequency of a primary frequency standard, simply tune a receiver to a WWV or WWVH channel and couple the RF signal from the receiver into the frequency meter's RF input. When the mixer is provided with a signal from the crystal oscillator that is exactly at the same frequency (or harmonic frequency) as WWV, a zero beat will be obtained in the headphones. When one of the crystal's harmonics does not fall on a WWV frequency, the VFO can be calibrated against WWV, then the VFO can serve as a standard for setting the frequency of the fixed crystal oscillator.

(c) The modulator makes it easier to keep track of the RF signal when the unknown cannot be found for comparison. The modulator also allows the VFO to be used as a signal generator for tuning and aligning receivers.

(d) See (a) above for explanation of how to measure unknown frequencies.

(e) Calibration check points provide an easy method for determining which harmonic of the crystal should be used, and for determining the proper range setting of the dials. When the frequency indication is not readable directly in kilohertz or megahertz, a numerical vernier indication may be compared against a like number in the calibration book, which lists the frequency that each numerical indication represents.

(f) Most frequency meters allow fairly easy interpolation of frequency readings because of the linearity between the dial readings and the frequency indications they represent. Thus, if a dial indicated a frequency to be between 4115 and 4116, the frequency would be proportionally between the two frequencies indicated. Assume that 4115 represents 152.75 MHz and 4116 represents 152.78 MHz. If the dial reading is two-thirds of the way from 4115 toward 4116, the frequency indicated will be proportionally the same between the two listed frequencies, or 152.77 MHz.

(g) When the switch in the output line from the VFO is placed in the position shown in the block diagram, the VFO portion of the frequency meter will serve as an accurate signal source, and can be used in conjunction with the audio modulator for aligning receivers.

(h) To qualify as a secondary transfer standard, a frequency meter must be calibrated against a primary standard at certain specified intervals (normally six months). However, frequent calibrations should be made to ensure consistent accuracy. Calibration checks should always be performed following a significant temperature change, after making any change in the frequency meter's tube complement or power supply, and after transportation of the device from one place to another.

Question 48: Draw a block diagram of an FM deviation (modulation) meter which includes the following stages:

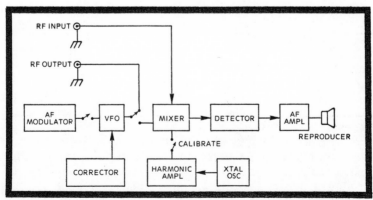

Fig. 5-13. Heterodyne frequency meter.

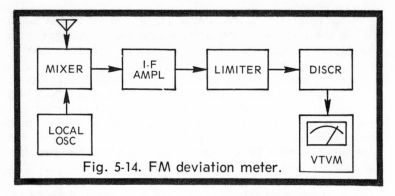

Fig. 5-14. FM deviation meter.

Mixer	Discriminator
IF amplifier	Peak reading voltmeter
Limiter	

(a) Explain the operation of this instrument.

(b) Draw a circuit diagram and explain how the discriminator is sensitive to frequency changes rather than amplitude changes.

(a) As can be seen by studying the block diagram of Fig. 5-14, a deviation monitor is nothing more than a simple FM receiver without the audio or squelch circuits. Since transmitter deviation is normally adjusted in the immediate vicinity of the instrument, the meter is not equipped with receiver circuits that provide a high degree of selectivity or sensitivity.

In operation, a signal from the transmitter under test is coupled into the mixer along with an appropriate-frequency signal from the monitor's local oscillator. The difference frequency is processed through the IF amplifier and limiter. (The limiter causes the IF signal to reach saturation so that AM components in the signal are minimized; that is, when an IF signal is amplified to saturation, there are no variations in signal amplitude and, consequently, little or no AM signal components.)

The discriminator recovers the audio from the IF signal, and provides a varying DC output voltage that is directly proportional to frequency deviation. Since the signal has been amplified to saturation via the limiter stage, the discriminator's input signal is of varying frequency but constant amplitude.

(b) The discriminator circuit is shown in Fig. 5-15. Note that two resistors (R1 and R2) appear across the output. When no modulation is applied to the transmitter under test, the voltages across R1 and R2 are equal and opposite. The capacitor on the primary of the discriminator transformer is

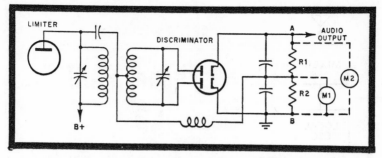

Fig. 5-15. Discriminator alignment connections.

adjusted for maximum deflection of meter M1. When modulation is applied, meter M2 (a peak-reading voltmeter or VTVM) will indicate a DC voltage that is proportional to deviation from the carrier frequency on modulation peaks.

Question 49: Describe the usual method, and the equipment needed, for measuring the harmonic attenuation of a transmitter.

The existence of harmonics may be observed using simple receiver, wavemeters, field-strength meters, and grid-dip meters. To measure attenuation, the detecting device must be calibrated in decibels so the harmonic signals may be compared with the strength of the fundamental signals.

The detecting device is placed at some fixed point in proximity to the transmitting antenna while the transmitter is operating. A calibrated attenuation control on the instrument is used to set the meter to 0 dB when it is tuned to the fundamental frequency. The device is then tuned to the desired harmonic and the negative-decibel reading noted. If the signal is not detectable, the attenuation is reduced incrementally until a reading is obtained. The attenuation, in decibels, will equal the meter reading plus the difference, in decibels, between the first setting and the second setting of the attenuation control. Each 10 dB represents an order of magnitude power change. Thus, if a 40 dB difference was noted between the fundamental and second harmonic, the transmitter's fundamental signal is 10,000 times more powerful than that of the harmonic.

Question 50: Why is it important that transmitters remain on frequency and that harmonics be attenuated?

If transmitters drift off frequency, or pass harmonics without insufficient attenuation, interference with other signals can hardly be avoided. All transmitters are required to remain on their assigned frequency and harmonics must be attenuated.

CHAPTER 6

Basic Radiotelephone, PART IV: Element 3

A battery is a simple source of electric power, whether it's a single cell or a combination of cells connected together in series for greater voltage, parallel for greater current, or series-parallel for greater voltage and current. A battery converts chemical energy into electrical energy and may be a primary (dry) cell which cannot be recharged and used again, or a secondary (wet) cell that may be recharged and used over again many times.

The dry cell consists of a zinc container forming the negative terminal with a paste type electrolyte of sal ammoniac and manganese dioxide separating it from the carbon rod in the center, which is the positive terminal. The cell offers 1.5 volts, which drops as the zinc is decomposed by the chemical action of the electrolyte, until it is of no further use and must be discarded. This type of cell is used for flashlights, small transistor radios, and other small devices requiring limited amounts of power.

The secondary cell, commonly referred to as a lead-acid storage cell or wet storage cell, has a normal output voltage of 2 volts per cell. The 12-volt auto battery consists of six of these cells connected in series for maximum voltage, and with proper care often lasts for several years. The construction and care of these batteries is reviewed more completely in the Q & A part of the chapter.

MOTORS AND GENERATORS

A motor converts electrical energy into mechanical energy and the generator does just the opposite—it changes mechanical energy into electrical energy. If a current is applied to a wire or coil inside a magnetic field, the wire will move in a direction according to factors involved. In order to allow continuous rotation, the current flowing through the coil must be reversed during each rotation and this switching is provided by the commutator. A DC motor uses an electromagnet in the field winding which is connected in series with the armature coil to provide a series-wound motor. The field winding may be connected in parallel with the armature winding, in which case we have a DC shunt motor.

Although a DC motor may be used as a DC generator and the generator as a motor, best performance is realized only when the unit is specifically designed for the intended use. The shunt-wound motor offers reasonably constant speed under varying loads, but some slow-down may be expected under heavier loads; torque is rather low, too. The voltage output from the shunt-wound generator is also fairly constant under various loads. A DC motor may be reversed by simply reversing the field or the armature winding connection. Since a running DC motor also generates an opposing voltage to that applied, counter EMF is only a little less than the applied voltage and it serves to reduce the current drawn by the motor. Actually, this current depends on the resistance of the motor, the voltage applied, and the counter EMF. The current drawn by the motor while running increases along with the load because that load increase slows the motor, causing the counter EMF to decrease; consequently, the current increases.

MICROWAVE EQUIPMENT

Conventional tubes, transistors, and other components become of little use at UHF frequencies, and of no use at all for microwave operation. The inductance in a fraction of an inch of wire, or the capacitance in adjacent equally short wires or leads are sufficient to unbalance circuits and cause all sorts of problems in the microwave region. So we proceed with an entirely different concept of values and circuit characteristics as the study of microwave communication equipment is undertaken. Actually, klystron, magnetron, and traveling wave tubes are much simpler than our conventional pentodes and other multi-element tubes if the principles of operation are understood.

Just about every loss conceivable increases with frequency in ordinary vacuum tube amplifiers until, at microwave frequencies, they fail to show an output as great as their input signal. The inductance in the element connecting leads, grid-cathode capacitance, dielectric loss, and electron transit time are all major factors against them. Electron transit time, or the time required for an electron to travel from cathode to plate, is comparatively short at low frequencies—about one-thousandth of a microsecond. This is about one-thousandth of a hertz at a frequency of 1 MHz, but at 1,000 MHz the electron transit time amounts to one hertz. Indications are that tube efficiency really drops excessively when transit time is greater than one tenth of a hertz, and if it reaches two or three times that figure, the tube becomes a big zero, since it will not amplify or even oscillate.

Using special designs eliminates or at least reduces some of the problems and extends the upper limit of the operating frequency of conventional tubes. The acorn, doorknob, lighthouse, and pencil types are a few of the original special designs for UHF operation; many have been replaced with solid-state devices in current design. However, there are definite limitations even today and the newer principles of operation found in the klystron with its velocity modulation and the magnetron with a high-power output at super-high frequencies are explained a little later. In a magnetron, the transit time between cathode and anode determines the frequency of operation and it may be varied by changing the position of the external magnet. Klystron and traveling wave tubes both utilize transit time, also, but in a different way.

Microwave Uses

Certain properties of microwaves make them especially attractive for special situations. Probably the most important feature of microwave operation is the narrow beam of radiated energy produced with parabolic reflector antennas of modest size. This facilitates point-to-point transmission such as studio-transmitter links where the narrow beam makes it possible to focus most of the radiated power on the receiving antenna. Interference is easy to avoid and reliability is assured with surprisingly low power. Radar also makes good use of the concentrated beams offered in microwave operation, but due to other requirements such as sweeping beams and distances involved, extremely high power is used. Radar operations are discussed fully in Chapter 8. The width of a microwave carrier also makes it possible to comfortably accommodate many voice channels at one time with multiplexing.

TROUBLESHOOTING

In your FCC exam on Element 3, you will probably face several questions on troubleshooting. The best suggestion is to use good common sense in answering them. Read the question over carefully and take your time answering. Don't look for something complicated; it's more likely to be something simple—but logical.

TWO-WAY RADIO

Familiarization with rules, regulations, procedures, and definitions pertaining to the mobile services should be undertaken in earnest at this point. Portions of the answers given are expanded where advisable to further enlighten the applicant and improve his understanding of the principles involved. After completing this element and passing the FCC exam, many doors will be opened because you will receive the second class radiotelephone license, which authorizes you to repair, adjust, and maintain the transmitters used in the various mobile services.

STUDY QUESTIONS

Question 1: How does a primary cell differ from a secondary cell?

The primary cell must be discarded after use, since it cannot be recharged like a secondary cell. An example of the primary cell is the common flashlight battery (dry cell), while a typical secondary cell is the lead-acid cell (storage battery) used in automobiles.

A primary cell may not be recharged, since one electrode has been partly destroyed by the chemical reaction. Recharging could not possibly restore it to its original condition. A secondary cell merely undergoes a chemical change when discharged, which the charging current reverses, since nothing has been dissolved or destroyed and the battery is restored to its charged condition.

Question 2: What is the chemical composition of the electrolyte of a lead-acid storage cell?

The electrolyte is a diluted solution of sulphuric acid in distilled water, with a specific gravity of 1.300 when completely charged. Actually the acid forms 25 percent of the mixture by volume.

Question 3: Describe the care which should be given a group of storage cells to maintain them in good operating condition.

Storage batteries require considerable care in order to keep them in top condition and to ensure maximum life. The water level is important and must not be too high or it will boil out while the cell is in use (either charging or discharging). The level should be maintained at about ¼ inch above the plates by adding pure distilled water only—never acid or electrolyte unless some of the original has been spilled. Cells should be kept fully charged, never allowed to stand in partly or fully discharged condition because this results in sulphation. Overcharging slightly about once a month will remove any sulphation. The charging rate should be low to eliminate excessive gassing or bubbling. Keep the battery terminals free of corrosion with a layer of petroleum jelly and wash away corrosion prior to this application with a solution of baking soda. Do not allow the solution to get into the battery cells. Adequate ventilation should be provided, also.

Question 4: What causes sulphation of a lead-acid storage cell?

Sulphation may be caused by local action, particularly in batteries with a fairly high internal resistance. This type of problem can be prevented by making certain the cell is charged fully before allowing it to stand idle for long periods. Another major cause of sulphation is operating the battery with insufficient electrolyte. When the level of the electrolyte drops below the surface of the tops of the plates, sulphation is almost surely the result. When excessive gassing occurs, sulphation is accelerated, too; to avoid this, be sure to avoid overcharging and overdischarging. Adding electrolyte to a fully charged cell can cause excessive gassing (the result of which is sulphation); this may be avoided by adding electrolyte only when some of the electrolyte in the battery has been lost by spillage. When the battery is fully charged, or when the battery is about to be charged, distilled water may be added to bring the electrolyte to its proper level.

Question 5: What is the result of discharging a lead-acid storage cell at an excessively high current rate?

The battery will tend to overheat, thereby accelerating the discharge rate and perhaps damaging the battery permanently. The capacity of a battery is reduced during periods of excessive heating. Excessive heating causes sulphation, plate buckling, and electrolyte boiloff.

Question 6: If the charging current through a storage battery is maintained at the normal rate but its polarity is reversed, what will be the result?

This would discharge the storage battery, but it would cause no damage unless permitted to continue. The battery would eventually be damaged if charged with reverse polarity for an extended period. Severe sulphation would also result, ruining the negative plates.

Question 7: What is the approximate fully charged voltage of a lead-acid cell?

The fully charged voltage of a lead-acid cell is about 2.06 volts, and when fully discharged 1.75 volts. Actual voltage is dependent on temperature also, but it would be close to these figures. Measuring the terminal voltage is one method of determining its condition, specific gravity of the electrolyte is the other. All cells are fully charged when the specific gravity reads 1.300; the battery should be recharged if it is below 1.140.

Question 8: What steps may be taken to prevent corrosion of lead-acid storage cell terminals?

Clean the top of the battery and cell terminals with a baking soda solution, then coat the terminals with petroleum jelly or Vaseline. Exercise care with the baking soda solution—do not let it get into the cells. Connections to the terminals should be clean and tight before applying the lubricant.

Question 9: How is the capacity of a battery rated?

The capacity of a battery is rated in ampere-hours, a multiple of current in amperes and time in hours. A fully charged battery rated at 100 ampere-hours should deliver 10 amperes continuously for 10 hours or 100 amperes for 1 hour, but, of course, the actual performance would be somewhat less as a result of heating and chemical changes. The rate of discharge has considerably effect on the efficiency, as does the ambient temperature. Extremely high discharge rates or cold temperatures could reduce the ampere-hour capacity to less than half the actual rating.

Question 10: What is "power factor"? Give an example of how it is calculated. Discuss the construction and operation of dynamotors.

Power factor is a measure of the phase difference between the voltage and current or it may be expressed as the figure by which the product of E and I must be multiplied to secure the true power of a circuit. The power factor varies between zero and unity. When the phase angle between voltage and current is 90 degrees, the power factor is zero; and when voltage is exactly in phase with current, the power factor is unity. A high power factor is definitely desirable in lines carrying power because circuit losses are greatly reduced and efficiency is better as a result. A low power factor is desirable in capacitors and inductors because the maximum phase angle reduces losses in these components. In order to find the true power of a circuit, the apparent power (E x I) must be corrected by the factor relating to the phase angle. Simply multiply EI by the cosine of the phase angle which equals Z over R. If the resistance and reactance are known, impedance Z is equal to the square root of R squared plus X squared; then the power factor is equal to R over Z.

A dynamotor is a combination of motor and generator in which both functions operate from a single magnetic field with two armatures, or two separate windings on a single armature, and independent commutators. A dynamotor was used in pretransistor days to convert mobile DC voltages to B+ voltages for use by electronic circuits. Dynamotors are notoriously inefficient energy converters.

Question 11: List the comparative advantages and disadvantages of motor-generator and transformer-rectifier power supplies.

The motor-generator may be operated independently from any AC supply. In mobile applications, the motor-generator (dynamotor) may be connected directly to the terminals of a battery. The efficiency of the dynamotor, however, is extremely low—on the order of 43 percent or so; thus, a great deal of power is required to operate such a unit. The dynamotor often proves to be the source of RF interference, too; the contacts make and break at an extremely high rate, and generate electrical impulses that can prove difficult to filter. On the other hand, dynamotors are capable of sustaining large current drains over long periods without overheating, so long as the battery supply is capable of delivering the required power. The dynamotor is typically characterized by a high-pitched whine, which can prove annoying and, in military and police applications, sometimes hazardous. On the positive side of the ledger, the output of a dynamotor is a relatively ripple-free DC that does not itself require filtering other than with ordinary bypass capacitors.

A transformer-rectifier operating at a frequency of 60 Hz requires a conventional power-line source, so its portable applications are limited. There are transformer-rectifier combinations capable of operating at extremely high frequencies, but all such combinations do require a source of AC power, whether it be the power line, a vibrator supply, or a pair of switching transistors. A low-frequency combination requires considerable filtering to remove the ripple content and smooth the output to a usable DC for most receivers and transmitters. A high-frequency combination requires little filtering, but may be the cause of inductively coupled whine (an audio signal at the switching rate) in the radio circuits it is powering. A low-frequency transformer-rectifier requires a transformer with a considerably heavy core mass—which means more cost, more weight, and more space consumption. A high-frequency combination means smaller transformer, less filtering, less weight, less space. At one time, the rectifiers were a major space consideration, too. Today, however, the space consumed by rectifiers—regardless of the circuit in which they are used—is negligible.

A transformer-rectifier combination is an extremely efficient energy converter. While a dynamotor can produce DC when connected to a battery, its efficiency is rarely more than 45 percent. A vibrator, transformer, and rectifier combination (assuming solid-state rectifiers are used) can convert battery voltage to B+ voltage with a total conversion efficiency of up to 70 percent. A solid-state switching circuit in concert with a transformer-rectifier circuit can change battery voltage to B+ with a conversion efficiency of up to 78 percent. Some switching circuits, which employ two transformers rather than one, can operate with conversion efficiencies as high as 98 percent.

The dynamotor has a relatively low reliability factor because it is a mechanical device with a moving assembly. The transformer-rectifier has a high reliability factor because it has no moving parts. When the transformer-rectifier is used with a vibrator supply, the reliability factor decreases considerably, because the vibrator is a mechanical make-break device; however, when a transformer-rectifier is used with a solid-state switching system to supply the necessary AC, the reliability can be quite high.

The disadvantages of the dynamotor today outweigh the advantages. And since the advent of inexpensive transistors capable of switching at extremely high rates (the higher the rate, the cheaper the transformer), the dynamotor has all but disappeared from the communications scene.

Question 12: **What determines the speed of a synchronous motor? An induction motor? A DC series motor?**

The speed of a synchronous motor depends on the frequency of the supply voltage and the number of pairs of poles. The speed of the induction motor is related to the same factors plus the load, to some extent.

The speed of a DC series motor depends chiefly on the load, but to some extent on the voltage, type and number of turns in the armature, number of turns in the field and number of poles.

Question 13: **Describe the action and list the main characteristics of a shunt-wound DC motor.**

Since the field winding and the armature winding of a shunt motor are in parallel, the field current and flux are independent of the armature current and of constant value. As usual, the armature current peaks with the load and is lowest with no load. Even though the shunt motor slows down noticeably with an increase in load, the variation in speed with load is limited enough for this type to be labeled the "constant-

223

speed" motor. The starting torque of the shunt motor is less than satisfactory for heavy loads, but the speed is readily controlled by a rheostat in series with the field. As more resistance is added, the field current decreases and the motor speed increases.

Question 14: Name the possible causes of excessive sparking at the brushes of a DC motor or generator.

Brushes not aligned, insulation between commutator segments too high, commutator dirty or rough, poles incorrectly connected, brushes binding in holders, incorrect tension, open or shorted armature coil, defective field coil, excessive load on armature.

Question 15: How may radio frequency interference, often caused by sparking at the brushes of a high-voltage generator, be minimized?

RF interference may be reduced by adding filter chokes in series with the brushes and bypass capacitors from the brushes to ground. Sparking interference often originates from generator components that form tuned circuits, with the power leads radiating at the frequencies of those tuned circuits, and the spark energizing their oscillations. All radiating leads must be effectively bypassed as close to the generator as possible in order to provide effective relief from this source of interference.

Question 16: How may the output voltage of a separately excited AC generator, at a constant output frequency, be varied?

The output voltage may be adjusted by means of a potentiometer connected in series with the field windings. The field windings carry DC to the generator from a separate voltage source. As the field voltage is decreased (by increasing the series resistance), the alternator's output voltage is reduced.

Question 17: What is the purpose of a commutator on a DC motor? On a DC generator?

The commutator in a DC motor provides current in the required direction for each armature coil to cause a torque which acts to turn the armature. This switching action causes the armature current to reverse periodically and become AC, in effect, so that any given point on the armature leaving one field pole is repelled from it and attracted to the next pole. The commutator maintains contact between the armature and the supply voltage.

The commutator on a DC generator makes a direct current output possible by switching the AC generated by armature coils. As the brushes contact each armature segment current flows in one direction in the output. The current in the armature windings is AC, and the output would also be AC except for the commutator action which switches in another coil just as the previous coil starts to reverse its current direction.

Question 18: What may cause a motor-generator bearing to overheat?

Common causes are improper lubrication, poor alignment of the motor to the generator, broken bearings, bearings not aligned with the shaft, dirty bearings, overload or a lack of ventilation. If a bearing overheats, the motor-generator should not be stopped; instead, remove the load and slow down the machine while making every effort to cool it by forced air and by applying oil and graphite. Continue running it slowly until the bearing cools to the normal temperature, then stop the motor and flush the bearing with light oil, followed by lubrication with regular weight oil. The bearing should still be in satisfactory condition, if heating was not too severe. Check the machine for overload and correct condition.

Question 19: What materials should be used to clean the commutator of a motor or generator?

If in reasonably good condition, the commutator may be cleaned with very fine sandpaper, light canvas material or special commutator polishing paste. Rough or burned spots may be smoothed down by fine sandpaper. Emery paper must never be used because the metallic dust may very easily short out segments or even windings! The chocolate brown color indicates a commutator is in proper operating condition. Care should always be exercised in servicing rotating machinery to avoid possible injury or shock.

Question 20: If the field of a shunt wound DC motor were opened while the machine is running under no load, what would be the probable result?

The speed of a shunt motor is dependent on the magnetic strength of the field; the higher the field strength, the slower the motor will turn. An open field would cut off the field, and the motor speed would increase beyond the design point. Such operation could seriously damage the motor.

Question 21: Describe the physical structure of a klystron tube and explain how it operates as an oscillator.

The reflex klystron usually performs as an oscillator and has a cathode, resonator or anode, and repeller. Electrons from the cathode are drawn into a beam by the focusing electrode. The electron beam is attracted to the cavity resonator by its positive charge. Passing through the gap in the resonator, the beam interacts with the fields of oscillations

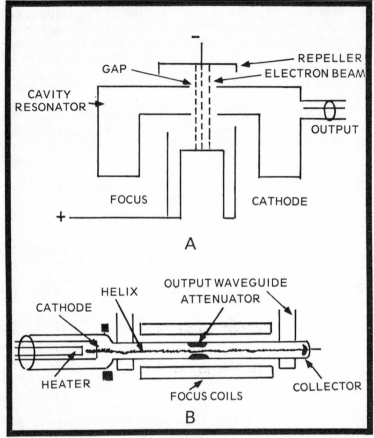

Fig. 6-1. Cross-sectional drawings: (A) reflex klystron, (B) traveling-wave tube.

in that cavity. When an electron passes through the gap in phase with the resonator oscillations, it passes on energy to the cavity fields and slows down. Passing through out of phase, the electron takes energy from the gap and picks up speed.

After passing through the gap, the electron beam is repelled by the strong negative charge of the repeller, which slows the beam to a stop and forces it to reverse direction. Passing through the gap again in the opposite direction, the electrons traveling at various speeds drift together in bunches. These bunches are in phase with cavity oscillations and give energy to the cavity to sustain oscillations. A layout sketch of the reflex klystron is shown in Fig. 6-1A.

Question 22: Draw a diagram showing the construction and explain the principles of operation of a traveling-wave tube.

Acting as an RF amplifier at frequencies above 3000 MHz, the traveling-wave tube offers an exceptional bandwidth of about 1000 MHz. As noted in Fig. 6-1B, the tube has no resonant circuits. The cathode and gun anode produce a beam aimed through the long helix and received by the collector at anode potential. The input signal enters the waveguide at the helix end nearest the gun, traveling along the helix to the opposite end where it arrives as an amplified signal to be coupled to the load through the output waveguide. In order to be amplified, the signal must travel at a lower velocity than the electron beam in order to receive energy from that source. This causes the wave to increase in amplitude as it reaches the output end of the helix. The electron beam must be slowed down to about one tenth its normal velocity (speed of light), and this is accomplished by the wave traveling around the turns of the helix at the speed of light but moving forward according to the pitch and diameter of the turns. By satisfactory design of the helix, forward progress of the wave may be limited to the desired speed. Focusing coils restrict the beam diameter and steer it through the center of the helix.

Question 23: Describe the physical structure and explain the operation of a multianode magnetron.

Fig. 6-2 illustrates the structure of the multianode magnetron, which roughly consists of a rod-shaped cathode in a copper cylinder (anode). Several cavities in the anode form resonant tank circuits with the centrally located cathode an output coupling and a very strong permanent magnet. Instead of being drawn to the anode directly, electrons from the cathode are bent as they pass through a strong magnetic field and whirl around the cathode, traveling in the same direction as determined by the field according to Fleming's rule. When the electrons pass the cavities or slots in the anode block, the cavities are shock-excited into oscillation and electrons passing the cavity slots out of phase take energy from the cavity, speed up and, being bent faster, return to the cathode. Electrons passing cavity slots in phase give energy to the cavity to sustain oscillations and slow down. Actually, most of the electrons contribute energy to the cavities and as a result of the short path of those that take away energy, the overall efficiency of the magnetron is not decreased to any great extent. In practice, operating efficiencies may be as high as 50 percent. Magnetrons are widely used in radar systems as pulsed power oscillators with peak power of 2 megawatts.

Question 24: Discuss the following with respect to waveguides.

(a) Relationship between frequency and size.

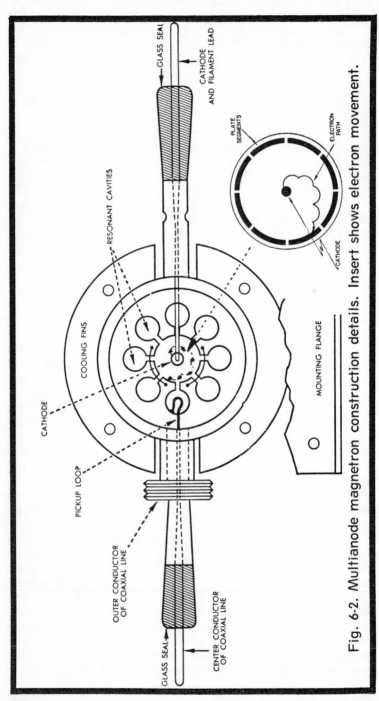

Fig. 6-2. Multianode magnetron construction details. Insert shows electron movement.

GLASS SEAL

CATHODE AND FILAMENT LEAD

PLATE SEGMENTS

ELECTRON PATH

CATHODE

RESONANT CAVITIES

COOLING FINS

MOUNTING FLANGE

CATHODE

PICKUP LOOP

OUTER CONDUCTOR OF COAXIAL LINE

GLASS SEAL

CENTER CONDUCTOR OF COAXIAL LINE

(b) Modes of operation.

(c) Coupling of energy into waveguides.

(d) General principles of operation.

(a) Waveguides are used in place of transmission lines at UHF or microwave frequencies. The inside dimension of the waveguide varies in accordance with the frequency for which it is designed. Inside dimensions decrease with an increase in frequency and the widest inside dimensions must equal at least one-half wavelength for the signal traveling through it. The narrow width of the rectangular waveguide is usually one-half the wider dimension. This is known as the "fundamental mode" (TE1, 0) and is superior to all others because no power is wasted. The wider dimension must be greater than one-half wavelength but no greater than one wavelength and the narrow width less than one-half wavelength.

(b) The mode of operation is based on the configuration of the electric and magnetic fields inside the waveguide. The modes are determined by the shape of the waveguide and are labeled TE or TM. In the TE (transverse electric) mode the electric field is at right angles to the direction of propagation and the magnetic field parallel in this direction. In the TM (transverse magnetic) mode the magnetic field is transverse or at right angles to the direction of propagation with the electric field parallel to that movement. Modes are readily identified by letters for the particular group followed by numerals.

(c) Energy is coupled into waveguides by any one of three basic methods. One is to insert a small loop of wire in the waveguide which inductively couples to the electromagnetic field in a way similar to the common transformer. A second coupling technique involves the use of a small straight probe inserted in the guide parallel to the electric field. Acting somewhat like a quarter-wave antenna, the probe couples to the electrostatic field. The third coupling method makes use of holes or slots in the wall of the waveguide; a current-carrying conductor parallel to these holes provides a link with the internal and external fields. The external conductor may add or absorb energy from the waveguide as desired.

(d) A waveguide permits transmission of microwave energy without the considerable loss encountered in conventional conductors. A waveguide has the ability to conduct electromagnetic waves within and, since the energy is completely contained in these waves, current-losses as encountered normally in wires is not a problem. The energy is in the electric and magnetic fields. Conventional electron flow as in a wire conductor is not required for waveguide transmission. Of course, the use of waveguides is restricted by practical dimensions, since the inside dimension of the guide must increase as the frequency of operation decreases. This makes their use practical for microwave frequencies only.

Question 25: Explain briefly the construction and purpose of a waveguide. What precautions should be taken in the installation and maintenance of a waveguide to insure proper operation?

A waveguide may consist of either round or rectangular pipes or channels for propagating microwave energy. Its purpose is clearly defined by the fact that it transmits high-frequency energy without excessive loss as would be unavoidable in the usual conductor. Precautions must be observed in installing sections of waveguides to be sure that all joints are strong mechanically and continuous electrically to reduce the possibility of loss. Tight, secure joints keep out moisture and dust particles which could adversely affect proper operation. Careful handling should eliminate bending, denting or otherwise altering the designed shape of the waveguide and its resonant cavity.

Question 26: Explain the operation of a cavity resonator.

The cavity resonator is a form of resonant circuit having an extremely high Q and intended for efficient operation in the microwave frequency range. Conventional LC resonant circuits are not practical due to the small physical size of inductance and capacity required in the microwave region. The resonant cavity is like a closed section of waveguide with the microwave energy therein reinforced at resonance, resulting in strong oscillations. This measured section of waveguide has a resonant frequency dependent on its dimensions. Cavities may be shaped in various ways—cylindrical, doughnut, rectangular and spherical. They are energized in the same manner as waveguides.

Question 27: How are cavities installed in vertical guides to prevent moisture from collecting? Why are long horizontal waveguides not desired?

Vertical sections should be installed with the end where the cavity is mounted through a choke joint at the bottom. Moisture-sealing gaskets should be used at each choke-coupling flange. Long horizontal waveguides have a tendency to collect moisture, making them undesirable. A small hole may be drilled at the lowest point in such existing installations to permit drainage of accumulated moisture.

230

TROUBLESHOOTING

The FCC's list of published study questions includes an appendix stating that several "troubleshooting" questions of the multiple-choice type will be asked on the exam. The questions will be accompanied by appropriate diagrams with numbered components. This section lists representative troubleshooting questions in the same manner as they are included in the actual test.

It will be helpful for you to remember certain specifics about amplifiers. Many of the questions may contain references to meter readings; if you have an idea as to the class of amplifier represented by the diagram, and have a basic idea as to the normal readings, you will be in a better position to predict the results of any given malfunction. A Class A amplifier draws current at all times (the constant current keeps the tube operating in the center of its linear region); a Class B amplifier is biased near cutoff, which means that it will draw current only during the positive half-cycles of input signal. A Class C amplifier will always contain tuned circuits—either in the input circuit or the output circuit, or both. Also, the Class C amplifier should draw current for only a small portion of the input signal's cycle, because the tube must be driven positive by some considerable portion of the input cycle before the tube starts conducting.

It is also helpful to bear in mind the basic function of biasing: to control the flow of electrons from cathode to plate. Without bias, the signal itself is the only control. Thus, if a Class C amplifier loses its bias for some reason, current flows uncontrollably in the tube; and since Class C amplifiers are designed to draw considerable current for short periods of

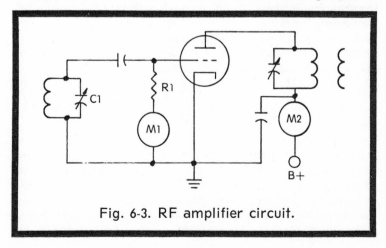

Fig. 6-3. RF amplifier circuit.

each cycle, a continuous current almost certainly will destroy the tube in short order.

Question 28: In the tuned-plate, tuned-grid oscillator circuit of Fig. 6-3, what would be the meter indication if capacitor C1 should short?

    (a) M1 would read higher

    (b) M1 would read lower

    (c) M2 would read lower

    (d) M2 would read zero

    (e) Both meters would read normal

If C1 shorts, there is no signal developed in the input tuned circuit, and consequently no signal applied to the grid. Under normal conditions, electrons flow from cathode to grid during positive half-cycles. The grid current charges the capacitor as it flows from the grid through the input tuned circuit. A portion of this charging current is diverted by the grid-leak resistor (R1), and so M1 will indicate a current flow. With C1 shorted, however, the input tuned circuit is effectively shunted to ground and can develop no signal. The grid, being at the same potential as the cathode, will have no curtailing effect on electron flow through the tube. The reading of M2 will increase, the reading of M1 will drop, and the circuit will cease to oscillate.

Question 29: If R1 should burn out (Fig. 6-3),

    (a) M1 would read zero

    (b) M2 would read lower

    (c) M1 would read higher

    (d) M2 would read higher

    (e) Both (a) and (d) above are true

When a resistor "burns out," it opens. With no resistor in the grid circuit, there is no discharge path for C2, so meter M1 would have to read zero. During the positive half of the grid signal, the grid becomes positive with respect to the cathode. The grid draws current and charges to the peak value of the grid signal so that plate of the capacitor connected to the grid becomes negative. The charge path is through the tube. During the negative half-cycle, the grid is driven negative with respect to the cathode. Ideally, C2 should discharge through R1 during negative half-cycles, and be charged during positive half-cycles—the bias being the average pulsating DC value of the varying charge. With no discharge path, the capacitor remains fully charged. With no discharge current through the grid-leak resistor, there is no DC bias voltage. With no bias voltage, there is no control element that may be used to check the flow of electrons in the tube from cathode to plate (other than the signal itself); thus, the reading of M2 would increase.

Question 30. If M1 reads normal while M2 is pinned against the maximum-current stop, there is an indication of:
  (a) Defective C1
  (b) R1 too low in value
  (c) Leaky C3
  (d) Open L2
  (e) Open L1

Plate voltage is applied to the oscillator tube through M2 and the output tank circuit. If M1 reads normal or low while M2 is pinned against its peg, there is an indication that excessive current is flowing in the plate circuit. If C1 is defective, plate current would drop. If R1 were too low in value, M1 would read higher than normal. An open L1 would remove the input signal and drop the reading of M1 to zero. If the bypass capacitor is leaky or shorted, however, the high voltage is effectively shorted to ground, and the reading of M2 would be excessive.

RULES AND REGULATIONS

Question 31: Define the following words or phrases:
  (a) Authorized frequency
  (b) Base station
  (c) Carrier
  (d) Citizen's radio service
  (e) Coast station
  (f) Disaster communications
  (g) Earth station
  (h) Fixed station
  (i) Harmful interference
  (j) Land mobile service
  (k) Land station
  (l) Maritime mobile service
  (m) Primary frequency standard
  (n) Public safety radio service
  (o) Repeater station
  (p) Space station
  (q) Type-accepted radio device

(a) Authorized frequency is the radio frequency of the carrier assigned and specified in the FCC authorization or license.

(b) A base station is a fixed land station communicating with mobile units in a land mobile service.

(c) The carrier is the RF emission without modulation and is the center frequency in an FM signal.

(d) The citizen's radio service is an FCC authorized communication service for use by any citizen for business or personal needs.

(e) A coast station is a land-based station in the maritime mobile service.

(f) Disaster communications are messages relating to the safety or protection of life and property during such disasters as floods, tornadoes and any actual emergency. Any station may assist in this type of communications, but must report such activity to the FCC as soon as possible and discontinue such operations following the emergency period.

(g) An earth station is one in the earth-space service and may be located on the earth's surface or an object in flight between points on the earth's surface.

(h) A fixed station provides radio communication between fixed points as specified.

(i) Harmful interference is any emission, radiation or induction outside the authorized frequency which endangers the normal functioning of a radionavigation service or seriously degrades, obstructs, or repeatedly interrupts any radio communication service operating in accordance with the FCC Rules and Regulations.

(j) The land mobile service is a communication service between base stations and mobile stations or units of any kind operating on land.

(k) A land station is one in the mobile service not intended for operation while in motion.

(l) The maritime mobile service provides communications between shore-based stations and boat stations or units of any class.

(m) The primary frequency standard is the signal of WWV or WWVH of the National Bureau of Standards, which the FCC requires all radio stations to use as the standard of comparison for their frequency of operation.

(n) The public safety radio service includes police, fire, ambulance as well as any other radio service dealing primarily with the public safety in relation to the protection of human life or property.

(o) A repeater station is a radio receiver-transmitter (transceiver) which automatically retransmits any signals received on the same or on a different frequency.

(p) A space station operates in the earth-space service or space service and is located on an object which is beyond or intended to proceed beyond the major portion of the earth's atmosphere but not intended for flight between points on the earth's surface.

(q) A type-accepted radio device is any piece of equipment, designed to generate RF signals, of which a prototype has been approved by the FCC.

Question 32: What is the frequency range associated with the following frequency designations:

(a) VLF
(b) LF
(c) MF
(d) HF
(e) VHF
(f) UHF
(g) SHF
(h) EHF

(a) Very low frequency (VLF), below 30 kilohertz (kHz).

(b) Low frequency (LF), 30 to 300 kHz.

(c) Medium frequency (MF), 300 to 3000 kHz.

(d) High frequency (HF), 3,000 to 30,000 kHz.

(e) Very high frequency (VHF) 30 to 300 megahertz (MHz).

(f) Ultra high frequency (UHF), 300 to 3,000 MHz.

(g) Super high frequency (SHF), 3,000 to 30,000 MHz.

(h) Extremely high frequency (EHF), 30,000 to 300,000 MHz.

Question 33: What is meant by the following emission designations: (a) A0, (b) A1, (c) A3, (d) A3A, (e) A5C, (f) F0, (g) F1, (h) F3, (i) F5, (j) P3D, (k) P3F.

Designations for various types of transmission are A (amplitude modulated, F (frequency or phase modulated), P (pulse modulated):

(a) A0 indicates continuous wave (CW) with no modulation.

(b) A1 indicates CW telegraphy using on-off keying.

(c) A3 indicates telephony with regular double sideband and carrier.

(d) A3A indicates telephony, single sideband with reduced carrier; also known as SSSC.

(e) A5C indicates regular amplitude modulated television (picture) emission with vestigial sideband.

(f) F0 indicates FM carrier without modulation.

(g) F1 indicates frequency-shift keying (no modulation).

(h) F3 indicates regular frequency modulated telephony such as used in FM broadcast stations.

(i) F5 indicates frequency modulated television.

(j) P3D indicates pulse modulated telephony with amplitude modulated pulses.

(k) P3F indicates pulse modulated telephony with phase modulated pulses.

Question 34: What is the basic difference between type approval and type acceptance of transmitting equipment?

Type approval is required for all transmitters in the commercial services and indicates testing by FCC personnel of submitted samples. If the transmitter meets frequency tolerance, harmonic suppression and stability requirements, it is placed on the type-approved list and you may use it. Type acceptance is based solely on information submitted by the manufacturer or individual prospective licensee.

Question 35: Define the following phrases:

　　(a) **Authorized bandwidth.**

　　(b) **Bandwidth occupied by an emission.**

　　(c) **Station authorization.**

　　(a) The authorized bandwidth is the maximum width of the band of frequencies, as specified in the authorization, to be occupied by an emission.

　　(b) The bandwidth occupied by an emission is the width of the frequency band (normally specified in kilohertz) containing those frequencies upon which a total of 99 percent of the radiated power appears, extended to include any discrete frequency upon which a power is at least 0.25 percent of the total radiated power.

　　(c) The station authorization is any construction permit, license, or special temporary authorization issued by the Commission.

Question 36: May stations in the public safety radio services be operated for short periods of time without a station authorization issued by the FCC?

No. No radio transmitter shall be operated in the public safety service except under and in accordance with a proper station authorization granted by the Federal Communications Commission.

What notification must be forwarded to the engineer in charge of the Commission's district office prior to testing a new radio transmitter in the public safety radio service, which has been obtained under a construction permit issued by the FCC?

The date on which the transmitter will first be tested in such a manner as to produce radiation, giving the name of the permitee, station location, call sign, and frequencies on which tests are to be conducted. This notification shall be made in writing at least two days in advance of the test date. FCC Form 456 may be used for this purpose.

Question 37: Where may standard forms applicable to the public safety radio services be obtained?

These standard forms may be obtained from the FCC office at Washington, D.C. 20554 or from any FCC field engineering office listed in this book.

Question 38: In general, what type of changes in authorized

stations must be approved by the FCC? What type does not require FCC approval?

Proposed changes which will result in operation inconsistent with any of the terms of the current authorization require that an application for modification of construction permit and-or license be submitted to the Commission on FCC Form 400. Proposed changes which do not depart from any of the terms of the outstanding authorization for the station involved may be made without prior Commission approval. Included is the substitution of equipment on the Commission's "List of Equipment Acceptable for Licensing," and designated for use in the public safety, industrial, and land transportation radio services—provided that substitute equipment employs the same type of emission and does not exceed the power limitations as set forth in the station authorization.

Changes of name and mailing address do not require a formal application for modification of license (without changes in ownership, control, or corporate structure and without changes in authorized location of the base or fixed station or the area of operation of mobile stations); however, the licensee shall notify the Commission promptly of these changes.

Question 39: The carrier frequency of a transmitter in the public safety radio service must be maintained within what percentage of the licensed value? Assume the station is operating at 160 MHz with a licensed power of 50 watts.

The carrier frequency of the transmitter must be within 0.0005 percent of its assigned frequency.

Question 40: What is the authorized bandwidth and frequency deviation of public safety stations operating at about 30 MHz? At about 160 MHz?

At 30 MHz the maximum bandwidth is 20 kHz and frequency deviation, plus or minus 5 kHz. At 160 MHz the authorized bandwidth is 20 kHz and the frequency deviation is also plus or minus 5 kHz. Actually, below 450 MHz these same figures apply, except in the case of transmitters authorized for operation before December 2, 1961, in the frequency band from 73.0 through 74.6 MHz; those stations may continue to operate with a 40-kHz bandwidth and a frequency deviation of plus or minus 15 kHz. A frequency tolerance of 0.005 percent is also permitted. In the frequency band from 450 to 1000 MHz, bandwidth is 40 kHz and the allowed deviation plus or minus 15 kHz.

Question 41: What is the maximum percentage of modulation allowed by the FCC for stations in the public safety radio services that utilize amplitude modulation (AM)?

The modulation percentage shall be sufficient to provide efficient communication and normally shall be maintained about 70 percent on peaks, but must not exceed 100 percent on negative peaks.

Question 42: Define "control point" as the term refers to transmitters in the public safety radio service.

A control point is an operating position which meets all of the following conditions:

(a) The position must be under the control and supervision of the licensee.

(b) All monitoring facilities required by this section must be installed at this position.

(c) The person immediately responsible for the operation of the transmitter is stationed at this position.

Question 43: Outline the transmitter measurements required by the FCC for stations in the public safety radio service.

The licensee of each station having a transmitter with a plate input power to the final RF stage in excess of 3 watts must employ a suitable procedure to determine that the carrier frequency of each transmitter is maintained within the tolerance prescribed and the results entered in station records:

(1) When the transmitter is initially installed.

(2) When any change is made which may affect the carrier frequency or stability of the transmitter.

(3) At intervals not exceeding one year for transmitters employing crystal-controlled oscillators.

(4) At intervals not exceeding one month for transmitters not employing crystal-controlled oscillators.

The licensee must employ a suitable procedure for determining the plate power input to the final RF stage of each base or fixed station transmitter over three watts to ensure operation within the maximum figure specified on the current station authorization. If direct measurement of plate current to the final stage is not practicable, the plate input power may be determined by a measurement of the cathode current in the final stage. In all such cases, the required entry shall indicate clearly the quantities measured, the values thereof, and the method of determining the plate power input from those figures. These measurements and entries in the station records shall be made following the initial installation, or after any change is made in the transmitter which may increase the power input, and at intervals not to exceed one year.

The licensee of each station shall employ a suitable procedure to determine that the modulation of each transmitter, authorized to operate in excess of 3 watts input power, does not exceed the limits specified in this part. This determination shall be made and entered in the station records when the transmitter is installed initially and when any change is made in the transmitter which could affect the modulation characteristics. Intervals of such measurements shall not exceed one year.

Question 44: What are the general requirements for transmitting identification announcements for stations in the public safety radio service?

The required identification for stations in these services shall be the assigned call signal at the end of each transmission or exchange of transmissions, or once for each 30 minutes of the operating period, as the licensee may prefer. However, a mobile station authorized to the licensee of the associated base station and which transmits only on the transmitting frequency of the associated base station is not required to transmit any identification.

Question 45: When a radio operator makes transmitter measurements required by the FCC's Rules for a station in the public safety radio service, what information should be transcribed into the station's records?

The results and dates of the transmitter measurements, as well as the name of the person making the measurements and expiration date of his license.

Question 46: What are the FCC's general requirements regarding the records that must be kept by stations in the public safety radio service?

The records shall be kept in an orderly manner and in such detail that the data required are readily available. Key letters or abbreviations may be used if proper explanation is given in the record. Each entry in the records shall be signed by a person qualified to do so, one who has an actual knowledge of the facts to be recorded. No record or portion thereof shall be erased, obliterated, or willfully destroyed within the required retention period (one year). Any necessary correction may be made only by the persons originating the entry who shall strike the erroneous portion, initial the correction made, and indicate the date of the correction.

Question 47: When servicing a radio transmitter where your license is not posted, what must you carry for proper identification?

A verification card from the FCC certifying that you have a valid operator's license.

Question 48: How long must an operating log be retained when it contains an entry regarding a distress call?

Whenever an operating log contains an entry pertaining to a distress call in any way, the log in question must be retained until permission is given by the FCC to destroy it.

CHAPTER 7

Basic Radiotelephone, Part V: Element 3

Although 80 to 90 percent of the troubles encountered in mobile equipment are defective tubes, the figure for transistorized units with defective transistors is considerably less. Learn to use test equipment whenever possible; it saves valuable time and makes the job much easier. Signal tracing is ideal for isolating defective stages in complicated circuits, then voltage readings pinpoint the defective component quickly. Voltage readings on PNP transistor types should be a few tenths of a volt more negative on the base than the emitter (meter leads + on emitter, - on base), and the collector reading should be negative in relation to the emitter by about the full supply voltage. When checking NPN type transistor voltages (schematic shows the emitter arrow pointing **out** or away from the base), all polarities mentioned above are reversed. That is, the base should be a few tenths of a volt more **positive** than the emitter, and the collector would be **positive** by the approximate amount of the power supply in regard to the emitter. Burned resistors are a common failure in solid-state (transistor) circuits and usually result from shorted (punctured) transistors drawing excessive current through them. The reason for the defective transistor could be the result of a power supply surge or even overdrive.

PREVENTIVE MAINTENANCE

Mobile equipment is designed for easy servicing. Numerous test points make it possible to eliminate as suspects those sections that are performing properly. The use of quality parts throughout ensures more reliable performance, and special test equipment reduces the time spent in locating and correcting circuit problems. Preventive maintenance is recommended to eliminate or reduce the number and severity of breakdowns; in other words, to eliminate "callbacks." It is much easier to go over the unit while it is on the service bench, replacing components that are below par even still working, than to risk imminent failure on the road.

RULES & REGULATIONS

The FCC Rules and Regulations pertaining to second class radiotelephone operators are listed in this chapter in the form of extracts from the official document and in the exact wording thereof. If any question comes to mind regarding the proper meaning of the regulations, refer to the extract listed for that exact wording and check it carefully.

FINAL PREPARATION

If you feel that sufficient preparation has been made, check your progress by using the 100 sample FCC type questions in this chapter. Take a sheet of paper and mark down your choice (a), (b), (c), (d), or (e) beside each question number, but don't check your answers until you have completed the sample test. Then, by checking your answers against the list in Chapter 13, you can easily grade your progress. Brush up on any specific areas where a need is shown, and check yourself on the sample test again. If you come up with 90 percent or better, refer to the FCC district office schedule (Chapter 13) for the necessary arrangements in your area. You are ready! After arrangements have been made, look over the questions missed and refresh yourself in these sections by a careful review.

TWO WAY RADIO

Most of the stations in the public safety radio service and land mobile radio service take advantage of FM's ability to suppress noise, a particularly important consideration in mobile operations. Automobile ignition noise may not be fully suppressed, but with FM it need be reduced only to a level slightly below that of the desired signal. As the noise generated by the car limits the range of the mobile unit, it must be reduced as much as possible in order to allow reliable communications.

Probably the best way to tackle the problem is to bypass or suppress the major potential noise sources. These include the generator, voltage regulator and ignition system. Since the noise may be considered as AC, a large capacitor to ground will provide a low resistance path for the alternating component while leaving the DC in the circuit free to circulate. The capacitor should be as close to the noise source as possible, even mounted directly on the offending unit if possible. A series resistor may be used in the high-voltage part of the ignition system, since the ignition coil pulses the spark plugs at 25,000 volts or more. The exceptionally high Q of the coil causes the duration of the pulse to be long, and by inserting a series resistor of about 10K, the duration is shortened with an appreciable reduction in total noise. Battery cables sometimes serve as noise radiators and should always be as short as practical. Resistors and capacitors used as noise suppressors in mobile installations must be special types to withstand existing conditions. All capacitors have an inductance factor to a small extent, at least, and for VHF operation, the coaxial capacitor is recommended for its high resonant frequency.

Ignition noise is a sharp, continuous, popping sound which varies in frequency with the speed of the motor, but it is stronger at idling speed. The installation of a suppressor between the coil and distributor will usually eliminate the problem. If further reduction is required, install a coaxial capacitor in the primary lead to the ignition coil (from the ignition switch) and resistor spark plugs, if special radio-resistance wire was not used in your system. Capacitors should not be used in high-voltage circuits, just as the use of resistors is not permissible in low-voltage circuits.

Voltage-regulator noise is similar to plug noise, except that it lacks smooth regularity. Voltage-regulator noise stops completely when the motor is turning slowly, while the plug noise increases at this point. Correct by installing bypass capacitors on battery (BAT) and armature (ARM) terminals of the regulator.

The generator offers a whining sound which increases in frequency as the motor speed increases. By installing a bypass capacitor on the generator case (connect the capacitor lead to terminal A, the thick wire), the noise is eliminated at its source. Check the brushes and commutator for excessive sparking and clean if needed.

Instrument noise is difficult to track down, since it can be produced by the fuel, temperature and oil gauges and may be corrected only at the source—never at the dash. Connect a bypass directly to the sending unit, not at the dash. The symptom is irregular popping only when the car is moving.

Front-wheel static results from a build-up of a charge while the car is moving. Grease insulates the hub from the car body. Cure by installing grounding springs inside the front hub caps.

FCC requirements for two-way radio maintenance include a valid second-class radio-telephone operator's license before working on the transmitter or even making adjustments that could alter the frequency or power output in any way. By getting that FCC license, the door is opened to unlimited opportunities for good pay while doing clean, pleasant work in this interesting phase of electronics. Demand increases daily as more and more communications are required in the land mobile services and the search for eligible men never ceases. Looking at the equipment, receivers and transmitters differ very little from those in use in other areas of communications. The squelch, although new to some, is quite simple and it is covered thoroughly, since it is very important in mobile work.

A typical system has a base station and any desired number of mobile units. Being a fixed station, the base is headquarters and the control point for the operator to handle messages to the various mobile units in automobiles or trucks. In some cases the system is further expanded to include hand-carried units known as walkie-talkies.

Section 2.551, program defined: In order to carry out its responsibilities under the Communications Act and the various treaties and international regulations, it is necessary for the Commission to ascertain that the equipment involved is capable of meeting the technical operating standards set forth in the said statutes, treaties and the Commission's Rules and Regulations. To facilitate such determinations in those services where equipment is generally standardized, to promote the improvement of equipment and to promote the efficient use of the radio spectrum, the Commission has designed two specific procedures for securing advance approval of equipment. These procedures are designed as type approval and type acceptance. Ordinarily, type approval is based on tests conducted by Commission personnel, while type acceptance is based on data concerning the equipment submitted by the manufacturer or the individual prospective licensee. The procedures described in this subpart are intended to apply to equipment in those services which specifically require either type approval or type acceptance. These procedures may also be applied to equipment components, such as RF power amplifiers, etc., to the extent specified in the rules of the particular service in which such components will be used.

PUBLIC SAFETY RADIO SERVICE

Section 89.1, basis and purpose. (a) The basis for this part is the Communications Act of 1934, as amended, and applicable treaties and agreements to which the United States is a party. This part is issued pursuant to authority contained in Title III of the Communications Act of 1934, as amended, which vests authority in the Federal Communications Commission to regulate radio transmissions and to issue licenses for radio stations.

(b) This part is designed to provide a service of radio communication essential either to the discharge of non-Federal governmental functions or to the alleviation of an emergency endangering life or property.

Section 89.3 Definitions. For the purpose of this part, the following definitions shall be applicable:

Definitions of Services

Fire radio service. A public safety service of radio communication essential to official fire activities.

Fixed service. A service of radio communication between specified fixed points.

Forestry-conservation radio service. A public safety device of radio communication essential to forestry-conservation activities.

Highway maintenance radio service. A public safety service of radio communication essential to official highway activities.

Land mobile service. A mobile service between base stations and land mobile stations, or between land mobile stations.

Local government radio service. A service of radio communication essential to official activities of states, possessions, and territories, including counties, towns, cities, and similar governmental subdivisions.

Mobile service. A service of radio communication between mobile and land stations, or between mobile stations.

Police radio service. A public safety service of radio communication essential to official police activities.

Public safety radio services. Any service of radio communication essential either to the discharge of non-Federal government functions or the alleviation of an emergency endangering life or property, the radio transmission facilities of which are defined as fixed, land, mobile, or radiolocation stations.

Radio location. Radio determination used for purposes other than those of radio navigation. (For the purposes of this part, radiolocation includes speed measuring devices.)

Radio service. An administrative subdivision of the field of radio communication. In an engineering sense, the subdivisions may be made according to the method of operation; as for example, mobile service and fixed service. In a regulatory sense, the subdivisions may be descriptive of particular groups of licensees; as for example, the groups and subgroups of persons licensed under this part.

Safety service. A radio communication service used permanently or temporarily for the safeguarding of human life and property.

Special emergency radio service. A public safety service of radio communication essential to the alleviation of an emergency endangering life or property.

State guard radio service. A public safety service of radio communication essential to official activities of state guards or comparable organizations of states, territories, possessions, or the District of Columbia.

Definitions of Stations

Base station. A land station in the land mobile service carrying on a service with land mobile stations.

Control station. An operational fixed station, the transmissions of which are used to control, automatically, the emissions or operation of another radio station at a specified location.

Fixed station. A station in the fixed service.

Fixed relay station. An operational fixed station established for the automatic retransmission of radio communications received from either one or more fixed stations or from a combination of fixed and mobile stations and directed to a specified location.

Interzone station. A fixed station in the police radio service using radiotelegraphy (A1 emission) for communication with zone stations within the zone and with interzone stations in other zones.

Land station. A station in the mobile service not intended to be used while in motion.

Mobile station. A station in the mobile service intended to be used while in motion or during halts at unspecified points.

Mobile relay station. A base station established for the automatic retransmission of mobile service communications which originate on the transmitting frequency of the mobile stations and which are retransmitted on the receiving frequency of the mobile stations.

Operational fixed station. A fixed station, not open to public correspondence, operated by and for the sole use of those agencies operating their own radio communication facilities in the public safety, industrial, land transportation, marine, or aviation services.

Radio location mobile station. A station in the radio location service intended to be used while in motion or during halts at unspecified points.

Repeater station. An operational fixed station established for the automatic retransmission of radio communications received from any station in the mobile service.

Zone station. A fixed station in the police radio service using radiotelegraphy (A1 emission) for communication with other similar stations in the same zone and with an interzone station.

Miscellaneous Definitions

Antenna structures. The term "antenna structure" includes the radiating system, its supporting structures, and any surmounting appurtenances.

Assigned frequency. The frequency appearing on a station authorization from which the carrier frequency may deviate by an amount not to exceed that permitted by the frequency tolerance.

Authorized bandwidth. The maximum width of the band of frequencies, as specified in the authorization, to be occupied by an emission.

Bandwidth occupied by an emission. The width of the frequency band (normally specified in kilohertz) containing those frequencies upon which a total of 99 percent of the radiated power appears, extended to include any discrete frequency upon which the power is at least 0.25 percent of the total radiated power.

Carrier frequency. The frequency of the carrier.

Harmful interference. Any emission, radiation or induction which endangers the functioning of a radio navigation service or of other safety services or seriously degrades, obstructs, or repeatedly interrupts a radio communication service operating in accordance with the classifications set forth in this chapter.

Landing area. A landing area means any locality, either land or water, which is used, or intended to be used, for the landing and takeoff of aircraft, whether or not facilities are provided for shelter, servicing, or repair of aircraft, or for receiving or discharging passengers or cargo.

Station authorization. Any construction permit, license, or special temporary authorization issued by the Commission.

Section 89.51 Station authorization required. No radio transmitter shall be operated in the public safety radio services except under and in accordance with a proper station authorization granted by the Federal Communications Commission.

Section 89.53 **Procedure for obtaining a radio station authorization and for commencement of operation.** (a) Persons desiring to install and operate radio transmitting equipment should first submit an application for a radio station authorization in accordance with Section 89.59(a).

(b) When a construction permit only has been issued for a base, fixed or mobile station and installation has been completed in accordance with the terms of the construction permit and the applicable rules of the Commission, the permittee shall proceed further as follows:

(1) Notify the engineer in charge of the local radio district of the date on which the transmitter will first be tested in such a manner as to produce radiation, giving the name of the permittee, station location, call sign, and frequencies on which tests are to be conducted. This notification shall be made in writing at least two days in advance of the test day. FCC Form 456 may be used for this purpose. No reply from the radio district office is necessary before the tests are begun.

(2) After testing, but on or before the date the station is used for operational purposes, mail to the Commission in Washington, D.C., 20554, an application on FCC Form 400 or in the case of microwave station on FCC Form 402 for a license or modification of license as appropriate in the particular case. The station may thereafter be used as though licensed, pending Commission action on the license application.

(c) When a construction permit and license for a new base, fixed or mobile station are issued simultaneously, the licensee shall notify the engineer in charge of the local radio district of the date on which the transmitter will be placed in operation, giving the name of licensee, station location, call sign, and operating frequencies. This notification shall be made in writing on or before the day on which operation is commenced. FCC Form 456 may be used for this purpose.

(d) When a construction permit and modification of license for a base, fixed or mobile station are issued simultaneously, operation may be commenced without notification to the engineer in charge of the local radio district, except where operation on a new or different frequency results by reason of such modification, in which event the notification procedure set forth in paragraph (c) of this section must be observed.

Section 89.55 **Filing of applications.** (a) To assure that necessary information is supplied in a consistent manner by all persons, standard forms are prescribed for use in connection with the majority of applications and reports submitted for Commission consideration. Standard numbered forms applicable to the public safety radio services are discussed in Section 89.59, and may be obtained from the Washington, D.C., 20554, office of the Commission or from any of its engineering field offices. Concerning matters where no standard form is applicable, the procedure outlined in Section 89.61 should be followed.

(b) Any application for a radio station authorization and all correspondence relating thereto shall be submitted to the Commission's office at Washington, D.C. 20554, directed to the attention of the Secretary. An application for a commercial radio operator permit or license may be submitted to any of the Commission's engineering field offices or to the Commission's office at Washington, D.C. 20554.

(c) Unless otherwise specified, an application shall be filed at least 60 days prior to the date on which it is desired that Commission action thereon be completed. In particular, applications involving the installation of new equipment shall be filed at least 60 days prior to the contemplated installation.

(d) Failure on the part of the applicant to provide all the information required by the application form or to supply the necessary exhibits or supplementary statements may constitute a defect in the application.

(e) Applications involving operation at temporary locations:

(1) When one or more individual transmitters are intended to be operated as a base station or as a fixed station at unspecified or temporary locations for indeterminate periods, such transmitters may be considered to comprise a single station intended to be operated at temporary locations. An application for authority to operate a base station or a fixed station at temporary locations shall specify the general geographic area within which the operation will be confined. The area specified may be a city, a county or counties, or a state or states.

(2) When a base station or fixed station authorized to operate at temporary locations remains at a single location for more than one year, an application for modification of the station authorization to specify the permanent location shall be filed within 30 days after expiration of the 1-year period.

Section 89.57 Who may sign applications. (a) Except as provided in paragraph (b) of this section, applications, amendments thereto, and related statements of fact required by the Commission shall be personally signed by the applicant, if the applicant is an individual; by one of the partners, if the applicant is a partnership; by an officer, if the applicant is a corporation; or by a member who is an officer, if the applicant is an unincorporated association. Applications, amendments, and related statements of fact filed on behalf of eligible government entities, such as states and territories of the United States and political subdivisions thereof, the District of Columbia, and units of local government, including incorporated municipalities, shall be signed by such duly elected or appointed officials as may be competent to do so under the laws of the applicable jurisdiction.

(b) Applications, amendments thereto, and related statements of fact required by the Commission may be signed by the applicant's attorney in case of the applicant's physical disability or of his absence from the United States. The attorney shall, in that event, separately set forth the reason why the application is not signed by the applicant. In addition, if any matter is stated on the basis of the attorney's belief only (rather than his knowledge) he shall separately set forth his reasons for believing that such statements are true.

(c) Only the original of applications, amendments, or related statements of fact need be signed; copies may be conformed.

(d) Applications, amendments, and related statements of fact need not be signed under oath. Willful false statements made therein, however, are punishable by fine and imprisonment, U.S. Code, Title 18, Section 1001, and by appropriate administrative sanctions, including revocation of the station license pursuant to Section 312(a)(1) of the Communications Act of 1934, as amended.

Section 89.59 Standard forms to be used. (a) Except as provided in paragraph (h) of this section, a separate application shall be submitted on FCC Form 400 for the following:

(1) New station authorization for a base or fixed station.

(2) New station authorization for any required number of mobile units (including hand-carried or pack-carried units) or any required number of units of a base station or fixed station to be operated at temporary locations in the same service. Note: An application for mobile units may be combined with an application for a single base station in those cases where the mobile units will operate with that base station in a single radio communication system.

(3) License for any class of station upon completion of construction or installation in accordance with the terms and conditions set forth in the construction permit.

(4) Modification of combined construction permit and station license for changes outlined in Section 89.75(a).

(5) Modification of construction permit.

(6) Modification of station license.

Any of the foregoing applications will, upon approval and authentication of the Commission, be returned to the applicant as a specifically designated type of authorization.

(b) When the holder of a station authorization desires to assign to another person the privilege to construct or use a radio station, he shall submit to the Commission a letter setting forth his desire to assign all rights, title, and interest in and to such authorization, stating the call sign and location of the station. This letter shall also include a statement that the assigner will submit his current station authorization for cancellation upon completion of the assignment. Enclosed with this letter shall be an application for assignment of authorization on FCC Form 400 prepared by and in the name of the person to whom the station is being assigned.

(c) (Reserved)

(d) A separate application shall be submitted on FCC Form 703 whenever it is proposed to change, as by transfer of stock-ownership, the control of a corporate permittee or licensee.

(e) An application not submitted on a standard form prescribed by the Commission is considered to be an informal application. Each informal application shall be submitted in duplicate, normally in letter form, and with the original properly signed. Each application shall be clear and complete within itself as to the facts presented and the action desired.

(f) FCC Form 456 "Notification of Completion of Radio Station Construction" may be used to advise the engineer in charge of the local district office that construction of the station is complete and that operational tests will begin.

(g) Application for renewal of station license shall be submitted on FCC 405A. All applications for renewal must be made during the license term and should be filed within 90 days but not later than 30 days prior to the end of the license term. In any case in which the licensee has, in accordance with the provisions of this chapter, made timely and sufficient application for renewal of license, no license with reference to any activity of a continuing nature shall expire until such application shall have been finally determined.

(h) Application for construction permit, license, modification or assignment thereof for an operational fixed station using frequencies above 952 MHz (a so-called microwave station) shall be submitted on FCC Form 402.

Section 89.75 Changes in authorized stations. Authority for certain changes in authorized stations must be obtained from the Commission before these changes are made, while other changes do not require prior Commission approval. The following paragraphs describe the conditions under which prior Commission approval is or is not necessary.

(a) Proposed changes which will result in operation inconsistent with any of the terms of the current authorization require that an application for modification of construction permit and-or license be submitted to the Commission and shall be submitted on FCC Form 400, or, in the case of microwave stations, on FCC Form 402, and shall be accompanied by exhibits and supplementary statements as required by Section 89.63.

(b) (Reserved)

(c) Proposed changes which will not depart from any of the terms of the outstanding authorization for the station involved may be made without prior Commission approval. Included in such changes is the substitution of various makes of transmitting equipment at any station, providing the particular equipment to be installed is included in the Commission's "List of Equipment Acceptable for Licensing" and designated for use in the public safety, industrial, and land transportation radio services and providing the substitute equipment employs the same type of emission and does not exceed the power limitations as set forth in the station authorization.

Frequency range MHz	All fixed and base stations	All mobile stations	
		Over 3 watts	3 watts or less
	Percent	Percent	Percent
Below 25	0.01	0.01	0.02
25 to 50	.002	.002	.005
50 to 1000	.0005 (1)	.0005	.005

Table 7-1. Carrier frequency tolerances.

Section 89.103 Frequency stability. (a) A permitee or licensee in these services shall maintain the carrier frequency of each authorized transmitter within the percentage of the assigned frequency shown in Table 7-1.

(b) For the purpose of determining the frequency tolerance applicable to a particular transmitter in accordance with the foregoing provisions of this section, the power of a transmitter shall be the maximum rated plate power input to its final radio frequency stage, as specified by the manufacturer.

Section 89.107 Emission limitations. (a) Each authorization issued to a station operating in these services will show, as a prefix to the emission classification, a figure specifying the maximum authorized bandwidth in kilohertz to be occupied by the emission. The specified band shall contain those frequencies upon which a total percent of the radiated power appears, extended to include any discrete frequency upon which the power is at least 0.25 percent of the total radiated power. Any radiation in excess of the limits specified in paragraph (c) of this section is considered to be an unauthorized emission.

(b) The maximum authorized bandwidth of emission corresponding to the types of emission specified in Section 89.105 (a) and (c), and the maximum authorized frequency deviation in the case of frequency or phase modulated emission, shall be as follows:

(1) For all type A3 emissions, the maximum authorized bandwidth shall be 8 kHz.

(2) For all F3 emission, the maximum authorized bandwidth and maximum authorized frequency deviation shall be as shown in Table 7-2.

(3) For all type A1 emissions, the maximum authorized bandwidth shall be 0.25 kHz.

(c) The mean power of emissions shall be attenuated below the mean output power of the transmitter in accordance with the following schedule:

(1) On any frequency removed from the assigned frequency by more than 50 percent up to and including 100 percent of the authorized bandwidths: at least 25 decibels.

(2) On any frequency removed from the assigned frequency by more than 100 percent up to and including 250 percent of the authorized bandwidth: at least 35 decibels.

(3) On any frequency removed from the assigned frequency by more than 250 percent of the authorized bandwidth: at least 43 plus 10 $\log_{10}$ (mean output power in watts) decibels or 80 decibels, whichever is the lesser attenuation.

Frequency band (MHz)	Authorized bandwidth (kHz)	Frequency deviation (kHz)
25 to 50	20	5
50 to 150	20	5
150 to 450	20	5
450 to 1000	40	15

Table 7-2. Bandwidth and frequency deviation maximum for F3 emissions.

(d) When an unauthorized emission results in harmful interference, the Commission may, in its discretion, require appropriate technical changes in equipment to alleviate the interference.

Section 89.109 Modulation requirements. (a) The maximum audio frequency required for satisfactory radiotelephone intelligibility in these services is considered to be 3000 Hz.

(b) When amplitude modulation is used for telephony, the modulation percentage shall be sufficient to provide efficient communication and normally shall be maintained above 70 percent on peaks, but shall not exceed 100 percent on negative peaks.

(c) Each transmitter shall be equipped with a device which automatically prevents modulation in excess of that specified in this subpart which may be caused by greater than normal audio level—provided, however, that this requirement shall not be applicable to transmitters authorized to operate as mobile stations with a maximum plate power input to the final radio frequency stage of 3 watts or less.

(d) Each transmitter in the frequency ranges 25 to 50, 150.8 to 162, and 450 to 460 MHz shall be equipped with an audio low-pass filter. Such a filter shall be installed between the modulation limiter and the modulated stage and shall meet the specifications contained in paragraph (h) of this section. The provisions of this paragraph do not apply to transmitters of licensed radio communications systems operated wholly within the limits of one or more of the territories or possessions of the United States, or Alaska or Hawaii.

(e) Each transmitter in the frequency ranges 72.0 - 73.0 and 75.4 - 76.0 MHz shall be equipped with a device which automatically prevents modulation in excess of that specified in this subpart which may be caused by a greater than normal audio level.

(f) Each transmitter in the frequency ranges 72.0 - 73.0 and 75.4 - 76.0 MHz shall be equipped with an audio low-pass filter. The required filter shall be installed between the modulation limiter and the modulated stage and shall meet the specifications contained in paragraph (h) of this section.

(g) Each transmitter in the frequency range 73.0 - 74.6 MHz first authorized after July 1, 1950, must be equipped with a device which automatically prevents modulation in excess of that specified in this subpart which may be caused by a greater than normal audio level. An audio low-pass filter is not required regardless of the date of authorization.

(h) At audio frequencies between 3 kHz and 15 kHz, the low-pass filter required by the provisions of paragraphs (d) and (f) of this section shall have an attenuation greater than the attenuation of 1 kHz by at least:

$$40 \log_{10} (f/3) \text{ decibels}$$

where f is the audio frequency in kilohertz. At audio frequencies above 15 kHz, the attenuation shall be at least 28 decibels greater than the attenuation at 1 kHz.

Section 89.113 Transmitter control requirements. (a) Each transmitter shall be so installed and protected that it is not accessible to or capable of operation by persons other than those duly authorized by the licensee.

(b) A control point is an operating position which meets all of the following conditions:

(1) The position must be under the control and supervision of the licensee;

(2) It is a position at which the monitoring facilities required by this section are installed;

(3) It is a position at which a person immediately responsible for the operation of the transmitter is stationed.

(c) Each station which is not authorized for unattended operation shall be provided with a control point, the location of which will be specified in the license. Unattended stations may be provided with a control point if authorized by the Commission. In urban areas the location will be specified "same as transmitter" unless the control point is at a street address different from that of the transmitter. In rural areas the location will be specified "same as transmitter" unless the control point is more than 500 feet from the transmitter, in which case the approximate location will be specified in distance and direction from the transmitter in terms of feet and geographical quadrant, respectively. It will be assumed that the location of the control point is the same as the location of the transmitter unless the application includes a request for a different location described in appropriate terms as indicated in this paragraph. Authority must be obtained from the Commission for the installation of additional control points.

(d) A dispatch point is any position from which messages may be transmitted under the supervision of the person at a control point who is responsible for the operation of the transmitter. Dispatch points may be installed without authorization.

(e) At each control point, the following facilities shall be installed:

(1) A carrier-operated device that will provide a continuous visual indication when the transmitter is radiating; or, in lieu thereof, a pilot lamp or meter which will provide a continuous visual indication when the transmitter control circuits have been placed in a condition to produce radiation— provided, however, that the provisions of this subparagraph shall not apply to hand-carried or pack-carried transmitters or to transmitters installed on motorcycles;

(2) Equipment to permit the person responsible for the operation of the transmitter to aurally monitor all transmissions originating at dispatch points under his supervision;

(3) Facilities which will permit the person responsible for the operation of the transmitter either to disconnect the dispatch point circuits from the transmitter or to render the transmitter inoperative from any dispatch point under his supervision;

(4) Facilities which will permit the person responsible for the operation of the transmitter to turn the transmitter carrier on and off at will.

Section 89.115 Transmitter measurements. (a) The licensee of each station shall employ a suitable procedure to determine that the carrier frequency of each transmitter, authorized to operate with a plate input power to the final radio frequency stage in excess of 3 watts, is maintained within the tolerance prescribed in this part. This determination shall be made, and the results thereof entered in the station records, in accordance with the following:

(1) When the transmitter is initially installed;

(2) When any change is made in the transmitter which may affect the carrier frequency or the stability thereof;

(3) At intervals not to exceed one year for transmitters employing crystal-controlled oscillators.

(4) At intervals not to exceed one month for transmitters not employing crystal-controlled oscillators.

(b) The licensee of each station shall employ a suitable procedure to determine that the plate power input to the final radio frequency stage of each base station or fixed station transmitter, authorized to operate with a plate input power to the final radio frequency stage in excess of 3 watts, does not exceed the maximum figure specified on the current station authorization. Where the transmitter is so constructed that a direct measurement of plate current in the final radio frequency stage is not practicable, the plate input power may be determined from a measurement of the cathode current in the final radio frequency stage. When the plate input to the final radio frequency stage is determined from a measurement of the cathode current, the required entry shall indicate clearly the quantities that were measured, the measured values thereof, and the method of determining the plate power input from the measured values. This determination shall be made and the results thereof entered in the station records in accordance with the following:

(1) When the transmitter is initially installed;

(2) When any change is made in the transmitter which may increase the transmitter power input;

(3) At intervals not to exceed one year.

(c) The licensee of each station shall employ a suitable procedure to determine that the modulation of each transmitter, authorized to operate with a plate input power to the final radio frequency stage in excess of 3 watts, does not exceed the limits specified in this part. This determination shall be made and the results thereof entered in the station records in accordance with the following:

(1) When the transmitter is initially installed;

(2) When any change is made in the transmitter which may affect the modulation characteristics;

(3) At intervals not to exceed one year.

(d) The determinations required by paragraphs (a), (b) and (c) of this section may, at the option of the licensee, be made by any qualified engineering measurement service, in which case the required record entries shall show the name and address of the engineering measurement service as well as the name of the person making the measurements.

(e) In the case of mobile transmitters, the determinations required by paragraphs (a) and (c) of this section may be made at a test or service bench; provided, the measurements are made under load conditions equivalent to actual operating conditions, and provided further, that after installation the transmitter is given a routine check to determine that it is capable of being satisfactorily received by an appropriate receiver.

Section 89.117 Acceptability of transmitters for licensing. (a) From time to time the Commission publishes a list of equipment entitled "Radio Equipment List, Part C, List of Equipment Acceptable for Licensing." Copies of this list are available for inspection at the Commission's Offices in Washington, D.C., and at each of its field offices. This list includes type approved and type accepted equipment and equipment which was included in this list on May 16, 1955. Such equipment will continue to be included on the list unless it is removed therefrom by Commission action.

(b) Except for transmitters used at developmental stations and transmitters authorized as of January 1, 1965, in police zone and interzone stations, each transmitter utilized by a station authorized for operation under this part must be of a type which is included on the Commission's current "List of Equipment Acceptable for Licensing" and designated for use under this part or be of a type which has been type accepted by the Commission for use under this part.

(c) Transmitters to be operated in any of the frequency bands between 952 and 12700 MHz, except the 8400-8500 MHz band, authorized under this part shall be type accepted if specified in an application filed after July 20, 1962, except that equipment authorized prior thereto may continue to be used, provided such operation does not result in harmful interference to other stations or systems which are conforming to the microwave technical standards in Section 89.121.

Section 89.153 Station identification. (a) Except as provided in paragraph (b) of this section, the required identification for stations in these services shall be the assigned call signal.

(b) In lieu of meeting the requirements of paragraph (a) of this section, mobile units in the police, fire, forestry-conservation, highway maintenance, and local government radio services operating above 30 MHz may identify by means of an identifier other than the assigned call signal—provided, that such identifier contain, as a minimum, the name of the governmental subdivision under which the unit is licensed; that the identifier is not composed of letters or letters and digits arranged in a manner which could be confused with an assigned radio station call signal; **and provided further** that the licensee notifies, in writing, the engineer in charge of the district in which the unit operates concerning the specific identifiers being used by the mobile units.

(c) Nothing in this section shall be construed as prohibiting the transmission of additional station or unit identifiers which may be necessary for systems operation—provided, however, that such additional identifiers shall not be composed of letters or letters and digits arranged in a manner which could be confused with an assigned radio station call signal.

(d) Except as indicated in paragraphs (e), (f), and (g) of this section, each station in these services shall transmit the required identification at the end of each transmission or exchange of transmissions, or once each 30 minutes of the operating period, as the licensee may prefer.

(e) A mobile station authorized to the licensee of the associated base station and which transmits only on the transmitting frequency of the associated base station is not required to transmit any identification.

(f) Except as indicated in paragraph (e) of this section, a mobile station shall transmit an identification at the end of each transmission or exchange of transmissions, or once each 30 minutes of the operating period, as the licensee may prefer. Where election is made to transmit the identification at 30-minute intervals, a single mobile unit in each general geographic area may be assigned the responsibility for such transmission and thereby eliminate any necessity for every unit of the mobile station to transmit the identification. For the purpose of this paragraph the term "each general geographic area" means an area not smaller than a single city or county and not larger than a single district of a State where the district is administratively established for the service in which the radio system operates.

Section 89.175 Content of station records. Each licensee of a station in these services shall maintain records in accordance with the following:

(a) For all stations, the results and dates of the transmitter measurements required by these rules and the name of the person or persons making the measurements.

(b) For all stations, when service or maintenance duties are performed, the responsible operator shall sign and date an entry in the station record giving:

(1) Pertinent details of all duties performed by him or under his supervision;

(2) His name and address, and

(3) The class, serial number and expiration date of his license—provided that the information called for by subparagraphs (2) and (3) of this paragraph, so long as it remains the same, need be entered only once in the station record at any station where the responsible operator is regularly employed on a full-time basis and at which his license is properly posted.

(c) For all base and fixed stations, except such stations which are authorized to be operated at temporary locations or for unattended operation, the name or names of persons responsible for the operation of the transmitting equipment each day, together with the period of their duty. Each such person shall sign—not initial—the record both when coming on and when going off duty.

(d) (Reserved)

(e) For stations whose antenna or antenna supporting structure is required to be illuminated, a record must be kept in accordance with the following:

(1) The time the tower lights are turned on and off each day if manually controlled.

(2) The time the daily check of proper operation of the tower lights was made.

(3) In the event of any observed or otherwise known failure of a tower light:

(i) Nature of such failure.

(ii) Date and time the failure was observed, or otherwise noted.

(iii) Date, time and nature of the adjustments, repairs, or replacements that were made.

(iv) Identification of the Flight Service Station (FAA) notified of the failure of any code or rotating beacon light or top light not corrected within 30 minutes, and the date and time such notice was given.

(v) Date and time notice was given to the Flight Service Station (FAA) that the required illumination was resumed.

(4) Upon the completion of the periodic inspection required at least once each three months:

(i) The date of the inspection and the condition of all tower lights and associated tower lighting control devices, indicators and alarm systems.

(ii) Any adjustments, replacements, or repairs made to insure compliance with the lighting requirements and the date such adjustments, replacements, or repairs were made.

Section 89.177 Form of station records. (a) The records shall be kept in an orderly manner and in such detail that the data required are readily available. Key letters or abbreviations may be used if the proper meaning or explanation is set forth in the record.

(b) Each entry in the records shall be signed by a person qualified to do so, one having actual knowledge of the facts to be recorded.

(c) No record or portion thereof shall be erased, obliterated, or willfully destroyed within the required retention period. Any necessary correction may be made only by the persons originating the entry who shall strike out the erroneous portion, initial the correction made and indicate the date of the correction.

ELEMENT 3
Basic Radiotelephone Sample Test Questions

1. What other expression would describe "difference of potential"?
   - (a) Electromotive force.
   - (b) IR drop.
   - (c) Voltage drop.
   - (d) EMF.
   - (e) Any of the above.

2. What is the basic unit of EMF?
   - (a) Coulomb
   - (b) Ohm
   - (c) Meter
   - (d) Volt
   - (e) Watt

3. What would be used to measure current in a circuit?
   - (a) A voltmeter.
   - (b) An ammeter.
   - (c) An ohmmeter.
   - (d) A potentiometer.
   - (e) None of the above.

4. What governs the ability of a material to conduct electricity?
   - (a) The number of free electrons.
   - (b) The type of insulation.
   - (c) Its flexibility.

(d) Its diameter.

(e) Its heat resistance.

5. What is a hertz?

    (a) An ampere.

    (b) A megohm.

    (c) A cycle.

    (d) A kilovolt.

    (e) None of the above.

6. What is the value of a resistor colored brown, green, brown?

    (a) 50 ohms.

    (b) 100 ohms.

    (c) 150 ohms.

    (d) 151 ohms.

    (e) None of the above.

7. What is "skin effect"?

    (a) The resistance to high-frequency current in the center of a conductor.

    (b) The insulation losses in a conductor.

    (c) The average reactance between two inductors.

    (d) The resistance to high values of direct current in conductors.

    (e) The effect of a nonconductor on audio voltages.

8. How many degrees would 1 hertz represent?

    (a) 45

    (b) 90

    (c) zero

    (d) 270

    (e) 360

9. What should be used to replace a condenser?

    (a) A capacitor.

    (b) A resistor.

    (c) An inductor.

    (d) A battery.

    (e) None of the above.

10. What is impedance?

    (a) The resistance offered by a capacitor to current flow.

    (b) The resistance offered by an inductance to the flow of current.

    (c) The total opposition to current flow at a specific frequency.

    (d) The opposition of an inductor to changes in current.

    (e) The opposition of a voltage divider to current changes.

11. What is the impedance of an ideal parallel resonant circuit?

    (a) Zero.

    (b) Infinite.

    (c) Twice the value of a series resonant circuit.

(d) One-half the value of a series resonant circuit.

(e) The reciprocal of a series resonant circuit.

12. **A relay having a resistance of 1,000 ohms requires a current of 50 mA from a 100-volt source; what value of series resistance is needed?**

(a) 150 ohms

(b) 1,500 ohms

(c) 15,000 ohms

(d) 100 ohms

(e) 1,000 ohms

13. **Why are interstage leads shielded?**

(a) To control stage gain.

(b) To reduce distortion.

(c) To increase magnetic coupling.

(d) To reduce magnetic coupling.

(e) None of the above.

14. **What is the advantage of matching impedances?**

(a) Reduces harmonics.

(b) Provides maximum power transfer.

(c) Eliminates parasitic oscillations.

(d) Reduces overmodulation.

(e) Eliminates the need for neutralization.

15. **What controls the amount of voltage induced in a conductor?**

(a) The strength of the magnetic field it cuts.

(b) The length of the conductor cutting the lines of force.

(c) The speed at which it cuts the lines of force.

(d) The angle between the conductor and the lines of force.

(e) Any of the above.

16. **What is the total resistance of three 150-ohm resistors connected in parallel?**

(a) 450 ohms.

(b) 300 ohms.

(c) 100 ohms.

(d) 50 ohms.

(e) 75 ohms.

17. **What is the actual value of a 10K resistor?**

(a) 10,000 ohms.

(b) 10 ohms.

(c) 100 ohms.

(d) 1,000 ohms.

(e) 10,000,000 ohms.

18. **What is the total value of two 0.005-mfd (uF) capacitors connected in series?**

(a) 0.010 uF

(b) 0.0001 uF

(c) 0.1 uF

(d) 0.0025 uF

(e) 0.00025 uF

19. If we change the 0.005-uF capacitor to picofarads how should the decimal point be moved?

(a) Six places to the left.

(b) Six places to the right.

(c) Three places to the right.

(d) Nine places to the left.

(e) Nine places to the right.

20. What effect does increasing the Q have on a tuned circuit?

(a) It increases the bandwidth.

(b) It decreases the gain.

(c) It decreases the bandwidth.

(d) It causes distortion and radiation.

(e) It inverts the output waveform.

21. What would cause the plates of a vacuum tube rectifier to become red hot?

(a) Shorted filter capacitor.

(b) Grounded filter choke.

(c) Shorted bleeder resistor.

(d) Short in the voltage divider or load.

(e) All of the above.

22. Which of the following could prolong the life of a vacuum tube?

(a) Increased filament voltage.

(b) Increased screen current.

(c) Excessive plate current.

(d) Insufficient grid bias.

(e) Insufficient filament voltage.

23. When will the current lag the voltage by 45 degrees?

(a) In a circuit having equal resistive and inductive reactance.

(b) In a circuit with equal resistive and capacitive reactance.

(c) A circuit with capacitive reactance and no resistive reactance.

(d) A circuit with inductive reactance but no resistance.

(e) In a circuit with equal capacitive and inductive reactance.

24. What is the main advantage of a tetrode over a triode?

(a) Greater voltage gain.

(b) Neutralization is not necessary.

(c) Distortion factor is reduced.

(d) Power output is considerably greater.

(e) Any of the above.

25. If a coil with an inductance of 100 millihenrys (mH) and 500 turns has 200 turns added, what is the new value of inductance?
> (a) 1,500 mH
> (b) 1,200 mH
> ⌐(c) 180 mH
> (d) 120 mH
> (e) 140 mH

26. How could low-impedance headphones be properly connected to a high-impedance plate circuit?
> (a) With a matching stub.
> (b) With a low-loss transmission line.
> (c) By connecting an RFC in series.
> (d) Through a modulation transformer.
> (e) With an output transformer.

27. If a wattmeter reads 220 watts, what power is used in 15 hours?
> (a) 330 watt-hours.
> (b) 33 kilowatt-hours.
> (c) 3,300W.
> ⌐(d) 3.3 kilowatt-hours.
> (e) 2,200W.

28. If the prefix "meg" is 1,000,000, what is micro?
> (a) 0.000001
> (b) 0.00001
> (c) 0.0001
> (d) 0.001
> (e) 0.0000001

29. How may feedback be prevented in audio amplifiers with a common power supply?
> (a) By reducing the plate voltage.
> (b) Increasing the grid bias.
> (c) Reducing the screen resistor value.
> (d) Increasing the value of the cathode bypass capacitor.
> (e) By using decoupling resistors and capacitors.

30. What is the negative electrode of a lead-acid storage battery?
> (a) Monel metal.
> (b) Pure nickel.
> (c) Pure sponge lead.
> (d) Pure zinc.
> (e) Lead peroxide.

31. What is the electrolyte in a lead-acid storage battery?
> (a) Vinegar and water.
> (b) Sulphuric acid and water.
> (c) Nitric acid and distilled water.

(d) Sodium hydroxide.

(e) Acetic acid and carbon tetrachloride.

32. How may a storage battery be checked for condition of charge?

    (a) A hydrometer.

    (b) A VTVM.

    (c) A voltohmmeter.

    (d) An ammeter.

    (e) None of the above.

33. What is the value of a mica capacitor, reading from left to right top row (white, yellow, violet), second row (green, silver, brown)?

    (a) 0.047 uF, plus or minus 20 percent.

    (b) 947 pF, plus or minus 10 percent.

    (c) 470 pF, plus or minus 10 percent.

    (d) 940 pF, plus or minus 5 percent.

    (e) 9,400 pF, plus or minus 10 percent

34. If a sine wave measures 150 volts peak, what is the effective voltage?

    (a) 135.0 volts.

    (b) 95.4 volts.

    (c) 212.1 volts.

    (d) 106.2 volts.

    (e) 75.1 volts.

35. What would replace the bleeder if more than one output is needed from the power supply?

    (a) A bridge rectifier.

    (b) A tapped filter choke.

    (c) A voltage divider.

    (d) A swinging choke.

    (e) A mercury-vapor rectifier.

36. What problem would result from an open bleeder resistor?

    (a) Improved regulation.

    (b) Choke overheating.

    (c) Rectifier damage.

    (d) Very little regulation.

    (e) Higher hum level.

37. What is the phase relationship between the grid and plate of a triode?

    (a) 0 degrees.

    (b) 360 degrees.

    (c) 180 degrees.

    (d) 270 degrees.

    (e) 90 degrees.

38. What is the main advantage of a Class B amplifier over one operating Class C?

(a) Greater harmonic output.
(b) More linear output.
(c) Greater plate efficiency.
(d) More economical.
(e) Greater stability.

39. What is an advantage of the push-pull amplifier?
(a) Even-order harmonics are cancelled.
(b) Odd-order harmonics are cancelled.
(c) Fundamental and other odd harmonics are cancelled.
(d) High-order harmonics are cancelled.
(e) Only the funamental is left in the output.

40. What is the cause of frequency shift?
(a) High plate voltage.
(b) Overmodulation.
(c) High screen voltage.
(d) Insufficient regulation.
(e) Excessive biasing.

41. Overmodulation usually causes:
(a) Attenuation of the lower sideband.
(b) Suppression of the carrier.
(c) Increased bandwidth.
(d) Improved signal-to-noise ratio.
(e) Higher noise level.

42. What advantage does grid modulation have over plate modulation?
(a) Offers better linearity.
(b) Requires much less audio drive.
(c) Much easier to control.
(d) Provides better stability.
(e) Overrides noise better.

43. Speaking of transistors, what is the "flow of holes"?
(a) Movement of positive carriers.
(b) Movement of negative carriers.
(c) Flow of electrons.
(d) Junction current flow.
(e) Reverse bias current.

44. What is the output power of a transmitter with 1.6 amps antenna current at a resistance of 50 ohms?
(a) 80 watts
(b) 128 watts
(c) 4,000 watts
(d) 96.4 watts
(e) 91.2 watts

45. What is the purpose of diversity reception?
(a) Practically eliminates fading.
(b) Eliminates image frequencies.
(c) Reduces electrical interference.

(d) Improves quality.

(e) Overrides weak signals.

46. What is the effect of an open cathode bypass capacitor on an audio amplifier?

(a) Increased output, improved quality.

(b) Less output, better quality.

(c) Greater output, some distortion.

(d) Practically no effect.

(e) Tube would be biased to cutoff.

47. What effect would a shorted plate bypass capacitor have on an amplifier?

(a) Output current would rise.

(b) Output voltage would drop to zero.

(c) Tube would be damaged.

(d) Cathode resistor would burn out.

(e) None of the above.

48. What is the mark of a Colpitts oscillator?

(a) Split tank inductance.

(b) Split tank capacitance.

(c) Isolation of the tank from the load.

(d) Unusual feedback loop.

(e) The quartz crystal.

49. What governs the speed of a DC series type motor?

(a) The frequency of the source.

(b) The strength of the field.

(c) The load.

(d) The applied voltage.

(e) None of the above.

50. What is the function of the commutator in a DC generator?

(a) Changes AC to DC.

(b) Controls the speed.

(c) Reduces the current on field windings.

(d) Prevents armature coils from overheating.

(e) Provides a smoothing action.

51. Where is the suppressor grid located?

(a) Between the screen grid and plate.

(b) Between the control grid and plate.

(c) Between the control grid and screen grid.

(d) Between the cathode and control grid.

(e) Between the cathode and filament.

52. What potential is supplied to the suppressor grid?

(a) Same as the screen grid.

(b) Slightly higher than the screen grid.

(c) Lower than the plate voltage.

(d) Higher than the control grid.

(e) Same as the cathode.

53. Which audio stage supplies information to the final RF amplifier?
    (a) Damper
    (b) Modulator
    (c) Limiter
    (d) Oscillator
    (e) Mixer

54. What may cause excessive grid current fluctuation during plate tuning?
    (a) Insufficient grid bias.
    (b) Poor voltage regulation.
    (c) Improper grid drive.
    (d) Improper neutralization.
    (e) None of the above.

55. What is "type approval" equipment?
    (a) Manufacturer's data submitted to FCC.
    (b) Tested by a licensed operator.
    (c) Tests by FCC personnel.
    (d) Test approved by an installation agent.
    (e) Approved and tested by the licensee.

56. How often should the carrier frequency of a 3-KW crystal-controlled transmitter be checked?
    (a) At least once a year.
    (b) At least once a month.
    (c) Twice a year.
    (d) Once a week.
    (e) Every 24 hours.

57. What is the maximum bandwidth for an AM broadcast station?
    (a) 2 kHz
    (b) 4 kHz
    (c) 8 kHz
    (d) 10 kHz
    (e) 20 kHz

58. What is required to prevent frequency drift in the crystal oscillator?
    (a) Low temperature operation.
    (b) Constant temperature.
    (c) Maximum crystal current.
    (d) Excessive feedback.
    (e) Any of the above.

59. What happens when excitation is lost in a Class C amplifier with grid leak bias?
    (a) The output increases.
    (b) Plate current is excessive.
    (c) Plate current drops to a low level.

(d) Self-oscillation takes place.

(e) Output is distorted.

60. What causes self-oscillation in an audio amplifier?

(a) Open grid resistor.

(b) Defective bypass capacitor.

(c) Leaky filter capacitor.

(d) Gassy tube.

(e) Any of the above.

61. What potential is required to bias a Class A amplifier?

(a) Positive

(b) Grid leak bias.

(c) No bias.

(d) Negative.

(e) Bias to cutoff.

62. What class of amplifier is most efficient?

(a) Class A

(b) Class AB

(c) Class B

(d) Class C

(e) None of the above.

63. What is the function of the screen grid?

(a) Decreases secondary emission.

(b) Reduces interelectrode inductance.

(c) Eliminates harmonic generation.

(d) Increases secondary emission.

(e) Lowers interelectrode capacitance.

64. What is the result of plate current reaching its maximum level?

(a) Plate saturation.

(b) Plate resonance.

(c) Demodulation.

(d) Parasitic oscillations.

(e) Plate cutoff.

65. What is the approximate efficiency of a Class A amplifier?

(a) 100 percent.

(b) 95 percent.

(c) 70 percent.

(d) 50 percent.

(e) 20 percent.

66. What is the output voltage of the usual primary cell?

(a) 4.5 volts.

(b) 1.5 volts.

(c) 2.1 volts.

(d) 9.0 volts.

(e) 22.5 volts.

67. What is a common type meter movement?

(a) Faraday
(b) Edison
(c) D'Arsonval
(d) Miller
(e) Marconi

68. Which of the following describes a primary cell?
    (a) Lead-acid cell.
    (b) A rechargeable cell.
    (c) A wet cell.
    (d) Large current cell.
    (e) None of the above.

69. Lightning is a type of:
    (a) Pulse modulation.
    (b) Phase modulation.
    (c) Frequency modulation.
    (d) Amplitude modulation.
    (e) Harmonic radiation.

70. How is field strength normally expressed?
    (a) Joules per square meter.
    (b) Microvolts per meter.
    (c) Microvolts per centimeter.
    (d) Kilowatts per mile.
    (e) Reactance per mile.

71. What is the bias level of a Class C amplifier?
    (a) Slightly positive.
    (b) Slightly negative.
    (c) Well below cutoff.
    (d) The cutoff value.
    (e) Zero.

72. What frequencies are covered by the high-frequency (HF) band?
    (a) 30 to 300 MHz.
    (b) 3 to 30 MHz.
    (c) 30 to 300 kHz.
    (d) 3 to 30 kHz.
    (e) 300 to 3,000 kHz.

73. What is referred to as an A5 transmission?
    (a) Television.
    (b) FM telephony.
    (c) AM telephony.
    (d) AM telegraphy.
    (e) Unmodulated AM.

74. What is the meter reading shown in Fig. 7-1?
    (a) 0.0258 volt
    (b) 2580 volts
    (c) 25,800 volts

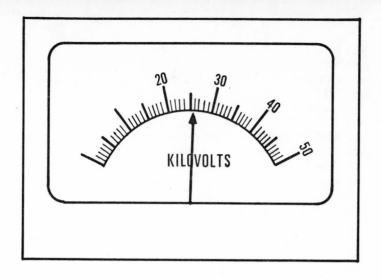

Fig. 7-1. High-voltage meter.

(d) 258,000 volts
(e) 2,580,000 volts

75. What is the effect of a decoupling circuit?
    (a) Introduces oscillations.
    (b) Improves regulation.
    (c) Provides better transfer of power.
    (d) Provides interstage shielding.
    (e) Isolates stages from each other.

76. What is the purpose of the limiter in an FM receiver?
    (a) Limits intermediate frequency bandwidth.
    (b) Removes amplitude variations.
    (c) Establishes AVC level.
    (d) Controls audio peaks.
    (e) Prevents overmodulation distortion.

77. What is the function of a traveling-wave tube?
    (a) UHF amplifier.
    (b) VHF oscillator.
    (c) FM modulator.
    (d) AM buffer amplifier.
    (e) LF intermediate-frequency amplifier.

78. What problem results from using long, horizontal waveguide sections?
    (a) Modes overlap.
    (b) Reflections are caused.
    (c) Moisture accumulates.

(d) Difficult to match impedances.

(e) Signal losses are increased.

79. **What is gained by the use of a capacitor input filter in place of the choke input type?**

    (a) Higher DC peak voltage.

    (b) Much improved regulation.

    (c) Lower ripple content.

    (d) Easier to maintain.

    (e) Less filtering required.

80. **If a transformer has more turns on the primary than the secondary, it would be called a:**

    (a) Push-pull transformer.

    (b) Step-down transformer.

    (c) Step-up transformer.

    (d) Modulation transformer.

    (e) Power transformer.

81. **Which type microphone requires a DC source?**

    (a) Crystal microphone.

    (b) Dynamic microphone.

    (c) Carbon microphone.

    (d) Ribbon microphone.

    (e) Ceramic microphone.

82. **What is a desirable quality of the ribbon type microphone?**

    (a) Has a wide frequency range.

    (b) Rugged construction.

    (c) High output level.

    (d) Low-impedance output.

    (e) All of the above.

83. **What components form an RC circuit?**

    (a) Resistor and a coil.

    (b) Resistor and a choke.

    (c) Resistor and a capacitor.

    (d) Relay and capacitor.

    (e) Relay and a coil.

84. **What is pre-emphasis?**

    (a) Low audio frequencies amplified more.

    (b) High audio frequencies amplified more.

    (c) High audio frequencies attenuated.

    (d) Low audio frequencies attenuated.

    (e) Lows attenuated, high frequencies boosted.

85. **What is "high-level" modulation?**

    (a) Modulation level over 100 percent.

    (b) Modulation input to the plate circuit of the final amplifier.

    (c) A modulation percentage below 85.

(d) When two modulators are used in parallel.

(e) When modulation is introduced in the grid of the final.

— 86. When an AM transmitter is modulated 100 percent with a sinusoidal tone, what is the percentage increase in antenna current?

(a) 22.5 percent.

(b) 25.5 percent.

(c) 60 percent.

(d) 85 percent.

(e) 100 percent.

—87. What characteristics of an audio tone determine the modulation percentage in an FM transmitter?

(a) Amplitude and phase of the tone.

(b) Amplitude and frequency of the tone.

(c) Only the frequency of the modulating tone.

(d) Only the phase of the modulating tone.

(e) The pulse interval of the tone.

— 88. In a quarter-wave transmission line, which of the following characteristics is not true?

(a) When shorting the far end, the input impedance is infinite.

(b) When the far end is terminated in an open circuit, the input is extremely low.

(c) A quarter-wave section always repeats its load.

(d) In the quarter-wave section, the input impedance reverses the output impedance.

(e) The greater the value of the terminating resistance, the lower the input impedance will be.

— 89. What is the advantage of terminating a transmission line in an impedance value equal to its characteristic impedance?

(a) Offers maximum power transfer.

(b) Greatly reduces line radiation.

(c Provides a 1:1 current ratio without losses.

(d) Provides an excellent standing wave ratio.

(e) All of the above.

— 90. What is the current in a 72-ohm transmission line witn an input of 10,000 watts?

(a) 12.38 amperes.

(b) 23.56 amperes.

(c) 11.78 amperes.

(d) 13.88 amperes.

(e) 138.8 amperes.

— 91. What is the purpose of using top loading in a standard broadcast antenna?

(a) Controls the power output.

(b) Increases the effective height of the antenna.

(c) Decreases the effective height of the antenna.

(d) Improves the vertical field intensity.

(e) Produces a directional radiation.

92. Which efficiency factor would be used when the authorized night-time power of a standard broadcast station is different from daytime power and the operating power is computed by the indirect method?

(a) Efficiency factor for minimum rated carrier power.

(b) Efficiency factor for maximum rated carrier power.

(c) Efficiency factor for regular daytime power.

(d) Efficiency factor for average rated carrier power.

(e) Efficiency factor for regular night-time power.

93. What is the center frequency of an FM broadcast station?

(a) The instantaneous output frequency.

(b) The frequency of the unmodulated carrier.

(c) The average between maximum and minimum peak values.

(d) The average difference between maximum and minimum excursions.

(e) The output frequency of the FM oscillator.

94. What method must be used to determine the operating power of an FM broadcast station?

(a) The Armstrong method.

(b) The electron coupled method.

(c) The indirect method.

(d) The direct method.

(e) E_p times I_p.

95. What is the function of the reactance tube in an FM broadcast transmitter?

(a) Prevents overheating the swinging choke.

(b) Provides better stability with plate modulation.

(c) Modulates the master oscillator.

(d) Improves power supply regulation.

(e) Stabilizes the modulator balancing.

96. What frequency tolerance is an international broadcast station allowed?

(a) 0.00005 percent.

(b) 0.0005 percent.

(c) 0.005 percent.

(d) 0.003 percent.

(e) 0.001 percent.

97. What is the necessary bandwidth of the IF strip in an FM receiver for acceptable quality?

(a) 25 kHz

(b) 50 kHz

(c) 75 kHz

(d) 100 kHz

~(e) 150 kHz

~ 98. What is the speed of a 220-volt 60-Hz, 4-pole, 3-phase induction motor?

(a) 2150 RPM.

(b) 1250 RPM.

~(c) 1750 RPM.

(d) 2250 RPM.

(e) 2500 RPM.

— 99. If a voltmeter with a 0-250 microampere scale and a suitable series resistor offers a full-scale reading of 500 volts, what is the ohms per volt rating of the meter?

~(a) 4,000 ohms per volt.

(b) 2,000 ohms per volt.

(c) 1,000 ohms per volt.

(d) 5,000 ohms per volt.

(e) 10,000 ohms per volt.

— 100. What accuracy at full scale is required of meters used to measure voltage and current in the final stage of a standard broadcast station?

(a) 10 percent.

(b) 5 percent.

~(c) 2 percent.

(d) 1 percent.

(e) 0.02 percent.

— 101. What is the purpose of the variable attenuator for a speech input system?

(a) Attenuates undesired background.

~(b) Provides control of the voltage gain.

(c) Attenuates undesired frequencies.

(d) Serves as an impedance match between the signal and the amplifier.

(e) Adjusts the amplifier frequency response.

— 102. What is the purpose of a line equalizer?

(a) Balances the input and output circuits.

~(b) Uniform frequency response at all times.

(c) Increased power transfer.

(d) Eliminates standing waves.

(e) Ensures correct impedance matching.

CHAPTER 8

Radar Endorsement: Element 8

The expansion of radar during recent years into the small boating and other hobby fields has resulted in additional opportunities for the licensed technician. Kits and other inexpensive radar type systems are available, but the installation, maintenance, and repair of such equipment requires a first or second class radiotelephone license with the **radar endorsement.** Small radar units are also being used in light planes and some guidance systems. Only a brief coverage of the subject is attempted here, but for those with a greater interest, many comprehensive books are currently available.

Radar is actually an abbreviation of "radio detection and ranging," a method of detecting objects by means of radio waves. A radar system radiates microwave energy in pulses which bounce off objects in their path. The reflections return to the system receiver and are displayed on the oscilloscope screen. The interval between transmission and reception of the pulses is timed to compute their distance away. Although there are other forms of radar transmission, we are interested in pulse transmission which is the type commonly used in search and direction-determining equipment.

RULES & REGULATIONS

Before proceeding with the actual radar equipment involved, a study of the Commission's Rules and Regulations governing operation, installation, and maintenance is covered in the first part of the question and answer section.

System Components

So that the operation of each system is clear and questions regarding their purpose may readily be answered, we review each unit individually in the question and answer section.

Echo Box

This is a device used for periodic system checks. It utilizes a high Q resonant cavity for a reference standard. The cavity may be varied in length to change the frequency as desired. Pulsing the transmitter shock excites the cavity resonator into oscillation, which continues for a short time after the transmitter pulse. A signal is returned to the receiver and appears as an artificial pattern on the CRT indicator. By measuring the length of the spokes or size of the intensified area on the screen when the system is in good working condition, a standard may be set for future checks, since a decrease in spoke length or distortion in shape would indicate improper performance.

Sample Test

The regular FCC type study questions and answers are followed by a 50 question sample test to evaluate your understanding. This will enable you to review any weak points before sitting for the FCC examination.

The FCC examination covering Element 8 consists of 50 questions of the multiple choice type, except for those requiring correction, completion or drawing diagrams pertaining to ship radar techniques.

Question 1: Within what frequency bands do ship radar transmitters operate?

The following bands are authorized: 2900 to 3100 MHz; 5460 to 5650 MHz; 9320 to 9500 MHz.

Question 2: What are the FCC license requirements for the operator who is responsible for the installation, servicing and maintenance of ship radar equipment?

Although fuses and receiving tubes may be replaced without a license, the operator responsible for the installation, maintenance and servicing of the ship radar equipment must hold a first or second class radiotelephone or radiotelegraph license as well as the ship radar endorsement.

Question 3: Who may operate radar equipment in the ship service?

The master of the ship may designate any crew member to operate a ship radar station during the course of normal duty.

Question 4: Under what conditions may a person who does not hold a radio operator license operate a radar station in the ship service?

Any crew member designated by the master of the ship may operate the radar station so long as the station does not possess external controls that affect the tuning, frequency, or other operating parameter of the equipment.

Question 5: Who may make entries in the installation and maintenance record of a ship radar station?

277

Entries in the maintenance and installation log may be made by the station's licensee or any authorized licensee who performs a maintenance adjustment or service of the equipment.

Question 6: What entries are required in the installation and maintenance record of a ship radar station?

The following entries must be made:

(a) Date and place of initial installation.

(b) Any required steps taken to eliminate any interference found to exist at the time of such installation.

(c) The nature of any complaint, including interference to radio communication arising following the initial installation and the date of same.

(d) Reason for complaint or trouble leading to same and the component or part responsible.

(e) Corrective measures taken and date.

(f) Name, license number and date of radar endorsement on the first or second class operator license of the responsible operator supervising or engaged in the installation, service or maintenance.

Question 7: Draw a block diagram of a radar system, labeling the antenna, duplexer, transmitter, receiver, timer, modulator and indicator.

See the sketch in Fig. 8-1.

Question 8: Explain briefly the principle of operation of a radar system.

A radar system transmits high-power RF pulses of very short duration but at regular intervals from a directional antenna. A portion of the energy from the pulse is reflected back from the target to the receiver in the system, with the direction determined by the position of the antenna and the distance of the target by the elapsed time required for the return of the reflected signal. The modulator or pulser in Fig. 8-1 controls the pulsing of the magnetron oscillator to permit extremely short duration pulses of high power to be generated and fed through a waveguide to a horn-type antenna which radiates them in a narrow, searchlight type beam. The antenna rotates continuously to permit scanning of the desired area.

The reflected signal picked up by the receiver is amplified and displayed on a cathode ray tube known as a PPI. The duplexer makes it possible to use the same antenna for transmitting the pulse and receiving the reflected echo by disconnecting the receiver during transmission and the transmitter between pulses to allow the echo to be received. The timer provides synchronization between the scope (PPI) and the pulse transmission to ensure accurate measurement of the elapsed time from pulse transmission to echo reception as shown by position on the PPI screen.

Question 9: What component determines pulse repetition rate (PRR) in radar?

The timer or synchronizer is responsible for determining the pulse repetition rate of a radar system.

Question 10: What is the purpose of the rotary spark gap used in some older radar sets?

Although not used in modern equipment, the rotary spark gap was a mechanical substitute for the modulator tube and offered a mechanical method for discharging the pulse-forming network and forming the output pulse by modulating the magnetron directly at a high level.

Question 11: What is the purpose of an artificial transmission line in a radar system?

Its function is to form the shape of the modulation pulses with an LC network that actually resembles a regular transmission line. This network accurately controls the length, shape and magnitude of the transmitted pulse.

Question 12: What is the peak power of a radar pulse if the pulse width is one microsecond, the pulse repetition rate (PRR) is 900 and the average power is 18 watts? What is the duty cycle?

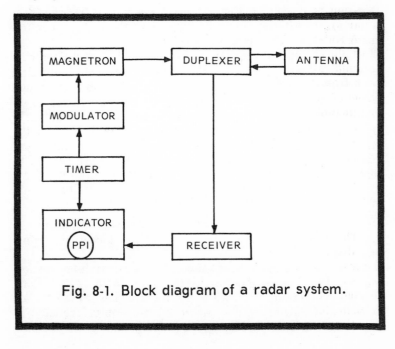

Fig. 8-1. Block diagram of a radar system.

Peak power in radar is the average power transmitted during a single pulse and average power is the average of the transmitted power during the pulse repetition period, or the start of a pulse to the start of the succeeding pulse. The period between pulses is always many times the pulse duration which makes the average power much lower than peak power. The duty cycle is that fractional part of each second during which pulses are transmitted, and is the result of multiplying the pulse width by the PRR. The peak power is found by dividing the average power by the duty cycle.

$$\text{Peak power} = \frac{\text{average power}}{\text{duty cycle}} = \frac{18}{0.0009} = 20,000 \text{ watts}$$

Question 13: Explain briefly why radar interference to a radiotelephone receiver is frequently characterized by a steady tone in the radio speaker?

The steady tone is the PRR of the radio transmitter or a harmonic thereof and it is detected by the receiver. The signal may be picked up through local power lines or by reception of the radiation. As the radar pulses are rich in harmonics as well as strong in peak power, they are not tunable.

Question 14: Describe how various types of interference from a radar installation may be apparent to a person when listening to a communications receiver.

When listening to radar interference with an AM or FM communications receiver, the sound is a characteristic musical buzzing, similar to ignition interference but at a much higher repetition rate. Often, such interference varies in intensity proportional to the radar's sweep. Most squelch-operated receivers "see" radar signals as noise; thus, the interference is not noticeable except when an accompanying communications signal defeats the squelch and is detected. In such cases, the radar pulses tend to desensitize the receiver, rendering it incapable of receiving faint signals that would otherwise be copyable.

Question 15: How are various types of radar interference recognized in auto-alarm equipment? In direction-finding equipment?

The characteristic audio indication of radar interference may be observed by listening to the auto-alarm or direction-finding equipment with an amplifier-speaker or a set of headphones. Owing to the nature of radar interference (its variation in intensity with range sweeping), it is often difficult to locate with direction-finding equipment. The most satisfactory method is to observe a signal strength indicator while monitoring during periods of peak disturbance, and take readings from several locations.

Question 16: On what frequencies should the radar serviceman look for radar interference to communication receivers on ships equipped with radar?

The frequencies susceptible to interference would depend on the type of interference (mixing, or intermod, for example, may occur on any frequency); however, UHF equipment in the 450 MHz region would be most vulnerable.

Question 17: Why is it important that all units of a radar installation be thoroughly bonded to the ship's electrical ground?

Grounding is important as a safety measure to eliminate the danger of electrical shock and to prevent radar interference to other electronic units.

Question 18: Would there be danger in testing or operating radar equipment aboard ship when explosive or inflammable cargo is being handled?

Definitely, radar equipment should never be operated or tested while explosives or inflammable cargo is being handled. The high-frequency radar pulses could dielectrically produce enough heat in the material to cause it to ignite, and possible arcing in the system would pose a threat as well.

Question 19: What precaution should a radar serviceman observe when making repairs or adjustments to a radar set to prevent personal injury to himself or other persons?

Power should be removed from the equipment before making adjustments. Electrolytics and filters should be discharged by shorting to ground for 30 seconds. The magnetron and other heat-producing elements should be allowed to cool in order to prevent possible burns.

Question 20: In checking a direction finder for interference from radar equipment, would it be advisable to rotate the D-F loop while checking?

Radar interference tends to be characterized by a constantly changing intensity, particularly where the interference signal is being radiated by the radar's revolving antenna. This lack of a continuous and stable source renders a direction finder useless unless it is held in a fixed direction during each radar sweep. The best approach is to take independent readings from a variety of directions without moving the loop during each reading. The readings may be compared following the taking of sample signals.

Question 21: List at least two types of indications on a loran scope that would signify that a radar system was causing interference to the loran.

The presence of unusual noise on the screen is the principal indication. Another indication is momentary weakening or loss of display or a shift in the display image.

Question 22: Would a radar installation be likely to cause interference to radio receivers if long connecting lines were used between the radar transmitter and modulator?

Yes.

Question 23: What steps may be taken by the radar serviceman to eliminate a steady-tone of interference to radio communication receivers, or interference to loran evidenced by "spikes"?

The serviceman should check to see that appropriate filters are installed in the receiving equipment and that the reciprocal filter types are installed and properly deployed on the radar equipment. Where the interference is attributable to leakage through the power lines, he should make certain that appropriate RF filter chokes have been used to isolate the radar gear from the lines.

Question 24: What steps may be taken by a radar serviceman to reduce "grass" on a loran scope or motor-generator noise in communication receivers?

There are two basic approaches: **passive** and **active**. Passive techniques involve methods by which the receiver can be made impervious to such interference, and these include additional filtering, installation of better shielding and ground connections, improved isolation from supply lines, etc. Active measures include those procedures designed to minimize the radiation at the source of interference, such as filtering the input and output lines to the motor-generator, shielding the generator, etc.

Question 25: Name at least four pieces of radio or electronic equipment aboard ship that might suffer interference from the radar installation.

ADF equipment, loran gear, auto-alarm equipment, radiotelephone installations and other communications equipment.

Question 26: What may cause bright flashing pie sections to appear on a radar PPI scope?

The flashing pie sections, sometimes referred to as "spoking," as displayed on the plan position indicator, normally signifies failure of the AFC circuit in the receiver. The cause is often a defective crystal in the AFC, but other possibilities include an improperly keyed magnetron or even failure of the magnetron. Irregular rotation of the deflection coil or yoke could also cause a similar indication and would be the result of a defective servo amplifier or mechanical binding in the assembly.

Question 27: What symptoms on a radar scope would indicate that the radar receiver mixer crystal is defective?

A defective crystal mixer is indicated by the presence of excessive noise. While a single-ended or unbalanced crystal mixer will not exhibit the noise-reduction and noise cancellation capability of a balanced or hybrid mixer, there is a noticeable difference in noise content on a radar signal when the mixer crystal begins to deteriorate. Similarly, crystal defects may take the form of phase-shifting of the displayed signal as well as a general diminishing of displayed-signal quality (amplitude and intensity).

Question 28: What tests may a radar serviceman make to determine whether or not the radar receiver mixer crystal is defective?

The crystal in a radar receiver's mixer stage is a high-quality germanium diode. Normally, the crystal is easily accessible, as it plugs directly into a waveguide section. To check the crystal element, it is only necessary to check the rectification capability of the device with an ohmmeter. When forward-biased, the device should indicate low resistance value; when reverse-biased, the resistance across the terminals should be quite high. The ratio of resistance between forward- and reverse-biasing should be at least 200 to 1. If the reverse-bias resistance reading is not on the order of hundreds of thousands of ohms, the crystal junction has probably deteriorated and excessive leakage is indicated.

Question 29: In a radar set, what are the indications of (1) a defective magnetron, (2) a weak magnet in the magnetron, (3) a defective crystal in the receiver converter stage?

When a magnetron is supplied with a rectangular plate-voltage pulse of proper magnitude and duration and is itself operating as it should, the ultrahigh-frequency output waveform should be a uniform wavetrain. If this output voltage is rectified and filtered, it appears as a square wave whose pulse width is equal to the duration of the wavetrain. If a nonrectangular pulse is supplied to the magnetron, or if the magnetron itself is not operating properly, the pulse envelope is not a square wave. Hence, observation of the pulse envelope from a transmitter gives an indication of the magnetron performance. In general, if the frequency or plate voltage of a magnetron changes, the power output changes, which also makes a change in the observed pulse-envelope height. As a further check on the operation of magnetrons, coaxial wavemeters are sometimes used to measure the wavelength of oscillation or to check the relative power outputs between different tubes.

Under certain conditions, the frequency of the magnetron is very sensitive to the RF tuning. In these cases, the mere variation in the impedance of the line resulting from faulty rotating joints or from other causes may shift the magnetron frequency by several megahertz.

A magnetron must not have its plate voltage applied when the magnetic field is not present. If this is done, the plate may be bombarded and the tube destroyed almost at once.

Another precaution to observe concerns the powerful permanent magnets which are frequently used to supply the magnetic field. Striking or jarring these magnets or touching them with a magnetic material such as a screwdriver greatly lowers their field strength.

Question 30: What is the purpose of a klystron in a radar set?

A klystron may be used as an amplifier, oscillator or mixer. It has a low power-output capability, and is typically used in the local oscillator in the receiver portion of a radar set. The klystron's output is heterodyned with the RF input to produce an intermediate frequency.

Question 31: Explain briefly the principle of operation of the reflex klystron.

A klystron tube, especially one using cavity resonators, is very critical to adjust since the tuning and spacing of the cavities are interdependent. Therefore, when it is desired to use a velocity-modulated tube as an oscillator only, a simplified form called the reflex klystron is used. This tube is so named because the same set of grids is used for both bunching and catching, and a negative repeller plate is provided to force the electrons to retrace their paths after their first passage through the grids.

By proper adjustment of the negative voltage on the repeller plate, the electrons which have passed the bunching field may be made to pass through the resonator again at the proper time to deliver energy to this circuit. Thus, the feedback needed to produce oscillations is obtained and the tube construction is simplified. Spent electrons are removed from the tube by the positive accelerator grid or by the grids of the resonator. Energy is coupled out of the cavity by a one-turn coupling loop. The operating frequency can be varied over a small range by changing the negative potential of the repeller. This potential determines the transit time of the electrons between their first and second passages through the resonator. The output of the oscillator is affected considerably more than the frequency by changes in the repeller voltage. This is because the output depends upon the fact that the electrons go back through the resonator just at the time when they are bunched and at exactly the decelerating half-cycle of oscillating resonator grid voltage. The volume of the resonant cavity is changed to change the oscillator frequency. The repeller voltage may be varied over a narrow range to provide minor adjustments of frequency.

Three typical tubes of the reflex klystron type are the McNally tube, using an external cavity with screw plugs for tuning; the Pierce (or Shepard) tube, using a cavity sealed in the tube and tuned by means of flexing the tube envelope to vary the grid spacing; and the klystron 417, a large tube whose cavity may be tuned by flexing the sides of the cavity. These reflex klystrons are by far the most widely used types of local or beating oscillators in ultrahigh-frequency receivers.

Question 32: What circuit element determines the operating frequency of a self-blocking oscillator?

The operating frequency depends mainly on the RC time constant in the grid circuit, but tube characteristics, operating voltage and transformer values have a limited effect. The iron-core transformer closely couples the plate circuit to the grid circuit in the self-blocking oscillator and as a result has some bearing on the frequency even though secondary.

Question 33: Draw a simple block diagram of a radar receiver, label the signal crystal, local oscillator, AFC crystal stage, IF amplifier, and discriminator.

See Fig. 8-2 for a block diagram of a radar receiver.

Question 34: What type of detector is used frequently in radar receivers?

The usual type of detector (mixer) is a crystal diode.

Question 35: What care should be taken when handling silicon crystal rectifier cartridges for replacement in radar superheterodyne receivers?

Silicon crystals are extremely sensitive to electrical field and static charges and should be wrapped in lead foil or kept in a lead container when not in use. The technician should touch a convenient ground to discharge static charges from his body before handling and inserting the exposed crystal in the set. Mechanical shock and strong electrical fields must be avoided while handling this type of diode.

Question 36: What nominal intermediate frequencies are commonly used in radar receivers?

The commonly used intermediate frequencies are 30 and 60 MHz.

Question 37: What is "sea return" on a radar scope?

Sea return is the reception and radar scope display of signals that strike ocean wave crests. Since the reflection of such signals depends on the angle of the wave surface at any given instant, the interference is not normally a long-term problem.

Question 38: Explain briefly the purpose of the sensitivity time control circuit in a radar set.

Receiver gain is reduced automatically for closer targets by the sensitivity time control, reducing sea return interference and overload of the receiver as a result of the strong reflections from nearby targets. The STC control should be carefully adjusted until the solid sea return pattern becomes weaker and the closer ship targets are readily observed.

Question 39: What is the purpose of the discriminator stage in a radar superheterodyne?

It serves as part of the automatic frequency control (AFC) circuit which prevents drift in the frequency of the local klystron oscillator. Any drift in the klystron frequency causes the intermediate frequency of the receiver to drift, developing a DC voltage across the discriminator output. After amplification, the DC voltage is impressed on the klystron repeller grid, causing it to return to the correct frequency.

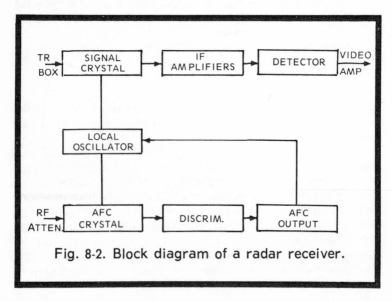

Fig. 8-2. Block diagram of a radar receiver.

Question 40: Draw a diagram of a cathode ray tube used in radar, showing the principal electrodes in the tube and the path of the electron beam.

See Fig. 8-3.

Question 41: What is the distance in nautical miles to a target if it takes 12.3 microseconds for a radar pulse to travel from the radar antenna to the target, back to the antenna and be displayed on the PPI scope?

The distance to the target would be one nautical mile. A radar pulse travels 1 nautical mile and returns in 12.3 microseconds.

Question 42: Explain the principle of operation of the cathode ray PPI tube and the function of each electrode.

Referring to Fig. 8-3, electrons are emitted by the cathode and accelerated by the first anode toward the face of the tube. The focusing coil confines the electron stream to a narrow

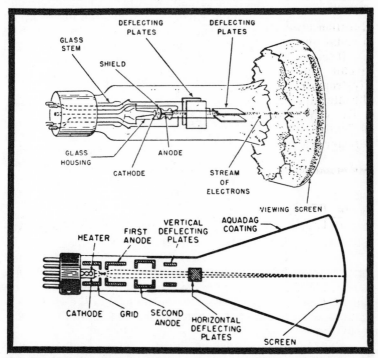

Fig. 8-3. The electron beam emitted by the cathode flows through the grid "cage" toward the phosphor-coated face of the tube. The first anode is the focusing element, and the second anode is the beam-accelerating element. The vertical and horizontal deflection plates allow the beam to be directed toward any part of the screen.

beam approaching a point at the face of the CRT. The Aquadag coating on the bell of the tube is the second anode, which, due to its high potential, accelerates the beam to a high velocity. Beam brightness is regulated by the amount of negative bias on the grid electrode, and the fluorescent material on the screen or face of the tube causes light wherever the beam strikes it. The deflection coils cause the beam to sweep across the screen according to the timing of the current flowing through them. In sets using PPI (plan-position-indicator), the deflection coils rotate around the neck of the tube in step with the rotation of the radar antenna. This means that the sweep line on the screen rotates radially around the center in sync with the antenna.

Question 43: What is the purpose of the Aquadag coating on radar cathode-ray tubes?

Aquadag is a conductive material of graphite particles used to paint the inside of cathode ray tubes to form a second anode. The entire painted surface assumes the high-voltage potential applied at the terminal on the side of the tube. The coating also forms an electrostatic shield to prevent external voltages from affecting the sweep of the electron beam.

Question 44: What is meant by the "bearing resolution" of a radar set?

This is the ability of the radar set to distinguish between targets having the same range but differing azimuth directions. The width of the radar beam is the determining factor in bearing resolution; a narrow beam affords better separation of targets at the same radial distance than would be possible with a wide beam. Naturally, resolution is affected considerably by the receiver components and the PPI indicator scope.

Question 45: Explain how heading flash and range-marker circles are produced on a radar PPI scope.

Heading flash is produced, as the radar beam points dead ahead, by a switch in the antenna system which provides a pulse of short duration to intensify the radial line representing the heading. This positive pulse on the grid of the PPI scope causes a bright sweep line and enables the operator to know exactly when the dead-ahead position is reached.

Range-marker circles on the PPI screen indicate range distances and enable the operator to quickly estimate target distance. The range-marker oscillator, along with squaring and peaking circuits, produces a series of short positive pulses or "pips" which are synchronized with the sweep and applied to the grid of the PPI. As the beam sweeps out from center to edge, the accurately spaced pips appear and form range-marker circles as the sweep rotates.

Question 46: What precautions should the service and maintenance operator observe when replacing the cathode-ray tube in a radar set?

Turn off the power supply system and completely discharge all high-voltage capacitors with a well-insulated screwdriver or similar tool. Extreme care must be taken when removing and handling the tube to avoid implosion of the glass envelope and possible serious injury to anyone in the vicinity. The glass spray is terrific and, aside from bad cuts, dangerous poisoning of the bloodstream may result from the fluorescent coating. So don't use force; keep others at a safe distance, and wear gloves and safety glasses.

Question 47: Draw a simple sketch showing a synchro generator located in the radar antenna assembly connected to a synchro motor located in the indicator to drive the deflection coils. Show the proper designation of all leads and where AC voltages (if needed) are applied.

See the sketch in Fig. 8-4. Some ship radar systems employ additional PPI indicators and it is necessary to synchronize the rotation of the sweep line on the CRT with the rotation of the radar antenna. This is normally handled by a servo system.

Question 48: In what range of frequencies do magnetron and klystron oscillators find application?

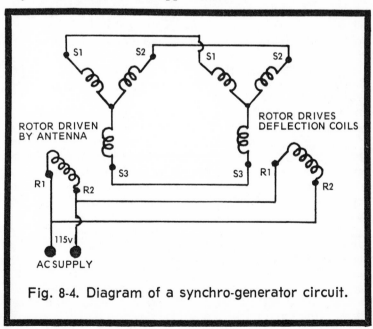

Fig. 8-4. Diagram of a synchro-generator circuit.

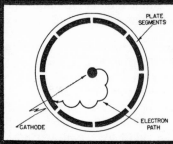

Fig. 8-5. Cross section of magnetron, showing plate segments (anode), cathode, and electron flow.

The frequency range normally covered by a magnetron oscillator is 600 to 30,000 MHz, while klystron oscillators operate in a range from 3,000 to 30,000 MHz.

Question 49: Draw a simple cross-section sketch of a magnetron showing the anode, cathode and direction of electron movement under the influence of a strong magnetic field.

Refer back to Fig. 6-2 for this drawing in its complete form. The insert of this drawing, showing electron movement is shown in Fig. 8-5.

Question 50: Explain briefly the principle of operation of the magnetron.

The plate element of the multianode magnetron is made up of cavity resonators which receive energy from the movement of electrons outside each cavity opening. If the electron is accelerated by the cavity field, energy is taken from the cavity, but if on the other hand, as is usually the case, the electron is slowed by the cavity field, then energy is given, which sustains oscillations. Magnetrons usually function as pulsed power oscillators with an extremely high output peak power.

Question 51: Why is the anode of a magnetron normally maintained at ground potential?

This is for the protection of personnel from high-voltage shock as well as simplification of the chassis insulating problem. A negative high-voltage pulse is fed to the cathode which is centered in the magnetron well out of reach. The metal shell around the magnetron is grounded, making construction simple and safe.

Question 52: Draw a simple mixer (converter) circuit as frequently used in a radar superheterodyne receiver and indicate the crystal stage.

Fig. 8-6 shows a common frequency converter circuit.

Question 53: Describe briefly the construction and operation of radar TR and anti-TR boxes. What is the purpose of a "keep-alive" voltage?

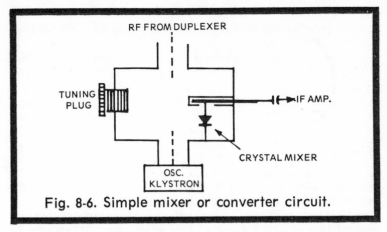

Fig. 8-6. Simple mixer or converter circuit.

Ship radar systems use a common antenna for transmitting and receiving, which makes it necessary to protect the receiver from the very high-powered pulse of the transmitter. On the other hand, the transmitter would absorb too much power from the reflected signal between pulses during reception. The duplexer is a type of switching arrangement made up of specific lengths of waveguide plus two spark-gap tubes. During transmission both spark gaps are fired and the gap resistance becomes very low. The waveguide input to the quarter-wave lines out to the gaps now becomes high. This makes it possible for most of the pulse energy to pass directly to the antenna with very little getting into the TR or anti-TR boxes with the very high input impedance as seen from the waveguide. During reception of the reflected echoes, the spark gaps do not operate because the received signal voltage is far too weak to break down the air gaps. The anti-TR box is now a half-wave transmission line shorted at the far end which makes its input impedance zero at the waveguide. The quarter-wave length between the waveguide entrance to the TR box and the entrance to the anti-TR box is thus terminated in zero impedance which makes its input impedance very high. The received signal, therefore, takes the lower impedance path to the receiver.

The TR box electrically isolates the receiver from the transmitter during pulse transmission to prevent damage to the receiver. The anti-TR box electrically isolates the transmitter from the receiver during reception of the reflected echo to avoid a loss in signal voltage.

The "keep-alive" voltage is a constant negative (1000 volts) applied to a third electrode inside one of the main electrodes. This keeps the gas and vapor slightly ionized to permit easier arcover during pulse transmission, and it also protects the receiver crystal.

Question 54: Describe briefly the construction of a waveguide. Why should the interior of the waveguide be clean, smooth and dry?

Waveguides are normally made of hollow brass tubing with a rectangular cross section. In some instances, weight considerations dictate the use of aluminum. Plating the inside with silver improves conductivity to a great extent and a gold or rhodium protective flashing prevents or retards corrosion. Smooth interiors prevent troublesome reflections and dirt must be avoided to eliminate transmission loss. Moisture also contributes to arcing and transmission problems.

Question 55: Why are waveguides used in preference to coaxial lines for the transmission of microwave energy in most shipboard radar installations?

Coaxial line losses are so great at the microwave frequencies required for radar that their use is not practical. When properly designed, waveguide losses are extremely low at microwave frequencies. The waveguide has neither the dielectric loss or the copper loss of the conventional coaxial line, since the waveguide has air for a dielectric and eliminates the thin inner conductor where most of the copper loss occurs. Thus, a waveguide having the same diameter as the coaxial line can carry much more power.

Question 56: Why are rectangular waveguides generally used in preference to circular cross-sectional waveguides?

The use of circular waveguides makes polarization of the wave more difficult to control and for this reason they are seldom used in radar. Since the electric field has a tendency to change direction at bends in circular waveguides, the polarization changes. With the rectangular waveguide, though, the desired polarization is readily maintained. A rotating joint permits free movement of the antenna with respect to the fixed waveguide; it must be circular, while the waveguide feeding the joint is rectangular. The frequency range at the dominant mode is limited to a greater extent in the circular waveguide than in the rectangular.

Question 57: Describe how the waveguide is terminated at the radar antenna reflector.

There are variations of the horn radiator which point into the parabolic reflector and form the energy into a narrow beam. The horn radiator must be large, compared to the operating wavelength, which is quite practical at these frequencies. The electromagnetic horn operates like an acoustic horn by matching the impedance of the waveguide to

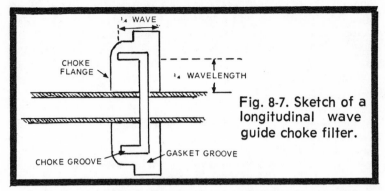

Fig. 8-7. Sketch of a longitudinal wave guide choke filter.

the impedance of free space. The parabolic reflector directs the energy into a narrow beam for accurate tracking.

Termination of the waveguide at the antenna may be achieved by means of a polystyrene window with the correct physical dimensions to provide the impedance match required. The window is placed at the focal point of the parabolic reflector and acts as a matching device between the waveguide, reflector and free space.

Question 58: What precautions should be taken when installing vertical sections of waveguides with choke-coupling flanges to prevent moisture from entering the waveguide?

Each guide section should have the end with the choke at the bottom to avoid collection of moisture in the choke joint. By using a gasket at each choke-coupling flange, the flange bolts may be tightened enough to ensure a rain-tight joint.

Question 59: Draw a longitudinal section of a waveguide choke joint and explain briefly its principle of operation.

See Fig. 8-7. The choke joint includes a slot-type groove having a depth of a quarter wavelength, making the input impedance across the circular groove infinite. By acting as a resonant element, the choke groove transfers energy across the junction without electrical contact. The distance from the groove to the waveguide is also a quarter-wave and it feeds into the infinite impedance at the input to the choke flange. Since this is a quarter-wave open line, its input impedance at the guide is zero and energy passes freely across the break at the flange without loss. Choke joints provide low-loss connections between parts of a system, provide mechanical isolation against vibration, and permit removal of sections for easy repair or replacements.

Question 60: Why are choke joints often used in preference to flange joints to join sections of waveguide together?

The cost of choke coupling is much less than direct contact flange joint coupling, which requires precision machining to ensure perfect contact all around and smooth, continuous inside surfaces. Perfect alignment is also important to avoid reflections and other losses and this adds considerably to the cost of the flange-joint. This precision work is not required with choke joint coupling, since electrical contact around the outside of the choke groove is desirable. Of course, the choke joint is somewhat inferior to the precision-machined direct contact flange joint from a loss standpoint, but the difference in signal losses certainly does not justify the much greater cost in most applications.

Question 61: When installing waveguides, why should long, perfectly level sections be avoided? Why is a small hole about one-eighth inch in diameter sometimes drilled on the underside of an elbow in a waveguide near the point where it enters the radar transmitter?

A slight slant in long horizontal sections of the waveguide permits condensed moisture to drain out through the small hole at the lowest point which has been drilled on the underside for this purpose.

Question 62: Describe how a radar beam is formed by the parabolic reflector.

The narrow beam of RF energy reflected by the parabolic reflector compares with the reflection of light by a parabolic reflector in an ordinary searchlight. Feeding the energy into the reflector at its focal point causes most of the RF to be focused into a narrow beam which is reflected by the "dish." The greater the diameter of the parabolic reflector, the narrower that beam will be.

Question 63: What effect if any does the accumulation of soot or dirt on the antenna reflector have on the operation of a ship radar?

A thin layer of soot, dirt or paint on the reflector will have little or no effect on the operation of the ship radar unit, since microwaves are able to penetrate an average accumulation with very little loss. An excessive amount of foreign material on the reflector surface, however, will decrease the efficiency of the system on weak targets; therefore, such matter should be cleaned off. Any accumulation of dirt on the plastic window will cause considerable loss and must not be permitted.

Question 64: What considerations should be taken into account when selecting the location of the radar antenna assembly aboard ship?

Obstructions must be avoided as much as possible when locating a radar antenna, and the scanning area around the ship should be reasonably clear of any objects that would interfere. It is most important that the forward or bow area be completely clear and the location of the antenna must not require a longer waveguide section from the transmitter than is necessary. It also must be accessible for routine maintenance.

Question 65: What is the purpose of an echo box in a radar system? Explain the principle of operation of the echo box. What indications may be expected on a radar scope when using an echo box and the radar set is operating properly? When the set is not operating properly?

The purpose of the echo box is to offer a phantom or artificial target for tuning the receiver and indicate or test the overall performance of a radar system.

An echo box is a resonant cavity with a very high Q, which is shock excited into oscillation by the transmitter pulse. The cavity rings or oscillates for several microseconds after the transmitted pulse ends, as a result of its high Q, and its radiation is received and displayed on the PPI scope. This appears as lines or spokes extending out from the hub, in the case of a motor tuned box, or as an intensified area or large spot in a box set at resonance.

When the radar system is operating properly, the spokes or intensified area will extend out quite a bit from the center of the display on the scope. If the radar is not functioning properly, the artificial target would be much smaller or even not visible at all. The echo box actually provides a useful reference signal for evaluating the performance of the radar system. Normal radar target signals do not furnish a satisfactory means of checking the system because of the many variables involved, such as atmospheric conditions, character of different signals, and the lack of adequate reference material.

Question 66: Draw a simple diagram of an artificial transmission line showing inductance and capacitance, source of power, the load and electronic switch.

To avoid the bulk of an actual line, an artificial line may be built of coils and capacitors which has approximately the same characteristics as the line but occupies a smaller space. The circuit for an artificial line is shown in Fig. 8-8. The distributed inductance and resistance of the line are lumped in several choke coils, while the distributed capacitance can be represented by capacitors, and the conductance is omitted entirely as it is too small even to consider. If the action of the actual transmission line with its evenly distributed R, L, and C is to be closely approximated, the sections must be small and numerous. In most cases, however, from three to eight sections produce as much of the required transmission line action as is needed for use in radar time-delay circuits.

Artificial transmission lines also may perform other duties in addition to introducing time delay or phase shift. These duties include action as filters to block or pass certain frequencies, and as models for laboratory demonstration of transmission-line action.

One important use in radar is the storage of energy and the subsequent delivery of the same energy at a predetermined rate to form pulses. In Fig. 8-8B, if switch S1 is closed, S2 remaining open, the artificial transmission line will charge through R to the voltage of E_D, the charge being retained on the capacitors as electrostatic field energy. In application, operating current may be obtained from the cathode circuit of an appropriate stage.

Question 67: Who has the responsibility for making entries in the installation and maintenance record of a ship-radar station?

The licensed operator doing the work and the station licensee are jointly responsible for making the proper entries in the installation and maintenance record.

Question 68: May fuses and receiving type tubes be replaced in ship-radar equipment by a person whose operator license does not contain a ship-radar endorsement?

Yes, receiving-type tubes and fuses may be replaced by unlicensed operators, but all other repairs, tests, and installations must be performed by a properly licensed technician, with no exceptions.

Question 69: What precautions should a radar serviceman take when working with or handling a magnetron to prevent weakening or damaging it?

A magnetron should be handled with the care and respect due any precision device; shocks and blows must be avoided. Steel tools or parts may not be in the proximity of the magnet and extreme heat will damage or weaken it.

Question 70: Draw a simple block diagram of a radar duplexer system; label the waveguide, TR box, anti-TR box, receiver and transmitter.

A block diagram of the duplexer is shown in Fig. 8-9.

Question 71: What is required to operate a ship-radar station?

Authorization by the ship's master permits any person so designated to operate the radar station.

Question 72: How does the "keep alive" potential lower the arc resistance in a TR box?

The constant "keep alive" voltage slightly ionizes the gas and vapor in the tube and lowers the breakdown resistance of the gap. A negative potential of about one thousand volts is used for this purpose.

Question 73: What causes receiver paralysis in radar and how may it be avoided?

Although TR and anti-TR boxes normally protect the receiver from paralysis or blocking, when a strong signal does get through, the tubes are overdriven and blocking results from the residual charges. The blocking or paralysis of the receiver may be avoided or greatly reduced by the application of a disabling rectangular pulse to the grid of one or more stages at the critical moment. However, better results overall are obtained by using a timing pulse to remove receiver B+ during the overload period.

Question 74: Why are RF amplifiers not employed in radar receivers?

RF amplifiers are just not practical at the microwave frequencies normally used for radar systems. Noise is high, gain is low and degenerative feedback is excessive as a result of the inductive reactance in the cathode leads.

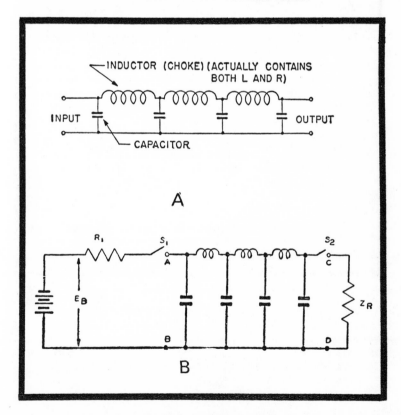

Fig. 8-8. Artificial transmission line.

Question 75: What limits the number of IF stages in a radar receiver?

Since each stage of IF amplification decreases the overall bandpass of the receiver, the number of stages employed is limited by the specific bandpass requirements of the radar system.

Question 76: Why is stagger-tuning commonly employed?

Stagger tuning broadens the bandpass of the IF amplifiers and either single or double-tuned coupling may be used.

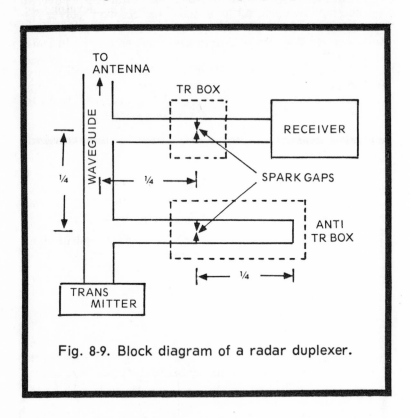

Fig. 8-9. Block diagram of a radar duplexer.

SAMPLE TEST QUESTIONS

1. Within what frequency bands do ship radar transmitters operate?
    (a) 5460 to 5650 kHz
    (b) 9100 to 9320 MHz
    (c) 9320 to 9500 MHz
    (d) 3340 to 3760 MHz
    (e) 5120 to 5420 kHz

2. What are the FCC license requirements for the operator who is responsible for the installation, servicing and maintenance of ship radar equipment?
    (a) First or second class radiotelegraph license.
    (b) Second class radiotelephone license.
    (c) First class radiotelegraph license.
    (d) First or second class radiotelephone or radiotelegraph license with radar endorsement.
    (e) Third class permit with radar endorsement.

3. What component determines the pulse repetition rate in a radar system?
    (a) Marker generator
    (b) Timer
    (c) Magnetron
    (d) Artificial transmission line
    (e) Echo box

4. What is the purpose of the rotary spark gap used in older radar?
    (a) Pulses the synchronizer
    (b) Eliminates the pulse-forming network
    (c) Modulates the magnetron directly
    (d) Controls the oscillator frequency
    (e) Protects the deflection coils

5. What precautions should a radar serviceman observe when making repairs or adjustments to a radar set to prevent personal injury to himself or others?
    (a) Check all protective devices.
    (b) Turn the power off and post a danger sign.
    (c) Wear gloves, goggles and other safety equipment.
    (d) Jumper interlock switches only after posting a warning.
    (e) Shut off the power, discharge the high-voltage capacitors with an insulated tool, and handle the CRT with extreme care.

6. Why is it important that all units of the radar system be thoroughly bonded to the ship's electrical ground?
    (a) Prevents accidental shock and interference to other equipment.

(b) Provides a high-impedance path for RF energy.

(c) Makes it easier to make electrical measurements.

(d) Provides a reference point for accurate comparison.

(e) Helps to lower the static charge peak.

7. What is the purpose of an artificial transmission line in a radar system?

(a) Determines the operating frequency.

(b) Provides trigger pulses for proper sweep.

(c) Determines the output of the video detector.

(d) Couples the flared waveguide to the reflector.

(e) Determines the shape and duration of the transmitted pulse.

8. What is the usual way of terminating a waveguide at the radar antenna reflector?

(a) Feeding it into a resonant cavity.

(b) By matching it with a quarter-wave stub.

(c) Connecting it to a choke joint.

(d) Forming a horn by flaring out the end.

(e) Matching it with a loading coil.

9. What is the peak power of a radar pulse if the pulse width is 2 microseconds, pulse repetition rate (PRR) is 700 and the average power is 14 watts?

(a) 10,000 watts

(b) 100 kilowatts

(c) 14,000 watts

(d) 70 kilowatts

(e) 1,000 KW

10. What is the duty cycle of the radar transmitter if the pulse width is 1 microsecond and the pulse repetition rate (PRR) is 900?

(a) 0.009

(b) 0.00009

(c) 0.0009

(d) 0.000009

(e) 0.00001

11. If we multiply the pulse width of a radar transmitter by its PRR, what would the product indicate?

(a) Average power

(b) Duty cycle

(c) Peak power

(d) Efficiency factor

(e) Bandwidth

12. What type of detector is used frequently in radar receivers?

(a) Ratio detector

(b) Selenium diode

(c) Grid leak

(d) Horizontal diode

(e) Silicon crystal diode

13. What are the indications of a defective crystal in the receiver converter (mixer) stage of a radar system?

(a) Low front-to-back ratio.

(b) Weak echo and no "grass" on the PPI scope.

(c) High reading on the crystal current meter.

(d) Low reading on the crystal current meter.

(e) High "grass" level and weak targets.

14. What is the purpose of the klystron tube in a radar set?

(a) Local oscillator in the receiver.

(b) Pulse amplifier.

(c) Drives the modulator grid.

(d) Determines the transmitter frequency.

(e) Controls the AFC circuit.

15. Weak echo signals may be received if the radar receiver has a:

(a) low signal-to-noise ratio.

(b) good RF amplifier.

(c) klystron mixer.

(d) high signal-to-noise ratio.

(e) narrow bandpass.

16. What determines the frequency of the radiated energy in a radar transmitter employing a magnetron?

(a) The timer circuit.

(b) The magnetron circuit.

(c) The reflex klystron circuit.

(d) The choke joint circuit.

(e) The parabolic reflector.

17. What are the indications of a weak magnet in the magnetron in a radar unit?

(a) AFC good and no change in oscillations.

(b) Oscillation amplitude less and frequency steady.

(c) Increased magnetron current and oscillations cease.

(d) Decrease in magnetron current and oscillations stop.

(e) Decrease in plate voltage and oscillations.

18. What symptoms on a radar scope would indicate a defective crystal in the receiver converter stage?

(a) Bright target with excessive noise.

(b) Pattern drifts across the PPI.

(c) Noise level below average.

(d) No target or "grass" with advanced gain.

(e) Weak or no target; "grass" high.

19. When checking the front-to-back ratio of the radar receiver mixer crystal with a good ohmmeter, what would be a resonable figure for a crystal in good operating condition?

(a) 5 to 1

(b) 1.5 to 1

(c) 8 to 1

(d) 10 to 1

(e) 20 to 1

20. In a radar set, what are the indications of a defective magnetron?

(a) Good AFC, no range marks.

(b) Poor AFC, fuzzy targets.

(c) No targets but stable frequency.

(d) Weak targets, current normal.

(e) High current, good AFC.

21. What care should be taken when handling silicon crystal rectifier cartridges for replacement in radar superheterodyne receivers?

(a) Discharge static body charges by touching the nearest ground.

(b) Wrap carefully in soft paper when storing.

(c) Grasp firmly when removing.

(d) Store near the transmitter for handy use.

(e) Wipe off dust particles when dropped.

22. What intermediate frequencies are common in radar receivers?

(a) 220 and 440 MHz

(b) 47.5 and 95 MHz

(c) 455 and 675 kHz

(d) 30 and 60 MHz

(e) 10.7 and 41.5 MHz

23. What is the purpose of the sensitivity time control circuit in a radar set?

(a) Balances the echo box.

(b) Regulates the pulse duration.

(c) Reduces the gain on nearby targets.

(d) Synchronizes the sweep with the transmitter.

(e) Raises the gain for sea return.

24. What is the purpose of the discriminator stage in a radar receiver?

(a) Part of the AVC circuit.

(b) Causes the IF amplifier to drift and develop a DC voltage.

(c) Supplies control voltage to the klystron for frequency correction.

(d) Eliminates unwanted targets or echoes.

(e) Applies a frequency correction potential to the magnetron.

25. What is the purpose of Aquadag coatings on radar cathode-ray tubes?

(a) Bunches electrons.

(b) Forms the second anode.

(c) Acts as a suppressor.

(d) Protects against dangerous shock.

(e) Prevents cathode blocking.

26. What is "sea return" on a radar scope?

(a) Radar signals returned over water.

(b) Echo from a distant target.

(c) Noise from an electronic buoy.

(d) Signals from a marine repeater.

(e) Reflection of the signal from sea waves.

27. What may produce bright flashing pie sections on a radar PPI scope?

(a) Defective TR box.

(b) Defective deflection coil.

(c) Defective parabolic reflector.

(d) Defective AFC circuit.

(e) Defective crystal holder.

28. How long does it take a radar pulse to reach a target one nautical mile away and return?

(a) 12.3 microseconds

(b) 1.23 microseconds

(c) 6.15 microseconds

(d) 24.6 milliseconds

(e) 1.235 seconds

29. What is indicated by the "bearing resolution" of a radar set?

(a) Consistent reception of long-range targets.

(b) The error factor between sea return and true target.

(c) Proper focusing of targets on the PPI screen.

(d) Ability to distinguish between targets with the same range but differing azimuth directions.

(e) Ability to distinguish between targets with the same azimuth directions but differing ranges.

30. If the elapsed time is 40 microseconds between transmission and reception of the radar signal, how far away is the target?

(a) 3,280 yards

(b) 6,460 yards

(c) 5,280 yards

(d) 1,640 yards

(e) 6,560 yards

31. Who may operate a ship radar station?

(a) Anyone holding a third class radiotelephone permit.

(b) Anyone holding a second class radiotelegraph license.

(c) The ship's master or anyone so authorized by him.

(d) Only the holder of a valid FCC license or permit.

(e) Only the ship's radio operator.

32. What license is required for the installation, servicing and maintenance of ship radar?

(a) First class radiotelegraph license.

(b) First or second class radiotelephone or telegraph.

(c) First or second class radiotelephone or telegraph with radar endorsement.

(d) Third class radiotelephone permit.

(e) Third class radiotelephone with broadcast endorsement.

33. What type of radar interference would be apparent to anyone listening to a communications receiver?

(a) A strong clicking like a rotating device.

(b) Intermittent buzzing and popping noise.

(c) A steady tone and hash from the radar motor-generator.

(d) Receiver paralysis or blocking.

(e) A series of popping sounds like ignition noise.

34. On what frequencies would the radar serviceman look for interference to communication receivers from a radar station?

(a) 2,900 to 3,100 MHz

(b) 9,320 to 9.600 MHz

(c) 30 to 60 MHz

(d) 5,460 to 5,650 MHz

(e) Any communication frequency

35. How would radar interference to auto-alarm equipment be recognized?

(a) By sparking of the relay contacts.

(b) Checking the tubes for internal arcing.

(c) Plugging phones into the alarm and listening for identifying sounds.

(d) Checking the supply voltage on the alarm.

(e) By shutting off the radar unit.

36. Why must the interior of waveguides be kept clean, smooth and free of moisture?

(a) To prevent shock hazard.

(b) To keep losses at a minimum.

(c) To prevent polarization.

(d) To eliminate serious rusting.

(e) To maintain resonance.

37. Why are waveguides used in perference to coaxial lines in most shipboard radar installations?

(a) Lower loss.

(b) Less expensive.

(c) Longer life.

(d) Neater appearance.

(e) Easier to terminate.

38. Why are rectangular cross-section waveguides usually preferred over circular cross-section waveguides?

(a) Rotating joints are easier to install.

(b) Electric field has greater tendency to change.

(c) Less frequency range at the dominant mode.

(d) Desired polarization easily maintained.

(e) Better harmonic attenuation.

39. What precautions should be taken when installing vertical sections of waveguides with choke-coupling flanges to prevent moisture from entering the waveguide?

(a) Use good gasket cement.

(b) Bend the flange to allow moisture to run off.

(c) Tape the outside with electrical tape.

(d) Use a gasket at each flange and tighten securely.

(e) Drill a hole in the bottom for the moisture to escape.

40. Why must long, perfectly level sections of waveguides be avoided?

(a) Prevent the accumulation of condensed moisture inside.

(b) This unbalances the magnetic fields.

(c) Prevents overloading the antenna.

(d) Makes impedance matching more difficult.

(e) Prevents too much loss in the TR box.

41. Why are choke joints generally used in preference to flange joints to join sections of waveguides?

(a) Electrical contact is better.

(b) Lower cost due to wider tolerances.

(c) Less signal loss.

(d) Easier to maintain.

(e) Overall efficiency is greater.

42. What is the purpose of an echo box in a radar system?

(a) Low Q cavity to absorb sea return interference.

(b) Provides a phantom target for tuning and evaluating performance.

(c) Controls and regulates the echo timing interval.

(d) Provides range indication by measuring the echo.

(e) Amplifies the returning echoes from weak targets.

43. Who may make entries in the installation and maintenance record of a ship radar station?

(a) Ship's master or person authorized by him.

(b) Any person with a valid FCC license.

(c) Only the station licensee.

(d) Licensed operator responsible for work or under his supervision.

(e) The ship's radio operator only.

44. **Why would it be dangerous to operate or test a radar system aboard ship when explosive or inflammable cargo was being handled?**

(a) Vibration from the scanning system.

(b) Reflections from targets.

(c) Friction produced in the waveguides.

(d) Static picked up by the receiver.

(e) Possible arcing in the radar set or RF arcing from the beam.

45. **What indication on a loran scope would result from radar interference?**

(a) Spikes moving across the screen and "grass" near the scanning lines.

(b) Spikes near the scanning lines not moving.

(c) Fuzzy detail on the screen.

(d) Flashing pie sections extremely bright.

(e) Radial spokes from the center of the scope.

46. **When the radar set is operating properly, which pattern would appear on the PPI screen as a result of the echo box?**

(a) Radial spoke pattern or intensified area.

(b) A non-sinusoidal wave.

(c) A series of spikes and some "grass."

(d) A damped RF pattern.

(e) A sine wave of varying intensity.

47. **Who has the responsibility for making proper entries in the installation and maintenance record of a ship radar station?**

(a) Only that person authorized to operate the station.

(b) The radio operator and the ship electrician.

(c) The person assisting in the work.

(d) Licensed operator doing the work and the station licensee jointly.

(e) The ship's master and his first officer jointly.

48. **How are heading flashes produced on a radar PPI scope?**

(a) The action of the antenna waveguide.

(b) By the local oscillator klystron.

(c) These are a function of the echo producing box.

(d) This is produced by the marker generator.

(e) Cam-operated microswitch closed when the antenna is dead ahead.

49. **How are range-marker circles produced on the radar PPI scope?**

(a) Intermittent shorting of the echo box.

(b) Blanking of the AFC circuit.

(c) Synchronized, short, positive pulses applied to the PPI grid.

(d) Continuous impulse applied to the PPI for ranging.

(e) Special CRT face-plate.

50. What is the purpose of the "keep alive" electrode in TR and anti-TR boxes?

(a) Eliminates overloading and damaging the main spark gap.

(b) Prevents an arc at the main gap when the transmitter is pulsed.

(c) Increases the spark gap impedance during conduction.

(d) Provides the proper delay in flash-over after pulsing.

(e) Permits easier arc-over during pulse transmission.

CHAPTER 9

Advanced Radiotelephone, Part I: Element 4

We are ready to proceed on the final leg of our journey and, if the path has been passable to this point, there can be no doubt of reaching our objective...it's already in sight! Most of the theory has already been digested and it will be easy to build onto that as we move one.

Actually, there are some additional rules and regulations that are applicable to first class radiotelephone operators since they may operate, test, adjust, modify or repair any AM, FM, or TV broadcast station regardless of power or directional or nondirectional antenna. Other than that, there is nothing new beyond what you have already studied in Element 3, except for a little more depth in the subjects covered.

AC CIRCUITS

AC current is always changing in amplitude and reversing direction every half hertz. Starting at zero, it rises to maximum positive voltage in the first quarter hertz or 90 degrees, falls back to zero the second 90 degrees, reverses direction and reaches maximum negative voltage at the end of the third quarter hertz (270 degrees), and falls to zero again during the fourth quarter as a full hertz is completed. It continues, repeating each step during each hertz thereafter. Although "cycles per second" may be used at times, we should remember that cycles and hertz are synonymous and the latter will replace the former universally in time. House current is now 60 hertz instead of 60 cycle. Its effective value or RMS (root mean square) is 0.707 times the maximum or peak value. If our meter reads RMS values, as many do, the peak value may be computed by multiplying by 1.414. AC voltages and currents vary with time as to quantity, while DC does not, and AC is represented by a sine wave or sinusoidal wave and DC is represented by a straight line. In using the formulas, always remember to convert properly; if the answer is in effective voltage and peak voltage is called for, multiply by 1.414; if you have peak voltage and need RMS or effective voltage for your answer, multiply by 0.707. In a few cases you may need average voltage when you have peak voltage figures, in which case you simply multiply by 0.637.

Phase

When an AC voltage is connected across a resistor, the voltage is in phase with the current as they reach maximum and minimum values at the same time, but this is not so when capacity or inductance is added. Capacity causes the AC current to lead the voltage, while inductance causes the AC current to lag the voltage. This may be clearer if we consider that a capacitor draws maximum current instantly as it is charging, tapering off until it is fully charged, then it draws minimum current. In a coil, the current supplies and removes energy for the magnetic field, causing it to lag the voltage. Inductive reactance is the opposite of capacitive reactance which is indicated in the impedance formula using a reactance value that is the difference between the two:

$$Z = \sqrt{R^2 + (XL-XC)^2}$$

The difference between the two reactances may be explained by understanding current flow. As a capacitor charges and discharges, it causes the flow of current, but the charging and discharging of an inductor's magnetic field opposes current flow.

Pulsating Waves

A pulsating wave changes in value but not in direction, and it may be a wave with DC and AC components. An example of such a wave is the output of a rectifier before it reaches the filtering section which removes the AC component and leaves only the DC. In practice, a capacitor and inductor (coil) are often used to combine the AC signal and the DC grid bias at the control grid of an amplifier tube, forming a pulsating wave. The capacitor blocks the DC by preventing it from entering that part of the circuit, but it permits the AC to enter freely. The inductor works the other way—keeping the AC out while permitting the DC to flow without opposition. A pulsating current is actually two currents, one AC and one DC, flowing together as one. During troubleshooting, while tracing through a circuit, it is always helpful to trace the path of each current separately, just as though the other did not exist.

AMPLIFIER PROBLEMS

Problems arise in the case of multistage audio amplifiers in which a common power supply is used. The impedance of the power supply filter capacitors becomes quite high at the low end of the audio range, and as a result, when a signal is applied to the grid of the amplifier, it is amplified and results in an AC component from the plate circuit which should be coupled into the next stage through the coupling capacitor that ordinarily would provide a lower impedance path than the plate resistor of the preceding stage.

However, it is not always practical to utilize a resistor that is high enough in value to block the AC component and force it to take the lower impedance path through the coupling capacitor. Therefore, the AC signal is passed at least partially through the plate resistor and gets into the po er supply. The same power supply is used for the plate circuit of the next stage, and the AC signal that it carries passes through the plate resistor and then through the coupling capacitor to reach the grid. Although that signal may be quite small, after it is amplified it becomes large, causing a greater voltage to be developed across the filter capacitor, thus increasing the feedback signal applied to the grid of the following stage. This larger signal is further amplified and the end result is oscillation. This oscillation is sustained only at very low frequencies and produces a sound similar to a "putt-putt" which is called motorboating. Elimination of the problem requires the use of decoupling filters consisting of a resistor in series with the plate resistor which is bypassed to ground from the plate side of the adder resistor. A decoupling filter should be used in the B+ lead of each stage.

Hum presents another problem in a multistage amplifier which, although not loud enough to be of importance in a single-stage amplifier, may override the signal if it enters early in a multistage amplifier. This problem is frequently caused by either insufficient filter capacity or a defective filter capacitor which has lost some of its capacity. In this case, the AC ripple is not filtered enough and it introduces a problem when subjected to higher amplification. Replacing a questionable filter, or substituting one of greater value, will resolve the trouble quickly.

Distortion is another problem common to amplifiers when any deviation from the original waveform appears at the output. We know that the output of any amplifier should be an exact but larger replica of the input signal, and any variation of gain with frequency is frequency distortion. If the gain is low at low frequencies, higher at the middle frequencies, and low once more at the high end of the audio range, there will be frequency distortion.

AUDIO EQUIPMENT

A microphone is an input device which transforms sound waves into tiny electrical waves, and many sizes, shapes, and types are available. In the questions and answers, we review the more popular microphones in detail and offer some comparison of the advantages and-or disadvantages of each.

Preamplifiers are normally used to boost the millivolt output of most microphones to a high enough level to overcome any noise pickup in the cable carrying the signal to the audio amplifiers. This requires placing the preamp as close to the microphone as possible before feeding its output to the longer cable connection to the main amplifier.

Tape and record players, line pads and equalizers, impedance matching, and amplifier fidelity, along with system maintenance, are discussed in the Q & A section. You will be enlightened on the problems frequently encountered in the broadcast studio, as well as shortcuts and corrective measures normally followed.

RF AMPLIFIERS

Although neutralization is not required with pentode RF amplifiers as a rule, it is important in triodes to prevent the amplifier from oscillating. Neutralization means cancelling one feedback voltage with another of equal level but opposite phase. A completely neutralized RF amplifier with normal loading will show maximum grid and minimum plate current at the same point in the tuning of the plate tank. When the plate is tuned either side of resonance, the grid will show an equal decrease from maximum on each side. Difficulty in neutralizing can be caused by lack of filament bypass, ground leads that are too long, neutralizing capacitors located too close to strong RF fields, insufficient shielding, magnetic coupling between plate and grid inductances, or induced current in shielding.

The need for neutralization in a transistor RF amplifier is much greater than it is for the vacuum tube type amplifier due to the larger values of internal capacity in solid-state devices. Interaction between stages of a multistage amplifier of the transistor type can be quite severe, making such stages hard to tune and causing them to oscillate. Improved designs are eliminating the need for neutralization in many circuits, and the grounded collector configuration, or emitter follower as it is also known, is comparable to the cathode follower in vacuum tube circuitry. This arrangement is very useful for impedance-matching purposes in RF amplifiers.

POWER SUPPLIES

Three-phase power supplies are utilized as the high-voltage source in large transmitters, since smaller rectifiers and less filtering is necessary than with single-phase. The 3-phase system is actually three separate AC voltages of equal amplitude, each 120 degrees out of phase with the other two. When 3-phase power is carried on a 3-wire line, with the wires designated as 1, 2, and 3, one of the AC voltages is delivered on wires 1 and 2, another on 2 and 3, and the third on 1 and 3. Even though we have three separate voltages, only three wires are necessary instead of six as would normally be expected.

Dealing with diode rectifiers of the silicon type, especially, peak inverse voltage is very important and should be carefully considered in selecting the proper diodes. The peak inverse voltage (PIV) is the maximum instantaneous voltage present during that portion of the hertz when the diode is reverse biased, and this is the time during which the diode is not conducting. If we exceed the inverse voltage rating, the life of the diode may be reduced or terminated because the voltage peak will puncture the diode and it will no longer act as a rectifier. If the power supply secondary has an output of 1,000 volts, the peak inverse voltage to which the diode would be subjected is 1.414 times 1,000 or 1,414 volts. This figure would hold true with a full-wave or bridge-type rectifier, but in the case of a half-wave capacitor filter input type, the peak would be 2.83 times 1,000 or 2,830 volts, so a rectifier rated at 3,000 PIV would be necessary. There should always be a reasonable margin allowed in choosing silicon diode PIV ratings, since possible line surges are multiplied considerably by transformer step-up ratios and the peak figure to be considered.

Filtering systems have been considered previously, one type simply using a capacitor across the rectifier output. But in many cases this does not prove adequate. The capacitor input is a basic type of filter, and when used in conjunction with other components, is quite useful, but the choke input type has many advantages no offered by other arrangements. The choke input filter, with the choke following the rectifier, tends to prevent current build-up due to the opposition of the choke when the rectifier conducts and yet maintains current through the load when the rectifier is not conducting. This offers much better regulation than is possible with a capacitor input type, but there is some sacrifice in voltage output. The choke filter is especially effective in the full-wave circuit because the smoothing action is more complete since there are twice as many pulses applied as there are in a half-wave rectifier. The capacitor and choke work together to provide optimum filtering action, since the capacitor stores energy while the applied voltage increases and releases energy when the applied voltage decreases. During this time, the choke opposes any change in current and thus assists the action of the capacitor in providing and maintaining a constant high-voltage level.

Voltage doublers, frequently used in TV receivers, offer a convenient way of obtaining a considerably higher voltage than would be available from the AC power line without the use of a step-up transformer. The saving in weight and cost is a big advantage, expecially with portables. Reasonable voltage regulation is provided in the doubler by using larger values of capacity which are able to store more energy between peaks.

Voltage regulation is of prime importance in many types of equipment, and special arrangements must be used to insure proper regulation under widely varying conditions. If the line voltage varies, the output of the power supply varies more. Transformer and choke windings also introduce resistance into the supply which results in a voltage drop that increases as the load increases, and thus causes a decrease in the supply output. Voltage regulation circuits compensate for these variations and may be either in the form of series or shunt systems. Zener diodes are used as shunt regulators when low voltages with normal currents must be regulated. Greater currents are handled more efficiently with series transistor regulation, and the load capacity may be increased by paralleling the series transistor with additional units as required. Voltage regulation may be expressed by:

$$\frac{E_{NL}-E_{FL}}{E_{FL}}$$

E_{NL} equals the no-load supply voltage
E_{FL} is the full-load supply voltage,
multiplied by 100 for a percentage figure.

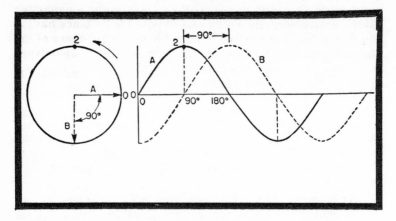

Fig. 9-1. Sine waves with 90 degrees phase difference.

QUESTIONS & ANSWERS

CHAPTER 9 (ELEMENT 4)

Question 1: Show by a simple graph what is meant by: "the current in a circuit leads the voltage." What would cause this?

When a sine-wave signal is processed through an inductor, the inductor opposes the changing current but offers no opposition to the voltage. As a result, the current through the inductor lags the voltage by 90 degrees. When a sinusoidal AC voltage is processed through a capacitor, the capacitor opposes the changing voltage but offers no opposition to the current. As a result, the voltage through a capacitor lags the current by 90 degrees. When a circuit is inductive, the net effect on the AC signal applied is the same as if the signal were applied to an inductor; when a circuit is capacitive in nature, the net effect is as if the signal were applied to a capacitor. Figure 9-1 shows the effect of applying a sinusoidal signal through a capacitance. Note that the current sine wave leads the voltage sine wave by 90 degrees. (In this sketch, sine wave A is the current cycle and sine B represents the voltage cycle.)

Question 2: List the fundamental frequency and the first 10 harmonic frequencies of a broadcast station licensed to operate at 790 kHz.

The fundamental (1st harmonic) is 790 kilohertz (kHz); the second harmonic is 1,580 kHz; the third, 2,370 kHz; the fourth 3,160 kHz; the fifth, 3,950 kHz; the sixth, 4,740 kHz; the seventh, 5,530 kHz; the eighth, 6,320 kHz; the ninth, 7,110 kHz; and the tenth, 7,900 kHz.

Question 3: A series-parallel circuit is composed of a 5-ohm resistor in series with the parallel combination of a capacitor having a pure reactance of 20 ohms and an inductance having a pure reactance of 8 ohms. What is the total impedance of the circuit? Would the total reactance be inductive or capacitive?

Solving for the impedance of the parallel combination, assume a voltage of 100 across the combination, thus:

$$I_c = \frac{E_a}{X_c} = \frac{100}{20} = 5 \text{ amps}$$

$$I_L = \frac{E_a}{X_L} = \frac{100}{8} = 12.5 \text{ amps}$$

$$I_p = I_L - I_c = 7.5 \text{ amps}$$

$$\text{so } Z_p = \frac{E_a}{I_p} = \frac{100}{7.5} = 13.3 \text{ ohms}$$

$$Z \text{ (total)} = \text{square root of } R^2 + X_L{}^2$$

$$= \text{square root of } 202 = 14.2$$

Therefore, the total circuit impedance is 14.2 ohms and the reactance is inductive.

Question 4: What does the Q of a coil mean?

The Q of a coil represents its degree of perfection and is equal to its reactance divided by its resistance. Usually, the higher the Q the more satisfactory the coil, and when above 10 it approximates the reciprocal of the power factor.

Question 5: What effect does mutual inductance have on the total inductance of two coils connected in series?

If connected so the fields are aiding, the total inductance increases, or, if connected with fields opposing, the inductance is reduced. Total inductance of two coils may be figured by:

$$L_T = L_1 + L2 \pm 2M$$

where LT equals the total effective inductance of henrys, L1 is the inductance of the first coil in henrys, L2 is the inductance of the second coil in henrys, M is the mutual inductance in henrys (add if the coil fields aid, subtract if the coil fields oppose).

Question 6: If the mutual inductance between two coils is 0.1 henry, and L1 has an inductance of 0.2 henry and L2 is 0.8 henry, what is the coefficient of coupling?

The extent to which two inductors are coupled is expressed by **coefficient of coupling** (K), which is the mutual inductance divided by the square <u>root of</u> the product of the individual inductances, or $K = M / \sqrt{L1 \times L2}$. The coefficient of coupling is always less than unity, since 1.0 means that 100 percent of the flux lines of one coil are cut by the turns of other—which can happen in theory only. In the case presented, K works out to 0.25.

Question 7: When two coils of equal inductance are connected in series with a maximum coefficient of coupling and the fields are in phase, what is the total inductance of the two coils?

The total inductance of the two coils is the sum of the two coils plus twice the mutual inductance between them, so M may be found by:

$$M = K \sqrt{L1 \times L2}$$

Since K equals 1 in this problem, the total inductance is LT equals L1 + L2 + 2L, which equals 4L. It is advisable to remember that 4L is the maximum inductance for a pair of coupled coils.

Question 8: What does the term power factor mean in reference to electric power circuits?

Power factor is a measure of the extent to which the current in a circuit leads or lags the voltage of that circuit. Ranging between zero and 1, the power factor is one when the current and voltage are in phase with each other and zero when the current is 90 degrees out of phase with the voltage. The lower the phase angle between current and voltage, the closer to unity the power factor will be. The power factor is equal to the true power used in the circuit over the circuit voltage times the circuit current, or the cosine of the angle of lead or lag between voltage and current in the circuit.

$$p.f. = \cos \Theta = \frac{Watts}{E \times I}$$

Question 9: What is meant by the time constant of a resistance-capacitance circuit?

The time constant in a resistance-capacitance circuit is a measure of the time required for a capacitor to charge or discharge through a specific resistor. The time required for charged capacitor C to discharge through shunt resistor R, until the actual voltage across C is reduced to 36.8 percent of its original value, is the time constant of that RC combination. By connecting R in series with C (uncharged) and applying a voltage to the terminals of the series combination, the time required for the capacitor to charge to 63.2 percent of the applied voltage is the time constant of that combination. The time constant of an RC circuit in seconds is equal to C in microfarads times R in megohms.

Question 10: A voltage of 110V is applied to a series circuit with an inductive reactance of 25 ohms, a capacitive reactance of 10 ohms and a resistance of 15 ohms. What is the phase relationship between the applied voltage and the current flowing in the circuit?

Circuit reactance is 25 –10 or 15 ohms, which is equal to the circuit resistance. When the circuit reactance is equal to circuit resistance, the phase angle must be 45 degrees. The phase angle for reactance and resistance in series is equal to the angle whose tangent is X over R, so the reactance divided by the resistance would provide the tangent figure and the "trig" tables would give the answer in degrees.

Question 11: What is the reactance of a capacitor at 1,200 kHz if the reactance is 300 ohms at 680 kHz?

Capacitive reactance is inversely proportional to the frequency, so:

The reactance will be less than 300 ohms by the same proportion that 1,200 kHz is greater than 680 kHz. Since 1,200 kHz is 1.7647 times greater than 680 kHz, the reactance at 1,200 kHz will be 300 divided by 1.7647, or 170 ohms.

Question 12: If an AC current of 5 amps flows in a series circuit composed of 12 ohms resistance, 15 ohms inductive reactance and 40 ohms capacitive reactance, what is the voltage across the circuit?

First find the voltage across individual components,

$$E_R = I \times R = 5 \times 12 = 60V$$

$$E_C = I \times X_C = 5 \times 40 = 200V$$

$$E_L = I \times X_L = 5 \times 15 = 75V$$

$$E_X = E_C - E_L \text{ or } 200V - 75V = 125V$$

$$E_T = \sqrt{E_X^2 + E_R^2} = \sqrt{(125)^2 + (60)^2} = 138.6V$$

Question 13: If a lamp rated at 100 watts and 155V is connected in series with an inductive reactance of 355 ohms and a

capacitive reactance of 130 ohms across a voltage of 220V, what is the value of the current flowing through the lamp?

The resistance of the lamp is:

$$R = \frac{E^2}{P} = \frac{115^2}{100} = 132.2 \text{ ohms}$$

So:

$$Z = \sqrt{R^2 + (X_L - X_C)^2}$$

$$= \sqrt{132.2^2 + (355 - 130)^2}$$

$$= 261 \text{ ohms}$$

$$I = \frac{E}{Z} = \frac{220}{261} = 0.843 \text{ amps}$$

Question 14: If an AC series circuit has a resistance of 12 ohms, an inductive reactance of 7 ohms, and a capacitive reactance of 7 ohms at the resonant frequency, what will be the total impedance at twice the resonant frequency?

As we double the frequency, the inductive reactance is doubled and the capacitive reactance halved. This changes X_L to 14 ohms and X_C to 3.5 ohms for a net reactance of 10.5 ohms:

$$Z = \sqrt{12^2 + 10.5^2} = 15.9 \text{ ohms}$$

Question 15: A series circuit has resistance, inductive reactance and capacitive reactance. The resistance is 7 ohms, the inductive reactance is 8 ohms. What value of capacitive reactance must the circuit have to total 13 ohms impedance?

$$Z = \sqrt{R^2 + X^2} \text{ or } 13 = \sqrt{7^2 + X^2}$$

and by squaring both sides,

$$13^2 = \sqrt{(7^2 + X^2)}$$

$$169 = 49 + X^2$$

$$X^2 = 169 - 49 \text{ or } 120$$

$$X = \sqrt{120}$$

$$X_C = 10.96 + 8 = 18.96 \text{ ohms}$$

Question 16: If in a given circuit the resistance, inductive reactance and capacitive reactance are each 11 ohms and the frequency is reduced to 0.411 of its original value at resonance, what is the impedance of the circuit at the new frequency?

Inductive reactance is directly proportional to frequency and capacitive reactance is inversely proportional, so:

$$X_{L(n)} = 0.411 \times 11 = 4.52 \text{ ohms}$$

$$X_{C(n)} = \frac{11}{.411} = 26.7 \text{ ohms}$$

$$X_{C(n)} = X_{Cn} - X_{Ln} = 26.7 - 4.5 = 22.2 \text{ ohms}$$

Since resistance R remains the same:

$$Z = \sqrt{R^2 + X^2} = \sqrt{11^2 + 22.2^2} = 24.8 \text{ ohms}$$

Question 17: If an AC voltage of 115V is connected across a parallel circuit composed of resistance 30 ohms, an inductive reactance of 17 ohms, and a capacitive reactance of 19 ohms, what is the total current required from the source?

$$I_R = \frac{E}{R} = \frac{115}{30} = 3.83 \text{ amps}$$

$$I_L = \frac{E}{X_L} = \frac{115}{17} = 6.76 \text{ amps}$$

$$I_C = \frac{E}{X_C} = \frac{115}{19} = 6.05 \text{ amps}$$

$$I_T = \sqrt{I_R^2 + (I_L - I_C)^2}$$

$$= \sqrt{(3.83)^2 + (6.76 - 6.05)^2}$$

$$= 3.9 \text{ amps}$$

Question 18: A parallel circuit has five branches as shown in Fig. 9-2; three branches are pure resistance of 7, 11, 14 ohms, with a fourth branch of 5 ohms inductive reactance and a fifth of 9 ohms capacitive reactance. What is the total impedance of the network? When power is applied, which branch will dissipate the most heat?

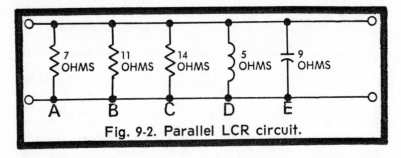

Fig. 9-2. Parallel LCR circuit.

In the circuit in Fig. 9-2, assume 100 volts is applied to the network. Current through each branch equals E over R as follows:

$$I_A = \frac{100}{7} = 14.28 \text{ amps}$$

$$I_B = \frac{100}{11} = 9.09 \text{ amps}$$

$$I_C = \frac{100}{14} = 7.14 \text{ amps}$$

$$I_D = \frac{100}{5} = 20.0 \text{ amps}$$

$$I_E = \frac{100}{9} = 11.11 \text{ amps}$$

The I_R total is 14.28 + 9.09 + 7.14 or 30.51 amps. The I_X total is 20.0 - 11.11 or 8.89 amps, since the inductive branch, I_D, is 180 degrees out of phase with the capacitive branch, I_E, and the smaller current branch is subtracted from the larger. Now, the I_R total may be combined with the I_X total as follows:

$$I_T = \sqrt{I_R^2 + I_X^2} = \sqrt{(30.51)^2 + (8.89)^2} = 31.8 \text{ amps}$$

$$Z_T = \frac{E}{I} = \frac{100}{31.8} = 3.14 \text{ ohms.}$$

The most heat would be dissipated by branch I_A, since it draws the most current of the resistance branches; inductors and capacitors do not consume any power, so they dissipate no heat.

Question 19: What factors determine the ratio of impedances which a given transformer can match?

The turns ratio is the determining factor, and it should be equal to the square root of the impedance ratio, with the winding having the most turns connected to the higher impedance.

Question 20: What value of capacitance must be shunted across a coil having an inductance of 56 microhenrys in order to provide resonance at 5,000 kHz?

$$C = \frac{1}{4\pi^2 F^2 L} =$$

$$\frac{1}{4 \times (3.14)^2 \times (5.000 \times 10^3)^2 \times 56 \times 10^{-6}}$$

$$= 18 \text{ picofarads}$$

Question 21: In a parallel circuit having an inductance of 150 microhenries and a capacity of 160 picofarads, what is the resonant frequency?

$$FR = \frac{1}{2\pi \sqrt{LC}} = \frac{1}{6.28\sqrt{1.5 \times 10^{-4} \times 1.6 \; 10^{-10}}}$$

$$= 1,028 \text{ kHz}$$

Question 22: What is secondary emission in a vacuum tube?

Secondary emission is caused by bombardment of the plate by the electron stream in the tube. The bombardment causes electrons to escape from the plate, resulting in nonlinear plate current. Although other electrodes may be involved in secondary emission, the plate is most important. The suppressor grid forces secondary electrons to return to the plate.

Question 23: What is the purpose of the screen grid in a vacuum tube?

The screen grid reduces interelectrode capacity between the plate and control grid to a very low value, thus preventing oscillations as a result of feedback. The screen grid acts as an electrostatic shield between the two critical elements.

Question 24: What is the meaning of "mutual conductance" and "amplification factor" in reference to vacuum tubes?

Mutual conductance or transconductance is the actual ratio of change in plate current to the change in grid voltage that produces the plate current change, with all other electrode voltages remaining constant. If the plate current changes 4 mA as the grid voltage changes 0.2V, mutual conductance of that tube is:

$$\frac{0.004}{0.2} = 20,000 \text{ micromhos}$$

Amplification factor in vacuum tubes refers to the effectiveness of voltages applied to that tube's plate and control grid. It is the ratio of a small plate voltage change required to balance a specified small change in grid voltage needed to keep plate current constant, while other voltages are maintained at a constant level.

Question 25: Define: Amplifier gain, percentage deviation, stage amplification, and percentage of modulation, while explaining the determination of each.

Although amplifier gain may refer to the power or voltage gain of an amplifier, unless otherwise specified, the reference is normally to voltage gain. Voltage gain is equal to the output signal voltage divided by the input signal voltage. Power gain is equal to the useful output power divided by the input signal power.

Percentage of deviation is the amount (in percentage) by which a quantity varies from a usual value, commonly in reference to an FM transmitter's variation from an assigned frequency.

Stage amplification is the voltage or power gain of a single amplifier stage and is figured by dividing the output voltage or power by the input voltage or power for that stage only.

Percentage of modulation in AM means half the difference between maximum and minimum amplitudes divided by the average amplitude and expressed as a percentage. In FM the reference is to the ratio of the frequency excursion to that needed for 100 percent modulation; it is also expressed as a percentage. As an example, FM broadcast transmitters require a frequency excursion of plus or minus 75 kHz for 100 percent modulation. When the actual excursion is plus or minus 50 kHz, the percentage of modulation is 66 percent.

Question 26: Under what circumstances will the gain-per-stage be equal to the voltage amplification factor of the tube employed?

This condition would be possible only in a resistance-coupled amplifier with an infinite load impedance. Since an infinite load impedance is not possible, the gain per stage must always be something less than the amplification factor of the tube in any resistance-coupled amplifier.

Transformer coupling does make it possible to equal the amplification factor of the tube, since a stepup transformer compensates for the loss of gain resulting from the less than infinite load impedance. Such gain may be obtained only with triodes from a practical standpoint.

Question 27: What is the stage amplification with a single triode operating with the following conditions: plate voltage 250V, plate current 20 mA, plate impedance 5,000 ohms, load impedance 10,000 ohms, grid bias 4.5V, amplification factor 24?

$$\text{Voltage gain} = \frac{uRL}{R_p + R_L} = \frac{24 \times 10,000}{5,000 + 10,000}$$

$$= \frac{240,000}{15,000} = 16$$

Question 28: Find the gain of a triode amplifier with a plate resistance of 50,000 ohms and a load resistance of 75,000 ohms with an amplification factor of 25.

$$\text{Voltage Gain} = \frac{uRL}{R_p + R_L} = \frac{25 \times 75,000}{50K + 75K}$$

$$= \frac{1,875 \ K}{125 \ K} = 15$$

Question 29: Draw a diagram of a push-pull Class B linear amplifier using triode tubes. Include a complete antenna coupling circuit and antenna circuit. Indicate the points at which various voltages are connected.

See Fig. 9-3.

Question 30: What is the principal advantage of a Class C amplifier?

High plate efficiency is the principal advantage of a Class C amplifier and a much greater output is possible from a given tube, with efficiencies of 60 percent or better likely.

Question 31: Name four causes of distortion in a modulated amplifier output.

Overmodulation, excessive RF drive, a defective tube or improper tuning of the final tank.

Question 32: What precautions should be observed when soldering transistors and repairing printed circuits?

A small soldering iron in the order of 25 watts or so should be used when soldering transistors or repairing printed circuits. It is considered good policy to keep your long-nose pliers clamped to the transistor leg, between the iron and the body, while soldering or unsoldering any transistor. Never hold the iron against the pattern of a PC board any longer than is absolutely necessary, since the pattern will raise and a major

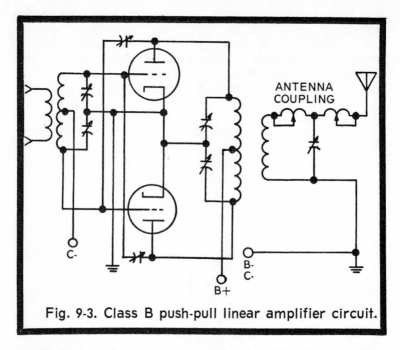

Fig. 9-3. Class B push-pull linear amplifier circuit.

repair job may be needed to get the circuit back in working order. Always hit and run!

Question 33: What is the gain factor of a transistor?

"Gain factor" is a little-used term that may refer to the alpha or beta of a transistor. The term may refer to **either** alpha or beta because they are related by the formula B $B = a/(1-a)$. Alpha is the emitter-to-collector current gain of a transistor in the common-base configuration and is always less than unity. Beta is the base-to-collector current in the common-emitter configuration.

Question 34: What are the major disadvantages of using transistors in place of vacuum tubes if costs are the same?

Today it would be hard to find a disadvantage with transistors. In the early days of semiconductors, however, the transistor was a great deal more susceptible to heat and was plagued with thermal noise problems. Transistors are more vulnerable than tubes to voltage excesses such as occur during atmospheric storms. The advantages, however, far out-weigh the disadvantages in virtually every category from construction simplicity to circuit performance.

Question 35: What is an audio frequency? What approximate band of frequencies is normally referred to as the audio-frequency range?

An audio frequency is any frequency in the audible spectrum, which extends from 20 to about 18,000 Hz. In hi-fi circles, the audio spectrum is considered to be 20-20,000 Hz, despite the fact that few individuals are capable of hearing sounds at or above 15 kHz.

Question 36: What causes sound and how is it transmitted in the air?

Sound is a disturbance of air molecules resulting in sound waves being set up at an audio frequency. Transmission of sound waves in air results when the compression and spreading of the air molecules at an audio rate forces the waves to move out from their point of origin at a high rate of speed (approximately 1120 feet per second).

Question 37. Sketch the physical construction of the following types of microphones and list their advantages or disadvantages: dynamic, crystal and ceramic, single-button (carbon), and ribbon. Which are normally used in broadcast studios and why?

Dynamic Microphone

The dynamic, or moving-coil, microphone (Fig. 9-4A) consists of a coil of wire attached to a diaphragm and is so constructed that the coil is suspended and free to move in a radial magnetic field. Sound waves impinging on the diaphragm cause the diaphragm to vibrate. This vibration moves the voice coil through the magnetic field, cutting the lines of force. This action generates a voltage in the coil that has the same waveform as the sound waves striking the diaphragm.

The dynamic microphone requires no external voltage source, has good fidelity (20-9000 Hz), is directional for high-frequency sounds, and has an output of the order of −85 dB. The impedance of the dynamic microphone is low (50 ohms or less). Therefore, it may be connected to relatively long transmission lines without excessive attenuation of the high frequencies.

Crystal and Ceramic Microphones

Crystal and ceramic microphones utilize a property of certain crystals (such as quartz and Rochelle salt) known as the piezoelectric effect. The bending of the crystal, resulting from the pressure of the sound wave, produces an EMF across the faces of the crystal or ceramic element. This EMF is applied to the input of an amplifier.

The microphone (Fig. 9-4B) consists of a diaphragm that may be cemented directly on one surface of the crystal, or in

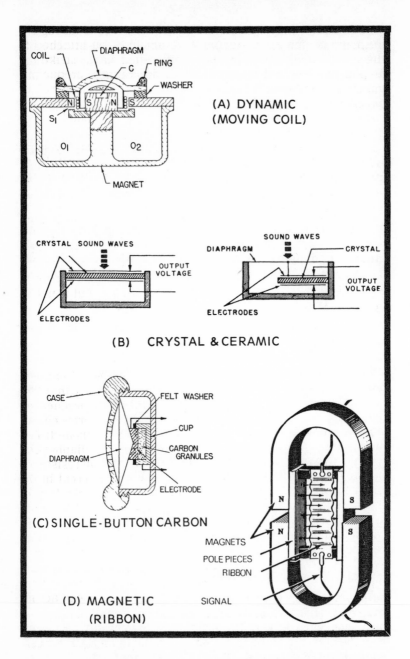

Fig. 9-4. Cross sections of dynamic (A) crystal and ceramic (B), single-button carbon (C), and magnetic, or ribbon microphones.

some cases it may be connected to the element through a coupling member. A metal plate, or electrode, is attached to the other surface of the crystal. When sound waves strike the diaphragm, the vibrations of the diaphragm produce a varying pressure on the surface of the crystal, and therefore an EMF is induced across the electrodes. This EMF has essentially the same waveform as that of the sound waves striking the diaphragm.

A large percentage of ceramic microphones employ some form of the bimorph cell. In this type of cell, two crystals, so cut and oriented that their voltages will be additive in the output, are cemented together and used in place of a crystal.

This type of microphone has high impedance, is light in weight, requires no battery, is nondirectional, has a high frequency response, and has an output of the order of −70 dB. However, the crystal microphone is sensitive to high temperature, humidity, and rough handling; therefore, its use is restricted where these conditions prevail. The ceramic microphone has almost the same limitations, but is not as susceptible to temperature extremes.

Single-Button Microphone

The single-button carbon microphone (Fig. 9-4C) consists of a diaphragm mounted against carbon granules that are contained in a small carbon cup or button. To produce an output voltage, this microphone is connected in a series circuit containing a battery and the primary of a microphone transformer. The pressure of the sound waves on the diaphragm, which is coupled to the carbon granules, causes the resistance of the granules to vary. Thus, a varying direct current in the primary produces an alternating voltage in the secondary of the transformer. This voltage has essentially the same waveform as that of the sound waves striking the diaphragm. The current through a carbon microphone may be as great as 100 mA and the resistance may vary from about 50 to 90 ohms. The voltage developed across the secondary depends upon the turns ratio and the rate of change in primary current. Normal output voltage of a typical circuit is from 3 to 10V peak across the secondary terminals.

Ribbon Microphone

One of the key disadvantages of most other microphone types is their inability to respond to sound waves from all directions. This disadvantage is overcome with the ribbon, or velocity, microphone. The operation of this type is fundamentally the same as that of the dynamic mike. Instead of the moving coil, through, a ribbon of corrugated metal is caused to vibrate in the magnetic field. The device is shown in Fig. 9-4D. The ribbon element functions in much the same manner as the diaphragm of other mike types. The ribbon is arranged in such a way that its length is perpendicular to (and its width is in the plane of) the magnetic lines of force. The pole pieces are constructed in such a way so that air passes freely through the microphone. When sound waves strike the ribbon, the ribbon vibrates in the magnetic field, which induces a voltage in the ribbon that is proportional to the strength of the field, the velocity of movement in the field, and the length of the ribbon in the field.

The ribbon is subject to winds out of doors, so its use is restricted for the most part to studios. A good ribbon mike can give essentially flat reproduction of signals between 20 and 15,000 Hz, and is sensitive enough to pick up sounds at considerable distances. The output is on the order of —90 dB at a very low impedance. In virtually all applications, the impedance must be raised by means of a matching transformer.

The ribbon microphone is the type most widely used in broadcast work (TV newscasts, panel discussions, studio recording). While it is resistant to temperature variations and humidity, the ribbon's delicate mounting makes the mike susceptible to rough handling, vibration, and shock.

Question 38: What is meant by "phasing" of microphones and when is this necessary?

Phasing means that each microphone has the same output polarity with a given sound pressure wave. The outputs must be in step to avoid some cancelling of each other. Phasing is necessary when connecting two or more microphones to a mixer to eliminate opposing outputs, resulting in a reduced and distorted overall output. The best operation of many AM transmitters requires proper phasing due to the unsymmetrical aspects of these waveforms.

Question 39: What is the difference between unidirectional, bidirectional, and omnidirectional microphones?

The unidirectional mike's pickup is in one direction only. A unidirectional picks up equally well from two directions, separated by 180 degrees, and the omnidirectional microphone responds equally to sounds from all directions.
Question 40: What is a decibel?

The decibel is a unit of relative power, either sound or electrical, and is equal to ten times the logarithm of the ratio of the two powers. The formula for such calculations is:

$$db = 10 \log \frac{P2}{P1}$$

where P2 is always the larger power and impedances are equal. When using db in relation to power, an increase of 1 db represents an increase of 25 percent in power, while an increase of 3 db actually doubles the power.

Question 41: VU meters are normally placed across transmission lines of what characteristic impedance?

VU meters measure "volume units" across 600-ohm lines, where the reference power level of 0 dBm, or 1 mW at an audio frequency of 1 kHz, is used as the standard "zero" point. The corresponding RMS voltage across the 600-ohm load is 774.6 mV. Incrementally, the VU is identical to the decibel—that is, a signal of 10 dBm is the same as a signal that measures +10 on a VU meter.

Question 42: Show by a circuit diagram a method of desensitizing a VU meter to cause it to read lower than normal.

See Fig. 9-5.

Question 43: Why are the diaphragms of certain microphones stretched?

Stretching a diaphragm shifts the natural resonant frequency of the diaphragm to a higher value and provides more uniform response to all frequencies.

Question 44: What type of microphone uses a coil of wire, attached to a diaphragm, which moves in a magnetic field as the result of the impinging of sound waves?

A dynamic microphone (frequently used in broadcast stations).

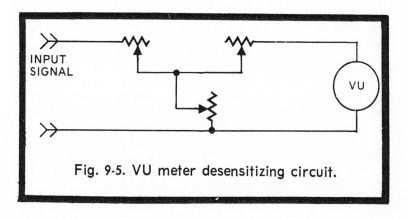

Fig. 9-5. VU meter desensitizing circuit.

Question 45: What is the most serious disadvantage of using carbon microphones with high fidelity amplifiers?

The high noise level or hissing which is a characteristic of the carbon microphone makes it unsatisfactory for quality use.

Question 46: What is the purpose of a variable attenuator in a speech-input system?

A variable attenuator controls the voltage gain of an amplifier and permits adjustment to a proper value according to the input signal level.

Question 47: Why is it important to keep the contact points on attenuator pads used in a broadcast studio console clean? How are they cleaned?

Contact points must be clean to provide reliable, noise-free operation of the pads. Points may be cleaned with a good TV tuner cleaner (spray) or carbon tetrachloride; then they should be wiped clean with a soft cloth. Wipers may be cleaned the same way, but be extremely careful not to bend or disturb their tension. After cleaning, a light lubrication with a TV tuner lubricant, or, if not available, petroleum jelly, will reduce wear of the contacts. In fact, a TV type lubricant will help keep the contacts clean.

Question 48: Why should impedances be matched in speech-input equipment?

Maximum transfer of energy to the load, as well as good frequency response, may be obtained only by matching the impedances. Impedance matching also eliminates line reflections which cause echo effects where long lines are used.

Question 49: What is a preamplifier?

A preamplifier is a high-gain audio amplifier used to increase low-level outputs from microphones, record or tape players to a more reliable and acceptable level before application to other audio equipment.

Question 50: Why are preamplifiers sometimes used ahead of mixing systems?

Preamplifiers are used ahead of mixing systems to provide a better output signal-to-noise ratio. Most pickup units have an extremely low output level, while the mixer has inherent noise which must be overcome for a satisfactory output.

Question 51: If a preamplifier, having a 600-ohm output, is connected to a microphone so that the power output is -40 db, and assuming the mixer system has a loss of 10 db, what voltage amplification is necessary in the line amplifier in order to feed +10 db into the transmitter line?

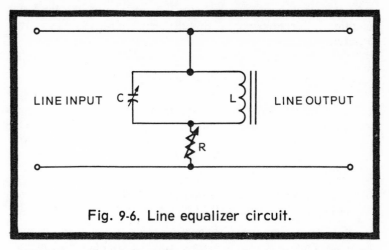

Fig. 9-6. Line equalizer circuit.

Raising a level of -40 db up to +10 db requires a gain of 40 + 10 or 50 db. Adding the 10 db loss in the mixer system, the total required gain is 50 + 10 or 60 db.

$$db = 20 \log A$$

where A is the voltage gain of the amplifier.

$$60 = 20 \log A, \quad \log A = \frac{60}{20} = 3$$
$$A = \text{antilog } 3 \text{ or } 1,000$$

Question 52: What is a line equalizer?

Higher frequencies are always attenuated by the distributed capacity in a telephone line, and by using a line equalizer the lower frequencies may be attenuated to ensure constant response of the line to all audio frequencies.

Question 53: Draw a diagram of an equalizer circuit most commonly used for equalizing wire-line circuits.

Fig. 9-6 is the circuit of a high-pass filter designed to attenuate low frequencies to a degree equal to the normal line attenuation of the highs.

Question 54: Given the gain of an amplifier which amplifies feedback and the overall voltage gain of a circuit, how is it possible to determine the amount of feedback used?

The gain of an amplifier without feedback is A. The feedback fraction is B. Assuming the initial amplifier input to be unity, or 1, the input with feedback is 1 plus AB for an output of A. If we label this 1-plus-AB input as X, the total gain is A minus X. The feedback fraction is equal to the reciprocal of A

331

minus X. If A is 100, and A minus X equals 79, the feedback fraction is the reciprocal of the difference, or 1 / 21 (just under 5 percent).

Question 55: What will occur if one tube is removed from a push-pull Class A audio-frequency stage?

Power output will be reduced, hum may be increased, second harmonic content will reappear, and other tubes may be damaged if a common resistor is used. There would also be a loss of gain if a cathode bypass capacitor was not used, and the outer transformer could be saturated, resulting in poor low-frequency response.

Question 56: If an audio-frequency amplifier has an overall gain of 40 db, and the output is 4 watts, what is the input?

With power, each 10 dB represents an order-of-magnitude increase. Thus, with 40 dB of gain, there have been four orders of magnitude increases. Write 4.0 watts as a decimal, and move the decimal point from places left (to represent the four orders of magnitude). The input power, then, is 0.0004 watt, or 0.4 milliwatt.

Question 57: What is the power output of an audio amplifier if the voltage across the load resistance of 500 ohms is 60V?

$$P = \frac{E^2}{R} = \frac{60^2}{500} = \frac{3,600}{500} = 7.2 \text{ watts}$$

Question 58: Why is degenerative feedback sometimes used in an audio amplifier?

Degenerative feedback is most useful in audio applications to reduce harmonic and intermodulation distortion. Other advantages include stabilization of amplifier gain, lowering of hum level, and a reduction of effective internal resistance of the stage. The only disadvantage worthy of note is a probable loss of gain which can readily be restored by additional voltage amplification.

Question 59: What is the result of deliberately introduced degenerative feedback in audio amplifiers?

Amplifier gain will be less and stability will be improved, but most important of all, distortion and noise will be noticeably reduced.

Question 60: In a low-level amplifier using degenerative feedback, at a nominal mid-frequency, what is the phase relationship between the feedback voltage and the input voltage?

Feedback voltage would be 180 degrees out of phase in relation to the input voltage.

Question 61: What is meant by the fidelity of an audio amplifier? Why is good fidelity an important consideration when replacing amplifiers in a broadcast station?

The fidelity of an audio amplifier is its ability to faithfully reproduce in its output an exact but amplified version of the input. Hum and noise components must be at a negligible level with linear amplitude response. In order to ensure broadcast signals of top quality, good fidelity is a primary consideration when replacing amplifiers in a broadcast station. Frequency and phase distortion must be held to an insignificant value.

Question 62: What type of playback stylus is generally used in broadcast station turntables and why?

Modern FM studios broadcasting quality music use elliptical-tip, diamond styli. The elliptical shape provides more accurate tracking than a spherical tip over the entire record surface area. The diamond stylus is preferred because of its longevity.

Question 63: How does dirt on the playback head of a tape recorder affect the audio output? How are such heads cleaned?

Dirt on the playback head of a tape deck tends to obscure the gap in the head, causing a marked decrease in high-frequency response. When the condition goes unchecked, the audio output will be increasingly distorted and will diminish in ampltiude. In extreme cases, a total loss of signal occurs.

Question 64: What is wow and rumble as referred to turntables? How can they be prevented?

Wow is characterized by a rapid but brief shift in the pitch of a program as a result of a momentary speed change. Rumble is an extremely low-frequency component introduced into a recorded program as a result of an inadvertent transfer of the table's mechanical energy to the pickup stylus. Rumble is particularly troublesome, as the condition is aggravated by tone arm resonances, environmental conditions, and acoustic feedback when monitor loudspeakers are set up in the area of the turntable.

Question 65: What factors may cause a serious loss of high frequencies in tape recordings?

High frequencies may be lost as a result of excessive head wear, poor head alignment, accumulated oxides on the head surface, and improper contact between head and tape

Question 66: Explain the use of a stroboscope disc in checking turntable speed.

To understand the function of a stroboscopic disc, it is first necessary to understand the character of certain types of light sources. Fluorescent and other gaseous light sources do not produce a continuous light. Rather, they flicker at twice the rate of the energizing AC voltage. Since a 117V 60-hertz light source (of the nonincandescent type) "sees" an applied voltage of zero twice during each cycle, there are two short periods of illumination and two short periods of darkness during each sixtieth of a second. If a revolving disc is marked with bars spaced so that a new bar passes a given fixed point during each illumination period, the speed of the revolving disc may be said to be stroboscopically synchronized.

At a speed of 33 1/3 rpm, a phonograph record requires 0.03 minute (1.8 sec) to complete a single revolution. Since there are two "light" periods for each cycle, and 60 cycles for each second, it can be seen that 1.8 (sec) x 120 (light pulses per sec) will equal the number of equally spaced bars (216) on a strobe disc used to calibrate a 33 1/3 rpm turntable. When viewed, the strobe disc will appear to be standing still if the turntable is rotating at the proper speed. If the turntable is revolving too fast, the strobe bars will appear to be moving gradually in a clockwise direction. If the turntable is rotating too slowly, the bars will appear to be rotating in a counterclockwise direction.

Question 67: Show how the frequency response of a pickup unit of either a tape recorder or a turntable may be tested.

A test tape, which contains a series of various tone frequencies ranging from 50 to 15 kHz, played on a tape recorder will reveal the frequency response of the unit. A VTVM connected to the playback amplifier output or the VU meter on the tape machine may be used as the output level indicator. The output reading for each tone can be used to plot a graph of frequency vs amplitude.

The frequency response of a turntable pickup is easily checked with a test record, which (like a test tape) contains tones ranging from 50 Hz to 50 kHz.

Question 68: What is an STL system?

An STL system is a "studio-to-transmitter" link that allows radio relay of program material from the broadcast studio to the transmitter/antenna site. A separate FCC authorization is required for operating an STL. The FCC has specific rules governing the deployment of such systems, which include the maintenance of a minimum field strength between sites, the use of directional antennas, the assignment of frequencies over which such relays may be set up, etc.

Question 69: What is a proof-of-performance?

A proof of performance is exactly what the term suggests—proof that the entire plant meets FCC engineering specifications. The "proof" measurements include an overall frequency response check from console to transmitter output, distortion measurements at prescribed intervals throughout the audio range for the class or type of station, and carrier shift measurements. "Proof" measurements must be made at regular intervals and be available for FCC inspection.

Question 70: What are limiting amplifiers? Why are they used in broadcast stations? Where are they normally placed in the program circuit?

A limiting amplifier is an audio stage that provides amplification and automatic gain-reduction of input signals. The amplifier is adjusted so that gain-limiting occurs at a point just below that where "overload" distortion of a signal would otherwise occur. These units are used in broadcast stations to keep the station's modulation within the legal requirement (and thus minimize the likelihood of adjacent-channel interference from splattering). In normal AM use, limiting amplifiers are placed between the input-signal preamplifier / conditioner and the speech amplifier (and modulator).

Question 71: Explain the operation of limiting amplifiers.

A limiting amplifier operates in much the same manner as an AVC circuit in a conventional AM receiver. The audio signal itself is rectified to form a DC bias voltage whose value is proportional to the signal amplitude. The bias voltage is used to control the stage gain; the higher the voltage, the greater the limiting.

Question 72: What are AGC amplifiers and why are they used?

An AGC is a gain-riding circuit that is used to keep a station's program material at a more or less constant level. Frequently, gain-riding, compression, and limiting are accomplished within a single circuit block.

Question 73: Explain the operation and uses of compression amplifiers.

The operation of a compression amplifier is similar to the action of normal AVC. Part of the output signal is rectified and fed back to the grid as a DC bias voltage. However, the design of the amplifier is such that not only are signal peaks attenuated, but signal nulls are accentuated. The result is a flattening or compression of the signal waveform, and a reduction in the signal's dynamic range. Remember that a limiter flattens peaks to prevent overmodulation, an AGC amplifier acts as a volume control to "ride again," and a compressor reduces dynamic range to permit a higher average level of modulation.

Question 74: Draw a diagram of an audio amplifier with inverse feedback.

See Fig. 9-7.

Question 75: What is the purpose of a line pad?

The line pad provides attenuation as desired between the amplifier and the line, while maintaining the necessary impedance match between the amplifier and the line. The line pad also effectively isolates the line from the amplifier.

Question 76: What are the purposes of H or T pad attenuators?

H and T pad attenuators provide a constant impedance between the source and load and take care of the attenuation as desired.

Question 77: Why is a high-level amplifier, feeding a program transmission line, generally isolated from the line by means of a pad?

The pad isolates the variations in amplifier impedance from the line and also provides adjustment of the amplifier output to a proper level for feeding into the line.

Question 78: Why are grounded center-tap transformers frequently used to terminate program wire lines?

The grounded center tap minimizes stray induction pickup by keeping the two sides of the line balanced to ground, and it improves the frequency response in many cases as well.

Question 79: Why is it preferable to isolate direct current from the primary winding of an audio transformer working out of a single vacuum tube?

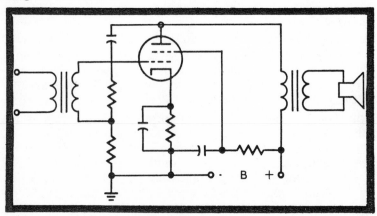

Fig. 9-7. Audio amplifier circuit with inverse feedback.

Magnetic saturation of the core lowers the primary impedance to such an extent that proper loading is no longer possible, efficiency is lower, output is reduced, along with the low-frequency response, and poor fidelity results. In a push-pull stage, there is no problem when the output transformer is used. The current flow through the two halves of the primary will set up fields that oppose each other and cancel.

Question 80: If a transformer having a turns ratio of 10 to 1 works into a load of 2000 ohms out of a circuit having an impedance of 15 ohms, what value of resistance may be connected across the load to effect an impedance match?

Since the impedance ratio is equal to the square of the turns ratio, the turns ratio squared is 100 and the proper impedance is 15 times 100 or 1,500 ohms. The parallel resistance across the 2,000-ohm load may be calculated by the usual formula:

$$1,500 = \frac{R1R2}{R1 + R2} = \frac{2,000X}{2,000 + X} \qquad X = 6,000 \text{ ohms}$$

Question 81: What is the formula for determining the db power or voltage gain in a circuit?

$$\text{Power gain} = 10 \log \frac{P1}{P2} \text{ db}$$

$$\text{Voltage gain} = 20 \log \frac{E1}{E2} \text{ db}$$

P1 and P2 are the input and output powers, E1 and E2 the input and output voltages, with the larger value always on top to make the fraction P1 over P2 or E1 over E2 greater than unity, thus simplifying the formula and reducing the chance of error.

Question 82: Draw the approximate equivalent circuit of a quartz crystal.

When placed in an electrical circuit, a crystal can act like a very high Q series-resonant circuit. The electrical circuits associated with a vibrating crystal can be represented by an equivalent circuit composed of resistance, inductance, and capacitance, as shown in Fig. 9-8. In this circuit, C1 represents the capacitance between the metal plates of the crystal holder. When the crystal is not vibrating, the circuit acts only as this capacitance. The series combination of L, C, and R represent the electrical equivalent of the vibrating crystal characteristics.

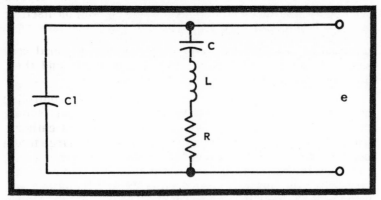

Fig. 9-8. Equivalent circuit of quartz crystal and holder.

Question 83: What factors affect the resonant frequency of a crystal? Why are crystal heaters often left on all night even though the broadcast station is not on the air?

In addition to such factors as the crystal cut, size, thickness, etc., there are environmental and circuit conditions that affect the resonant frequency of a crystal. Unless the crystal has a temperature coefficient of resistance equal to zero, temperature variations will affect the frequency; the greater the temperature variation from the crystal's intended operating temperature, the greater the frequency variation. The capacitance of the crystal holder itself will influence the ultimate frequency, too. Normally, crystal's are cut and mounted in their holders with some foreknowledge on the part of the manufacturer as to the type of circuit the crystal will ultimately be used in. A series-resonant circuit, for example, requires a different holder capacitance than a parallel-resonant circuit. And if a crystal designed for one circuit is used in the other circuit type, the resonant frequency will not be as marked on the crystal holder. Most commercial radio units are equipped with trimmer capacitors in the oscillator circuits to compensate for any slight variations in cut, capacitance, and the like; however, when a series-resonant circuit is used with a crystal designed for a parallel-resonant circuit, the trimmer will not be able to rubber the crystal enough to compensate for the difference.

Crystals are so dependent upon a constant temperature that most communication oscillator circuits incorporate a system for housing the crystal in a thermally controlled enclosure, or oven. Because of the time required for one of these ovens to reach its design temperature, and the additional time required for an accompanying crystal to be stabilized by this temperature, broadcast stations normally keep the crystal oven operating all the time, even when the station itself is required to shut down at the close of each day.

Question 84: Explain by simple drawings the physical construction and operation of mercury thermometer and thermocouple types of crystal heater controls.

In Fig. 9-9A, a simplified sketch of a mercury-controlled oven is shown. In operation, electrons flow from chassis ground through the heater coil and into the tube's cathode, from where they are attracted across the space charge to the plate by virtue of the applied B+. The mercury column, contained in the oven, adjacent to the heater coil, serves as a switch. When the temperature is low, the "switch" is open, allowing current to flow through the heater. When the heater has been energized for some time, the temperature in the oven rises, causing the mercury to touch the upper contact. When this occurs, a high negative bias is applied to the grid of the tube, thus cutting off the tube's conduction and stopping further cathode current from flowing. By continuous recycling, the oven maintains a fairly constant temperature.

The circuit shown in Fig. 9-9B is that of a conventional "bimetal strip" thermostat. This consists of two strips of different types of metal, which have an electrical contact as shown. At ambient temperature, both strips are perfectly

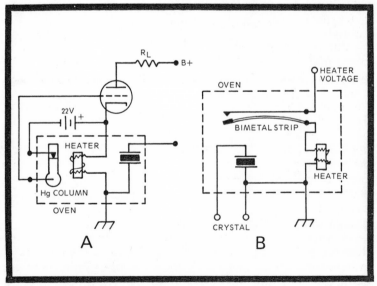

Fig. 9-9. Crystal heater circuits: (A) mercury type, and (B) thermocouple type.

straight and the contacts come together, thus allowing voltage to be fed to the heater coil. As the coil heats, the metal strips absorb the heat and expand. One of the two strips, with a higher rate of expansion than the other, buckles in the center, which separates the contacts. This breaks the heater circuit until the buckled strip cools. This arrangement, or some variation of it, is the same thermostat element used in such appliances as toasters, coffeemakers, fry pans, etc. It is not particularly accurate with respect to consistency of temperature but it is quite economical.

Question 85: What is the maximum allowable temperature variation at the crystal from the usual operating temperature when using X-cut or Y-cut crystals? When using low temperature coefficient crystals?

The X or Y-cut type crystal temperature cannot vary more than 0.1 degree C, while a low temperature coefficient type can vary as much as 1.0 degree C.

Question 86: Why are tubes used in linear RF amplifiers not normally biased Class A?

Due to the low efficiency of Class A operation, a reduction in power and the prohibitive costs would result in larger amplifiers with a carrier efficiency of about ten percent. Such amplifiers are normally biased Class B, which provides an efficiency of better than 30 percent.

Question 87: Indicate, by a simple diagram, the shunt-fed plate circuit of a radio frequency amplifier.

In Fig. 9-10, an RF choke prevents the RF output of the tube from flowing through the plate supply and forces it

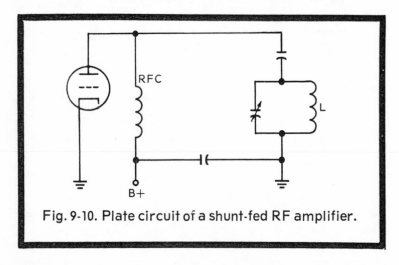

Fig. 9-10. Plate circuit of a shunt-fed RF amplifier.

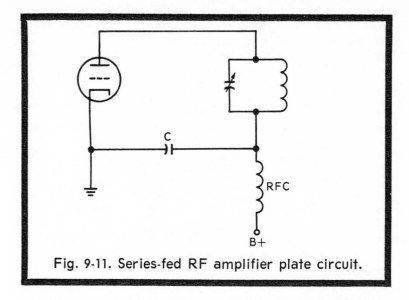

Fig. 9-11. Series-fed RF amplifier plate circuit.

through the tank circuit. The capacitor prevents the DC in the plate circuit from being shorted to ground through L.

Question 88: Indicate, by a simple diagram, the series-fed plate circuit of an RF amplifier.

Fig. 9-11 is readily identified by the fact that the plate tank C1-L1 is connected in series between the plate supply and tube. In this case, capacitor C keeps the plate RF out of the plate supply by providing a low-impedance path to ground.

Question 89: When adjusting the plate tank circuit of an RF amplifier, would minimum or maximum plate current indicate resonance?

Minimum plate current indicates resonance because the plate tank impedance is maximum at resonance and, as a result, current flow is minimum. Remember, the parallel LC impedance is always high at resonance and low off-resonance, so more current flows due to the lower impedance until the resonant point is reached.

Question 90: If, while tuning the plate circuit of a triode RF amplifier, the grid current varies, what defect is indicated?

Some variation in DC grid current during plate-tank tuning is to be expected when fixed bias is used, but excessive variation may result from improper neutralization, excessive RF drive or incorrect grid bias.

Question 91: Why are grounded-grid amplifiers used at very high frequencies (VHF)?

The grounded grid acts as a shield between plate and cathode, reducing interelectrode capacity and making neutralization of the triode unnecessary. Triodes are more desirable than pentodes as VHF RF amplifiers due to their lower noise figure.

Question 92: Draw a diagram of a grounded-grid amplifier.

See Fig. 3-7, which shows the difference between a grounded-grid and the conventional amplifier circuitry. The grid is at RF ground and the signal is applied to the cathode circuit. The output is taken between the grid and plate.

Question 93: What effect does a loading resistance have on a tuned RF circuit?

A loading resistor is connected across the resonant circuit and has the effect of reducing the Q of that circuit. This broadens the tuning as well as bandwidth. However, since the effective impedance is lower, the gain per stage is reduced. Loading resistors are commonly used to widen the frequency band being amplified, as is frequently done in a video IF amplifier.

Question 94: What is the purpose of neutralizing an RF amplifier stage?

Neutralization prevents oscillation resulting from regenerative feedback from the plate to the grid through the interelement capacity in the tube. This positive feedback may cause the amplifier to break into sustained self-oscillation, especially on peaks. If this regeneration is not cancelled by neutralizing, the least effect it could have would be distortion of the modulation envelope with AM.

Question 95: Why is it necessary to remove the plate voltage from the tube being neutralized?

Removal of the plate voltage from a tube when neutralizing simplifies the procedure and insures more accurate results by preventing the stage from amplifying. Also, the danger of shock is eliminated in cases where such hazards exist. When grid drive is applied, any current indicated in the plate tank must be passed by the interelectrode capacity between the grid and plate, verifying the need for neutralization.

Question 96: Under what conditions is neutralization of a triode RF amplifier not necessary?

Neutralization of a triode RF amplifier is not required when the stage acts as a frequency multiplier, or when operating in a grounded-grid arrangement.

Question 97: How are radio signals transmitted and received when amplitude modulation is used?

When using amplitude modulation, the amplitude of the radio wave is varied in direct proportion to the level of the information being transmitted. The varying amplitude radio wave is picked up by the receiving antenna, amplified, rec-

342

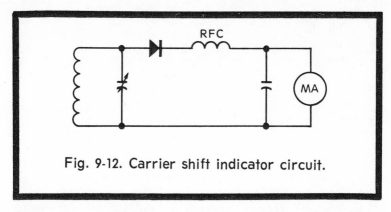

Fig. 9-12. Carrier shift indicator circuit.

tified, and amplified again by the receiver. The output, following detection, is directly proportional to the amplitude of the input signal and it varies in amplitude in exactly the same way as the original information, in fact, an exact reproduction of the original intelligence.

Question 98: If a frequency doubler stage has an input frequency of 1,000 kHz and the plate inductance is 60 microhenrys, what value of plate capacitance is required for resonance, disregarding stray capacitances?

Since the plate tank circuit has a frequency of 2,000 kHz, the value of capacitance for resonance is:

$$C = \frac{1}{4\pi^2 f^2 L}$$

$$= \frac{1}{4 \times (3.14)^2 \times (2{,}000 \times 10^3)^2 \times 60 \times 10^{-6}}$$

$$= \frac{1}{39.4 \times 4 \times 10^{12} \times 60 \times 10^{-6}}$$

$$= \frac{1}{9{,}546 \times 10^6} = 105.5 \text{ pf}$$

Question 99: What is carrier shift and how is it measured?

Carrier shift to the amplitude, not frequency, and it occurs when the relative positive and negative modulation peaks are not symmetrical. Fig. 9-12 is a simple carrier shift indicator circuit which determines the average value of the modulated and unmodulated transmitted wave. The inductance of the test equipment is placed near the transmitter stage to be monitored and adjusted for about a half-scale reading on the milliammeter. Now, the transmitter is modulated while observing the meter, which should remain still if no carrier shift or overmodulation exists. If the meter reading shows an increase, the carrier shift is positive and negative if a decrease in the reading appears.

Question 100: In a Class C RF amplifier stage feeding the antenna system, if there is a positive shift in carrier amplitude under modulation conditions, what trouble may be expected?

Positive carrier shift could result from overmodulation, parasitics, or insufficient neutralization.

Question 101: What is a Doherty amplifier?

This is a special type linear RF amplifier having a much greater efficiency than the usual RF linear amplifier. The amplifier uses an additional tube which is operated Class C to carry positive modulation peaks, while the regular amplifier tube, biased Class B, may operate at a higher average level to allow plate saturation on modulation peaks. Since the peaks are taken care of by the other tube, no distortion occurs.

Question 102: The DC input to a final amplifier measures 1,800V at 600 mA and the antenna resistance is 8.2 ohms with an antenna current of 10 amps. What is the plate efficiency of the final amplifier?

Output power or power in the antenna is:

$$P(out) = I^2R = 10^2 \times 8.2 = 820 \text{ watts}$$
$$P(in) = EI = 1,800 \times 0.6 = 1,080 \text{ watts}$$

$$\text{Efficiency} = \frac{output}{input} = \frac{820}{1,080}$$
$$= 0.759 = 75.9 \text{ percent}$$

Question 103: Draw a schematic of a final amplifier with capacitance coupling to the antenna which will discriminate against the transfer of harmonics.

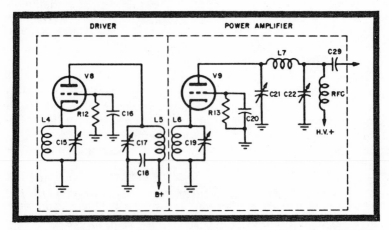

Fig. 9-13. Final amplifier-to-antenna coupling circuit with a low-pass pi network.

The circuit of Fig. 9-13 shows an rf driver, the final amplifier, and a pi-network matching system capacitively coupled to the antenna. The coupling capacitor (C29) prevents B+ from being passed from the plate circuit to the antenna. The pi network (consisting of L7, C21, and C22) serves as a low-pass filter that shunts signals to ground that are higher in frequency than intended for the antenna.

Question 104: Why are electrostatic shields used between the windings in coupling transformers?

An electrostatic shield eliminates any coupling other than magnetic, which reduces unbalanced line noise and RF pickup. Harmonic transfer is greatly reduced and circuit stability is improved.

Question 105: What material is used in shields to prevent stray magnetic fields near RF circuits?

RF shielding against magnetic fields requires a good non-magnetic conductor such as aluminum or copper; one or the other is often used for this purpose. A high permeability material is desirable for adequate shielding from power lines or audio magnetic fields; Permalloy or similar nickel-iron alloy should be used. Needless to say, iron or steel are not satisfactory due to their low permeability.

Question 106: What effect will doubling the excitation voltage of a Class B linear RF amplifier have on the RF output power?

Doubling the excitation voltage doubles the output voltage of a linear amplifier and, since the power of any circuit is proportional to the square of the voltage, the output power would be four times that value before the input was doubled.

Question 107: What is the value of the voltage drop across the elements of a mercury-vapor rectifier tube under normal conducting conditions?

The normal voltage drop is 15 volts.

Question 108: Why is it important to maintain the operating temperature of mercury-vapor tubes within specified limits?

The maximum peak current is low when the operating temperature of the tube is too low, and when too high, the maximum peak inverse voltage of the tube is reduced.

Question 109: What is meant by "arc back" or "flash back" in a rectifier tube?

This condition refers to arcing between the anode and the cathode or filament of a rectifier tube. The result is a reverse electron flow. This is normally caused by too high an inverse voltage being applied to the tube, and it may damage the tube permanently.

Question 110: What is meant by the "peak inverse voltage" of a rectifier?

The peak inverse voltage (PIV) rating is the maximum voltage that may be applied to the rectifier in the reverse direction (anode to cathode) without causing arc-back or breakdown.

Question 111: Why is a time delay used to apply high voltage to the anodes of mercury-vapor rectifier tubes following the application of the filament voltage?

The time delay is necessary to prevent damage to the tube, which must be allowed to reach the normal operating temperature before applying plate voltage. Otherwise, the voltage drop across the tube would be high enough to cause serious damage to the cathode surface from positive ion bombardment. Besides heating the filament, mercury deposits on the emitting surface of the cathode require vaporizing before plate voltage can be turned on.

Question 112: When mercury-vapor tubes are connected in parallel in a rectifier system, why are small resistors placed in series with the plate leads of the tubes?

The connection of low, equal value resistors in each plate lead of parallel mercury-vapor tubes provides an equal division of current between the tubes, a condition which would not exist under ordinary conditions. It also prevents one tube from ionizing ahead of the others, thus dropping the voltage across the others to a point where ionization would not be possible. This would place the full load on one or two tubes instead of the entire group.

Question 113: How is the inverse peak voltage to which tubes of a full-wave rectifier will be subjected determined from the known secondary voltages of the power transformer?

By multiplying the effective secondary voltage (end to end) by 1.414, less the actual voltage drop across the conducting tube. As an example, a mercury-vapor full-wave rectifier tube is connected to the secondary of a center-tapped transformer having a 500-volt output either side of the center tap. So the inverse peak is 500 + 500 or 1000 volts end to end, times 1.414, which equals 1414 volts, less the usual drop between cathode and anode of the mercury rectifier tube (15V) which is 1,399 volts PIV.

Question 114: If a power transformer has a primary voltage of 4,400V, a secondary voltage of 440V with an efficiency of 95 percent when delivering 11 amps of secondary current, what is the value of the primary current?

Secondary power, P + E x I equals 440 x 11 or 4,840 watts. If the efficiency is 95 percent, the primary power is 4,840 divided by 0.95 or 5,094.7 watts. Since the primary power is 5,094.7 watts at 4,400V, the current must be 5.094.7 divided by 4,400 or 1.57 amps.

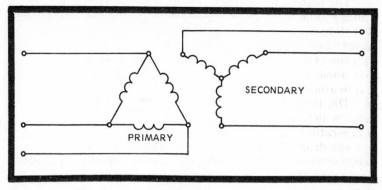

Fig. 9-14. Three-phase transformer with delta primary and Y secondary connections.

Question 115: What factors determine the core losses in a transformer?

The core losses in a transformer are eddy current losses and hysteresis losses. The former is easily reduced by laminated core construction, since an eddy current loss results from the circulating currents induced in the core by a varying magnetic field. Hysteresis loss is the actual energy consumed as the core molecules are reversed for each cycle (hertz) against molecular friction which increases with frequency.

Question 116: What determines the "copper" loss of a transformer?

Copper loss in a transformer is the result of the resistance in ohms to the flow of current in the primary and secondary windings. Power lost in a winding is equal to I squared times R, and the total copper loss is the sum of the primary and secondary losses. Therefore, copper losses are the result of the current flow through the transformer windings and the resistance opposing that flow as offered by the copper wire in those windings.

Question 117: What system of connections for a 3-phase, 3-transformer bank will provide maximum secondary voltage?

The delta-Y connection, with the primary connected in delta and the secondary connected in Y, provides maximum secondary voltage.

Question 118: Draw a wiring diagram of the 3-phase transformer with delta connected primary and Y connected secondary.

Fig. 9-14 shows the delta connection, with the primary forming a triangle (Greek letter "delta") and the secondary forming a Y as illustrated.

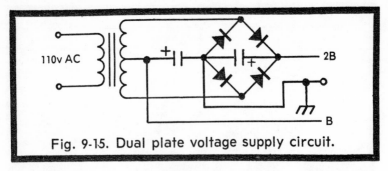

Fig. 9-15. Dual plate voltage supply circuit.

Question 119: Three single-phase transformer, each with ratio of 220 to 2,200V, are connected across a 220V three-phase line, with the primaries in delta. If the secondaries are connected in Y, what is the secondary line voltage?

As shown in Fig. 9-14, in a Y connection two windings are in series across any two of the three wires in the 3-phase line. This means the output voltage is greater than that across a single winding, but not double because of the phase angle. Actually, the voltage in the Y connection is 1.732 times the single winding. The illustration clearly shows the delta primary connection, with each winding directly across the 220V line; therefore, the primary input is 220V and the secondary 1.732 times 2,200 or 3,810 volts.

Question 120: Draw the circuit of a rectifier system which will supply two plate voltages, with one about twice the other, using one high-voltage transformer with a single center-tapped secondary.

Fig. 9-15 shows the use of the center tap for providing a rectified voltage based on half the secondary voltage, along with the full voltage based on the full transformer winding.

Question 121: Draw a diagram of a full-wave bridge rectifier that does not require a center-tapped transformer. Indicate the polarity of the output.

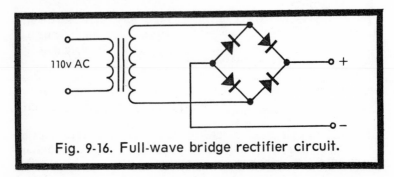

Fig. 9-16. Full-wave bridge rectifier circuit.

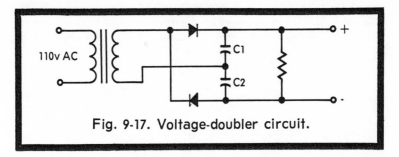

Fig. 9-17. Voltage-doubler circuit.

Fig. 9-16 is a bridge rectifier which works on both half waves, giving full-wave output.

Question 122: Draw a diagram of a voltage-doubling power supply using two half-wave rectifiers.

Fig. 9-17 is a conventional voltage doubler offering up to twice the peak of the AC input voltage, depending on the load. Capacitors C1 and C2 are charged to the peak value of the transformer secondary on alternate half cycles and, being in series, the output across the pair is the sum of the two voltages or about twice the peak input voltage.

Question 123: What is a "low-pass" filter and a "high-pass" filter?

A low-pass filter will pass all frequencies **below** a specific value or cutoff point and attenuate all above that point. A high-pass filter will pass all frequencies **above** the cutoff point for which it is designed, while attenuating all frequencies below that specific value.

Question 124: Draw a diagram of a simple low-pass filter.

Fig. 9-18 is representative of the usual type low-pass and high-pass filters. Notice the inductor passes the low frequencies, the capacitor the high frequencies, and they connect in series with the line to pass or in parallel (shunt) to reject (short).

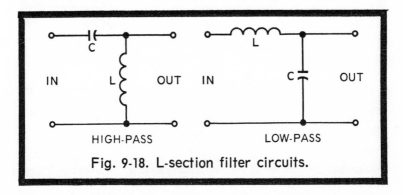

Fig. 9-18. L-section filter circuits.

Question 125: Why is it not advisable to operate a filter reactance in excess of its rated current value?

Since excessive current through a filter reactance will cause magnetic saturation of the core, its reactance and filtering capability are greatly reduced. The voltage drop across a choke also increases with the current, which upsets voltage regulation, reduces the voltage output and unnecessarily heats the choke windings, with possible permanent damage resulting.

Question 126: How may a capacitor be added to a choke input-filter system to increase the full load voltage?

The addition of a shunt capacitor across the rectifier output before the choke will raise the output voltage and change the name of the choke input filter to a capacitor filter input system.

Question 127: What is the predominant ripple frequency in the output of a single-phase full-wave rectifier when the primary source of power is 110V at 60 Hz?

The lowest and predominant ripple frequency would be 120 Hz or twice the line frequency with full-wave rectification.

Question 128: If a power supply has a regulation of 11 percent when the output voltage at full load is 240V, what is the output voltage at no load?

Since regulation is 11 percent, the change between full load and no load is 0.11 x 240V or 26.4V. Therefore, the no load voltage is 240V + 26.4V or 266.4 volts.

Question 129: If a power supply has an output voltage of 140V at no load and the regulation at full load is 15 percent, what is the output voltage at full load?

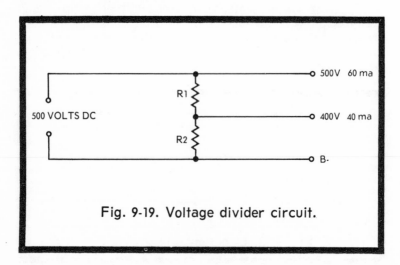

Fig. 9-19. Voltage divider circuit.

Since the regulation is 15 percent, the no-load voltage must be 15 percent greater than the full-load output which makes the no-load 115 percent of the full load. Full load voltage is:

$$\frac{140}{1.15} = 121.7 \text{ volts.}$$

Question 130: A rectifier-filter power supply furnishes 500 volts at 60 mA to one circuit and 400 volts at 40 mA to another circuit. The bleeder current in the voltage divider is to be 15 mA. What value of resistance should be placed between the 500 and 400V taps of the voltage divider?

In Fig. 9-19, the bleeder current through R2 is 15 mA and the current through R1 is equal to the current drawn by the 400V tap plus the bleeder current or 55 mA. The voltage drop across R1 is 500-400 or 100 volts, so the resistance needed for R1 is 100 divided by 0.055 equals 1818 ohms.

CHAPTER 10

Advanced Radiotelephone, Part II: Element 4

In this chapter, we continue reviewing some of the material covered earlier in Element 3. While you may find that some questions in Element 4 are very similar to those asked in Element 3, most Element 4 questions are on a higher level. These could not possibly be answered correctly without adequate preparation, and we are working toward this end as we continue to add to the basic material already mastered.

OSCILLATORS

Most oscillators use grid-leak bias so that the bias level is completely dependent on the grid signal level. Oscillations begin to build as soon as the power is turned on and the bias increases quickly until it reaches the Class C level. This means top efficiency, since plate current flows only in a short burst during each cycle. The flywheel effect provides a true sine wave and the short pulse replaces the energy used during the preceding cycle. Oscillations continue as the necessary energy is fed to the tank circuit. Class C operation requires grid-leak bias to be self-starting, otherwise there would be no input signal to the grid of the oscillator. Initially, the grid bias is zero, since there is no feedback, but heavy plate current results the moment power is turned on and oscillations build-up rapidly to quickly bias the oscillator at Class C. Thus, the grid-leak biased oscillator has the advantage of being self-starting and self-adjusting in Class C operation.

MODULATION

Actually, modulation is nothing more than a process of applying sound or information to a radio transmitter. Getting in a little deeper, modulation varies the amplitude, frequency, or phase of a wave with time. In order to modulate a transmitter, the output must be varied in step with the audio or other signal to be transmitted. The simplest way to do this is by varying the plate supply voltage of the final amplifier at the modulating signal rate, so that the AC transmitter output applied to the antenna is in step with the audio or other signal.

Amplitude modulation or AM is used by some broadcast stations and is a method of transmission in which the amplitude of the transmitted signal varies according to the instantaneous amplitude of the audio signal, at a rate corresponding to the frequency of that audio intelligence. The swing of the audio (AC) wave adds to the amplitude of the transmitter output during positive excursions and subtracts from that output level during negative swings. There are several ways of accomplishing amplitude modulation, such as plate modulation, as briefly described above, grid modulation, cathode modulation, screen grid modulation, and several modifications which are covered later. Before leaving the subject of amplitude modulation, it should be remembered that the antenna current is increased by exactly 22.5 percent during **100 percent AM modulation**; this is not true with other forms of modulation.

Frequency modulation as used by FM broadcast stations, as well as the sound portion of television, is angle modulation of the carrier where the instantaneous frequency of the modulated wave differs from the carrier by the amplitude of that modulating wave. The simplest way to vary the frequency of the carrier is to vary the frequency of its source—the oscillator. This is easily accomplished by varying the capacitance of the oscillator grid (LC) circuit so that the resonant frequency is varied in step with the audio signal. The resonant frequency of the grid circuit determines the output frequency of the oscillator, and eventually, after multiplication, the frequency of the output signal to the antenna. Notice that the amplitude of the oscillator output does not change, so the antenna current is unaffected by modulation. The rate at which the carrier swings is equal to the frequency of the modulating voltage, but the width of that swing is dependent on the amplitude of the modulating voltage. The **amount of deviation** is proportional to the volume of the voice or music, but the **rate of deviation** is governed by the pitch or frequency (the higher the note, the faster the rate) of the audio modulating voltage.

Phase modulation may be called indirect or Armstrong modulation, although it is really frequency modulation, since the frequency of the output depends on the audio modulating voltage. However, it does result from varying the phase of the carrier rather than its deviation, but the output is normally called FM, whether it is converted before transmission or not. This form of modulation is commonly used with mobile transmitters so that they may use crystal-controlled oscillators. This eliminates frequency control problems without the usual elaborate frequency control circuits.

DEMODULATION

Actually stripping the modulating wave from the carrier, demodulation is the detection of the information received from the modulated carrier signal. The high-frequency carrier is removed in the process, leaving only the audio which is amplified and fed to the speaker. This is what happens in the case of AM detection, but FM is a bit more complicated. Several circuits are required to remove the desired audio from the frequency modulated wave. The discriminator (Foster-Seeley) has been studied and, needless to say, is superior to others but more costly. Better quality receivers use this discriminator which requires a limiter circuit ahead to restore the constant amplitude of the FM wave. Even though FM is constant in amplitude as transmitted, noise and interference may be added before being picked up by the receiver, and this usually results in amplitude changes which would distort the output of the discriminator. The ratio detector demodulates the FM signal without a limiter, since it is incapable of responding to amplitude variations.

It should be noted that the two circuits (the Foster-Seeley discriminator and the ratio detector) are quite similar in many respects. The big difference in the ratio detector is that the diodes are reversed and the time constant of the RC circuit is lengthened considerably to maintain a constant voltage across the diodes. When a few hertz of RF are changed in amplitude due to noise, the battery effect of the RC network maintains the total voltage at a constant level and no noise can get through. This is why the limiter is not needed with the ratio detector.

TRANSMISSION LINES

The purpose of a transmission line is to transfer RF energy efficiently from the source to the load. Coaxial cable or the parallel wire arrangement are common. A transmission line has inductance and resistance in each wire, plus capacitance and leakage between the two wires. The leakage is small enough to disregard, and the others may be treated as lumped constants for short sections of line. So in reality, the velocity factor is determined by the dielectric constant of the insulating material between the conductors, with air being the lowest at unity. Since the line must be supported by a solid insulating material at regular intervals and since the dielectric constants of such supports are higher than air, the velocity of the wave must be decreased as a result. Ceramic insulator supports could give a velocity factor of around 97 percent in an open-wire line, but the velocity figure of a twin-lead solid plastic line could run as low as 65 percent.

WAVELENGTH

A wavelength is the distance occupied by one cycle on a transmission line and may be found by dividing the velocity of propagation by the frequency. As wavelength in feet is usually required, the formula is 984 divided by the frequency in MHz. The velocity factor must be considered, since all transmission lines are less than 1, so the wavelength figure for a transmission line is multiplied by the velocity figure as supplied by the manufacturer.

TRANSMITTERS

Harmonics present a problem in transmitters, as well as being the desired product in frequency multipliers. Push-pull amplification cancels even harmonics, and the Faraday shield has proven most helpful in eliminating unwanted harmonics in a transmitter output. Interstage coupling helps, too, and specified bias voltages are also a benefit. Parasitic oscillations are a big problem because they sometimes appear when least expected and without apparent cause. However, we may pinpoint a few of the causes of such parasitics as being due to improper neutralization, shielding, feedback loops between undesirable components, and a lack of proper bypassing. Impedance coupling between stages may also cause parasitics or harmonics, and filters are especially useful in eliminating such harmonics. Low-pass filters prevent high-frequency harmonics, bandpass filters allow only a specified frequency to pass, and high-pass filters suppress all frequencies below the designed cutoff point.

PRE-EMPHASIS AND DE-EMPHASIS

The low audio frequencies are amplified more than the highs in audio amplifiers, making it necessary to provide additional amplification for the highs at the transmitter, a technique known as pre-emphasis. High frequencies are more susceptible to interference during transmission, which makes this feature quite important. However, with pre-emphasis a correction is needed at the receiver to prevent the program from sounding tinny or unnatural from a frequency response standpoint. This is overcome by a de-emphasis circuit which attenuates the highs by the same amount of boost added at the transmitter. This reverse procedure at the receiver evens things and restores normal output.

TRANSMITTER PROBLEMS AND PROCEDURES

Unmodulated transmitters form a basis for further consideration of modulating methods. The unmodulated transmitter has an oscillator to generate RF energy. The oscillator is usually followed by a buffer amplifier to protect it from loading which could cause its frequency to change. Since the load varies considerably, the buffer isolates the critical oscillator from these variations and assists in maintaining a constant frequency output to the frequency multiplier stage. Doublers, triplers, and even quadruplers may be used as required to multiply the oscillator frequency to the desired assigned carrier frequency. The power amplifier then boosts the carrier power to the authorized level before coupling into the antenna. Some of our high-powered transmitters use an intermediate power amplifier to provide the necessary drive for the grid of the final, which in many cases is quite high.

Transmitter power amplifiers, as a result of the large amounts of power handled, are subject to many types of unwanted oscillations. These oscillations absorb power and reduce the output of the amplifier by that amount, and the spurious oscillations may reach the antenna, causing interference with other stations. The parasitic oscillations must be taken seriously because they may cause signal distortion in linear amplifiers and modulators. Excessive voltage may be produced in portions of the circuit and modulate the carrier, resulting in the radiation of sideband frequencies. Such parasitics could overheat the amplifier tube and cause damage to the tube or associated components.

Undesirable harmonics may be reduced to a minimum by the use of low LC ratio tank circuits, correct grid drive, low-pass filters, link coupling between stages, and the Faraday screen in the output between the tank and antenna coupling coil. RF chokes should be used in power leads between the high-power transmitter and power supply, especially with a motor-generator. The choke keeps RF out of the motor-generator commutator where it could cause sparking. RF chokes also protect the generator from high-voltage spikes wherein greater than normal voltages are developed across the armature windings due to line transients which may produce arcing and insulation breakdown.

Exposed metal parts in high-powered transmitters must be well grounded for the protection of operating personnel and a reduction of electrostatic coupling. The operator must be certain that no interference with other stations will result when making any adjustments on the transmitter while it is connected to the antenna. Interference may occur when the carrier deviates from its assigned frequency or if over-modulated. Many adjustments are possible with the transmitter connected to a dummy or phantom antenna, which is a non-radiating impedance designed with the same resistance and reactance values of the regular antenna. Its function is to check the operation of the transmitter without radiation which may be undesirable at the time.

Question 1: Draw a diagram and describe the electrical characteristics of an electron-coupled oscillator circuit.

In an electron-coupled oscillator (Fig. 4-9) the isolation of the tank circuit from the load results in exceptional frequency stability by preventing load variations from reflecting back to the tank circuit.

Question 2: If an oscillator circuit consists of two identical tubes with the grids connected in push-pull and the plates in parallel, what relationship will hold between the input and output frequencies?

If biased and excited as a Class C amplifier, even harmonics of the excitation frequency will appear in the output and the fundamental and all odd harmonics will cancel. This push-push arrangement is often used as a frequency doubler where the plate tank is tuned to twice the fundamental. If the circuit were operated Class A, the output would be insignificant.

Question 3: Draw a simple diagram of a multivibrator oscillator circuit.

See Fig. 4-10 for the common multivibrator.

Question 4: What determines the fundamental operating frequency range of a multivibrator oscillator?

The operating frequency is mainly determined by value of the grid resistor and coupling capacitor for each tube (R1-C1 and R2-C2). The formula is:

$$F = \frac{0.6}{R1C1 + R2C2}$$

Increasing the value of either grid resistor or coupling capacitor will cause the operating frequency to decrease.

Question 5: What precautions may be taken to ensure crystal oscillator operation at one frequency?

Use a separate power supply; maintain a constant temperature on the crystal; isolate the oscillator with a buffer stage, make sure of rigid construction; keep the RF crystal current low, and provide adequate shielding. Always purchase crystals from a reliable source.

Question 6: What are the advantages of mercury thermostats over bimetallic thermostats?

Mercury types are more sensitive, not subject to pitting or corrosion, more accurate, and more reliable.

Question 7: Would maximum stability be obtained when the tuned circuit of a crystal oscillator is tuned to the exact crystal frequency?

Absolutely not. The best stability is obtained by tuning slightly higher than the crystal frequency, thus making the plate circuit tuning slightly inductive.

Question 8: What is the ratio of unmodulated carrier power to instantaneous peak power with 100 percent modulation at a standard broadcast station?

If the modulation waveform is sinusoidal, the ratio is one to four. However, considerable variation from this figure may be expected with other waveforms.

Question 9: What percentage increase is obtained in the average output power with 100 percent sinusoidal modulation versus average unmodulated carrier power?

Output power with 100 percent sinusoidal modulation is 50 percent more than the power output without modulation.

Question 10: If a transmitter has an output of 1,000 watts and the efficiency of the final modulated stage is 50 percent with 60 percent efficiency in the modulator, what plate input to the modulator is required for 100 percent sinusoidal modulation of the transmitter?

The final has an efficiency of 50 percent, so the power input is 1,000 divided by 0.50 or 2,000 watts and the modulator must provide 50 percent as much power as the final or 1,000 watts. The modulator operates with an efficiency of 60 percent, and its input power requirements are 1,000 divided by 0.60 or 1,666.7 watts.

Question 11: During 100 percent modulation, what percentage of the average output power is in the sidebands?

At 100 percent modulation, one third of the total power being radiated is in the sidebands. This means that 50 percent or half of the carrier power would be in the sidebands.

Question 12: If modulation is decreased from 100 percent to 50 percent, by what percentage has the power in the sidebands been decreased?

Sideband power varies as the square of the modulation percentage which is 100 squared divided by 50 squared; 10,000 divided by 2,500 equals 4. This indicates that a reduction in modulation from 100 percent to 50 percent would decrease the sideband power by a ratio of 4 to 1 or to 25 percent of its value at 100 percent. Therefore, the sideband power has been reduced by 75 percent (100 to 25).

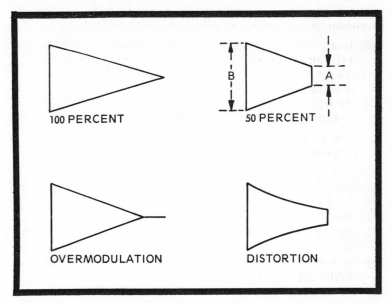

Fig. 10-1. Trapezoidal scope patterns indicating various modulation percentages.

Question 13: When the power output of a modulator is decreased from 1,000 watts to 10 watts, how would the loss in power be expressed in db?

Each order-of-magnitude decrease is equal to 10 db. Since 10W is two orders of magnitude lower than 1000W, the loss would be 2 x 10, or 20 db.

Question 14: What percentage of modulation capability is required of a standard broadcast station?

The station must be able to modulate at least 95 percent, and with the modulation percentage ranging between 85 and 95 percent, the output harmonic content may not exceed 7.5 percent. If the modulation is less than 85 percent at any time, the harmonic content of the output may never be more than 5 percent. During normal operation, the modulation must be maintained at the highest possible level consistent with good quality transmission, and under no circumstances below 85 percent on positive peaks or above 100 percent on negative peaks.

Question 15: Draw a simple sketch of the trapezoidal oscilloscope pattern indicating a low percentage of modulation without distortion.

The scope patterns in Fig. 10-1 show different modulation percentages. The 100-percent modulation pattern forms a perfect triangle, and overmodulation adds a straight line or "tail" to the triangle. Notice the curvature of the sides of the pattern caused by distortion. The percentage of modulation may be figured by the dimensions of A and B, shown in the sketch, using the formula:

$$\text{Modulation percentage} = \frac{B-A}{B+A} \times 100$$

$$\frac{2-1}{2+1} = \frac{1}{3} \times 100 = 33\%$$

Assume that B is twice as long as A, or B equals 2, A equals 1.

Question 16: What is the effect of 10,000-Hz modulation of a standard broadcast station on adjacent-channel reception?

The 10-kHz modulation would produce sidebands wide enough to beat with adjacent-channel carrier frequencies to cause a serious heterodyne that would interfere with the quality of their signals.

Question 17: Define high-level and low-level modulation.

High-level modulation is applied to the RF carrier in the plate circuit of the final RF amplifier. Low-level modulation is introduced before the plate circuit or the output of the final RF amplifier.

Question 18: What is the last audio-frequency amplifier stage which modulates the RF stage termed?

This is called the modulator or modulator stage.

Question 19: Draw a simple schematic diagram of a grid-bias modulation system, including the modulated RF stage.

See Fig. 4-33.

Question 20: Draw a simple schematic diagram of a Class B audio high-level modulation system, including the modulated RF stage.

See Fig. 10-2.

Question 21: What are the advantages and disadvantages of Class B modulators?

Class B modulators offer exceptionally high output from the modulator tubes with a high overall efficiency. The principal disadvantage, especially at high and low signal level extremes, is the large increase in distortion over Class A operation.

Question 22: How is the modulator load determined when modulating the plate circuit of a Class C RF stage?

The load at the secondary of the modulation transformer is the effective DC resistance of the plate circuit in the modulated stage. This figure is equal to the DC plate voltage divided by the DC plate current in the modulated stage.

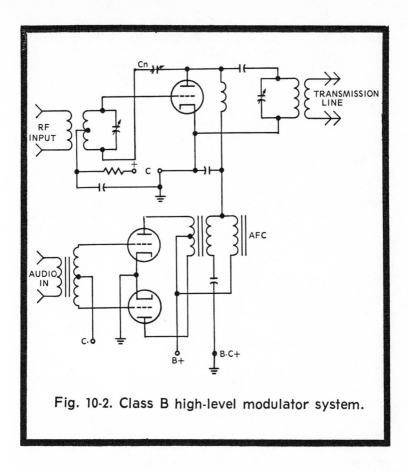

Fig. 10-2. Class B high-level modulator system.

Question 23: A Class C amplifier with a plate voltage of 1,000 volts and a plate current of 150 mA is modulated by a Class A amplifier with a plate voltage of 2,111 volts at 200 mA into a plate impedance of 15K. What is the proper turns ratio for the coupling transformer?

It may be assumed that the proper load impedance for the modulator is twice its plate impedance or 30K, which will be matched to the effective resistance of the modulated stage (final). R equals E over I; 1000 divided by 0.150 equals 6,666 ohms, and the turns ratio for the matching transformer is the square root of the impedance ratio:

$$\text{Turn ratio} = \sqrt{\frac{30,000}{6,666}} = \sqrt{4.5} = 2.12 : 1$$

361

The modulator would feed the high side of the transformer.

Question 24: In a modulated amplifier, when will the plate current vary on a DC meter?

Under normal operating conditions, there should be no variation in the plate current when modulation is applied and any such variation would be regarded as carrier shift. Positive carrier shift is an increase in carrier amplitude with modulation, while negative carrier shift is a decrease in carrier amplitude with modulation.

Carrier shift should never be confused with frequency shift, since the former does not refer to a change in frequency but only a change in amplitude. Any actual change in carrier frequency during modulation would be referred to as "dynamic instability" of the carrier, which is quite serious because it means undesirable frequency modulation in the transmitter output.

Positive carrier shift means that the average increase in plate current during the positive portion of the modulation envelope is greater than the average decrease in plate current during the negative half of the modulation cycle. The cause may be improper or insufficient neutralization, over-modulation or parasitics. In most linear RF amplifiers, positive carrier shift results from excessive negative bias and-or a low output impedance.

Negative carrier shift shows less than the average increase in plate current over the unmodulated value during the positive swing than the average decrease in plate current below the unmodulated value during the negative portion of the envelope. The causes are several, including insufficient modulator bias, insufficient audio, overloading of the modulated stage, low filament voltage, a too high impedance bias supply, a weak tube, improper matching with the modulated stage, plate and antenna circuits not tuned, or the cathode bypass on the final may be too small. In most linear amplifiers, negative carrier shift may be caused by excessive RF drive or insufficient bias.

Question 25: In a properly adjusted grid-bias modulated RF amplifier, under what circumstances will the plate current vary on a DC meter?

A slight variation in the DC plate current may be expected during high percentages of modulation, but any pronounced variation would indicate improper tank circuit adjustment or overmodulation.

Question 26: What frequency swing is defined as 100 percent modulation for FM broadcast stations?

The FCC defines a frequency swing of plus and minus 75 kHz as 100 percent modulation for an FM broadcast transmitter.

Question 27: What characteristic of an audio tone determines the percentage of modulation of an FM broadcast transmitter?

Disregarding pre-emphasis, the modulation percentage is governed entirely by the amplitude of the tone, but pre-emphasis is important and always used in FM broadcasting. In practice the percentage of modulation is dependent on the amplitude and frequency of the modulating tone. The greater the amplitude and the higher the frequency, the greater the swing and the higher the percentage of modulation.

Question 28: If the transmission line current of an FM transmitter is 7.5 amps without modulation, what is the transmission line current when the percentage of modulation is 90 percent?

The power output of an FM transmitter is always the same no matter what the percentage of modulation may be, so the current in the transmission line remains the same at 7.5 amps.

Question 29: How does the amount of audio power required to modulate a 1,000-watt FM broadcast transmitter compare with the amount of audio power required to modulate a 1,000-watt standard broadcast transmitter to the same percentage of modulation?

The power required to fully modulate an FM transmitter is in the order of a fraction of 1 watt, while the power needed to plate modulate (high-level) a standard AM broadcast transmitter 100 percent is 600 or 700 watts. Even the theoretical power, disregarding normal losses, would be 500 watts. Using low-level modulation, with its numerous disadvantages, would require nearly 30 watts of audio power to modulate a 1,000-watt AM transmitter.

Question 30: What is a ratio detector?

The ratio detector is a type of FM demodulator. An advantage of the ratio detector over the discriminator type detector is that it does not require a limiter for noise rejection. The output of the ratio detector is proportional to the ratio of the IF input voltages rather than their amplitude.

Question 31: Draw a diagram of an FM broadcast receiver detector circuit.

See Figs. 10-3 and 5-15 for the ratio detector and discriminator circuits.

Question 32: Why is an inert gas placed within concentric RF transmission lines?

The gas under pressure prevents a condensation of moisture around the inner conductor and eliminates the chance of insulation breakdown, arcing, and dielectric losses. Nitrogen is commonly used.

Question 33: When the spacing of the conductors in a 2-wire RF transmission line is doubled, what change may be expected in the surge impedance of the line?

Doubling the spacing will increase the surge impedance by 276 log 2 or 83.2 ohms. If the original impedance was 75 ohms and the distance between conductors is doubled, the impedance of the line, as a result, would be 75 + 83.2 or 158.2 ohms.

Question 34: If the conductors in a 2-wire RF transmission line are replaced by larger conductors, how would the surge impedance be affected with no change in spacing between centers?

By increasing the diameter of the conductors, the surge impedance is reduced according to the following formula:

$$Z_o = 276 \log\frac{2D}{d}$$

where D is the center-to-center spacing between conductors and d is the diameter.

Question 35: Explain the properties of a quarter-wave section of an RF transmission line.

Looking into a quarter-wave line shorted at the far end, we see a very high (actually infinite) impedance, but if the far

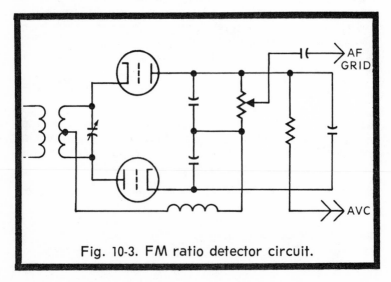

Fig. 10-3. FM ratio detector circuit.

end is open, the input impedance is extremely low or zero in the ideal line with no losses. If we terminate the far end with a resistance, the greater the resistance the lower the input impedance will be, or the smaller the resistance the larger the input impedance of the line. The quarter-wave section inverts the load at the other end, which makes it quite useful as a matching device.

Question 36: What is the ratio between the currents at the oppsoite ends of a transmission line, one-quarter wavelength, terminated in an impedance equal to its surge impedance?

If the line loss is negligible, the current will be the same at both ends regardless of the length of the line, as long as it is terminated by the equivalent of its surge impedance. Line losses must be insignificant in all cases.

Question 37: What is the primary reason for terminating a transmission line in an impedance equivalent to the characteristic impedance of the line?

Such termination of a transmission line eliminates line reflections and standing waves, reduces line radiation, and ensures maximum power transfer.

Question 38: If the power input to a 72-ohm concentric line is 5,000 watts, what is the RMS voltage between the inner conductor and sheath?
Since

$$E = \sqrt{PR} = \sqrt{72 \times 5,000} = 600 \text{ volts (RMS)}$$

Peak voltage would be 1.414 times this value or 848 volts.

Question 39: The power input to a 72-ohm concentric line is 5,000 watts, what is the current value?

$$I = \sqrt{P/R} = \sqrt{5,000/72} = \sqrt{69.44} = 8.336 \text{ amps}$$

Question 40: An antenna is fed by a properly terminated two-wire transmission line and the current at the input end is 3 amps. The surge impedance of the line is 500 ohms. How much power is supplied to the line?

$$P = I^2 R = 3^2 \times 500 = 4,500 \text{ watts}$$

Question 41: A long transmission line delivers 10 KW to an antenna with a line current of 5 amps at the transmitter end and 4.8 amps at the coupling end. If properly terminated with

negligible losses, what is the power loss in the transmission line?

$$\text{Line impedance} = \frac{P}{I^2} = \frac{10,000}{(4.8)^2} = 434 \text{ ohms}$$

$$\text{Pin} = I^2R = 5^2 \times 434 = 10,850 \text{ watts}$$

Power loss in the transmission line is 10,850 - 10,000 or 850 watts.

Question 42: A 50-KW transmitter uses six tubes in push-pull parallel in the final Class B linear stage while operating with a 50-KW output at an efficiency of 33 percent. If all heat radiation is transferred to the water cooling system, what amount of power must be dissipated from each tube?

Since the transmitter operates at an efficiency of 33 percent, the power input to the final is 50,000 divided by 0.33 or 151,500 watts. Total dissipated power is 151,500 - 50,000, which is 101,500 watts or 101.5 KW to be divided between the six tubes, each handling 16.9 KW.

Question 43: The daytime transmission line current of a 10-KW transmitter is 12 amps. At sunset the transmitter must be reduced to 5KW. What is the new value of transmission line current?

Since the power is proportional to the current squared,

$$\frac{P1}{P2} \quad \frac{I1^2}{I2^2} \quad \text{or} \quad \frac{10}{5} \quad \frac{12^2}{I2^2} \, , \quad I2^2 = \frac{5 \times 12^2}{10} = 72,$$

$$I2 = \sqrt{72} = 8.48 \text{ amps}$$

Question 44: What is the purpose of an auxiliary transmitter?

An auxiliary transmitter must be maintained to be put into operation immediately for the transmission of regular programs upon failure of the main transmitter. Regular programs may be transmitted during maintenance or modification work on the main transmitter, necessitating discontinuance of its operation for a period not to exceed five days. The auxiliary transmitter may be used upon request to a duly authorized representative of the Commission.

366

Question 45: How frequently must the auxiliary transmitter of a standard broadcast station be tested?

The auxiliary transmitter must be tested at least once a week. Tests should be conducted only between midnight and 9 AM local standard time.

Question 46: Draw a simple schematic diagram showing a method of coupling the RF output of the final power amplifier stage of a transmitter to a 2-wire transmission line. Show a method of suppression of second and third harmonic energy.

The circuit in Fig. 10-4 uses a Faraday screen as an electrostatic shield between the coupling windings to eliminate the transfer of harmonic energy by electrostatic coupling from the final to the transmission line. The parallel circuits in the transmission line are resonant at the second harmonic and offer a high impedance to that harmonic but pass the fundamental freely. The series circuits are tuned to the third harmonic and permit that energy to pass to ground.

Question 47: What units are used to measure the field intensity of a broadcast station?

Field strength or field intensity is normally measured in microvolts per meter, although millivolts per meter is used on some occasions.

Question 48: How does the field strength of a standard broadcast station vary with distance from the antenna?

The field strength is inversely proportional to the distance when only the groundwave is considered and losses are ignored. However, ground losses become increasing important as distance from the transmitter increases until the ratio no longer applies. Ground losses vary according to the ground conductivity; over sea water conductivity it is excellent. The rule is applicable to 100 miles. Ground losses are much greater at higher frequencies, and for distances over a few hundred miles the field strength of the ground wave approaches zero. The effective field strength then depends entirely on the sky wave for which there is no simple rule.

Question 49: If the power output of a broadcast station is quadrupled, what effect will this have on the field intensity at a given point?

Field intensity varies according to the square root of the radiated power, so quadrupling the radiated power provides a field intensity that is doubled at the given point.

Question 50: If positive modulation peaks are greater than the negative peaks in a transmitter with a Class B modulator, what steps should be taken to determine the cause?

Check the modulator tubes for balance. If their characteristics are not reasonably close, replace with a balanced pair. The modulated amplifier may be improperly neutralized and should be checked if the modulator tubes are not at fault.

Question 51: What may cause a decrease in antenna current during modulation of a Class B RF linear amplifier?

Insufficient modulation capability in the modulated stage, or the linear amplifier following that stage, causes the problem and may result from excessive drive, insufficient loading, low filament emission, or low filament voltage.

Question 52: What may cause unsymmetrical modulation of a standard broadcast transmitter?

This may be caused by distortion in the audio system from the microphone through the modulated stage and even in a succeeding linear amplifier. Although possible causes are quite numerous, the most likely are the modulator tubes.

Question 53: What would cause downward deflection of the antenna current meter when modulation is applied?

Using plate modulation, the possible causes may be defective tubes, poor power supply regulation, insufficient bias on the final, a defective filter capacitor, faulty neutralization or the antenna may be improperly tuned.

Question 54: What do variations in the final plate current of a transmitter indicate when using low-level modulation?

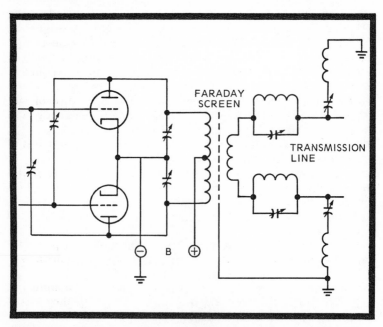

Fig. 10-4. Final amplifier coupling to a transmission line. Notice the use of a Faraday shield.

Such variations in the plate current if noticeable could indicate that the modulation capability of the amplifier was being exceeded under the conditions, but not necessarily overmodulated. Improper adjustment, incorrect bias, drive or loading conditions could cause the modulation capability to be exceed considerably lower than 100 percent. These danger signals often appear as the result of a defective component.

Question 55: What undesirable effects result from over-modulation of a broadcast transmitter?

The most serious effect of overmodulation is the increased radiated bandwidth which interferes with stations on adjacent channels. The transmitted signal becomes distorted and spurious harmonic frequencies are generated.

Question 56: What is the maximum carrier shift permissible at a standard broadcast station?

Carrier shift, regardless of modulation percentage, must not exceed 5 percent. Once again, a word of caution: Carrier shift means only a variation in the amplitude of the carrier current with modulation and has nothing to do with frequency.

Question 57: What is the meaning of the term "center frequency" in reference to FM broadcasting?

The center frequency is the frequency of the unmodulated carrier or the average frequency of the emitted wave modulated by a symmetrical signal. During modulation, the instantaneous frequency swings to either side of the center frequency.

Question 58: What is the meaning of the term "frequency swing" in reference to FM broadcasting stations?

Frequency swing is the instantaneous departure of the frequency of the emitted wave from the center frequency as a result of modulation.

Question 59: What determines the rate of frequency swing of an FM broadcast transmitter?

The rate of the frequency swing is determined by the audio frequency of the modulating signal and alternates according to that input.

Question 60: What is the frequency swing of an FM broadcast transmitter when modulated 60 percent?

Since 100 percent modulation is considered to be plus and minus 75 kHz, 60 percent modulation of the FM transmitter would be 0.60 x 75 or plus and minus 45 kHz.

Question 61: If an FM transmitter employs a doubler, a tripler, and a quadrupler, what is the carrier frequency swing when the oscillator frequency swing is 2 kHz?

The multipliers equal a total of 24 (2 x 3 x 4); therefore, since the oscillator has a swing of 2 kHz, the frequency swing following the multipliers would be 48 kHz.

Question 62: An FM transmitter operates on 98.1 MHz with a reactance tube-modulated oscillator on 4.905 MHz. What is the oscillator frequency swing when the transmitter is modulated 100 percent by a 2,000-Hz tone?

Frequency multipliers in the transmitter are 98.1 divided by 4.905 or 20, and the oscillator frequency swing must be one-twentieth of the 100 percent modulation figure of plus or minus 75 kHz or 3.75 kHz.

Question 63: An FM transmitter is modulated 50 percent by a 7,000-Hz test tone. If the test tone frequency is changed to 5,000 Hz and the percentage of modulation unchanged, what is the frequency swing of the transmitter?

At 100 percent modulation in an FM transmitter the frequency swing is plus or minus 75 kHz, so at 50 percent modulation the frequency swing would amount to plus or minus 37.5 kHz with either test tone.

Question 64: An FM transmitter is modulated at 40 percent by a 5,000-Hz test tone. If the percentage of modulation is doubled, what is the frequency swing of the transmitter in this case?

Since doubling the modulation would increase it to 80 percent, the frequency swing would be 0.80 x 75 kHz or plus and minus 60 kHz.

Question 65: What is the purpose of a "reactance tube" in an FM broadcast transmitter?

The reactance tube offers a simple way of modulating the master oscillator in an FM transmitter. By connecting the reactance tube in parallel or shunt with the master oscillator tank circuit, and with a phase shifting network, the tube acts as an additional reactance in the tank, causing the total value of the tank to vary with the modulation. Thus the operating frequency of the master oscillator varies in direct response to the modulating signal.

Question 66: What are the common methods of obtaining frequency modulation in an FM broadcast transmitter?

The direct frequency modulation of the carrier wave, sometimes called the Crosby system, uses a reactance tube in shunt with the oscillator tank which acts to vary the total frequency-determining reactance. This variation conforms to the amplitude of the modulation.

The Armstrong system of indirect frequency modulation operates by converted phase modulation and mixes two carrier frequencies with a 90-degree phase differential. One carrier is amplitude modulated by the modulating signal and the other is constant in amplitude. The mixing results in phase modulation which must be changed to frequency modulation, so the audio to the modulator is attenuated in proportion to the frequency. The phasitron method requires a special tube to secure phase modulation with a much greater phase shift than is possible with the Armstrong system. The phase shift is then converted to frequency modulation.

Question 67: What is meant by pre-emphasis in an FM broadcast transmitter?

In FM broadcasting, pre-emphasis refers to the practice of amplifying the higher audio frequencies of the modulating signal to a greater degree than the lower frequencies. This definitely improves the signal-to-noise ratio as the noises that are especially annoying to the listener are crowded in the upper end of the audio frequency range. So the extra amplification of the highs causes a greater percentage of modulation than a low of equal intensity at the start and enables them to override the irritating noise that may be present. A de-emphasis circuit must be incorporated in the receiver to level the highs and lows to their original relationship, so the lower signals are now amplified to a greater extent than the higher audio signals. In the original audio, high-frequency notes are usually low in amplitude and may easily be overamplified without chancing overmodulation of the transmitter.

Question 68: What is the audio-frequency range capability required of an FM broadcast station?

An audio frequency range of 50 to 15,000 Hz.

Question 69: Why is frequency modulation undesirable in the standard broadcast band?

Since frequency modulation actually requires a much wider channel than amplitude modulation, the number of stations operating at the same time would be considerably reduced with frequency modulation.

Question 70: How is the operating power of an FM broadcast station determined?

The operating power of an FM broadcast station must be figured by the indirect method and is determined by input power to the final RF amplifier stage times the efficiency factor. The efficiency factor is established by the transmitter manufacturer at the time FCC approval of the equipment is secured and should be clearly stated in the instruction book supplied with the FCC approved transmitter. The input power to the final RF amplifier is, of course, the plate voltage times the plate current of that stage, and the operating power of the FM transmitter where F is the efficiency factor, is: $E_p \times I_p \times F$ equals the operating power (indirect method).

Question 71: What is the tolerance in operating power of FM broadcast stations?

The operating power must be as close to the authorized operating power as is practicable and must not exceed 5 percent above or 10 percent below the authorized power unless an emergency exists.

Question 72: What is the frequency tolerance of an FM broadcast station?

The frequency must be maintained within 2,000 Hz of the assigned center frequency, except in the case of an FM educational station with a power of 10 watts or less which is allowed a frequency tolerance of 3,000 Hz or less from the assigned center frequency.

Question 73: What is the power specified in the instrument of authorization for a standard broadcast station called?

The power specification is called "authorized power" or "licensed power."

Question 74: What is the power that is actually transmitted by a standard broadcast station termed?

This is referred to as "radiated power."

Question 75: Define the maximum rated carrier power of a broadcast station transmitter.

The standard broadcast station's "maximum rated carrier power" is the maximum power for satisfactory performance of the transmitter as determined by its design, number and type tubes used in the final RF stage.

Question 76: Are the antenna current, plate current, and other values used in the Rules and Regulations of the FCC for modulated or unmodulated conditions?

They are unmodulated values.

Question 77: Define the plate input power of a broadcast station transmitter.

The broadcast station "plate input power" refers to the plate voltage applied to the tubes of the final RF stage times the DC current drawn by those tubes, measured without modulation.

Question 78: Describe the various methods by which a broadcast station may compute its operating power and state the conditions for each method used.

The operating power of a standard broadcast station must be figured by the direct method of measurement as follows: The antenna input power, as determined by direct measurement, is I squared times R, where I is the antenna current and R is the antenna resistance at the point of current measurement and at the operating frequency. Direct measurement of antenna input power will be accepted as the operating power of the station, providing the data on antenna resistance measurements are submitted under oath with a detailed description of the method used and data taken. Antenna current must be measured with an ammeter of accepted accuracy, and with directional antenna systems the current and resistance shall be measured at the point of the common RF input to that directional antenna system.

The indirect method may be used for computing the operating power of a standard broadcast station only in case of an emergency where the licensed antenna has been destroyed or damaged by storm or other cause beyond the control of the licensee or pending the completion of changes in the antenna system as authorized. The operating power as determined by indirect measurement from the plate input power of the last radio stage is the product of plate voltage, plate current (total) of the final stage, and the efficiency factor. The efficiency factor (F) may vary from 0.35 to 0.80 and may be found in the FCC Rules & Regulations or in the extracts from "Part 73" herein, under "Technical Operation." See the answer to Question 70 for the method of determining the operating power of an FM broadcasting station.

Question 79: What are the permissible tolerances of power for a standard broadcast station?

The operating power of a standard broadcast station may never exceed the authorized power by more than 5 percent or drop more than 10 percent below that authorized power. Operation must be as near the authorized figure as practicable at all times.

Question 80: When the transmitter of a standard broadcast station is operated at 85 percent modulation, what is the maximum permissible combined audio harmonic output?

The output may not contain more than 7.5 percent harmonics at a modulation percentage of 85 percent.

Question 81: If the plate ammeter in the last stage of a broadcast transmitter burns out, what should be done?

If no replacement within the required specifications is available, operation may continue without the defective instrument, pending its repair or replacement for a period not in excess of 60 days without further authority of the Commission. However, the station log must show the date and time the meter was removed from, and restored to, service. The engineer in charge of the radio district in which the station is located shall be notified immediately after the instrument is found to be defective and immediately after the repair or replaced instrument has been installed and is functioning properly. If conditions beyond the control of the licensee prevent the restoration of the meter to service within the above allowed period, informal request must be filed with the engineer in charge of the radio district in which the station is located for such additional time as may be required to complete repairs of the defective instrument.

Question 82: What is the frequency tolerance which must be maintained at the present time by a standard broadcast station?

The operating frequency of each standard broadcast station shall be maintained within 20 Hz of the assigned frequency.

Question 83: What is the frequency tolerance allowed an international broadcast station?

The operating frequency of an international broadcast station shall be maintained within 0.003 percent of the assigned frequency.

Question 84: Under what conditions may a standard broadcast station be operated by remote control?

A station which is authorized for nondirectional operation with a power of 10 KW or less may, upon prior authorization from the FCC, be operated by remote control at the point which shall be specified in the station license. Remote control operation shall be subject to the following conditions:

(a) The equipment at the operating and transmitting positions shall be so installed and protected as not to be accessible to, or capable of operation by, persons other than those duly authorized and a licensee.

(b) The control circuits from the operating position to the transmitter shall provide positive on and off control and shall be such that open circuits, short circuits, grounds, or other line faults will not actuate the transmitter, and any fault causing a loss of such control will automatically place the transmitter in an inoperative condition.

(c) Control and monitoring equipment shall be installed to allow the licensed operator either at the remote control point or at the transmitter to perform all the functions in a manner required in the FCCs Rules.

CHAPTER 11

Advanced Radiotelephone, Part III: Element 4

FM receivers, motors, measuring instruments, and antennas are covered briefly in this chapter to augment the material already familiar to you, adding a little detail on the specific purpose of these circuits.

MEASURING INSTRUMENTS

The required accuracy of measuring instruments used in radio broadcast and television stations is clearly stated in the FCC Rules, and we will go over these one by one to insure a complete understanding. You will be responsible for the accuracy of all tests and measurements, including the reliability of monitoring equipment. Most test instruments have detailed manuals to follow, and becoming familiar with the technical information presented will make the work a lot easier and save much valuable time as well. Most of the regular instruments are explained in detail in the Element 3 text, but additional information follows on this important subject in the questions and answers in this chapter, even the protection of your instruments against lightning and what to do if it fails. The measuring equipment used is indeed very expensive, and the more we learn about it in the beginning, the longer it will perform with the accuracy and reliability intended, so don't overlook those technical manuals supplied by the manufacturer.

ANTENNAS

Radiation patterns show us where the radiated energy goes after leaving the antenna, since it is frequently directional as in many of our broadcast stations, to concentrate the radiated power into heavily populated areas for better coverage and more advertising dollars and to protect co-channel and adjacent-channel stations. Mobile base stations usually have an omnidirectional pattern to provide satisfactory coverage of their mobile units operating in all directions around the hub. A bidirectional pattern is used where operations between the base station and mobile units are confined to a narrow corridor running in opposite directions. Two of the more popular types of antennas are the Hertz, which is ungrounded and usually a half-wavelength, and the Marconi which is grounded and a quarter-wavelength tall. A correct match between the antenna and transmission line reduces line losses and insures maximum transfer of energy. Some of the more frequently used methods of obtaining an accurate match include the quarter-wave stub, quarter-wave matching section or transformer, and the delta match.

The power gain of an antenna is the ratio of the power supplied to give a specified field voltage intensity when compared to the power supplied to a standard antenna to produce an equal field voltage intensity. In calculating the power gain, the ratio of our field intensity voltage is squared, or if the voltage is 3 to 1, the power gain is 3 squared or 9. This means that an antenna with a power gain of 9 would produce the same results with 1 KW of power that would be produced by a power of 9 KW using the standard antenna.

Many useful formulas are included in this section and must be retained for the FCC exam, since they will be needed to correctly answer several of the questions. This may seem difficult, but by practicing with several examples, you will be surprised how well they stick and how long they will stay with you by reviewing them occasionally.

RULES AND REGULATIONS

Additional rules pertaining to first class radiotelephone operators conclude this chapter and must be studied carefully as you will be asked questions on most of them in your FCC test. Knowing them thoroughly will enable you to easily answer the questions and after passing you will be a better broadcast engineer as a result of that extra effort you are making at this time.

Question 1: How wide a frequency band must the intermediate frequency amplifier of an FM broadcast receiver pass?

Since an FM signal may vary 75 kHz either side of the center frequency, a bandwidth of not less than 150 kHz is satisfactory. Actually, a bandwidth of 240 kHz would be required for distortionless reproduction of the highest audio frequency of 15 kHz at 100 percent modulation, but cutting off high-order sidebands does not cause objectionable distortion.

Question 2: What is the purpose of a de-emphasis circuit in an FM broadcast receiver?

By increasing the modulation percentage at the higher frequencies, the signal-to-noise ratio is improved considerably, which is the reason for the standard practice of amplifying the higher frequencies of the modulating signal to a greater degree than the low audio frequencies. However, at the receiver it is necessary to reverse this process in order to reproduce the low audio frequencies in their original ratio. In the receiver, by amplifying the low frequencies more than the high audio frequencies, the original ratio of the audio is restored. The circuit which accomplishes this in the receiver is known as the de-emphasis circuit and it compensates for the pre-emphasis that takes place in the transmitter.

Question 3: Draw a diagram showing how automatic volume control (AVC) is accomplished in a standard broadcast receiver.

Fig. 4-36 shows a typical automatic volume control circuit.

Question 4: If a frequency of 500 Hz is beat with a frequency of 550 kHz, what will be the resultant frequencies?

If the mixed frequencies are not passed through a nonlinear device, such as a diode, the only frequencies will be original ones, 500 Hz and 550 kHz. However, when the original frequencies are passed through a crystal diode or similar device, the output will carry many frequencies besides the original, but the sum and difference frequency resulting from the originals will be of greatest interest. In the case stated, the sum would be 550 kHz + 0.5 kHz or 550.5 kHz and the difference, 549.5 kHz. The harmonics of the original frequencies will also be in the output, and they will beat with each other to form sum and difference frequencies, as well as beating with the original frequencies to form still others in the output.

Question 5: What is the purpose of a limiter stage in an FM broadcast receiver?

The limiter stage removes the amplitude modulation due to noise and other interference from the IF before the signal is applied to the discriminator. A signal of constant amplitude is offered to the discriminator as a result.

Question 6: Draw a diagram of a limiter stage in an FM broadcast receiver.

See Fig. 5-5.

Question 7: What is the purpose of a discriminator in an FM broadcast receiver?

The discriminator converts the frequency modulated RF signals to amplitude variations at the audio rate of the original modulating wave.

Question 8: Draw a diagram of a shunt-wound DC motor.

Fig. 11-1 is a diagram of a shunt-wound motor, including the starting box.

Question 9: What is the approximate speed of a 220V, 60-Hz, 4-pole, 3-phase induction motor?

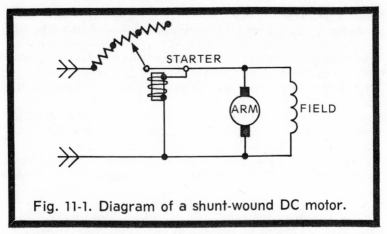

Fig. 11-1. Diagram of a shunt-wound DC motor.

Revolutions per minute of a synchronous motor is the line frequency times 60 over the number of pairs of poles. Actually, the voltage and number of phases have no bearing on the speed. As it is a 4-pole motor, there are two pairs of poles. So the motor speed is:

$$\frac{60 \times 60}{2} = 1,800 \text{ RPM}$$

The true speed of an induction motor would be possibly as much as 5 percent less than the figure arrived at with the above formula.

Question 10: What is the ohms-per-volt rating of a voltmeter constructed of a 1 mA DC milliammeter and a suitable resistor which makes a full-scale reading 500V?

The 1 mA meter is 1,000 ohms per volt regardless of the full-scale indication, since the ohms-per-volt rating of a meter is the reciprocal of the current applied for a full-scale deflection.

$$\text{Ohms per volt} = \frac{1}{0.001} = 1,000$$

$$R = \frac{E}{I} = \frac{500}{.001} = 500K$$

The series resistor required for a full-scale reading at 500 volts is 500,000 ohms or 500K.

Question 11: What type of voltmeter absorbs no power from the circuit under test?

A vacuum-tube voltmeter (commonly known as a VTVM) of the plate detector type with voltage applied to a negative control grid draws no current at all from the circuit under test.

There are other types of vacuum-tube voltmeters that draw very little power from the circuit or component being tested, but even these may be considered to absorb no power for all practical purposes. Input impedances range from 11 megohms up; needless to say, the loading effect of such values is nil.

Question 12: What type of meter is suitable for measuring the AVC voltage in a standard broadcast receiver?

Although DC voltmeters as low as 20,000 ohms per volt may suffice, for accurate measurement of such critical circuits a VTVM should always be used.

Question 13: What is the required full-scale accuracy of the plate ammeter and plate voltmeter in the final radio stage of a standard broadcast transmitter?

At least 2 percent of the full-scale reading is required, and the length of the scale may not be less than 2.3 inches with a minimum of 40 divisions. The full-scale reading shall not be greater than five times the minimum normal indication. These specifications apply to both meters of the final stage, plate voltmeter and plate ammeter.

Question 14: In accordance with the FCC Standards of Good Engineering Practice, what determines the maximum permissible full-scale reading of indicating instruments required in the last radio stage of a standard broadcast transmitter?

The full-scale reading of the instrument must not exceed five times the normal minimum plate current drawn by the final radio stage.

Question 15: What is the required accuracy of the instruments indicating the plate current and the plate voltage of the last radio stage or the transmission line current or voltage at an FM broadcast station?

The requirements for FM are the same as for a standard broadcast station, 2 percent on a scale at least 2.3 inches long, having 40 divisions or more, with the full-scale reading no greater than five times the normal minimum.

Question 16: Exclusive of monitors, what indicating instruments are required in the transmitting system of an FM broadcast station?

An FM broadcast station must be equipped with indicating instruments for reading direct plate voltage and current of the final radio stage and the transmission line RF current, voltage or power.

Question 17: How may a standard broadcast antenna ammeter be protected from lightning?

A suitable air-gap type protector may be used between the antenna side of the meter and electrical ground. The gap should be sufficient to prevent possible flashover on modulation peaks. If the tower radiator is provided with proper lightning protection, it is not likely for the antenna ammeter to be damaged even if the tower is struck, so the protective device for the meter is not necessary. In a few cases, for severe lightning storms the antenna ammeter could be connected on a make-before-break switch to permit its quick removal from the circuit at critical periods. An RF choke in the antenna lead at the meter and a ball gap on the antenna side, where protection is needed, is advisable.

Question 18: What type of meter is suitable for measuring peak AC voltage?

A peak reading VTVM is quite satisfactory because it uses a peak rectifier with a good sensitive DC meter. The ordinary AC voltmeter reads effective (RMS) voltage only, and although the peak reading is 1.414 times the effective value, this holds true for sine waves only. If the voltage being measured is not a pure sine wave, the actual peak conversion factor above does not apply. A peak reading vacuum-tube voltmeter should be used for measurement of nonsinusoidal waves.

Question 19: What type of a meter is suitable for measuring RF currents?

A thermocouple meter is suitable for measuring RF current.

Question 20: A current-squared meter has a scale divided into 50 equal divisions; when 45 mA flows through the meter the needle deflection is 45 divisions. What is the current flowing through the meter when the scale deflection is 25 divisions?

The deflection of the needle is proportional to the square of current through the meter, so:

$$\frac{D1}{D2} = \frac{I1^2}{I2^2} \text{ or } \frac{25}{45} = \frac{I1^2}{45^2}$$

$$I1^2 = \frac{25 \times 45^2}{45} = 25 \times 45, \quad I1 = \sqrt{1125} = 33.54$$

The current flowing through the meter when the needle reads 25 divisions is 33.5 mA.

Question 21: What portion of the scale of an antenna ammeter having a square law scale is considered as having acceptable accuracy for use at a broadcast station?

The upper two-thirds of the scale is acceptable if no scale division in that upper two-thirds is more than one-thirtieth of full scale. Since the lower third is not acceptable, full scale must not be greater than three times the normal minimum reading.

Question 22: How frequently must a remote reading ammeter be checked against a regular antenna ammeter?

All remote reading ammeters must be checked for calibration against the regular meter at least once a week.

Question 23: Broadcast stations using the direct method of computing output power require antenna current measurement at what point in the antenna system?

The antenna current must be measured at the point where the resistance of the antenna is measured. In a directional antenna system, antenna resistance must be measured at the common RF input point, with the operating power determined by I squared times R.

Question 24: What factors enter into the determination of power of a broadcast station which employs the indirect method of measurement?

Determining the power of a standard broadcast station by the indirect method requires measurement of plate supply voltage of the final RF stage (E_p) plate current of the final RF stage (I_p) and the efficiency factor F: Operating power equals E_p x I_p x F. The efficiency factor (F) for a standard AM broadcast transmitter is determined by the type and power classification of the final radio stage according to the table given in the FCC Rules & Regulations. Indirect measurement is not permitted for standard AM broadcast stations except in emergencies or pending the direct method measurement.

Question 25: Draw a schematic diagram of test equipment capable of detecting carrier shift in a radiotelephone transmitter output.

See Fig. 9-12. With no carrier shift, the needle is stationary with modulation; with positive carrier shift, the needle advances noticeably with modulation; with negative carrier shift, the needle reading decreases noticeably with modulation.

Question 26: Where are phase monitors located and what is their function?

A phase monitor is part of a directional antenna system where two or more radiators are used. The phase monitor provides a continuous indication at the transmitter of the relative phase of currents in the various tower radiators forming the antenna array. The current is normally coupled at the base of each tower and fed to the phase monitor through individual transmission lines. The pattern of directivity for the array is directly controlled by the phase relationship between currents in various tower elements and, in order to maintain the necessary directivity pattern, the FCC requires frequent checking of phase relationships between the current in each tower by means of the phase monitor.

Question 27: What is the device used to derive a standard frequency of 10 kHz from a standard frequency oscillator operating on 100 kHz?

This is a frequency divider and it is normally done with a multivibrator circuit.

Question 28: Describe the technique used in frequency measurements employing a 100-kHz oscillator, a 10-kHz multivibrator, a heterodyne frequency meter of known accuracy, a suitable receiver, and standard frequency transmission.

After thorough warm-up of the test equipment, couple the output of the 100-kHz crystal to the receiver and pickup the 5,000-kHz signal of WWV (National Bureau of Standards, Fort Collins, Colorado). The 50th harmonic of the 100-kHz crystal should beat with WWV, forming an audio beat in the receiver. After the modulation on WWV goes off, adjust the compensator control on the 100-kHz crystal for a zero-beat in the receiver output. This assures accurate calibration of the 100-kHz crystal. The signal to be measured may now be coupled to the heterodyne frequency meter. The oscillator dial on the meter is varied until the meter oscillator frequency is zero-beat with the unknown being measured, and the latter is read on the oscillator dial, along with the calibration chart, to within 0.1 percent, which is far from close enough for broadcast transmitter frequency measurement where an accuracy of 0.002 percent is required for a station on 1,000 kHz. After carefully noting the dial reading for the unknown frequency, uncouple from the frequency meter and couple the multivibrator in its place. Now turn the heterodyne frequency meter dial toward a lower frequency zero beat between the meter oscillator and the 10-kHz multivibrator; record the reading on the meter dial and proceed to turn to a higher frequency zero beat, which will be the next harmonic of the 10-kHz multivibrator beating with the meter oscillator. After recording this reading, the frequency of the unknown signal may now be pinpointed to a high degree of accuracy by interpolation. The multivibrator may be coupled to the calibrated 100-kHz oscillator so that its frequency is synchronized with it.

Question 29: In frequency measurements using the heterodyne "zero beat" method, what is the best ratio of signal EMF to calibrate the heterodyne oscillator EMF?

Under normal conditions, the 1:1 ratio is best because it is the equivalent to 100 percent modulation and, therefore, produces the highest amplitude beat frequencies.

Question 30: If a heterodyne frequency meter, having a straight-line relationship between frequency and dial reading, has a dial reading 31.7 for a frequency of 1,390 kHz and a dial reading of 44.5 for a frequency of 1,400 kHz, what is the frequency of the ninth harmonic of the frequency corresponding to a scale reading of 41.2?

Since the frequency difference between the two dial readings is 10 kHz and the dial division difference is 12.8, the frequency per division is 781.2 Hz. Solving for the frequency represented by a dial reading of 41.2, we have 3.3 divisions difference below the 44.5 reading for 1,400 kHz. The frequency per division being 781.2 Hz, 3.3 divisions would be 2,577.96 Hz from 1,400 kHz or 1,397.422 kHz, the actual frequency for the 41.2 dial reading. The ninth harmonic of this frequency is 12,576.79 kHz or 12.5768 MHz.

Question 31: If a broadcast station receives a frequency measurement report indicating that the station frequency was 45 Hz low at a certain time, and the transmitter log for the same time shows the measured frequency to be 5 Hz high, what is the error in the station frequency monitor?

The actual frequency is 45 Hz low and the monitor measurement 5 Hz high, so the station frequency monitor is in error 50 Hz.

Question 32: What procedure should be adopted if it is found necessary to replace a tube in a heterodyne frequency meter?

After any such change, the frequency meter calibrations must be rechecked with a known accurate source.

Question 33: What is the reason certain broadcast station frequency monitors must always receive their energy from an unmodulated stage of the transmitter?

The sideband frequencies of the modulated wave would affect the accuracy of the frequency monitor readings.

Question 34: What is the required frequency range of the indicating device on the frequency monitor at an FM broadcast station?

The FM frequency monitor must have a coverage of at least 2,000 Hz above to 2,000 Hz below the assigned frequency.

Question 35: What is the purpose of using a frequency standard or service independent of the transmitter frequency monitor or control?

Such a regular check on the accuracy of the station's frequency monitor guarantees operation of the station on its assigned frequency or well within the tolerance permitted.

Question 36: If the two towers of a 950-kHz directional antenna are separated by 120 electrical degrees, what is the tower separation in feet?

When tower separation is measured in degrees, 360 degrees is one wavelength and 120 degrees is one-third of a wavelength. The formula for wavelength in feet is 984,000 divided by the frequency in kHz:

$$\frac{984,000}{950} = 1,036 \text{ feet}; \quad 120^0 = \frac{1,036}{3} = 345.3 \text{ feet}$$

Therefore, the tower separation is 345.3 feet.

Question 37: What is the direction of maximum radiation from two vertical antennas at 180 degrees and having equal in-phase currents?

The radiation pattern is bidirectional with maximum radiation directed perpendicular to the plane of the antennas.

Question 38: What must be the height of a vertical radiator one-half wavelength high if the operating frequency is 1,100 kHz?

The height in feet of a half-wavelength antenna is 492,000 divided by the frequency in kHz:

$$\frac{492,000}{1,100} = 447.27 \text{ feet}$$

Question 39: If vertical antenna is 405 feet high and operating on 1,250 kHz, what is its physical height in wavelengths?

Wavelength in feet is 984,000 divided by the frequency of operation in kHz:

$$\frac{984,000}{1,250} = 787.2 \text{ ft}, \quad \frac{405}{787.2} = 0.5415 \text{ wave length}$$

Question 40: If a field intensity of 25 mV per meter develops 2.7V in a certain antenna, what is its effective height?

Since 25 mV is induced in each meter of effective height, the effective height is 2.7 volts divided by 25 millivolts, or exactly 108 meters. This may be changed to feet by multiplying by 3.28 (354.2 feet).

Question 41: Why do some broadcast stations use top-loaded antennas?

Top loading makes it possible to increase the effective height of an antenna and actually provides good efficiency even though the physical height is less than may be desired. There are at least two important considerations involved—cost and government restrictions. Top loading may be in the form of an umbrella, ring, or other provision for lumped capacitance at the top of the tower, and it may be connected either directly to the tower or through a coil. The same vertical field pattern intensity as that from an unloaded vertical a full quarter-wavelength may be realized with top loading.

Question 42: What is the importance of ground radials in standard antenna systems?

Since most broadcast stations use a vertical antenna system, with considerable importance placed on the conductivity of the ground beneath, the ground radials provide that function in many cases where the earth is found to be less than a good conductor. The ground conductors or radials actually offer an ideal approximation of the perfect ground.

Question 43: What effect do broken or corroded radials have on a standard broadcast antenna?

Broken or corroded ground radials increase the ground resistance in the direction of the broken conductor, which seriously affects the radiation pattern of the antenna system. The intensity of the radiation may also be reduced in varying degrees, depending on the conditions involved, such as the number of radials defective, the distance of the defect from the tower base, and the moisture content of the earth in the proximity of the break or faulty connection.

Question 44: How does a directional antenna array at an AM broadcast station reduce radiation in some directions and increase it in other directions?

As a result of cancellation or addition, depending on the phasing of the currents fed to the elements, with in-phase currents in the direction of radiation desired and out-of-phase in the direction to be reduced.

Question 45: What factors can cause the directional antenna pattern of an AM station to change?

External conditions such as temperature, humidity, large masses of metal in buildings, etc., broken radiators or reflectors, and leakage in transmission lines are some of the more common causes of a change in directional patterns.

Question 46: What adjustable controls are normally provided at an AM broadcast station to maintain the directional pattern?

Current controls and current phasing controls are used to alter the power to individual antenna elements of a directional array. The amount of power is determined by the setting of the controls and the desired pattern results from phase relationships between them. The adjustments require extreme care as they are "touchy."

Question 47: If the power output of a broadcast station has been increased so that the field intensity at a given point is doubled, what increase has taken place in the antenna current?

Field intensity varies as the square root of the radiated power, so doubling the field intensity necessitates quadrupling the antenna power, but this only requires doubling the actual antenna current. (Antenna power equals I squared times R).

Question 48: If the day input power to a certain broadcast station antenna having a resistance of 20 ohms is 2,000 watts, what would be the night input power if the antenna current were cut in half?

Since the power is proportional to the square of the current, which in this case is halved, the power is reduced to one-fourth the original (daytime) value.

$$Power = I^2R, \ 2,000 = I^2 20, \ I^2 20 = 2,000 \ I^2$$

$$= \frac{2,000}{20} = 100$$

so I is 10 amps. The antenna current is reduced to half at night, and night power is:

$$(5)^2 20 \ or \ 25 \ X \ 20 = 500 \ watts$$

Question 49: What is an STL system?

An STL is a studio-transmitter link, a one-way radio link from a broadcast studio to the transmitter site, using microwaves in the 942-952 MHz channel. Intercity relay stations may also use the same type equipment in the same frequency band for relaying sound (audio) programs from city to city.

Question 50: What is meant by "antenna field gain" of a television broadcast antenna?

The field gain of a TV transmitting antenna is found by dividing the effective free-space field intensity at one mile and in the horizontal plane, as expressed in millivolts per meter for a 1-KW antenna input power, by 137.6. This field gain figure is a comparison of the field intensity with that of a simple dipole under the above conditions, and, in the case of the complex TV antenna system over the simple dipole, it represents quite a sizable improvement. The large field gain results from the concentration of radiated energy in a specific direction or directions.

Question 51: Explain the operation of a turnstile TV antenna.

A turnstile antenna consists of two dipoles at right angles, with their axes intersecting at the midpoints. Ordinarily, the currents fed to the dipoles are equal in amplitude and 90 degrees out of phase. The result is an omnidirectional horizontal pattern.

Turnstile antennas used in TV broadcasting consist of two bat-wing sections at right angles. Such antennas produce a horizontally polarized signal, and feature a low angle of radiation.

Question 52: Why is horizontal polarization used for television?

Horizontal polarization was selected after extensive trials in the field and laboratory. Tests indicated stronger signals and fewer reflection problems resulting in ghosts. Since most man-made noise is vertically polarized, much relief was apparent from this source of trouble, since horizontally polarized receiving antennas were not susceptible to most noise pickup.

Question 53: If the antenna current is 9.7 amps for 5 KW, what current is necessary for a power of 1 KW?

Using the formula:

$$\frac{I1^2}{I2^2} = \frac{P1}{P2} \;,\; \frac{9.7^2}{I2^2} = \frac{5}{1} \;,\; 5(I2)^2 = 9.7^2$$

$$I2^2 = \frac{94.09}{5} \;,\; I2 = \sqrt{18.8} = 4.33 \text{ amps}$$

Question 54: What is the antenna current when a transmitter is delivering 900 watts into an antenna having a resistance of 16 ohms?

$$I = \sqrt{P/R} = \sqrt{900/16}, \text{ or } \sqrt{56.25} = 7.5 \text{ amps}$$

Question 55: The ammeter connected at the base of a Marconi antenna has a certain reading that is increased 2.77 times, what is the increase in output power?

Output power is proportional to the square of the current and 2.77 squared is 7.673, which means that the output power under these conditions will be increased to 7.67 times its original value.

Question 56: The currents in the elements of a directional broadcast antenna must be held to what percentage of their licensed value?

Plus or minus 5 percent.

Question 57: Draw a simple schematic diagram of a T-type coupling network suitable for coupling a coaxial line to a standard broadcast antenna. Include a means for harmonic attenuation.

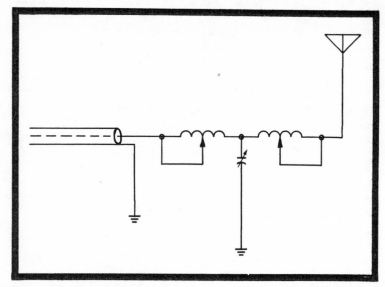

Fig. 11-2. T coupling used to connect a coaxial line to a standard broadcast antenna.

Fig. 11-2 illustrates a method of coupling a coaxial line with harmonic suppression.

Question 58: Explain why high-gain antennas are used at FM broadcast stations.

As a result of the small dimensions required for antennas at the high frequencies used for FM broadcast, it is possible to stack several bays or elements to concentrate much of the radiated energy near the ground where most receiving antennas are located. Therefore, the signal strength is greatly improved at ground level and very little is lost to the sky wave which is of no use at these frequencies.

Question 59: An FM transmitter has 320 watts plate input power to the last RF stage and an antenna field gain of 1.4. If the efficiency of the last RF stage is 60 percent and the efficiency of the antenna transmission line is 70 percent, what is the effective radiated power?

The input to the last RF stage is 320 watts at an efficiency of 60 percent, so the power output is 0.60 x 320 or 192 watts and the transmission line has an efficiency of 70 percent leaving 0.70 x 192 or 134.4 watts reaching the antenna. The antenna power gain is the square of the antenna field gain or 1.4 squared, which is 1.96. The effective radiated power is 1.96 x 134.4 or 263.4 watts.

CHAPTER 12

Advanced Radiotelephone, Part IV: Element 4

This is the last lap in our study of Element 4 and it deals with television and its monochrome and color transmitters which you may someday have as your responsibility. It's a wide field, full of big opportunities and still growing, but you can't get in until you get that "ticket" from the FCC!

Logs, definitions, and pulses are included in this chapter, plus SCA, EBS, and Special Broadcast Services. Antenna tower lighting and maintenance winds up the actual study material, along with the sample test.

TELEVISION

Two separate transmitters supply a common transmitting antenna. The audio or sound transmitter is frequency modulated, while the video or picture transmitter is amplitude modulated. Before transmission, the video is fed through a filter which removes part of the lower sideband (vestigial sideband transmission) and the audio and video signals reach the common antenna through a diplexer which prevents undesirable interaction. The minimum video modulation in the transmitted wave is 12.5 percent of the total carrier and occurs while the camera tube is scanning maximum white; maximum black areas require 75 percent modulation. Negative transmission is used here, since it is the reverse of the actual pickup tube output, which is maximum while scanning white and zero while scanning black. This negative transmission technique is more practical because less interference results under adverse conditions. The synchronizing pulses are sent in the 25 percent of the carrier envelope above the black level at 75 percent so they are not visible on the screen of the picture tube.

SUBSIDIARY CARRIER AUTHORIZATION

The purpose, standards, uses, and regulations governing SCA (subsidiary carrier authorization), stereophonic transmission, EBS, and special broadcast services are reviewed in the study guide answers of this section. Antenna tower lighting and maintenance is extremely important in many parts of the country and the subject is well covered in the answers to numerous study guide questions.

FCC TYPE SAMPLE TEST ON ELEMENT 4

After this element has been reviewed to the point where you feel confident, the sample FCC test should be taken to evaluate your preparations. After completing your answers to the 50 questions, check yourself on the list of answers given in Chapter 13. If you show weakness in any specific area, review that section thoroughly before testing yourself again.

Question 1: What are the radio operator requirements of the person on duty at an experimental television broadcast station?

One or more radio operators holding radiotelephone first-class or radiotelephone second-class operator licenses shall be on duty where the transmitting apparatus of any experimental television broadcast station is located and in actual charge of its operation. The licensed operator on duty and in charge of a broadcast transmitter may, at the discretion of the licensee, be employed for other duties, such as the operation of another station or stations in accordance with the class of operator's license which he holds and the Rules and Regulations governing such stations. However, such duties may in no way whatsoever interfere with the operation of the broadcast transmitter.

Question 2: What are the licensed operator requirements for a TV broadcast station? An FM broadcast station? A 5-KW night-time directional standard broadcast station?

The TV broadcast station requirement is that one or more licensed radiotelephone first-class operators must be on duty where the transmitting equipment is located and in actual charge thereof when the equipment is in operation. The original license or FCC Form 759 of each operator must be posted at the place where he is on duty.

An FM broadcast station with a power of more than 10 KW must abide by the same operator requirements as listed above for a TV broadcast station. However, if the power is 10 KW or less, the operator may hold any class of license or permit, providing the equipment is so designed that the stability of the frequency is maintained by the transmitter itself. Operators holding other than a first-class radiotelephone license are limited in their duties to the following: (1) putting the transmitter on and off the air in a routine manner; (2) making such external adjustments as may be required as a result of variations of primary power supply; (3) making external adjustments as may be required to ensure proper modulation. Should the transmitting equipment be observed to be operating improperly, an operator holding a license other than first-class must shut down the equipment and call a man holding a first-class license to make the necessary repairs and adjustments. Every station must have at least one first-class licensed operator in full-time employment, whose primary duty shall be to ensure the proper operation of the equipment.

Standard broadcast stations using a directional antenna meet the same operator license requirements as the TV broadcast station listed above. If no directional antenna is used and station power is 10 KW or less, the operator requirements are the same as those for an FM broadcast station of 10 KW or less, also listed above.

Question 3: What is meant by "equipment," "program," and "service" tests where these are mentioned in the FCC Rules and Regulations?

"Equipment tests" are made on the equipment of a radio station upon completion of the construction of the station in exact accordance with the terms of the construction permit. Equipment tests are made prior to filing an application for a station license. "Service" or "program" tests are made after the construction and equipment tests have been completed and a station license application filed. Program tests shall be automatically terminated by final determination upon the application for a station license.

Question 4: Referring to broadcast stations, what is meant by the "experimental period"?

The "experimental period" refers to the time between midnight and local sunrise. This period may be used for experimental purposes in testing and maintaining apparatus by the licensee of any standard broadcast station on its assigned frequency and with its authorized power, provided no interference is caused to other stations maintaining a regular operating schedule within such period. No station licensed for "daytime" or "specified hours" of operation may broadcast any regular or scheduled program during this period.

Question 5: Under what conditions may a standard broadcast station be operated at a reduced power other than that specified in the station license?

The licensee of a broadcast station must maintain the operating power of the station within the prescribed limits of the licensed power at all times, except that, in an emergency when due to causes beyond the control of the licensee, it becomes impossible to operate with the full licensed power, the station may be operated at reduced power for a period not to exceed 10 days, and provided that the FCC and the inspector in charge shall be notified in writing immediately after the emergency develops.

Question 6: When the authorized night-time power for a standard broadcast station is different from the daytime power and the operating power is determined by the "indirect" method, which of the efficiency factors established by the FCC Rules is used?

The efficiency factor given for the maximum rated carrier power of the station should be used in this case.

Question 7: Define an auxiliary broadcast transmitter and state the conditions under which it may be used.

The term "auxiliary transmitter" refers to the transmitter maintained only for transmitting regular station programming in case of failure of the main transmitter. Its installation may be at the main transmitter site or at another station. A licensed operator must be in control whenever an auxiliary transmitter is put into operation. It must be maintained so that immediate operation is possible at any time for the following purposes:

(a) The transmission of regular programs upon the failure of the main transmitter.

(b) The transmission of regular programs during maintenance or modification work on the main transmitter, necessitating discontinuance of its operation for a period not to exceed five days, or if such operation is required for periods in excess of five days, an informal application shall be made.

(c) Upon request by a duly authorized representative of the Commission.

Question 8: Why must the auxiliary transmitter be tested weekly and when may such tests be omitted?

Testing of the auxiliary transmitter is required at least once each week to ascertain if it is in proper working order and adjusted to the proper frequency. The test may be omitted on any week during which the transmitter has been used for such purposes as outlined above, providing that operation proved satisfactory.

Question 9: If a broadcast transmitter employs seven tubes of a particular type, how many spare tubes of the same type are required to be on hand in accordance with FCC regulations?

Three spares would be required in this case. The rule for spares is as follows:

Number of same type tubes used	Number of required spares of same type
1 or 2	1
3 to 5	2
6 to 8	3
9 or more	4

Question 10: How wide is an FM broadcast channel?

The FM broadcast channel is 200 kHz wide.

Question 11: What type of antenna is required at an STL station?

Broadcast STL or FM intercity relay stations must use a directional antenna system.

Question 12: Draw a block diagram of a typical monochrome television transmitter, indicating the function of each part.

Fig. 12-1 is a complete block diagram of a monochrome (black-and-white) television transmitter.

Question 13: What is a monitor picture tube at a television broadcast station?

A monitor picture tube (CRT) is used at the transmitter to permit the operator to visually observe the transmitted television picture and check for any possible technical problems. Several monitor tubes are normally used, being connected at various points in the picture circuit. This assists in the quick location of picture problems at the point in the video where they are introduced. The monitor also shows the horizontal and vertical synchronization and blanking signals.

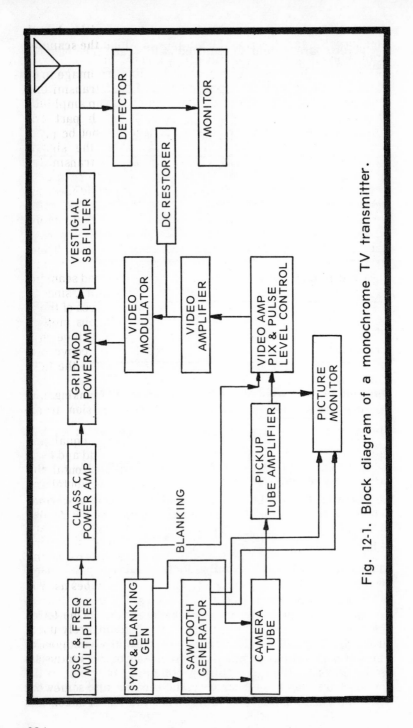

Fig. 12-1. Block diagram of a monochrome TV transmitter.

Question 14: Describe scanning as used by television broadcast stations, and describe the manner in which the scanning beam moves across the picture in the receiver.

Scanning is actually a process of dividing the image to be televised into many very small parts and then transmitting each in succession, providing a signal which has an amplitude proportional to the light actually striking each part and composing the complete picture. Since it would not be practical to transmit the whole picture at once, the signals representing each of the many elements must be transmitted in consecutive order. There are 525 lines in each frame, 30 frames per second, and two fields per frame. The odd-line field trace, the odd-line field retrace, the even-line field trace, and the even-line field retrace are the four periods of the scanning process at the transmitter and receiver. In the first period, odd-numbered lines are scanned from top to bottom. Then, the scanning beam is returned to the top of the picture and even lines are scanned to the bottom. This interlaced scanning method eliminates flicker from the television picture, since 60 fields are scanned per second, which is well in excess of the 40 pictures per second required for smooth, continuous motion. The electron beam scans the face of the picture tube in a receiver in a manner similar to the camera tube, converting the electrical variations of the video signal back to the light and dark variations of the picture.

Question 15: Make a sketch showing equalizing, blanking, and synchronizing pulses of a standard U.S. television transmission.

The waveform sketched in Fig. 12-2 shows equalizing pulses, which maintain correct interlacing of the odd and even fields of each frame, and a continuous string of horizontal and vertical synchronizing pulses that are fed to the horizontal and vertical scanning circuits. The synchronizing pulses maintain a correct scanning pattern and lock in the action of the receiving tube scanning beam with the beam in the camera tube. The blanking pulses turn off the electron beam during retrace by applying a short negative pulse to the grid of the electron gun at both transmitter and receiver.

Question 16: What are the main types of camera tubes used in television?

The iconoscope, vidicon, and image orthicon. Due to its comparative lack of sensitivity, the iconoscope is rarely used.

Question 17: What are the advantages and disadvantages of the vidicon TV camera tube in comparison to the image orthicon type?

The image orthicon is more costly, heavier, and somewhat more critical than the vidicon. Until recently, the orthicon was

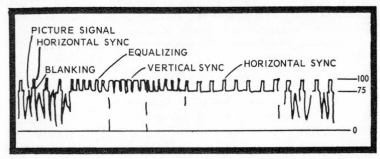

Fig.12-2. TV waveform showing equalizing, blanking and sync pulses.

used for professional broadcast applications because of its superior sensitivity and better resolution. Advances in technology in recent years, however, have resulted in vastly improved vidicons with low-light level sensitivity comparable to that of the image orthicon. As a result, the vidicon, with its simple and compact construction and ease of replaceability, has become the standard image tube used by broadcasters.

Question 18: Besides the camera signal, what other signals and pulses are included in a complete television broadcast signal?
The complete television signal includes the following:
1. The FM sound (carrier and sidebands).
2. Horizontal sync pulses.
3. Vertical sync pulses.
4. Horizontal blanking pulses.
5. Vertical blanking pulses.
6. Equalizing pulses.
7. Video carrier.
8. A DC component.

Question 19: Describe the procedure and adjustments necessary to couple properly a typical VHF visual transmitter to its load circuits.
A television video transmitter must pass a very wide band of frequencies, which necessitates a means of indication other than meters for tuning and coupling the transmitter to its load. The coupling circuit must pass all sideband frequencies uniformly, and this may best be checked with a sideband response analyzer. This offers a visual indication of all parts of the sideband to facilitate proper adjustments of the circuits involved. The plate and output circuits are tuned separately to different frequencies and then coupled together; the degree of coupling depends on the uniformity of the response obtained.

Question 20: What is the frequency tolerance for television broadcast transmitters?

The visual carrier frequency must be maintained within 1 kHz of the assigned carrier frequency, and the center frequency of the audio transmitter shall be maintained 4.5 MHz (plus or minus) 1 kHz above the visual carrier.

Question 21: What is meant by vestigial sideband transmission of a television broadcast station?

Vestigial sideband transmission is a system wherein one of the generated sidebands is partially attenuated at the transmitter. Actually, 2.75 MHz of the lower sideband is suppressed, so only partial radiation of this sideband takes place.

Question 22: How is operating power determined for the video transmitter at a television broadcast station? For the audio transmitter?

The operating power of the video transmitter is measured at the output terminals of the transmitter, including the vestigial sideband and harmonic filters as normally used. Average output power should be measured with a dummy load of zero reactance and a resistance equal to the characteristic impedance of the transmission line. During such measurement, the transmitter shall be modulated only by a standard synchronizing signal with blanking level at 75 percent of the peak amplitude as observed in an output monitor, and with this blanking level amplitude maintained throughout the time interval between synchronizing pulses.

The audio transmitter operating power shall be determined by either the direct or indirect method. Using the direct method, the power shall be measured at the transmitter output terminals operating into a dummy load of substantially zero reactance and a resistance equal to the characteristic impedance of the transmission line. The transmitter is to be unmodulated during this measurement, and if electrical devices are used to determine the output power, these must permit the determination of power to an accuracy of plus or minus 5 percent of the power indicated by a full-scale reading of the electrical indicating instrument of the device. When using temperature and coolant indicating devices to determine output power, determination of this power shall be permitted to within an accuracy of 4 percent measured average power out. During such measurement, the direct plate voltage and current of the last RF stage and the transmission line shall be read and a comparison made with similar readings taken when the dummy load is replaced by the antenna; the readings shall be in substantial agreement.

Using the indirect method, the operating power is determined by the formula, E_p x I_p x F, where E_p is the plate voltage, I_p the plate current of the last RF stage, and F the efficiency factor established by the transmitter manufacturer, approved by the Commission and supplied to the transmitter customer in the instruction books for the transmitter. Where composite equipment is used, the factor (F) shall be furnished to the FCC by the applicant, with a proper statement of the basis used in determining the factor.

Question 23: What is the figure representing the "aspect ratio" of the transmitted picture?

The ratio is 4 to 3 (4 wide by 3 high).

Question 24: Draw a block diagram of a color TV broadcast transmitter, complete from microphone-camera inputs to antenna outputs. State the purpose of each stage and explain briefly the overall operation of the transmitter.

In Fig. 12-3, the sound portion is exactly the same as for a monochrome transmitter, as well as the scanning and sync circuitry for the color pickup. The monitoring equipment and controls have been increased in number to handle additional problems presented by the color requirements. Three camera tubes form the color TV camera, with each tube responding only to the light relating to its filter (red, green, or blue). These color outputs are mixed in the matrix for the Y-signal (brightness) and the color-difference (I & Q) signals. The I and Q signals, applied to the balanced modulators, amplitude modulate the 3.58-MHz color subcarrier, which is then suppressed; only the sidebands are fed to the adder. No color subcarrier signals are needed for white or gray pictures at the receiver, since the color difference signals are zero for these shades; therefore, the Y signal controls the level at the receiver so the picture appears in black and white on monochrome receivers, even though a color transmission is in progress.

The Y signal is subtracted from the R, B, and G signals, and only two color signals are needed because the third color is reproduced at the receiver. The color sync signal used to trigger the color circuits in the receiver is produced by a 3.58-MHz signal injected into a gating circuit that is pulsed into conduction for a short burst on the horizontal frequency. This is fed into the adder with the other signals, forming the composite signal for transmission.

Question 25: Where on the synchronizing waveform do the color bursts for color transmission appear?

The color burst is on the back porch of the horizontal blanking pulse and has a duration of at least 8 Hz.

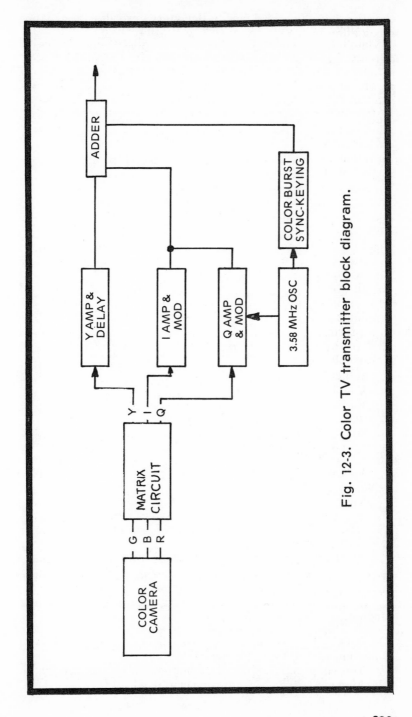

Fig. 12-3. Color TV transmitter block diagram.

Question 26: Why is grid modulation more desirable than plate modulation in television video transmitters?

Since television transmitters are required to handle low frequencies, high frequencies, synchronizing pulses, and blanking voltages, the necessary circuitry for leveling and clamping is more easily handled. The extremely high frequencies in video signals cannot be amplified through ordinary modulation transformers with iron cores, so grid modulation ensures better performance with fewer difficulties.

Question 27: What items must be included in a television station's operating log? In its maintenance log?

The operating log entries include:

An entry of the time the station begins to supply power to the antenna and the time it stops.

Entry of each interruption of the carrier wave, where automatically restored, its cause and duration, followed by the signature of the person restoring operation (if a licensed operator other than the operator on duty).

An entry at the beginning of operation and at intervals not exceeding one-half hour of the following (actual readings observed prior to making any adjustments to the equipment) and, when appropriate, an indication of the corrections made to restore parameters to the normal operating values:

(a) Operating constants of last RF stage of the audio transmitter (total plate voltage and plate current).

(b) Transmission line meter readings for both transmitters.

Maintenance log entries include:

An entry each week of the time and result of the test of the auxiliary transmitters.

A notation each week of the calibration check of any automatic recording devices.

An entry of the method used and the results of comparing the frequency deviation of the station with an external frequency source whenever the local video or audio frequency reference source becomes defective.

An entry of the date and time of removal from and restoration to service of any of the following equipment in the event it becomes defective:

(a) Video modulation monitoring equipment or audio modulation monitor.

(b) Video or audio frequency monitor.

(c) Final stage plate voltmeters of the audio and video transmitters.

(d) Final stage plate ammeters of the audio and video transmitters.

(e) Video and audio transmitter transmission line RF voltage, current, or power meter.

Record of tower light inspections where required.

Entries shall be made so as to describe fully any experiemental operation.

Question 28: Define the following terms as they apply to television broadcast stations:

(a) Aspect ratio.

(b) Audio (aural signal) transmitter.

(c) Aural center frequency.

(d) Blanking level.

(e) Chrominance.

(f) Chrominance subcarrier.

(g) Color transmission.

(h) Effective radiated power.

(i) Field.

(j) Frame.

(k) Free-space field intensity.

(l) Frequency swing.

(m) Interlaced scanning.

(n) Luminance.

(o) Monochrome transmission.

(p) Negative transmission.

(q) Peak power.

(r) Reference black level.

(s) Reference white level.

(t) Scanning.

(u) Scanning line.

(v) Standard television signal.

(w) Synchronization.

(x) Television broadcast band.

(y) Television channel.

(z) Television transmission standards.

(aa) Vestigial sideband transmission.

(bb) Video (visual signal) transmission power.

(a) Aspect ratio; the ratio of picture width to picture

(b) Aural transmitter: the radio equipment for the transmission of the aural signals only.

(c) Aural center frequency: (1) the average frequency of the emitted wave when modulated by a sinusoidal signal; (2) the frequency of the emitted wave without modulation.

(d) Blanking level; the level of the signal during the blanking interval, except the interval during the scanning synchronizing pulse and the chrominance subcarrier synchronizing burst.

(e) Chrominance; the colorimetric difference between any color and a reference color of equal luminance, the reference color having a specific chromaticity.

(f) Chrominance subcarrier: the carrier which is modulated by the chrominance information.

(g) Color transmission: the transmission of color television signals which can be reproduced with different values of hue, saturation, and luminance.

(h) Effective radiated power: the product of the antenna input power and the antenna power gain. This product should be expressed in kilowatts and in decibels above 1 kilowatt (dbk). (If specified for a particular direction, the effective radiated power is based on the antenna power gain in that direction only. The licensed effective radiated power is based on the average antenna power gain for each horizontal plane direction.)

(i) Field; scanning through the picture area once in the chosen scanning pattern. In the line interlaced scanning pattern of two to one, a field is completed when the alternate lines of a picture area have been scanned once.

(j) Frame; scanning all of the picture area once. In the line interlaced scanning pattern of two to one, a frame consists of two fields.

(k) Free-space field intensity; the field intensity that would exist at a point in the absence of waves reflected from the earth or other reflecting objects.

(l) Frequency swing; the instantaneous departure of the frequency of the emitted wave from the center frequency resulting from modulation.

(m) Interlaced scanning; a scanning process in which successively scanned lines are spaced an integral number of line widths, and in which the adjacent lines are scanned during successive cycles of the field frequency.

(n) Luminance; luminous flux emitted, reflected or transmitted per unit; the solid angle per unit projected from the area of the source.

(o) Monochrome transmission; the transmission of television signals which can be reproduced in gradations of a single color only.

(p) Negative transmission; where a decrease in the initial light intensity causes an increase in the transmitted power.

(q) Peak power; the power over an RF cycle corresponding in amplitude to the synchronizing peaks.

(r) Reference black level; the level corresponding to the specified maximum excursion of the luminance signal in the black direction.

(s) Reference white level of the luminance signal; the level corresponding to the specified maximum excursion of the luminance signal in the white direction.

(t) Scanning; the process of analyzing successively, according to a predetermined method, the light values of picture elements constituting the total picture area.

(u) Scanning line; a single continuous narrow strip of the picture area containing highlights, shadows, and half-tones, determined by the process of scanning.

(v) Standard television signal; a signal which conforms to the television transmission standards.

(w) Synchronization; the maintenance of one operation in step with another.

(x) Television broadcast band; the frequencies in the band extending from 54 to 890 MHz, which are assignable to television broadcast stations. These frequencies are 54 to 72 MHz (Channels 2 through 4), 76 to 88 MHz (channels 5 and 6), 174 to 216 MHz (channels 7 through 13) and 470 to 890 MHz (channels 14 through 83).

(y) Television channel; a band of frequencies 6 MHz wide in the television broadcast band and designated either by number or by the extreme upper and lower frequencies.

(z) Television transmission standards; the standards which determine the characteristics of a television signal as radiated by a television broadcast station.

(aa) Vestigial sideband transmission; a system of transmission wherein one of the generated sidebands is partially attenuated at the transmitter and radiated only in part.

(bb) Visual transmitter power; the peak power output when transmitting a standard television signal.

Question 29: What is the effective radiated power of a television broadcast station if the output of the transmitter is 1,000 watts, antenna transmission line loss 50 watts, and antenna power gain 3?

Power to the antenna is 1,000 - 50 or 950 watts, and with a power gain in the antenna of 3, the effective radiated power of the station is 3 times the input power to the antenna of 950 watts or 2,850 watts.

Question 30: What constitutes 100 percent modulation of the aural transmitter in a television broadcast station?

The television sound transmitter has 100 percent modulation when the frequency swing is plus or minus 25 kHz from the center frequency.

Question 31: Why is the field frequency made equal to the frequency of the commercial power supply?

This prevents ripple from the 60-Hz power source from moving across the screen and being noticeable to the viewer.

As the field frequency is equal to the line, filtering requirements are reduced at the receiver and this lowers its cost considerably.

Question 32: What is SCA and what are some possible uses of SCA?

Subsidiary Carrier (Subcarrier) Authorization (SCA) is used to provide limited types of subsidiary services on a multiplex basis. Possible uses include transmission of programs of a broadcast nature, but of interest primarily to limited groups of the public wishing to subscribe to the service. Services include background music, storecasting, detailed weather forecasting, special time signals, and other material of a broadcast nature expressly designed and intended for business, professional, educational, religious, trade, labor, agricultural or other groups engaged in any lawful activity.

SCA may be used for the transmission of signals which are directly related to the operation of FM broadcast stations; for example, relaying broadcast material to other FM and standard broadcast stations, remote cueing and order circuits, remote control telemetering functions associated with an authorized STL operation, and similar uses. SCA operations may be conducted without restriction as to time, so long as the main channel is programmed simultaneously.

Question 33: What items should be included in the SCA operating log?

Each licensee or permittee shall maintain a daily operating log of SCA operations in which the following entries shall be made, excluding subcarrier interruptions of five minutes or less:

(1) Time the subcarrier generator is turned on.

(2) Time that modulation is applied to subcarrier.

(3) Time that modulation is removed from subcarrier.

(4) Time the subcarrier generator is turned off.

Question 34: How are SCA subcarriers modulated? What frequencies are used for subcarriers?

Frequency modulation of the SCA subcarriers shall be used. The instantaneous frequency of the SCA subcarriers at all times shall be within the range 20 to 75 kHz; provided, however, that when the station is engaged in stereophonic broadcasting, the instantaneous frequency of the SCA subcarriers at all times shall be within the range 53 to 75 kHz.

The arithmetic sum of the modulation of the main carrier by SCA subcarriers shall not exceed 30 percent; provided, however, that when the station is engaged in stereophonic broadcasting, the arithmetic sum of the modulation of the main carrier by the SCA subcarriers shall not exceed 10 percent. The total modulation of the main carrier, including SCA subcarriers, shall meet the requirements of 85 to 100 percent modulation.

Frequency modulation of the main carrier caused by SCA subcarrier operation in the frequency range 50 to 15,000 Hz shall be at least 60 db below 100 percent modulation; provided, however, that when the station is engaged in stereophonic broadcasting, frequency modulation of the main carrier by the SCA subcarrier operation in the frequency range 50 to 53,000 Hz shall be at least 60 db below 100 percent modulation.

Question 35: What are the stereophonic transmission standards provided by the FCC Rules?

The modulating signal for the main channel shall consist of the sum of the left and right signals.

A pilot subcarrier at 19,000 Hz (plus or minus 2 Hz) shall be transmitted that shall frequency modulate the main carrier between the limits of 8 and 10 percent.

The stereophonic subcarrier shall be the second harmonic of the pilot subcarrier and shall cross the time axis with a positive slope simultaneously with each crossing of the time axis by the pilot subcarrier.

Amplitude modulation of the stereophonic subcarrier shall be used.

The stereophonic subcarrier shall be suppressed to a level less than one percent modulation of the main carrier.

The stereophonic subcarrier shall be capable of accepting audio frequencies from 50 to 15,000 Hz.

The modulating signal for the stereophonic subcarrier shall be equal to the difference of the left and right signals.

The pre-emphasis characteristics of the stereophonic subchannel shall be identical with those of the main channel with respect to phase and amplitude at all frequencies.

The sum of the sidebands resulting from amplitude modulation of the stereophonic subcarrier shall not cause a peak deviation of the main carrier in excess of 45 percent of the total modulation (excluding SCA subcarriers) when only a left (or right) signal exists; simultaneously, in the main channel the deviation when only a left (or right) signal exists shall not exceed 45 percent of the total modulation (excluding SCA subcarriers).

Total modulation of the main carrier, including pilot subcarrier and SCA subcarriers, shall meet the requirements of 85 to 100 percent modulation, with maximum modulation of the main carrier by all SCA subcarriers limited to 10 percent.

At the instant when only a positive left signal is applied, the main channel modulation shall cause an upward deviation of the main carrier frequency, and the stereophonic sub-carrier and its sideband signals shall cross the time axis simultaneously and in the same direction.

Question 36: Define the following terms as they apply to FM broadcast stations:

(a) Multiplex transmission.
(b) Crosstalk.
(c) Left (or right) signal.
(d) Left (or right) stereophonic channel.
(e) Main channel.
(f) Pilot subcarrier.
(g) Stereophonic separation.
(h) Stereophonic subcarrier.
(i) Stereophonic subchannel.

(a) Multiplex transmission: the simultaneous transmission of two or more signals within a single channel. Multiplex transmission as applied to FM broadcast stations means the transmission of facsimile or other signals in addition to the regular broadcast signals.

(b) Crosstalk: an undesired signal present in one channel caused by a signal in another channel.

(c) Left (or right) signal: the electrical output of a microphone or combination of microphones placed so as to convey the intensity, time, and location of sounds originating predominantly to the listener's left (or right) of the center of the performing area.

(d) Left (or right) stereophonic channel: the left (or right) signal as electrically reproduced in reception of FM stereophonic broadcasts.

(e) Main channel: the band of frequencies from 50 to 15,000 Hz per second which frequency modulate the main carrier.

(f) Pilot subcarriers: a subcarrier serving as a control signal for use in the reception of FM stereophonic broadcasts.

(g) Stereophonic separation: the ratio of the electrical signal caused in the right (or left) stereophonic channel to the electrical signal caused in the left (or right) stereophonic channel by the transmission of only a right (or left) signal.

(h) Stereophonic subcarrier: a subcarrier having a frequency which is the second harmonic of the pilot subcarrier frequency and which is employed in FM stereophonic broadcasting.

(i) Stereophonic subchannel: the band of frequencies from 23 to 53 kHz per second containing the stereophonic subcarrier and its associated sidebands.

Question 37: Define the following terms which apply to the Emergency Broadcast System:
  (a) Emergency Broadcast System (EBS)
  (b) National Defense Emergency Authorization (NDEA).
  (c) Emergency Action Notification.
  (d) Emergency Action Termination.
  (e) Emergency Action Condition.
  (f) Emergency Broadcast System Plan.

(a) The Emergency Broadcast System consists of broadcast stations and interconnecting facilities which have been authorized by the Commission to operate in a controlled manner during a grave national crisis or war.

(b) National Defense Emergency Authorization is an authorization issued by the FCC permitting controlled operation of broadcast stations on a voluntary organized basis during an Emergency Action Condition.

(c) Emergency Action Notification is the notice to stations in the radio broadcast service to operate in accordance with the Emergency Broadcast System Plan.

(d) Emergency Action Termination is the notice to stations in the radio broadcast services to discontinue controlled operations imposed by an outstanding Emergency Action Notification and return to normally licensed operations.

(e) Emergency Action Condition is the condition which exists after the transmission of an Emergency Action Notification and before the transmission of the Emergency Action Termination.

(f) The Emergency Broadcast System Plan is a plan containing, among other things, approved basic concepts and designated national level systems, arrangements, procedures, and interconnecting facilities as stated in Sec. 73.911.

Question 38: Describe the Emergency Action Notification attention signal.

The Emergency Action Notification attention signal is: cut the transmitter carrier for 5 seconds, return the carrier for 5 seconds, cut the carrier for 5 seconds, return the carrier and broadcast a 1,000-Hz steady-state tone for 15 seconds.

Question 39: Under normal conditions all standard, FM, and TV broadcast stations must make what provisions for receiving Emergency Action Notification and Termination Notices?

All broadcast station licensees must install and operate, during their hours of broadcast operation, equipment capable of receiving Emergency Action Notifications or Termination Notices transmitted by other radio broadcast stations. This equipment must be maintained in operative condition, including arrangements for a human listening watch or automatic alarm devices, and shall have its termination at each transmitter control point. However, where more than one broadcast transmitter is controlled from a common point by the same operator, only one set of equipment is required at that point.

Question 40: What type of station identification shall be given during an Emergency Action Condition?

No broadcast of station call letters shall be made during an Emergency Action Condition, but area identification shall be given.

Question 41: Must stations operate in accordance with Section 73.57 of the Commission's Rules during an Emergency Action Condition?

Definitely not.

Question 42: How often and at what times must EBS tests be sent?

The first method, twice a week (Sat. 9:30 AM and Sun. 8:30 PM EST); the second method, once a week at a selected time; the third method, once a week on a random basis between 8:30 AM and local sunset.

Question 43: What is the uppermost power limitation imposed on remote pickup broadcast stations? STL stations? Intercity relay broadcast stations?

A remote pickup broadcast station has a licensed power output not to exceed that required for satisfactory service. The station license specifies the power and in no event may that figure be exceeded by more than 5 percent. Similar power limitations apply to STL stations as well as intercity relay broadcast stations.

Question 44: What records must be maintained for each licensed remote pickup broadcast station?

The licensee shall maintain adequate records of the operation to include the hours of operation, program transmitted, frequency check, pertinent remarks concerning transmission, points of program origination and receiver location, antenna structure information and illumination where required.

Question 45: What is the basic difference between STL and intercity relay broadcast stations?

An STL station uses telephony for the transmission of all programming from a station's studio to its transmitter, and an intercity relay station uses the telephony for the transmission of aural program material between broadcast stations.

Question 46: What is the frequency tolerance provided by the Commission's Rules for an STL or intercity relay broadcast station?

The licensee of each aural STL and Intercity Relay station must maintain the operating frequency within 0.005 percent of the assigned frequency.

Question 47: Under what two general conditions must antenna structures be painted and lighted?

Antenna structures shall be painted and lighted when:

(a) They require special aeronautical study.

(b) They exceed 200 feet in height above the ground.

The FCC may modify the above requirement for painting and-or lighting of antenna structures, when it is shown by the applicant that the absence of such marking would not impair the safety of air navigation or that a lesser marking requirement would ensure the safety thereof.

Question 48: What colors should antenna structures be painted? Where can paint samples be obtained?

Antenna structures shall be painted throughout their height with alternate bands of aviation surface orange and white, terminating with aviation surface orange bands at both top and bottom. The width of the bands shall be equal and approximately one seventh the height of the structure; provided, however, that the bands shall not be more than 40 feet nor less than 1½ feet in width. All towers should be cleaned or repainted as often as necessary to maintain good visibility. Paint samples and information may be obtained from General Services Administration, Federal Supply Service Center, 7th & D Sts., S.W., Washington, D.C. 20407.

Question 49: If a tower is required to be lighted and the lights are controlled by a light-sensitive device and the device malfunctions, when should the tower lights be on?

If the light-sensitive device malfunctions, all lights shall be left on continuously, bypassing the control device as required.

Question 50: As a general rule, a light-sensitive device used to control tower lights should face which direction?

The north sky which offers the best light.

Question 51: If the operation of a station's tower lights is not continuously monitored by an alarm device, how often should the lights be visually checked?

The tower lights should be checked at least once every 24 hours.

Question 52: How often should automatic control devices and alarm circuits associated with antenna-tower lights be checked for proper operation?

At intervals not to exceed three months, all automatic or mechanical control devices, indicators, and alarm systems associated with the tower lighting system shall be inspected to ensure that such apparatus is functioning properly.

Question 53: What items regarding the operation of antenna tower lighting should be included in the station's miaintenance log?

The licensee of any radio station with an antenna structure requiring illumination shall make the following entries in the station record of the inspections required by Section 17.47:

(a) The time the tower lights are turned on and off each day, if manually controlled.

(b) The time the daily check of proper operation of the tower lights was made, if an automatic alarm system is not provided.

(c) In the event of any observed or otherwise known extinguishment or improper functioning of a tower light:

(1) Nature of such extinguishment or improper functioning.

(2) Date and time the extinguishment or improper functioning was observed or otherwise noted.

(3) Date, time, and nature of the adjustments, repairs, or replacements made.

(4) Identification of the Flight Service Station (Federal Aviation Administration) notified of the extinguishment or improper functioning of any code or rotating beacon light or top light not corrected within 30 minutes and the date and time such notice was given.

(5) Date and time notice was given to the Flight Service Station (Federal Aviation Administration) that the required illumination was resumed.

(d) Upon completion of the periodic inspection required at least once each three months:

(1) The date of the inspection and the condition of all tower lights and associated tower lighting control devices, indicators, and alarm systems.

(2) Any adjustments, replacements, or repairs made to insure compliance with the lighting requirements and the date such adjustments, replacements, or repairs were made.

Question 54: Generally speaking, how often should the antenna tower be painted?

All towers shall be cleaned or repainted as often as necessary to maintain good visibility.

Question 55: Is it necessary to have available replacement lamps for the station's antenna tower lights?

Spare lamps shall be maintained in su ficient supply for the immediate replacement of tower lights at all times.

Question 56: Generally speaking, how soon after a defect in the antenna tower lights is noticed should the defect be corrected?

Replacement or repair of lights, automatic indicators, or automatic alarm systems shall be accomplished as soon as practicable.

Question 57: What action should be taken if the tower lights at a station malfunction and cannot be immediately repaired?

The station licensee shall report immediately by telephone or telegraph to the nearest Flight Service Station or office of the Federal Aviation Administration any observed or otherwise known extinguishment or improper functioning of a code or rotating beacon light or top light not corrected within 30 minutes. Further notification by telephone or telegraph shall be given immediately upon resumption of the required illumination.

Sample test questions

1. A coil having an inductive reactance of 25 ohms, a capacitor with a capacitive reactance of 25 ohms, and a resistor of 50 ohms are connected in series. What is the impedance of the circuit?

    (a) 12.5 ohms
    (b) 25 ohms
    (c) 37.5 ohms
    (d) 50 ohms
    (e) 100 ohms

2. If a standard broadcast station has a fundamental frequency of 790 kHz, what is the frequency of its eighth harmonic?

    (a) 3,160 kHz
    (b) 6,320 kHz
    (c) 9,480 kHz
    (d) 12,640 kHz
    (e) None of the above.

3. If a coil has an inductive reactance of 50 ohms at 5 MHz, what is its reactance at 15 MHz?

    (a) 16.7 ohms
    (b) 33.3 ohms
    (c) 50 ohms
    (d) 100 ohms
    (e) 150 ohms

4. If a signal measures 15 volts RMS, what is its average value?

    (a) 9.4 volts
    (b) 10.5 volts
    (c) 13.5 volts
    (d) 14.2 volts
    (e) 21.2 volts

5. If the signal voltage is 18V RMS, what is the peak voltage?

   (a) 29.7 volts

   (b) 25.5 volts

   (c) 16.2 volts

   (d) 13.3 volts

   (e) 12.7 volts

6. What is known as the power factor in an AC circuit?

   (a) The ratio of resistance to impedance.

   (b) The voltage times the current.

   (c) The current times the resistance.

   (d) The impedance times the current.

   (e) The ratio of the reactance to the resistance.

7. What is the advantage of a Class C biased amplifier?

   (a) More linear output.

   (b) Lower efficiency.

   (c) Better stability.

   (d) Higher efficiency.

   (e) Good regulation.

8. If the primary of a transformer draws 1 ampere at 115 volts and the secondary provides 6.3 volts at 14 amperes, what is its percentage of efficiency?

   (a) 63 percent

   (b) 78.7 percent

   (c) 88.4 percent

   (d) 92.5 percent

   (e) 76.7 percent

9. How many spares are required for a standard broadcast transmitter using five tubes of a single type?

   (a) 2.

   (b) 3.

   (c) 4.

   (d) 5.

   (e) 1.

10. Why is degenerative feedback useful in an audio amplifier?

   (a) It improves linearity.

   (b) It increases sensitivity.

   (c) Provides greater output.

   (d) Reduces harmonic distortion.

   (e) Reduces overall stability.

11. Where would a limiter be used in a broadcast station?

   (a) In the speech-input amplifier.

   (b) Between the oscillator-buffer.

   (c) In the frequency multiplier.

   (d) Following the final amplifier.

   (e) In the pre-emphasis network.

12. What is the function of a limiting device in transmitting?

(a) Holds modulation to a preset value.

(b) Maintains the transmission line characteristic impedance.

(c) Prevents harmonic distortion.

(d) Limits amplifier output impedance variations.

(e) Regulates the frequency response of the final amplifier.

13. What eliminates the movement of hum bars across a television screen?

(a) Additional filtering in the vertical circuit.

(b) A field frequency equal to the line frequency.

(c) Interlaced scanning.

(d) The blanking pulses.

(e) The equalizing pulses.

14. In television, the upper video sideband and part of the lower video sideband are transmitted; this is called:

(a) Single-sideband transmission.

(b) Vestigial sideband transmission.

(c) Double-sideband, suppressed carrier transmission.

(d) Single-sideband, partially suppressed carrier transmission.

(e) Lower level suppressed carrier transmission.

15. What is the aspect ratio used in television broadcasting?

(a) 4 wide by 3 high

(b) 5 wide by 4 high

(c) 4 wide by 5 high

(d) 3 wide by 4 high

(e) 3 wide by 2 high

16. What is the effect of loading on a tuned circuit?

(a) Increases the Q.

(b) Peaks the frequency response.

(c) Broadens the bandwidth.

(d) Eliminates harmonic radiation.

(e) Reduces parasitics.

17. What is the usual characteristic impedance for a VU meter transmission line?

(a) 600 ohms

(b) 300 ohms

(c) 150 ohms

(d) 75 ohms

(e) 72 ohms

18. Where is a preamplifier normally required?

(a) Before the oscillator-mixer.

(b) Ahead of the RF amplifier.

(c) Following the microphone output.

(d) Between the audio driver and modulator.

(e) None of the above.

19. How may turntable speeds be accurately checked?
   (a) By a frequency meter
   (b) RMS meter
   (c) Strobe disc
   (d) Deviation percentage indicator
   (e) Line equalizer

20. What is the frequency tolerance of a standard broadcast station operating on 1150 kHz?
   (a) 3.45 kHz
   (b) 575 Hz
   (c) 238 Hz
   (d) 34.5 Hz
   (e) 20 Hz

21. Frequency stability is normally ensured with a quartz crystal by:
   (a) A feedback loop
   (b) The AVC circuit
   (c) A line equalizer
   (d) A crystal oven
   (e) A stabilizing network

22. What is the advantage of negative feedback?
   (a) Improves frequency response.
   (b) Reduces distortion.
   (c) Less gain variation.
   (d) Reduced hum and noise.
   (e) All of the above.

23. What type stylus is normally used in broadcast studios?
   (a) Sapphire
   (b) Carbon steel
   (c) Diamond
   (d) Nichrome
   (e) Germanium

24. What type bias is not satisfactory for linear RF amplifiers?
   (a) Class C
   (b) Class BC
   (c) Class B
   (d) Class AB
   (e) Class A

25. If an amplifier has an input of 3 milliwatts and the output power is 300 milliwatts, what is the power gain in decibels?
   (a) 10 db
   (b) 20 db
   (c) 30 db
   (d) 18 db
   (e) 60 db

26. A matched line would be:

(a) Short
(b) Long
(c) Capacitive
(d) Inductive
(e) Resistive

27. What is a waveguide?
    (a) An antenna
    (b) A transmission line
    (c) A transformer
    (d) A parabolic reflector
    (e) An attenuator

28. What is the purpose of an interlock?
    (a) Disconnects the transmission line from the antenna.
    (b) Cuts off dangerous voltages when the cabinet is open.
    (c) Removes filament power during an overload.
    (d) Provides a safety factor against lightning.
    (e) Reduces power during minor repairs.

29. What is the frequency tolerance of the video carrier in a television transmitter?
    (a) 20 Hz
    (b) 0.5 kHz
    (c) 1 kHz
    (d) 2 kHz
    (e) 5 kHz

30. What is the purpose of the blanking pulse?
    (a) Starts the vertical oscillator.
    (b) Cuts off the CRT beam during retrace.
    (c) Triggers the horizontal oscillator.
    (d) Shorts out the boost circuit between frames.
    (e) Prevents hum bars in the picture.

31. What is the modulation index for an FM broadcast station?
    (a) 1
    (b) 2
    (c) 5
    (d) 10
    (e) 15

32. What is the oscillator frequency of an FM station using two doublers, one tripler, and a quadrupler whose center frequency is 105.6 MHz?
    (a) 2.2 kHz
    (b) 6.6 kHz
    (c) 2.2 MHz
    (d) 4.4 MHz
    (e) 6.6 MHz

33. If an FM transmitter has a final RF amplifier plate voltage of 2 KV at 1.5 amps, what is the power output with an efficiency factor of 70 percent?

(a) 2,100 watts
(b) 2,800 watts
(c) 2.5 KW
(d) 3 KW
(e) None of the above.

34. If a broadcast station gets a frequency measurement report showing the station frequency 27 Hz high and the transmitter log shows 6 Hz low at that time, what is the actual error?

    (a) +33 Hz
    (b) +27 Hz
    (c) +21 Hz
    (d) -21 Hz
    (e) -33 Hz

35. If a transmitter has an output of 1 KW with an efficiency in the final of 70 percent, and the modulator functions at 60 percent, what plate input power is required to the modulator for 100 percent modulation?

    (a) 480 watts
    (b) 595 watts
    (c) 600 watts
    (d) 1190 watts
    (e) 675 watts

36. What is the major concern in a three microphone pickup?

    (a) Proper frequency response
    (b) Proper phasing
    (c) Audio feedback
    (d) Output level
    (e) Modulation control

37. What is the function of a diplexer?

    (a) Allows a single antenna to be used for television transmission.
    (b) Minimizes the effects of cross modulation.
    (c) Provides impedance matching of the visual and aural transmitters to the antenna.
    (d) Forms a bridge with antenna elements.
    (e) All of the above.

38. What is the blanking pulse level in the composite video signal?

    (a) 25 percent
    (b) 65 percent
    (c) 75 percent
    (d) 85 percent
    (e) 100 percent

39. What is the frequency difference between the aural and visual carriers?

(a) 4.5 MHz
(b) 3.58 MHz
(c) 1.25 MHz
(d) 5.75 MHz
(e) 6.00 kHz

40. What type modulation is required for the SCA subcarrier?
(a) Amplitude modulation
(b) Frequency modulation
(c) Vestigial sideband
(d) Single sideband
(e) Double sideband, suppressed carrier

41. What type of modulation is required for the subcarrier in stereo FM broadcasts?
(a) Amplitude modulation
(b) Frequency modulation
(c) Single sideband
(d) Single sideband, suppressed carrier
(e) Double sideband, suppressed carrier

42. What type emission is used by the aural transmitter in a television station?
(a) A1
(b) A3
(c) A5
(d) F3
(e) F5

43. What time is considered to be the "experimental period"?
(a) Midnight to 6 AM.
(b) Midnight to local sunrise.
(c) Time following the construction permit.
(d) Local sunset to midnight.
(e) None of the above.

44. What is known as "night-time operation"?
(a) Local sunrise to sunset.
(b) Midnight to local sunrise.
(c) Local sunset to midnight.
(d) Nightfall to dawn.
(e) 8:30 P.M. to 5:30 A.M.

45. What are "equipment tests"?
(a) Testing equipment during the experimental period.
(b) Testing equipment upon completion of station construction.
(c) Testing equipment prior to completion with a dummy load.
(d) Program testing under working conditions.
(e) Testing equipment under abnormal overloads.

46. What is the frequency of the ripple voltage in a full-wave rectifier?

(a) 30 Hz
(b) 60 Hz
(c) 120 Hz
(d) 150 Hz
(e) 180 Hz

47. If a transformer has 600 volts from center tap and a drop of 10 volts across the full-wave rectifier, what is the peak inverse voltage the rectifier must handle?

(a) 1,687 volts
(b) 849 volts
(c) 839 volts
(d) 2,482 volts
(e) 1,697 volts

48. How long will a 5 uF capacitor require to discharge to 37 percent of its peak voltage through a 500K resistor?

(a) 5 seconds
(b) 2.5 seconds
(c) 10 seconds
(d) 25 seconds
(e) 12.5 seconds

49. If a ¾ wavelength transmission line is shorted at its far end, what is the input impedance at the other end?

(a) A short circuit
(b) A very low impedance
(c) A high impedance
(d) Infinite impedance
(e) None of the above

50. If a television station operates on Channel 8, what is the center frequency of the sound transmitter?

(a) 179.75 MHz
(b) 181.25 MHz
(c) 191.75 MHz
(d) 175.25 MHz
(e) 185.75 MHz

CHAPTER 13

FCC Rules

For study as well as reference purposes, the following extracts from the FCC Rules should be helpful. Included are the appropriate parts on tower marking and lighting, technical operation and remote pickup broadcast stations.

EXTRACTS FROM PART 17, SPECIFICATIONS FOR OB-STRUCTION MARKING AND LIGHTING OF ANTENNA STRUCTURES

Section 17.21 **Painting and lighting; when required.** Antenna structures shall be painted and lighted when:

(a) They exceed 200 feet in height above the ground or they require special aeronautical study.

(b) The Commission may modify the above requirement for painting and-or lighting of antenna structures when it is shown by the applicant that the absence of such marking would not impair the safety of air navigation or that a lesser marking requirement would ensure the safety thereof.

Section 17.23 **Specifications for the painting of antenna structures in accordance with Sec. 17.21.** Antenna structures shall be painted throughout their height with alternate bands of aviation surface orange and white, terminating with aviation surface orange bands at both top and bottom. The width of the bands shall be equal and approximately one-seventh the height of the structure, provided, however, that the bands shall not be more than 40 feet nor less than 1½ feet in width.

Section 17.25 **Specifications for the lighting of antenna structures over 150 feet up to and including 300 feet in height.** (a) Antenna structures over 150 feet, up to and including 200 feet in height above ground, which are required to be lighted as a result of notification to the FAA under Sec. 17.7, and antenna structures over 200 feet, up to and including 300 feet in height above ground, shall be lighted as follows:

(1) There shall be installed at the top of the structure one 300 mm electric code beacon equipped with two 500-, 620-, or

700-watt lamps (PS-40 Code Beacon type), both lamps to burn simultaneously, and equipped with aviation red color filters. Where a rod or other construction of not more than 20 feet in height, incapable of supporting this beacon, is mounted on top of the structure and it is determined that this additional construction does not permit unobstructed visibility of the code beacon from aircraft at any normal angle of approach, there shall be installed two such beacons positioned so as to ensure unobstructed visibility of at least one of the beacons from aircraft at any normal angle of approach. The beacons shall be equipped with a flashing mechanism producing not more than 40 flashes per minute nor less than 12 flashes per minute, with a period of darkness equal to approximately one-half of the luminous period.

(2) At the approximate midpoint of the overall height of the tower there shall be installed at least two 100-, 107-, or 116-watt lamps (no. 100 A21-TS, no. 107 A21-TS, or no. 116 A21-TS, respectively) enclosed in aviation red obstruction light globes. Each light shall be mounted so as to ensure unobstructed visibility of at least one light at each level from aircraft at any normal angle of approach.

(3) All lights shall burn continuously or shall be controlled by a light-sensitive device adjusted so that the lights will be turned on at a north sky light intensity level of about 35 foot-candles and turned off at a north sky light intensity level of about 58 foot-candles.

Section 17.27 Specifications for the lighting of antenna structures over 450 feet up to and including 600 feet in height. (a) Antenna structures over 450 feet up to and including 600 feet in height above the ground shall be lighted as follows:

(1) There shall be installed at the top of the structure one 300 mm electric code beacon equipped with two 500-, 620-, or 700-watt lamps (PS-40 Code Beacon type), both lamps to burn simultaneously, and equipped with aviation red color filters. Where a rod or other construction of not more than 20 feet in height and incapable of supporting this beacon is mounted on top of the structure and it is determined that this additional construction does not permit unobstructed visibility of the code beacon from aircraft at any normal angle of approach, there shall be installed two such beacons positioned so as to ensure unobstructed visibility of at least one of the beacons from aircraft at any normal angle of approach. The beacons shall be equipped with a flashing mechanism producing not more than 40 flashes per minute nor less than 12 flashes per minute, with a period of darkness equal to approximately one-half of the luminous period.

420

(2) At approximately one-half of the overall height of the tower, one similar flashing 300 mm electric code beacon shall be installed in such a position within the tower proper that the structural members will not impair the visibility of this beacon from aircraft at any normal angle of approach. In the event this beacon cannot be installed in a manner to ensure unobstructed visibility of it from aircraft at any normal angle of approach, there shall be installed two such beacons at each level. Each beacon shall be mounted on the outside of diagonally opposite corners or opposite sides of the tower at the prescribed height.

(3) On levels at approximately three-fourths and one-fourth of the overall height of the tower, at least one 100-, 107-, or 116-watt lamp (No. 100 A21-TS, No. 107 A21-TS, or No. 116 A21-TS, respectively) enclosed in an aviation red obstruction light globe shall be installed on each outside corner of the tower at each level.

(4) All lights shall burn continuously or shall be controlled by a light-sensitive device adjusted so that the lights will be turned on at a north sky light intensity level of about 35 foot-candles and turned off at a north sky light intensity level of about 58 foot-candles.

Section 17.47 Inspection of tower lights and associated control equipment. The licensee of any radio station which has an antenna structure requiring illumination pursuant to the provisions of Section 303(q) of the Communications Act of 1934, as amended, as outlined elsewhere in this part:

(a) (1) Shall make an observation of the tower lights at least once each 24 hours, either visually or by observing an automatic properly maintained indicator designed to register any failure of such lights to insure that all such lights are functioning properly as required; or alternatively.

(2) Shall provide and properly maintain an automatic alarm system designed to detect any failure of such lights and to provide indication of such failure to the licensee.

(b) Shall inspect at intervals not to exceed three months all automatic or mechanical control devices, indicators, and alarm systems associated with the tower lighting to insure that such apparatus is functioning properly.

Section 17.48 Notification of extinguishment or improper functioning of lights. The licensee of any radio station which has an antenna structure requiring illumination pursuant to the provisions of Section 303(q) of the Communications Act of 1934, as amended, as outlined elsewhere in this part:

(a) Shall report immediately by telephone or telegraph to the nearest Flight Service Station or office of the Federal

Aviation Administration any observed or otherwise known extinguishment or improper functioning of a code or rotating beacon light or top light not corrected within 30 minutes. Further notification by telephone or telegraph shall be given immediately upon resumption of the required illumination.

(b) An extinguishment or improper functioning of a steady burning side or intermediate light or lights shall be corrected as soon as possible, but notification to the FAA of such extinguishment or improper functioning is not required.

Section 17.49 Recording of tower light inspections in the station record. The licensee of any radio station which has an antenna structure requiring illumination shall make the following entries in the station record of the inspections required by Sec. 17.47:

(a) The time the tower lights are turned on and off each day if manually controlled.

(b) The time the daily check of proper operation of the tower lights was made, if an automatic alarm system is not provided.

(c) In the event of any observed or otherwise known extinguishment or improper functioning of a tower light:

(1) Nature of such extinguishment or improper functioning.

(2) Date and time the extinguishment or improper functioning was observed, or otherwise noted.

(3) Date, time, and nature of the adjustments, repairs, or replacements made.

(4) Identification of the Flight Service Station (Federal Aviation Administration) notified of the extinguishment of improper functioning of any code or rotating beacon light or top light not corrected within 30 minutes, and the date and time such notice was given.

(5) Date and time the notice was given to the Flight Service Station (Federal Aviation Administration) that the required illumination was resumed.

(d) Upon completion of the periodic inspection required at least once each three months:

(1) The date of the inspection and the condition of all tower lights and associated tower lighting control devices, indicators and alarm systems.

(2) Any adjustments, replacements, or repairs made to insure compliance with the lighting requirements and the date such adjustments, replacements or repairs were made.

Section 17.50 Cleaning and repainting. All towers shall be cleaned or repainted as often as necessary to maintain good visibility.

Section 17.51 Time when lights shall be exhibited. All lighting shall be exhibited from sunset to sunrise unless otherwise specified.

Section 17.52 Spare lamps. A sufficient supply of spare lamps shall be maintained for immediate replacement purposes at all times.

Section 17.53 Lighting equipment and paint. The lighting equipment, color of filters, and shade of paint referred to in the specifications are further defined in the following government and-or Army-Navy Aeronautical specifications, bulletins, and drawings: (lamps are referred to by standard numbers).

Section 17.54 Rated lamp voltage. To provide satisfactory output by obstruction lights, the rated voltage of the lamp used should, in each case, correspond to or be within three percent higher than the average voltage across the lamp during the normal hours of operation.

Section 17.56 Maintenance of lighting equipment. Replacing or repairing of lights, automatic indicators or automatic alarm systems shall be accomplished as soon as practicable.

Section 17.57 Report of radio transmitting antenna construction, alteration and-or removal. Any permittee or licensee who, pursuant to any instrument of authorization from the Commission to erect or make changes affecting antenna height or location of an antenna tower for which obstruction marking is required, shall, prior to start of tower construction and upon completion of such construction or changes, fill out and file with the Director, U.S. Coast and Geodetic Survey, C & GS Form 844 (Report of Radio Transmitting Antenna Construction, Alteration and-or Removal) in order that antenna tower information may be provided promptly for use on aeronautical charts and related publications in the interest of safety of air navigation.

SECTION 73, TECHNICAL OPERATION

Section 73.51 Operating power; how determined. (a) Except as provided in paragraph (b) of this section, the operating power shall be determined by the direct method; i.e., as the product of the antenna resistance at the operating frequency (see Section 73.54) and the square of the antenna current at this frequency, measured at the point where the antenna resistance has been determined.

(b) The operating power shall be determined on a temporary basis by the indirect method described in paragraphs (c) and (d) of this section, in the following circumstances:

(1) In an emergency, where the authorized antenna system has been damaged by causes beyond the control of the licensee or permittee (see Sec. 73.45), or (2) pending completion of authorized changes in the antenna system, or (3) if changes occur in the antenna system or its environment which affect or appear likely to affect the value of antenna resistance or (4) if the antenna current meter becomes defective (see Sec. 73.58). Prior authorization for determination of power by the indirect method is not required. However, an appropriate notation shall be made in the operating log.

(c) (1) Operating power is determined by the indirect method of applying an appropriate factor to the plate input power, in accordance with the following formula: Operating power equals E_p x I_p x F, where, I_p is the plate voltage of the final radio stage; I_p is the total plate current of the final radio stage; F is the efficiency factor.

(2) The value of F applicable to each mode of operation shall be entered in the operating log for each day of operation, with a notation as to its derivation. This factor shall be established by one of the methods described in paragraph (d) of this section which are listed in order of preference. The product of the plate current and plate voltage, or alternatively, the computed operating power, shall be entered in the operating log under an appropriate heading for each log entry of plate current and plate voltage.

(d) (1) If the transmitter and the power utilized during the period of indirect power determination are the same as have been authorized and utilized for any period of regular operation, factor F shall be the ratio of such authorized power to the corresponding plate input power of the transmitter for regular conditions of operation, computed with values of plate voltage and plate current obtained from the operating logs of the station for the last week of regular operation. However, if the station has been regularly authorized for operation with a directional antenna, and temporary authority has been granted for nondirectional operation with the regularly authorized power, during the period that power is being determined indirectly, an adjusted factor F shall be employed, which is derived by dividing the factor, as determined above, by a constant (0.925 for authorized powers of 5 KW or less; 0.95 for powers above 5 KW).

(2) If a station has not been previously in regular operation with the power authorized for the period of indirect power determination, if a new transmitter has been installed, or if, for any other reason, the determination of the factor F by the method described in paragraph (d) (1) of this section is impracticable:

424

(i) The factor F shall be obtained from the transmitter manufacturer's letter or test report retained in the station's files, if such a letter or test report specifies a unique value of F for the power level and frequency utilized; or

(ii) By reference to Table 13-1.

Factor (F)	Method of modulation	Maximum rated carrier power	Class of amplifier
0.70	Plate	0.25 - 1.0 KW	
.80	Plate	5 KW and over	
.35	Low level	0.25 KW and over	B
.65	Low level	0.25 KW and over	BC[1]
.35	Grid	0.25 KW and over	

1. All linear amplifier operation where efficiency approaches that of Class C operation.

Table 13-1. Efficiency factors for various power levels and modulation methods.

(3) When the factor F is obtained from Table 13-1 this value shall be used even though the operating power may be less than the maximum rated carrier power of the transmitter.

Section 73.52 Operating power; maintenance of. (a) The operating power of each station shall be maintained as near as practicable to the licensed power and shall not exceed the limits of five percent above and ten percent below the licensed power, except that in an emergency when, due to causes beyond the control of the licensee it becomes impossible to operate with full licensed power, the station may be operated with reduced power for a period not to exceed 10 days; provided, that the commission and the engineer in charge of the radio district in which the station is located shall be notified immediately after the emergency develops and also upon the resumption of licensed power.

(b) In addition to maintaining the operating power within the above limitations, stations employing directional antenna systems shall maintain the ratio of the antenna currents in the elements of the system within five percent of that specified by the terms of the license or other instrument of authorization.

Section 73.54 Antenna resistance and reactance; how determined. (a) The resistance of an omnidirectional series-fed antenna shall be measured at the base of the antenna, without intervening coupling networks or components. For a shunt-excited antenna, the antenna resistance shall be measured at the point when the RF energy is fed to the slant wire or other feed wire circuit without intervening networks or components.

(b) The resistance and reactance of a directional antenna shall be measured at the point of common RF input to the directional antenna system. The following conditions shall be obtained:

(1) The antenna shall be finally adjusted for the required radiation pattern.

(2) The reactance at the operating frequency and at the point of measurement shall be adjusted to zero, or as near thereto as practicable.

(c) (1) The resistance of an antenna shall be determined by the following procedure: A series of discrete measurements shall be made over a band of frequencies extending from approximately 25 kHz below the operating frequency to approximately 25 kHz above that frequency, at intervals of approximately 5 kHz. The measured values shall be plotted on a linear graph, with frequency as the abscissa and resistance as the ordinate. A smooth curve shall be drawn through the plotted values. The resistance value corresponding to the point of intersection of the curve and the ordinate representing the operating frequency of the station shall be the resistance of the antenna.

(2) For a directional antenna, the reactance of the antenna shall be determined by a procedure similar to that described in subparagraph (1) of this paragraph.

(d) The license of a station with a directional antenna and an authorized power of 5 KW or less shall specify an antenna resistance 92.5 percent of that determined at the point of common input; for a station with directional antenna and authorized power exceeding 5 KW, the license shall specify an antenna resistance 95 percent of that determined at the point of common input.

(e) Applications for authority to determine power by the direct method shall specify the antenna or common-point resistance, and shall include the following supporting information.

(1) A full description of the method used to make measurements.

(2) A schematic diagram showing clearly all components of coupling circuits, the point of resistance measurement, location of antenna ammeter, connections to and characteristics of all tower lighting isolation circuits, static drains, and any other fixtures, sample lines, etc., connected to or supported by the antenna, including other antennas and associated circuits.

(3) Make and type of each calibrated instrument employed, manufacturer's rated accuracy, together with the date of the last calibration of the instrument, the accuracy of the calibration, and the identity of the person or firm making the calibration.

(4) A tabulation of all measured data.

(5) Graph(s) plotted from this data.

(6) The qualifications of the engineer(s) making the measurements.

Section 73.55 **Modulation.** The percentage of modulation shall be maintained as high as possible consistent with good quality of transmission and good broadcast practice. In no case is it to exceed 100 percent on negative peaks of frequent recurrence. Generally, it should not be less than 85 percent on peaks of frequent recurrence; but where necessary to avoid objectional loudness, modulation may be reduced to whatever level is necessary, even if the resulting modulation is substantially less than 85 percent on peaks of frequent recurrence.

EXTRACTS FROM PART 74 REMOTE PICKUP BROAD-CAST STATIONS

Section 74.435 **Power limitations.** Remote pickup broadcast stations are licensed with a power output not in excess of that necessary to render satisfactory service. The license for these stations specifies the maximum authorized power. The operating power shall not be greater than necessary to carry on the service and in no event more than 5 percent above the maximum power specified. Engineering standards have not been established for these stations. The efficiency factor for the last radio stage of transmitters employed will be subject to individual determination, but it shall be in general agreement with values normally employed for similar equipment operated within the frequency range authorized.

Section 74.481 Logs. (a) The licensee of a remote pickup broadcast base or mobile station shall maintain an operating log to show when and for what purpose the station is operated. The following basic data shall be recorded.

(1) The date and time of operation.

(2) The purpose of the operation.

(3) The location of the transmitter, if a mobile or portable station.

(4) The station with which it communicates.

(5) Frequency check, if made.

(6) Entries required by Section 17.49 of this chapter concerning daily observations of tower lights and quarterly inspections of the condition of the tower lights and associated control equipment and an entry when towers are cleaned or repainted as required by Section 17.50 of this chapter.

(7) Any pertinent remarks concerning the transmissions or equipment deemed desirable or necessary by the operator.

(b) In cases where a series of intermittent transmissions relating coverage of a single event are made, an entry showing the time of the beginning of the series and time of the conclusion of the series will suffice. A notation such as "intermittent transmissions in connection with coverage of automobile accident at Main and Fern Streets" will explain the purpose of the operation and location of the transmitter. The station with which it communicates could be the base station (call sign) or the associated broadcast station (call sign). Intermittent but unrelated transmissions shall be logged separately. A single time entry may be made for short transmissions of less than one minute duration. The time of beginning and ending shall be logged for longer transmissions. In all cases, the purpose of the transmission shall be shown and the approximate location of the mobile unit. If the mobile unit is halted, the exact location should be known.

(c) In cases where a base station is used for dispatching mobile units, a running log may be kept at the base station, containing entries for both the base station and one or more mobile units. Each entry should be identified by the call sign of the station making the transmission. The operator in the mobile unit shall keep a record of all transmissions by the mobile unit which are not acknowledged by the base station so that these missed transmissions may be inserted at the appropriate place in the log kept at the base station.

(d) In cases where only mobile units are used, the logs shall be kept by the operators in the mobile units. A rough log may be kept by the operator in the mobile unit and these notes entered in a permanent log at the end of the tour of duty.

(e) An entry shall be made of any frequency check made pursuant to the requirements of Section 74.462.

(f) If the station instrument of authorization requires painting and the lighting of the antenna structure, the log entries concerning lighting shall be made daily, whether or not the transmitter is used.

(g) Station records shall be kept in such a manner as to be available for inspection by a duly authorized representative of the Commission upon request. The records shall be retained for a period of two years.

AURAL BROADCAST STL AND INTERCITY RELAY STATIONS

Section 74.501 Classes of stations. (a) Aural broadcast STL station. A fixed station utilizing telephony for the transmission of aural program material between a studio and the transmitter of a broadcasting station other than an international broadcasting station, for simultaneous or delayed broadcast.

(b) Aural broadcast intercity relay station. A fixed station utilizing telephony for the transmission of aural program material between broadcasting stations, other than international broadcasting stations, for simultaneous or delayed broadcast.

Section 74.536 Directional antenna required. Each aural broadcast STL and intercity relay station is required to employ a directional antenna. Considering one kilowatt of radiated power as a standard for comparative purposes, such an antenna shall provide a free-space field intensity at one mile of not less than 435 mV/ m in the main lobe of radiation toward the receiver and not more than 20 percent of the maximum value in any azimuth 30 degrees or more off the line to the receiver. Where more than one antenna is authorized for use with a single station, the radiation pattern of each shall be in accordance with the foregoing requirement.

Section 74.561 Frequency tolerance. The licensee of each aural broadcast STL and intercity relay station shall maintain the operating frequency of the station within plus or minus 0.005 percent of the assigned frequency.

LATE AMENDMENTS TO FCC
RULES & REGULATIONS

Sections 2, 81, 83 are amended to adopt a schedule for conversion to single sideband, technical standards, and conditions applicable to availability of frequencies in the band 2,000 - 2,850 kHz. Amendments of Sections 81 and 83 set forth a duplex frequency plan, simplex frequency plan, and the condition of use.

Section 2.803 Part 2 is amended to prescribe regulations governing the sale or import or shipment for sale of devices which are capable of causing harmful interference to radio communications.

Section 15.63 Radiation interference limits. (d) Notwithstanding the provisions of paragraph (a) this section and subject to the prohibition against emissions on the frequencies listed in Section 15.215(c), the level of emission of RF energy from the receiver used with a radio control for a door opener shall not exceed the values listed below when measured in accordance with the procedures laid down in FCC Technical Division Report T-7001, latest issue.

Frequency MHz	Field Strength at 100 Ft. in Microvolts per Meter
Over 25 to and including 70	32.
Over 70 to and including 200	50.
200 to and including 1,500	50-500 (linear variation)
Over 1,500	500.

Section 73.1205 Section 73.124, 73.299 and 73.678 amended and new section 73.1205 are adopted to add language prohibiting fraudulent billing practices, concerning misrepresentation of the quantity of advertising broadcast or the time of day or date at which it was broadcast.

Section 73. Parts 0, 1 and 73 are amended to require licensees to conform to non-discriminatory hiring practices and programs concerning sex and minority groups.

Section 74.437 Licensee of each low power broadcast auxiliary station shall maintain adequate records at the main studio or transmitter of the broadcast station with which auxiliary is principally used, records will accurately show current location of all transmitting units, periods of operation, and any pertinent remarks concerning transmissions. All records must be retained for at least 2 years.

Section 87.501 Date after which no further radar altimeters operated in the 1,600 to 1,660 MHz band can be licensed is changed to read "July 1, 1971 rather than Jan. 1, 1971."

Section 87.513 (a) (4) 2372.5 kHz, 1.7F1 emission, 400 watts maximum power. When using a direct-printing telegraph system other than 60 words per minute, 5 unit (start-stop) code, station identification shall be made by means of A1, A3A or A3J emission.

Section 91. Parts 2, 89, 91 and 93 are amended to provide a geographic relocation of UHF-TV channels 14 through 20 to land mobile radio services within 10 of the 25 largest urbanized areas of the United States.

Section 91.3 "Signal Booster" definition has been added as follows: (5-21-71). In the Business Radio Service, a device operated for the sole purpose of retransmitting the signals of one or more base stations by amplifying and reradiating such signals which have been received directly through space, without significantly altering any characteristic of the incoming signal other tha   t amplitud

Section 91.555 Exemption from technical standards. Transmitters licensed in this Service which have a power input to the final radio frequency stage not exceeding 200 milliwatts are exempt from the technical requirements set out in Subpart C of this part: Provided, however, that the sum of the bandwidth occupied by the emitted signal plus the bandwidth for frequency tolerance shall be so adjusted that any emission appearing on a frequency 40 kHz or more removed from the assigned frequency is attenuated at least 30 db below the unmodulated carrier. Such transmitters may operate in the continuous carrier transmit mode.

Section 89.15 **Frequency coordination procedures.**
(amended 8-6-71) add: (b) A report based on a field study,
indicating the following: (1) The degree of probable interference to existing stations operating on the same channel
within 75 miles of the proposed station and a signed statement
that all existing co-channel licensees within 75 miles of the
proposed station have been notified of applicant's intention to
file his application, and (2) The degree of probable interference to existing stations located 10 to 35 miles from the
proposed station operating on a frequency within 15 kHz and a
signed statement that the licensees of all such stations have
been notified of applicant's intention to file his application. In
no instance will an application be granted where the proposed
station is located less than 10 miles from an adjacent channel
station 15 kHz removed.

FCC Field Engineering Offices

Dist. No.	Office Location	Examination Schedule at Office
1	Boston, Mass. 02109 1600 Custom House India & State Streets Phone: Area Code 617 223-6608	C & A - Wednesday, Thursday and Friday 8:30 AM to 10:00 AM
2	New York, N. Y. 10014 748 Federal Building 641 Washington Street Phone: Area Code 212 620-5745	C & A - Tuesday through Friday 9:00 AM to 12:00 Noon
3	Philadelphia, Pa. 19106 1005 U.S. Customhouse 2nd & Chestnut Streets Phone: Area Code 215 597-4412	P - Monday, Tuesday and Wednesday 10:00 AM to 2:00 PM T & A - Monday, Tuesday and Wednesday 9:00 AM to 10:00 AM
4	Baltimore, Md. 21202 415 U.S. Customhouse Gay and Water Streets Phone: Area Code 301 752-8460	P - Monday, Wednesday, and Friday 8:30 AM to 2:00 PM T & A - Monday and Friday 9:00 AM
5	Norfolk, Va. 23510 405 Federal Building Granby and York Streets Phone: Area Code 703 627-7471	P - Wednesday and Friday 9:00 AM T & A - Friday 9:00 AM to 10:00 AM
6	Atlanta, Ga. 30303 2010 Atlanta Merchandise Mart 240 Peachtree St., N.E. Phone: Area Code 404 526-6381	C & A - Tuesday and Friday 8:30 AM
6S	Savannah, Ga. 31402 238 Post Office Building York & Bull Streets Phone: Area Code 912 232-7602	P - Monday through Friday By appointment only T & A - 2nd & 4th Tuesday each month By appointment only
7	Miami, Fla. 33130 919 Federal Building 51 S.W. First Avenue Phone: Area Code 305 350-5541	P - Monday through Friday 9:00 AM T & A - Thursday 9:00 AM
7T	Tampa, Fla. 33602 738 Federal Building 500 Zack Street Phone: Area Code 813 228-7711	C & A - Monday through Friday By appointment only

Dist. No.	Office Location	Examination Schedule at Office
8	New Orleans, La. 70130 829 Federal Building South 600 South Street Phone: Area Code 504 527-2094	P - Monday, Tuesday and Wednesday 9:00 AM T & A - Monday 8:30 AM
8M	Mobile, Ala. 36602 439 U.S. Court & Custom House 113 St. Joseph Street Phone: Area Code 205 433-3581	C & A - Wednesday By appointment only
9	Houston, Tex. 77002 5636 Federal Building 515 Rusk Avenue Phone: Area Code 713 228-0611	P - Tuesday, Wednesday and Thursday 9:00 AM T & A - Tuesday 9:00 AM
9B	Beaumont, Tex. 77701 239 Federal Building 300 Willow Street Phone: Area Code 713 835-3911	P - Tuesday and Thursday By appointment only T & A - Tuesday By appointment only
10	Dallas, Tex. 75202 707 Thomas Building 1314 Wood Street Phone: Area Code 214 749-3243	P - Tuesday, Wednesday and Thursday 8:00 AM to 10:00 PM T & A - Tuesday 8:00 AM to 1:00 PM
11	Los Angeles, Calif. 90014 Mezzanine Room 50 849 South Broadway Phone: Area Code 213 688-3276	P - Tuesday and Thursday 9:00 AM and 1:00 PM T & A - Wednesday 9:00 AM and 1:00 PM
11SD	San Diego, Calif. 92101 Fox Theatre Building 1245 Seventh Avenue Phone: Area Code 714 293-5460	C & A - Wednesday By appointment only
11SP	San Pedro, Calif. 90731 1300 Beacon Street Phone: Area Code 213 832-2389	Examinations are not normally conducted at San Pedro. Contact the FCC office at Los Angeles, California.
12	San Francisco, Calif. 94111 323A Custom House 555 Battery Street Phone: Area Code 415 556-7700	P - Monday and Tuesday - 8:30 AM T - Tuesday - 8:30 AM A - Friday - 8:30 AM
13	Portland, Ore. 97205 441 U.S. Court House 620 S.W. Main Street Phone: Area Code 503 226-3361	P - Tuesday, Wednesday and Thursday - 8:45 AM T - Tuesday and Thursday - 8:45 AM A - Friday - 8:45 AM

Dist. No.	Office Location	Examination Schedule at Office
14	Seattle, Wash. 98104 806 Federal Office Building 1st Avenue & Marion Street Phone: Area Code 206 583-7653	P - Tuesday, Wednesday and Thursday - 8:00 AM T - Tuesday - 9:00 AM A - Friday - 8:45 AM
15	Denver, Colo. 80202 5024 New Customhouse 19th St. between California and Stout Streets Phone: Area Code 303 297-4053	P - 1st & 2nd Friday and by appointment - 9:00 AM T - 1st & 2nd Thursday - 9:00 AM A - 1st & 2nd Thursday - 8:00 AM
16	St. Paul, Minn. 55102 208 Federal Courts Building 6th & Market Sts. Phone: Area Code 612 228-7819	C - Thursday - 8:45 AM A - Friday - 8:45 AM
17	Kansas City, Mo. 64106 1703 Federal Building 601 East 12th St. Phone: Area Code 816 374-5526	C & A - Thursday & Friday 8:30 AM to 11:00 AM
18	Chicago, Ill. 60604 1872 U.S. Courthouse 219 South Dearborn Street Phone: Area Code 312 353-5386	C - Thursday - 9:00 AM A - Friday - 9:00 AM
19	Detroit, Mich. 48226 1029 Federal Building Washington Blvd. & LaFayette St. Phone: Area Code 313 226-6077	C - Tuesday and Thursday - 9:00 AM A - Wednesday and Friday - 9:00 AM
20	Buffalo, N. Y. 14203 328 Federal Office Building Ellicott & Swan Streets Phone: Area Code 716 842-3216	P - 1st & 3rd Thursday - 9:00 AM T & A - 1st & 3rd Friday - 9:00 AM
21	Honolulu, Hawaii 96808 502 Federal Building P.O. Box 1021 Phone: 588-640	P - Monday through Friday - 8:00 AM T & A - Tuesday and Wednesday - 8:00 AM and by appointment
22	San Juan, Puerto Rico 00903 322 U.S. Post Office & Courthouse P.O. Box 2987 Phone: 722-4562	P - Thursday and Friday 8:00 AM to 2:00 PM T - Friday 8:00 AM A - Friday 9:00 AM
23	Anchorage, Alaska 99501 54 U.S. Post Office Building 4th Avenue between F & G Streets Phone: Area Code 907 272-1822	C & A - Monday through Friday By appointment only

Dist. No.	Office Location	Examination Schedule at Office
24	Washington, D.C. 20555 204 - 521 Building 521 12th Street, N.W. Phone: Area Code 202 393-3620	P - Tuesday, Wednesday and Friday 8:30 AM to 3:30 PM T & A - Friday 9:30 AM and 1:00 PM
25	Gettysburg, Pa. 17325 P.O. Box 441 Phone: Area Code 717 334-3109	A - 1st & 3rd Tuesday By appointment only (Amateur Exams ONLY are conducted at Gettysburg, Pa.)

Times listed are normal examination starting times.

Key to chart

C - Commercial exam
A - Amateur exam
P - Radiotelephone exam
T - Radiotelegraph exam

This schedule is subject to change. No examinations are conducted on Sundays or legal holidays. When legal holidays fall on Saturday, Federal offices are closed the preceding Friday. When legal holidays fall on Sunday, Federal offices are closed the following Monday.

436

Answers to Sample Questions

Element 1: Basic Law

1. (b)	6. (b)	11. (d)	16. (c)
2. (c)	7. (b)	12. (d)	17. (d)
3. (e)	8. (c)	13. (e)	18. (c)
4. (d)	9. (b)	14. (a)	19. (c)
5. (a)	10. (d)	15. (b)	20. (d)

Element 2, Series 0: Basic Operating Practice

1. (a)	6. (a)	11. (b)	16. (e)
2. (a)	7. (c)	12. (d)	17. (c)
3. (d)	8. (c)	13. (d)	18. (e)
4. (c)	9. (d)	14. (a)	19. (b)
5. (a)	10. (c)	15. (b)	20. (a)

Element 2, Series M: Maritime Operating Practice

1. (c)	6. (c)	11. (b)	16. (c)
2. (a)	7. (e)	12. (a)	17. (a)
3. (c)	8. (b)	13. (a)	18. (a)
4. (a)	9. (d)	14. (e)	19. (a)
5. (b)	10. (a)	15. (c)	20. (b)

Element 9: Broadcast Endorsement

1. (d)	6. (e)	11. (c)	16. (a)
2. (b)	7. (a)	12. (a)	17. (b)
3. (d)	8. (e)	13. (b)	18. (c)
4. (b)	9. (d)	14. (b)	19. (a)
5. (c)	10. (a)	15. (d)	20. (a)

Element 3: Basic Radiotelephone

1. (e)	6. (c)	11. (b)	16. (d)
2. (d)	7. (a)	12. (e)	17. (a)
3. (b)	8. (e)	13. (d)	18. (d)
4. (a)	9. (a)	14. (b)	19. (b)
5. (c)	10. (c)	15. (e)	20. (c)
21. (e)	26. (e)	31. (b)	36. (d)
22. (e)	27. (d)	32. (a)	37. (c)
23. (a)	28. (a)	33. (c)	38. (b)
24. (b)	29. (e)	34. (d)	39. (a)
25. (c)	30. (c)	35. (c)	40. (d)
41. (c)	46. (b)	51. (a)	56. (a)
42. (b)	47. (b)	52. (e)	57. (c)

43. (a)	48. (b)	53. (b)	58. (b)
44. (b)	49. (c)	54. (d)	59. (b)
45. (a)	50. (a)	55. (c)	60. (e)

61. (d)	66. (b)	71. (c)	76. (b)
62. (d)	67. (c)	72. (b)	77. (a)
63. (e)	68. (e)	73. (a)	78. (c)
64. (a)	69. (d)	74. (d)	79. (a)
65. (e)	70. (b)	75. (e)	80. (b)

81. (c)	86. (a)	91. (b)	96. (d)
82. (e)	87. (b)	92. (b)	97. (e)
83. (c)	88. (c)	93. (b)	98. (c)
84. (b)	89. (e)	94. (c)	99. (a)
85. (b)	90. (c)	95. (c)	100. (c)

101. (b)	103. (a)
102. (b)	104. (c)

Element 8: Radar Endorsement

1. (c)	14. (a)	27. (d)	40. (a)
2. (d)	15. (d)	28. (a)	41. (b)
3. (b)	16. (b)	29. (d)	42. (b)
4. (c)	17. (c)	30. (e)	43. (d)
5. (e)	18. (e)	31. (c)	44. (e)
6. (a)	19. (e)	32. (c)	45. (a)
7. (e)	20. (b)	33. (c)	46. (a)
8. (d)	21. (a)	34. (e)	47. (d)
9. (a)	22. (d)	35. (c)	48. (e)
10. (c)	23. (c)	36. (b)	49. (c)
11. (b)	24. (c)	37. (a)	50. (e)
12. (e)	25. (b)	38. (d)	51. (e)
13. (d)	26. (e)	39. (d)	52. (b)

Element 4: Advanced Radiotelephone (Element IV)

1. (d)	11. (a)	21. (d)	31. (c)	41. (e)
2. (b)	12. (a)	22. (e)	32. (c)	42. (d)
3. (e)	13. (b)	23. (c)	33. (a)	43. (b)
4. (c)	14. (b)	24. (e)	34. (e)	44. (c)
5. (b)	15. (a)	25. (b)	35. (d)	45. (b)
6. (a)	16. (c)	26. (e)	36. (b)	46. (c)
7. (d)	17. (a)	27. (b)	37. (e)	47. (a)
8. (e)	18. (c)	28. (b)	38. (c)	48. (b)
9. (a)	19. (c)	29. (c)	39. (a)	49. (d)
10. (d)	20. (e)	30. (b)	40. (b)	50. (e)

Index